POLITICAL POSTERS
IN CENTRAL AND EASTERN EUROPE 1945–95

POLITICAL POSTERS
IN CENTRAL AND EASTERN EUROPE 1945–95
SIGNS OF THE TIMES

James Aulich
and Marta Sylvestrová

MANCHESTER UNIVERSITY PRESS

MANCHESTER AND NEW YORK

distributed exclusively in the USA by St. Martin's Press

Published to coincide with the exhibition
'Sign of the Times'
17 November 1999 – 31 January 2000
Exhibition organised by the Moravian Gallery in Brno in association
with Manchester Metropolitan University, the Czech Ministry of
Culture, Visiting Arts and the EU 'Raphael Programme'.

Published by Manchester University Press
Oxford Road, Manchester M13 9NR, UK
and Room 400, 175 Fifth Avenue, New York, NY 10010,USA
http://www.man.ac.uk/mup

Distributed exclusively in the USA by
St. Martin's Press, Inc., 175 Fifth Avenue, New York,
NY 10010, USA

Distributed exclusively in Canada by
UBC Press, University of British Columbia,
6344 Memorial Road, Vancouver, BC, Canada V6T 1Z2

British Library Cataloguing-in-Publication Data
A catalogue record for this book is available from the British Library

Library of Congress Cataloging-in-Publication Data applied for

ISBN   0 7190 5418 4   hardback
          0 7190 5419 2   paperback

First published 1999

06 05 04 03 02 01 00 99   10 9 8 7 6 5 4 3 2 1

Designed and typeset by Axis, Manchester

Printed in Singapore by Craft Print Pte Ltd.

CONTENTS

ACKNOWLEDGEMENTS

This book is the product of a research project initiated by James Aulich in 1994 with the support of the Department of Art and Design Research Group at Manchester Metropolitan University. A sabbatical from the university in summer 1998 allowed much of the writing to be completed. Marta Sylvestrová was appointed as a Research Assistant with a substantial travel budget to collaborate on the project from 1994–96, and with further assistance from the Moravian Gallery in Brno she played a key role, making use of her extensive contacts established as Curator of Applied Arts at the Moravian Gallery and through her work with the Brno Biennale.

Marta Sylvestrová has played an active part in the history of the poster in the region since the 1980s and the project would never have come to a successful conclusion without her specialist knowledge and intrepid determination to travel to the countries of the former Soviet bloc to search out material for the book and to collect posters for the Moravian Gallery Poster Collection in Brno. War inhibited research in the former Yugoslavia and finance led us to the decision to exclude Albania and Bulgaria. Marta researched archives and collections, interviewed designers and other participants, photographed posters, photocopied rare catalogues and obtained material on behalf of the project for further joint analysis and selection. Since 1988 she has visited places as diverse as Moscow, St Petersburg, Kiev, Ljubljana, Zagreb, Bratislava, Cluj, Łodź, Pécs, Rostock, Tallinn, Timişoara, Wrocław, Berlin, Riga, Vilnius, Bucharest, Warsaw, Poznań, Kiev, Budapest, Minsk, Prague and Brno. Thanks must go to René Wanner, who sponsored and helped with the research in Romania and who provided the benefit of his advice.

In this book the names of countries are given as those contemporaneous with the object under discussion. The names of party leaders are followed by dates giving the period of their incumbency. Posters are listed with the designer's name first, followed by a translation of the caption and date, country of origin and collection in which the poster is held.

From 1996 to 1998 we were funded by the Central European University Research Support Scheme as a group project. This allowed James Aulich and Marta Sylvestrová to continue to travel and research and enabled the project to appoint Mariusz Knorowski, who provided specialist knowledge of the Polish poster during his time at the Poster Museum, Wilanow, and then with other important collections in Poland. His research took him to Lublin, Łodź, Poznań, Bydgoszcz, Warsaw and Cracow. His unpublished essay, 'A Kite in the Wind of History', was used by the authors of the book and we thank him for his contribution to the project. The RSS funding also allowed group meetings to take place in Berlin, Warsaw and Manchester, while the Brno Biennale provided the opportunity for further meetings and research.

Translations of captions from the Czech and Russian were carried out by Marta Sylvestrová and Geraldine Cavalir-Holubová, from the Polish by Mariusz Knorowski, from the Hungarian by Katalin Bakos and from the German by James Aulich. Prose was translated from the Russian and Czech by Marta Sylvestrová, other translations from the Czech are by Ivan Leudar, and Kazimierz Aulich translated extensive material from the Polish.

The authors would like to offer their particular thanks to Peter Zimmermann at the Archive of the Academy of Fine Art in Berlin; Katalin Bakos at the Hungarian National Gallery in Budapest; Lenka Fencková and Jiří Pokorný at the All Trade Union Archive in Prague; Petr Štembera at the Prague Museum of Decorative Arts, Thomas Hill in Berlin and later in The Celyn, Longtown (UK); Boris Bučan in Zagreb; Lenka Bajžel in Ljubljana; Gunārs Lūsis in Riga, Juozas Galkus in Vilnius; Konstantin Geraimovich; Alexander Lozenko and Mikhail Avvakumov in Moscow; Alexander Faldin in St Petersburg; István Orosz in Budapest; Artur Rudzitski in Kiev; Maria Rus in Cluj and Constantin Prut in Bucharest, who were all extremely generous with their time, knowledge and assistance.

Thanks must also go to Rashit Akmanov, Svetlana Artamonova, Lajos Bajtai, István Balogh, Ferenc Baráth, Dana Bercea, Stane Bernik, Olga Binatovska, Ilmārs Blumbergs, Jan Bokiewicz, Szymon Bojko, Jānis Borgs, Klara Bourne, Juri Boxer, Alf Bückert, Bea Bückert, Andrzej Brachvogel, Uldis Briēdis, Jerzy Brukwicki, Andrei Budnik, Feliks Büttner, Manfred Butzmann, Genadii Bykov, Natasha Bykov, Vladimir Chaika, Alexander Chantsev, Erazm Ciołek, Vasilii Cygankov, Juris Dimiters, Pedrag Došen, Lex Drewinski, Krzysztof Ducki, Krzysztof Dydo, Libuše Eliášová, Wolfgang Erler, Anke Feuchtenberger, Janina Fialkowska, Martin Figura, Zoran Filipović, Dagmar Finková, Josef Flejšar, Jasna Galjer, Mikhail Gordon, Philip Granville, Wiktor Gorka, Thomas Gubig, Igor Gurovich, Jitka Hanicová, László Haris, Dalida and Bojan Hadžihalilović, Joseph W. Huber, István Ihász, Katalin Jalsovsky, Wolfgang Janisch, Zbigniew Juzwa, Vytautas Kaušinis, Éva Kemény, György Kemény, Jelena

Vote communist, 1946, Czecholsovakia, Museum of Working Class History, Prague.

Kitaeva, Želimir Koščević, Andrei Kolosov, Jitka Kohlová, Valeria Kovrigina, Juraj Králik, Irena Krasnická, Alena Křižová, Miroslav Kudrna, Viktor Kundyshev, Edmund Lewandowski, Māra Lindberga, Andrei Logvin, Sorin Lupsa, Linda Luse, Jan Lukas, Miron Lukianov, Jindřich Marco, Piotr Młodożeniec, Kálmán Molnár, Valentin Muntianu, Boris Mysliveček, Timotei Nādāsan, Aleš Najbrt, Tatiana Nemkova, André Novák, Olga Vladimirova Ovčarova, Bob Pacholík, Snjezana Pavičić, Josef Peterka, Tadeusz Piechura, Sàndor Pinczehélyi, Miroslava Pluháčková, Péter Pócs, Darko Pokorn, Jan Rajlich sen, Hubert Riedel, Vlado Rostoka, Artur Rudzitsky, Maria Rus, Ivar Sakk, Tomasz Sarnecki, Jan Sawka, Guy Schockaert, Zdzisław Schubert, Petr Šejdl, Laimonis Šēnbergs, Serge Serov, Václav Ševčík, Andrei Sheliuto, Vitalii Shostia, Joska Skalník, László Sós, Andrzej Stawarz, Jindřich Štreit, Janez Suhaldolc, Irina Subotić, Marijan Susovski, Olga Świerzewska, Waldemar Świerzy, Tibor Szentpétery, Maria Terenia, Efim Tsvik, Valerii Vasiliev, Matjaz Vipotnik, Valerii Viter, Henning Wagenbreth and Florian Zieliński.

The photography was carried out in Manchester by Stephen Yates; in Brno by Irena Armutidisová and Alena Urbanková; in Warsaw by Tadeusz Stanl, Michal Sielewicz, Piotr Syndoman and Joanna Tolloczko; in Posnań by Jerzy Nowakoski; in Budapest by Zsuzsanna Berenyi; in Bucharest by Gheorghe Ciurea; and in Berlin by Roman Marz.

The EU 'Raphael Programme' has provided funds to enhance the quality of this publication and assisted with the funding of the associated exhibition, website and international conference on political posters to be held at the Moravian Gallery, Brno. Our success with the latter would not have been possible without the collaboration of Angela Weight at the Imperial War Museum, London; the Moravian Gallery, Brno; the Hungarian National Gallery, Budapest; the Archive of the Academy of Fine Arts, Berlin; and Hrvatski Povijesni Muzej, Zagreb, Croatia.

The following archives and collections have contributed to the project: Academy of Art, Bucharest, Romania; Academy of Fine Arts, Timişoara, Romania; All Trade Union Archives, Prague, Czech Republic; APN Photography Archive, Moscow, Russia; Archive of the Academy of Art, Berlin, Germany; Archive of the Verband der Grafik-Designer, Berlin, Germany; Art Union, Bucharest, Romania; Mikhail Avvakumov Collection, Moscow, Russia; Berlinische Galerie, Berlin, Germany; Biennale of Industrial Design, Museum of Architecture, Ljubljana, Slovenia; Andrei Budnik Collection, Kiev, Ukraine; Jerzy Brukwicki Collection, Warsaw, Poland; City Art Gallery, Collection of Art Photography, Zagreb, Croatia; Culture Foundation, Riga, Latvia; Editura Humana, Archive of Photography, Bucharest, Romania; Juozas Galkus Collection, Vilnius, Lithuania; Gallery of Contemporary Art, Zagreb, Croatia; Mikhail Gordon, St Petersburg, Russia; Phillip Granville, Lord's Gallery, London, England; Thomas Hill Collection, Berlin, Germany; Historical Archive of the Czech Army, Prague, Czech Republic; Hrvatski Povijesni Muzej, Zagreb, Croatia; Hungarian National Museum, Department of Photography, Budapest, Hungary; Hungarian National Gallery, Budapest, Hungary; Hungarian National Museum, Department of Contemporary History,

Miron Lukianov, *Twenty-seventh Congress of the Communist Party of the Soviet Union*, 1985, Soviet Union offset placard, Alexander Lozenko Archive, Moscow.

Agitation Centre for the National Committee Elections, undated, Czechoslovakia, Museum of Working Class Movement, Prague.

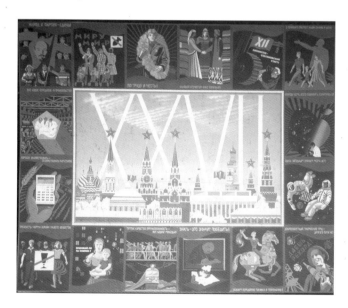

Budapest, Hungary; Künstlerhaus Bethanien, Berlin, Germany; Lenin State Library, Poster Collection, Moscow, Russia; Edmund Lewandowski Collection, Warsaw, Poland; Library of the Academy of Fine Art, Cracow, Poland; Library Poster Collection, University of Zagreb, Croatia; Alexander Lozenko Collection, Moscow, Russia; Lublin State Archive and Historical Museum, Lublin, Poland; Moravian Gallery, Brno, Czech Republic; Valentin Muntianu, Bucharest, Romania; Museum of Arts and Crafts, Zagreb, Croatia; Museum of Decorative Arts, Prague, Czech Republic; Museum of Fine Arts, Bucharest, Romania; Museum of History of Kiev, Ukraine; Museum of Independence, Warsaw, Poland; Museum of Modern Art, Ljubljana, Slovenia; Museum of Peasant History, Bucharest, Romania; Museum of Revolution, Moscow, Russia; Museum of the Working Class Movement, Graphics Collection, Moravian Museum, Brno, Czech Republic; Museum of the Working Class Movement in Prague, Czech Republic; National Art Museum, Cluj, Romania; National Museum, Poznań, Poland; National Museum, Beograd, Yugoslavia; National Gallery, Bucharest, Romania; National Library, Riga, Latvia; Panorama Publishing House, Moscow, Russia; Poster Museum at Wilanow, Warsaw, Poland; Rabbit and Solution Studio, Bratislava, Slovak Republic; Regional Museum, Bydgoszcz, Poland; State Russian Museum, St Petersburg, Russia; Ukrainian House of Culture, Kiev, Ukraine; Union of Estonian Graphic Designers, Tallinn, Estonia; Victoria and Albert Museum, London, England; Valery Viter, Kiev, Ukraine; René Wanner Poster Collection, Föhrenweg, Switzerland; Florian Zieliński Collection, Poznań, Poland.

The authors would also like to thank John Taylor for being there, reading the text and correcting the grammar; John Hewitt for his advice; Chris Paul for his knowledge of the corridors of the European Union; Jane Bedford for her clerical assistance beyond the call of duty; Matthew Frost our editor, for his enthusiasm; and, last but not least, Lynn Aulich, Ivo Lahoda and Marie Lahodová for putting up with us and for looking after our young families when our research took us far from home. The book is dedicated to Alice, John and Marek.

J.A.

M.S.

Jan Lukas, *Photograph of contemporary magazines and newspapers at the time of Stalin's death*, Gottwald died nine days later, on 14 March 1953. Czechoslovakia, Photographic Collection of the Moravian Gallery, Brno, the photographer.

Anon., *New Poland*, 1951, Czechoslovakia, All Trade Union Archive, Prague.

Rozsevačka

JOSEF VISSARIONOVIČ

CTENAR

ZLEPŠOVATEL A VYNÁLEZCE

J. V. Stalin (1879–1953)

DŘEVO

UZDRAV

ZÁVODNÍ ČASOPIS LÉKAŘSKÉ FAKULTY
A FAKULTNÍCH NEMOCNIC V PRAZE
1953 BŘEZEN 20   Cena 3 Kčs   ČÍSLO 10

LODNÍ SPORTY

JOSEF VISSARIONOVIČ STALIN

Josef Vissarionovič Stalin zemřel 5. března 1953

JEZDECTVÍ STŘELBA-ŠERM

HÁZENÁ ČESKÁ HÁZENÁ

LETECKÝ MODELÁŘ

ODBORÁŘ

ZEMŘEL J. V. STALIN

CYKLISTIKA

JOSEF VISSARIONOVIČ STALIN

TENNIS

JOSEF VISSARIONOVIČ STALIN

HUDEBNÍ ROZHLEDY

KOVOŠROT

Za velkým J. V. Stalinem

ZLEPŠOVATEL A VYNÁLEZCE

KR

INTRODUCTION

Ten years after the collapse of the Soviet sphere of influence in Europe it is an appropriate
time to examine the political poster. This book is intended as a general comparative
introduction to the political poster produced under communism since 1945. As one of the
most widely discredited and closely policed aspects of cultural life in the former communist
bloc it is one of our major contentions that its production, reception and control can provide
an index to the history of the public facade of the regimes in their pursuit of
legitimacy with an unwilling people.

The poster in communist Europe had a decisive political and cultural status. At first, as a weapon in a social struggle for human emancipation and later, as a medium of artistic expression independent of the commercial pressures of the market place, it had an authority it could rarely aspire to in Western democracies. It played an important role in communist ceremony and ritual, but its status shifts from that of a temporary agitational tool to that of an exhibitionary object caught up in the institutional framework of museums and galleries, curators and collectors. Paradoxically, as other media like television became more important for the purposes of state propaganda, the poster gained in symbolic significance. The region saw the birth of the 'art poster' and Jan Sawka, the Polish artist exiled since 1976, likened the role of the poster designer to that of Polish funerary sculptors under Russian imperial rule, forgotten but free.

As the invocation of the communist future became increasingly hollow, and as a generation came of age which had not known any other system, so the nature of the political poster moves from the empty rhetoric of political sloganeering to become a weapon of criticism and resistance. The hand-made street graphics of 1956, 1968, 1981 and 1989 pictured this process in the most vivid ways. The quest to develop a discourse separate from the party and the state was part of a continuous process. After Stalin's death the imperatives developed by 'national communism' encouraged designers to adopt styles drawn from indigenous pre-war traditions and the contemporary international graphic design arena. Designed to increase the currency of the political message, such stylistic strategems created degrees of ambiguity in the interpretation of the posters beyond legislation which had long-term implications for the regimes.

The unofficial political poster as an expression of the predicament of the individual or as a challenge to the official rhetoric corresponded to the development of a counter political sphere. Aided by the complexities and permeability of the systems of censorship and control, posters dealing with aspects of the environment or the anti-nuclear movement engaged the founding myths of the communist state. Significantly, their essential ambiguity represented a shift from the monologic to the dialogic: from a visual analogue of absolute power to the expression of something more anarchic or nationalist, but nevertheless circumscribed by the available language provided by the rhetoric of the state and the party.

It is a story of aesthetic, political and, finally, national liberation. Socialist-realist conventions established in the late 1940s had insisted on orthodox communist content, but these slowly gave way to individualist, liberal humanist critiques of contemporary communist and capitalist mores. Aesthetic leadership moved away from the centre, Moscow, to the periphery of the Soviet sphere of influence, to Poland, Czechoslovakia, Hungary, Yugoslavia, eventually to return to Leningrad and Moscow through the Ukraine and the Baltic States as what became known as the 'poster of perestroika'.

The study has taken a transnational comparative approach, researching the foremost private and public collections in Byelorussia, Croatia, the Czech Republic, Estonia, Germany, Hungary, Latvia, Lithuania, Poland, Romania, Russia, the Slovak Republic, Slovenia and the Ukraine. The approach has underlined the cultural diversity of the region and demonstrated the limited impact of cultural directives emanating from Moscow. Consistency is found in the ideological message rather than in the visual style. Quantitative analyses outlined in the second half of the book revealed a number of dominant themes and preoccupations of communist rhetoric, from the great leader to the socialist future: picturing a reality which did far more to conceal than to reveal existing conditions.

(detail of Jan Lukas, *Photograph of contemporary magazines and newspapers at the time of Stalin's death,* see p. ix)

CHAPTER ONE

THE POLITICAL POSTER AND COMMUNISM

Understanding central and eastern Europe is distorted by deeply held Cold War stereotypes which
have a fertile after-life in contemporary popular culture. Once the ignored hinterland of Soviet
influence, the region has become the imagined source of the threat of internecine war, uncontrollable
immigration, nuclear terrorism, drugs, AIDS, the far right, environmental disaster, and political and
financial gangsterism. Such prejudicial stereotypes in combination with the pressures of Western
tourism ensure the region remains as obscure as it did under Soviet occupation.

The political poster in central and eastern Europe was a closely monitored and legislated aesthetic expression of communist ideology. Suffused by a combination of nationalism and the utilitarian rationality inherent in modern technology and Marxist-Leninist thought, it was the site of a particular kind of late and reactionary modernism. In the attempt to establish the primacy of politics and the state over economics and the market, the posters pictured military-industrial necessities as national virtues. They were romantic in so far as they depicted a technological utopianism and a tempered determination to control the future, but, interestingly, there was little or no attempt to recapture a mythic and distant past. Instead, the aesthetic standards represented by socialist realism and its legacy of political control replaced moral norms. Theoretically communism embraced the modernizing impulses of individual emancipation associated with the Enlightenment, but in practice rejected them.

Visions of technological achievement – trains, electricity, industrial plant and collectivized farming – carried a natural and scientifically determined image of man within a conservative and deindividualized aesthetic. But as this book demonstrates, the discourse of the political poster was subject to challenge from both inside and outside the communist party as the winds of national communism, Cold War, *détente* and the 'changes' of 1989 blew across the Soviet empire. The communist regimes beyond the Iron Curtain[1] stretching from the Baltic to the Mediterranean lasted only half a century. But so profound were the assaults on human rights and autonomous social institutions, and so traumatic was the effect on political and material culture, that communism in Europe represents an entire historical period. Built on the unsure and abject foundations of the dislocations and destruction of war and invasion, communism contributed to a human tragedy on an unimaginable scale.[2] The mass deportations and population loss under Nazi occupation and

the subsequent Stalinist reorganization of the geopolitical structure of the region created opportunities for new communist elites. The Jewish population had been murdered and most ethnic Germans were transported to what became, in 1948, the German Democratic Republic. Poland, for example, had been one-third ethnic minorities before the war, but by 1948 it was ethnically almost homogeneous. In other areas the attempt was made to render the culture Soviet, or, more accurately, Russian. The Soviets had historical claims to sovereignty over the Baltic States and large numbers of Russians emigrated to Lithuania, Latvia and Estonia. The scale of the displacement wrecked traditional ways of life. At the same time fear, material need and arbitrary Soviet authority made people dependent upon the state. But under the communists repressive government was perceived to be marginally less terrible, even affording something of a relief to many who had already suffered expropriation and worse under the Nazis.[3]

The communist political poster was designed to give the new social and political forms visual shape.[4] It provided a field for the regimes to picture themselves to themselves and their people. It was part of a state-sponsored spectacle of visual and verbal rhetoric, a legitimating discourse which depicted the communist future, its hallowed leaders, the new socialist people and their internal and external enemies:

> The aim of political activity is to create and implement representations (mental, verbal, pictorial, dramatic) of the social world, by which the thinking of the actors in society, and thereby the social world itself, can be influenced; or, more precisely, to create and remove social groups – and with them, the social actions by which these groups could change the social world in accordance with their interests – by producing, maintaining, or destroying the representations which enable these groups to see themselves or be seen by others.[5]

The posters in this book were intended as affirmations, or challenges to communist ideology. They picture a discourse

(detail of 1.1)

of power and partake of 'manifold relations of power which permeate, characterize and constitute the social body … [which] cannot themselves be established, consolidated nor implemented without the production, accumulation, circulation and functioning of a discourse'.[6] Simultaneously, this discourse has its parameters in politics and aesthetics and subjects individuals to imaginary identities.

Cold War interpretations of Soviet cultural policy saw it as a means of maintaining ideological influence over subject populations. However, the relations of the satellites to Moscow were more nuanced.[7] It would be foolish to suggest that Soviet power did not play a crucial part in the development of cultural policy. But it does little to explain the aesthetic diversity across the region in countries with different national traditions and divergent recent histories. During the war, Warsaw had been razed to the ground, but Prague had escaped virtually unscathed; in the Cold War, East Berlin was in direct confrontation with the West, while the civilian population of Budapest was subject to the might of the Red Army in 1956 and Prague was occupied by the Warsaw Pact in 1968. It can be of no surprise that their material cultures are no less distinct.

This book concerns itself with the posters produced during the period of relative democracy between 1945 and 1947, the posters of freedom produced between 1986 and 1989 and what the communists called visual agitation and the 'fighting or militant poster'.[8] With them all the intention was to articulate an 'idea', but for the latter it was a weapon in the battle to build socialism in the class struggle and the fight for national liberation against the imperialists, intended to inspire love and defence of the party's achievements and hatred of its enemies. It must react quickly to political, cultural and economic events and popularize the historical struggle of the party: 'We want to see in the poster an agitator who can expose and defeat the enemy, who with the weapon of satire, irony and ridicule fights with the remnants of the old in the consciousness of working people. Soldiers of agitation. We are building socialism, socialism is a march to the music of fanfare.'[9] The nineteenth-century Russian political theorist Georgy Valentinovich Plekhanov defined visual agitation in similar terms: 'a propagandist presents many ideas to one or few persons; an agitator presents only one or a few ideas, but presents them to a mass of people.'[10] The term 'fighting poster' cannot easily describe the hopes for the future inscribed into the surfaces of the political posters of the three years leading up to 1948, the year Stalin consolidated his power. Nor can the epithet be applied to the products of individual designers who found the freedom to express, almost without fear, the oppression, disillusion and cynicism generated by the failure of communism. The

fighting or militant poster will always be associated with Moscow and the propagandists of the central committee and the state security apparatus.

Because the infrastructure of the region was so badly damaged in World War II communications were virtually non-existent. With little or no radio, and television but a distant luxury, the political poster became one of the most important means of communication. As a mass medium it was the perfect tool for the dissemination of propaganda for the party of the masses. Posters were distributed as 'the daily companions of our work and struggle', in the factory, office, street, in houses of culture and in the many clubs established through the trade unions and other party organizations.[11] They celebrated the new socialist national holidays and every important political anniversary. As the art of the streets, 'A Gallery for the Millions', they were intended to inform the populace of the nature of the dictatorship of the proletariat and to shape the behaviour, attitudes and tastes of working people in representations which also physically marked out the public space the people inhabited.[12]

The 'fighting poster' is a site of ideological conflict, where battles over meaning and cognition are won and lost. In the 1940s and 1950s it helped establish the official discursive framework of Marxism-Leninism, defining civil society, human rights, technological and scientific progress and revolution as the only valid models of social change. It illustrated the dominant discourse as a system of exclusion or prohibition where social and cultural norms of the good and the bad were articulated, value and social identity defined. As a discursive system it operated through institutional practices like censorship and, normatively, through the discourses of socialist realism and the cultural and educational policies of the state. Enacted within a system of binary oppositions, such negative categories as 'bourgeois-individualist', 'anti-humanist', 'anti-socialist' and 'irrational' were causally linked with late eighteenth-century romanticism, nationalism, fascism, post-war existentialism and alienation under capitalism. There was no room for ambiguity and there could be no lack of political commitment.

The historical significance of the communist political poster lies not so much in its aesthetic value as in the fact that it reproduces the official narratives upon which the state made its claims to legitimacy, insinuating various historiographies and theoretical concepts into the speech and thought patterns of everyday life. In political posters affirmation or opposition demanded conformity to established and internalized mind sets. As a result, the poster acquired a paradigmatic status in the imaginative life of the people. In the Czechoslovakian film *Larks on a*

String (1969) the poster provides an episteme, or grounding of knowledge, for those who labour for the atonement of their anti-socialist values.[13] Based on a story by Bohumil Hrabal, the film is a product of the scepticism and hopes of the Prague Spring and subjects the hyperbolic iconography of socialist progress to gentle but relentless interrogation. In the steel works in Kladno, workers discuss Kant's aesthetics as a foil to the desolation of their communist reality. Idle workers are surrounded by posters displaying the slogans 'Why not rejoice? We're working for ourselves' and 'Beat the capitalists to the finishing line.' The guard is obsessed by his domestic situation and neglects his duties. The women prisoners are amorous and pleasure seeking, with little thought of conscientious labour. A trade union official stands in front of Jan Čumpelík's poster *Don't be daunted by your enemies: Exhibition of the History of Revolutionary Struggles* (1949) (1.1), which features a Hussite fighter, a follower of Jan Žižka, the fifteenth-century national hero, reformist and Hussite leader who led the Czech people to victory against the German crusaders. The official speaks of the passing of the old bourgeois order and for the national values embodied in the original historical meaning of Žižka before he was appropriated to communist history and the defeat of Nazism.

In front of another poster a couple are filmed by a propagandist. They are a beautiful *émigré* and a young Jewish cook who refuses to work on Saturdays. They are told to look longingly into each other's eyes, while the commentary reads, 'We're doing all this for your future. For the future of our new young people, who love, raise families, have lovely children … who will never see war or suffering, only everlasting peace.' And who, in the film as in life, are denied all these things by the party. The ironies of the story contrast with the moral authority bestowed upon the poster in communist mythology: '[it] had no rival in art history. War veterans recall how front-line soldiers took posters with them into battle, as valuable personal belongings, how the German command issued orders to shoot at posters raised by Soviet soldiers in the front line. These examples explain their political authority and moral standing … .'[14]

But, as Hrabal insists, the official rhetoric is unsustainable: it defined dictatorship as a means of democratization; Soviet domination as a mechanism of self-determination; repression as a condition of freedom; privilege as necessary for equality; and the humanistic claims of Marxism-Leninism as the justification of human rights abuses. With the easing of the Cold War, internal stagnation and the increasing but unadmitted dependence of the Soviet satellites on the West, there were oppositional and dissident attempts to resolve the institutionalized double standards produced by these contradictions. In 1975

the Helsinki Final Act recognized the territorial *status quo* in Europe, but the so-called Third Basket committed all signatories to respect 'civil, economic, social and other rights and freedoms, all of which derive from the inherent dignity of the human person'.[15] Subsequently, 'socialism with a human face', democratic socialism, the third way, Charter 77, Solidarity and reform movements in the German Democratic Republic all emerged to find expression in posters.

Defined in relation to the disintegrating order, these movements failed to supply democratic or even commercial languages and modes of behaviour. László Béke, the Hungarian cultural historian, noted 'the reaction of commercial advertising to political styles on posters … The slogans of the Hungarian Insurance Company during the election campaign were: "You are the winner of the elections. We support your Party".'[16] There is no point outside the discourse from which to speak the 'truth'. The public discourse is tied to the structures of power, however dilapidated and in need of repair they may be. The poster charts the failure of the official culture to create authenticity or cohesion. But, paradoxically, the vacuity of official Marxism-Leninism, combined with the centrality assigned to culture, made inflections of style and symbolic meanings penetrate the culture as a whole. The ultimate struggle was to rewrite and re-inscribe the master narrative and to transfigure the boundaries of the discourse, to open up new spaces beyond Marxism-Leninism, religious revival and the reclamation of national identity.[17]

Official political poster designers responded to the needs of the leadership. Posters were commissioned by official political, military and cultural institutions; slogans were taken from the speeches of the leaders and the writings of Lenin, Stalin and other Marxist-Leninist theorists. Slogans have a single value, they are unambiguous. Meanings remain vague while value is clear. The language is often archaic and always repetitive. To say it makes it true; desires are already fulfilled. Without verbs the slogans are beyond contradiction. The copywriters and editors were named on the designs as well as the designers, while committees made judgements on the 'quality' of the posters and censored the output. The committees were constituted of members of the comissioning organization, a design 'expert' and a party *apparatchik*. But the members were often fellow designers, with less than hard-line sympathies. The 'rules of the game' were well known and most posters were censored before they came anywhere near the scrutiny of the party at large, or the general public. The design passed from studio to publishing house and party-controlled outlets, in a manner which created latitude for degrees of censorship.[18]

Under Stalin, bureaucratic institutions proliferated in an atmosphere of anxiety and fear. The national unions of artists, directly or indirectly under the control of the party, dispensed materials and regulated publishing and exhibiting. They furnished a social and intellectual milieu and the structures necessary for professionalization. But their primary role was to subject production to the authority of the state: 'Those who deny the state the right to influence cultural development, those who maintain that the state should not mix in cultural or artistic affairs, in my opinion, … underestimate the enormous importance of culture and art in the people's education … .'[19] In Poland, Henryk Szemberg, the director of Artistic and Graphic Publications (WAG),[20] described the organization as 'clearly political', promoting for critics, editors and designers a 'proper grasp of the subject' in an 'atmosphere of friendly, creative criticism'.[21] Officially the intention was not to limit the imagination, merely to shift production away from the glib demands of market capitalism to those of the 'people', who were, in fact, excluded from this politicized closed circuit of party control. Designers were free only in so far as they fulfilled their party-defined ideological responsibility to the audience.

In the Soviet Union each publishing house had its stable of artists among whom commissions were shared. The principal publisher in Moscow, Plakat, was controlled by the Communist Party Central Committee rather than the artists' union. Designers received a flat fee and designs were offered to party organizations to be printed in response to demand.[22] Effectively the people paid for their own propaganda in a nascent and tightly controlled market. After 1985 in the wake of Mikhail Gorbachev's reforms the system collapsed: 'political and social themes are not conducive to large-scale printing: who, for example, really wants to buy a poster against bureaucracy?'[23]

Political posters, unlike cultural posters, were produced for mass consumption in a graphic design process linked with industrial manufacture. Yet its origins are in commercial practice as a studio-based authorial skill, complemented by the artisanal base of the printing trade. From small print workshop to large volume press, the poster was shaped by economies of scale, degrees of political control and state cultural policy. By the 1960s the communist party claimed that the conditions for the mass dissemination of culture, free of the demands of the commercial market place, were in place. Contrary to contemporary left-liberal analyses of mass culture in the West, communist rhetoric claimed it was produced by the people, for the people.[24] The polemicists of culture were never keen to recognize the interceding role of the party and the central committee: control, they maintained, had been devolved to the people through the various party organizations which controlled cultural production to the exclusion of any alternative which did not carry with it the danger of persecution or prosecution. The system was bureaucratic and legislative rather than organic.

The participation of the people was guaranteed by their membership of the various party organizations such as trade unions, young pioneers, sports clubs and women's associations. Under these circumstances the old bourgeois distinctions between active creators and passive audiences were now obsolete. In the 1960s there was a fear of descending to superficiality, or simple and vacuous entertainment, but communist thought supplied a remedy in a characteristically circular argument: if culture is saturated with authentic value because it is of the people and is therefore political, the participation of the masses in forging culture will further increase political consciousness. The logic of the 'New Faith' was described by Czesław Miłosz: 'Everything proves that it is right. Dialectics: I predict the house will burn; then I pour gasoline over the stove. The house burns; my prediction is fulfilled. Dialectics: I predict a work of art incompatible with socialist realism will be worthless. Then I place the artist in conditions in which such a work is worthless. My prediction is fulfilled.'[25]

Mass culture was also defined by the technical means of production. Lenin had written: 'It is essential to learn that without machines, without discipline, it is impossible to live in modern society. It is necessary to master the highest technology or be crushed.'[26] Advanced communications are universally identified with scientific rationalism and modernity. The leading pre-war Soviet poster designer, Gustav Klutsis, who epitomized the thinking which led Stalin to adopt Frederick R. Taylor's management philosophies as keenly as had Henry Ford, had recognized 'artists of a totally new nature – activists, specialists in mass political and cultural work …'.[27] According to Marxism-Leninism, the internal contradictions of capitalism and the scientific-technical revolution could bring only alienation and manipulative, standardized mass media. In contrast, under communism, the mass media were widely regarded as a technical guarantee of the democratic mass character of culture and the means by which socialist society reproduces itself. Consequently, the poster was credited with the status of a universal form of mass communication. Grandiose Five Year Plans were liable to failure, but the mass communications revolution was the measure of socialist progress and the new man.

Posters were only one facet of the party propaganda machine. Equally important were the newspapers, magazines, film, radio and television (1.2). The telephone was altogether more problematic, with its capacity for enabling individual and mutual communication, and telephone tapping was widespread. By the late 1960s the poster had began to lose its omniscience (1.3). The art historian Volker Handloik remarked:

> In the GDR the media had changed since the 1970s. Every second household was in possession of a TV set … posters and placards were no longer exclusively used for regulations of the authorities and government. The public city broadcast and the public address car were no longer used, the Russian garrison commanders no longer pasted their daily orders on the walls, and on advertising pillars one could see more art than administration. Just as the socialist society fell more and more apart into individuals and the mass movements turned into empty hulks, so the posters became more and more individual and only rarely the categorical imperative was used: 'Build up, German youth, build up'.[28]

People who had grown up in the immediate post-war years remembered the all-pervading presence of political posters on the streets, in the schools, clubs, factories, theatres, cinemas and canteens. But with television and the possibility of receiving Western broadcasts, especially in the German Democratic Republic, the political poster as an organ of state power began to lose its authority. According to the Czech poster designer Václav Ševčík:

> In the 1950s, Czech cities were overflowing with 'political' posters … after a short while nobody paid them any attention … and to Western visitors they signified the atmosphere of the eastern part of Europe … In the 1960s, however, we began to feel the time had passed for just wasting printed paper; if a 'political poster' must exist, then let it speak to somebody, let it make people think.[29]

The political poster became marginalized and found a new freedom and audience among a disenfranchised and anti-capitalist class of people who owed their cultural loyalties to the pre-war intelligentsia. The political poster took to the drawing rooms, salons and spaces of the gallery as a conversation piece, an object of subversive aesthetic pleasure and as a weapon of resistance.

Since the end of the 1960s public ritual, propaganda and indoctrination, physical coercion and terror had not been the primary means of maintaining social order. Instead, socialist industrialization provided universal state employment in a system of dependence.[30] State employment was measured, classified and policed, but many designers discovered possibilities for entrepreneurial and critical dispositions. This was particularly true of designers who produced unique posters as critical or artistic statements, or who were commissioned to produce small editions by cultural organizations involved with film, theatre and youth culture. As such, the independent art poster provided a means of self-employment. The existence of this new field challenged the ideological blueprint of communism. The craft was practised in an artisanal world and often displayed a conscious distance from the conventions of power and its language. Consequently, it attracted individuals of a bohemian disposition, self-exiles on the margins of official society who were criticized for possessing petty bourgeois life styles and egotistic attitudes. The art poster, with its existential bias and capacity for individual expression, was implicitly subversive in ways far greater than any equivalent activity in the West, where culture and politics are less integrated and self-expression is but another form of conformity. In Marxist-Leninist dogma, culture was defined only in relation to its effort in building socialism. Anything which could be perceived as a challenge was seen as a threat to the communist order.

In Czechoslovakia it was known as the 'grey zone': a territory grudgingly tolerated at home, but subject to opportunistic and self-interested praise from the authorities abroad. It was a paradigm of the larger picture where attempts to reform from within were abandoned in favour of dissent, however mute or covert, from without. It also marked a sea change in the nature of the profession, from being part of the technical and creative intelligentsia, identifying with the broad aims of the party, to becoming an intellectual class identified with bohemianism and the outsider mentality associated with the European avant garde. Paradoxically, artists were also driven by a desire to change the world, much as Marx had demanded.

Expression free of direct party influence was held to be retrogressive and dangerously irrational by the party faithful. In this sense the art poster was understood to be antagonistic to the nature and role of mass communications in modern society. During the 1970s in Poland theatres were allowed to sell posters and a rudimentary consumer-led market developed in response to the demand created by collectors. By the end of the 1970s in Poland and Hungary poster production had become a nuanced part of an incipient consumer economy wedded to intellectual dissent, carried along less by materialistic imperatives than by the despair engendered by economic inefficiency, corruption and the cynicism generated by official ideology. The phenomenon was symptomatic of deep democratizing impulses. In Poland and Hungary, where small private sectors first evolved, there were negotiated rather than pressured withdrawals from state communism, even if precipitated by mass demonstrations.

SOCIALIST REALISM

Communism and its ideology were articulated in images which shared with Eastern Orthodox thinking a lack of distinction between the 'represented and that which is represented'.[31] As Ulf Abel has emphasized, the painted icon communicates something about God in a process of magic identification where the distinctions between the picture and the real are blurred. Assisted by posters, ideology acquires a substance all its own which ultimately serves to show that everything socialism had set out to achieve had failed. Jindřich Štreit's photographs of communist Czechoslovakia capture the essential paradox between the posters and life as it was lived. Communist posters reflect, according to Marxist-Leninist theory, not 'the present state of things' but the 'real movement which abolishes the present state of things'[32]. Their terms of production define posters as analogues of scientific rationalism. But, displayed in everyday conditions, they are as incapable of connecting with reality as the rhetoric of Marxism-Leninism they embody. They cannot support the emancipatory political programme to which they lay claim. Their systems of representation are at the heart of one of the contradictions of modernity: the pursuit of scientific rationalism was to have liberated human beings from the burdens of tradition and myth, yet under communism it succeeded only in reproducing traditional systems of subjection and domination. (1.4, 5)[33]

Socialist realism was the method through which the political poster was to propagate ideologically defined party views on history, class and the nation.[34] It was a practice not so much negotiated between individual practitioners as played out in party institutions such as the artists' unions and the daily press. In contrast to Western art and design practice, rooted in art for art's sake and commercialism, the obligation was to the social and the political. The poster designer was defined by state policy as a teacher and philosopher and was expected to instil *narodnost*, or 'peopleness'; to be popular but in a non-commercial, folkish sense; to display *klassovost*, or 'classness', as the engine of struggle and historical progress; and through an awareness of *partiinost*, or 'partyness', to identify with the party and its aims.[35] Most important, the mission was to portray the 'typical', not to show people as they were, but as they might become under socialism: educated, culturally developed and ideologically aware.

The communist regimes had no real legitimacy with the people and their authority relied on political coercion effected through the various security organs of the state. After Stalin's death the Kremlin policy of 'national communism' was designed to help overcome the problem by a partial return to national traditions, provided they were suitably 'progressive' and 'humanistic'. The policy echoes wider developments which saw nationally based cultural agendas take hold throughout the industrialized world during the 1950s.

For party ideologues, posters had to be legible, populist and middlebrow. To this end, Stalinist culture owed its inspiration to traditional European classical, Renaissance and baroque models, combined with Russian nineteenth-century eclectic and realist precedents. Anti-experimental and unchallenging, these forms were the product of a process of social change. Vera Dunham has remarked on a new career-oriented class, born of the party and the *nomenklatura*, and driven by aims of personal and domestic improvement: this class 'represents today, as it did before, a middle class mentality that is vulgar, imitative, greedy, and ridden with prejudice. Both deficiency of spirit and the defensive mechanisms of philistinism are implicit ... .'[36] The aesthetic tastes of this class were essentially conservative.

Conceived as the bearer of pre-formulated philosophical messages and state myths, the communist political poster is didactic and conforms to the tastes of an aspirant class with antagonistic relations to the critical or avant-garde forms of the radical intelligentsia. Dunham saw it as the product of a puritanical culture of manners providing proper rules of conduct intolerant of those who take ideas seriously. Its consumers and producers had positions of social leadership, but at the same time they were subject to controls and the fear of denunciation by rivals. In this way the middlebrow is absorbed into the political arena and dispenses *ersatz* participation in the political process by invading the spaces of everyday life and, under Stalin, by rendering subjects realistic. Subsequently it structured them in notions of the contemporary and the new. This was achieved through a veneer of commercial internationalism and *la moderne*. Art Deco in pre-war Europe and the international style in the post-war West had adapted modernism as a market-oriented signal for a socially and technologically advanced and *chic* audience. Superficially the observer can find easy identification, but the striving for contemporaneity serves, to use a Marxist phrase, only to obscure rather than reveal real conditions of existence.

Indigenous traditions of graphic design could not always fulfil the ideological demands for which they were intended under communism. Unlike Soviet socialist-realist posters, typographical designs were common, the transparency of language sufficient for Marxist-Leninist claims to realism, even when used in punning and subversive ways (1.6–11, 4.2). Styles and symbols can have several meanings and can be used ambiguously. The medium was potentially unreliable and presented to the viewer gaps, interruptions and interludes which at once critically reorganized experience and opened up space for interpretative uncertainty. The rhetoric of communism had ensured the status of Marx's philosophy as descriptive

1.1

1.2

1.1
Jan Čumpelík, *Don't be daunted by your enemies. Exhibition of the History of Revolutionary Struggles*, 1949, Czechoslovakia, Moravian Museum, Brno.

1.2
Viktor Govorkov, *Listen, Moscow speaks!*, 1949, Soviet Union, Academy of Fine Arts, Berlin.

1.3
Klaus Wittkugel, *East German television broadcast. To struggle and triumph*, 1967, GDR, Academy of Fine Arts, Berlin.

1.4
Jindřich Štreit, *Village monument, Albrechtice*, 1981, Czechoslovakia, the photographer.

1.3

1.4

rather than a 'danger zone of philosophical transcendance'.[37] The contradiction between theory and practice ensured the cultural sphere was crucial in the battle for minds and in the maintenance of the political status quo. Everybody has to believe in the communist myth to live, to survive. But, at the same time, the myth had become transparent. As Stefan Heym, the German Democratic writer, once noted, people read only the sports pages in the newspapers: the one place where the communist authorities did not lie. The invalidity and illegitimacy of official discourses encouraged an increased sense of value in the aesthetic sphere, not least because it was safer than the openly political. Or, at least, safer most of the time. Jindřich Štreit's photograph of frosted portraits of decorated hero workers was controversial (1.12). Culture was important. Jan Sawka tells the story of his expulsion from Poland and a bad-tempered exchange with a communist official because he was not prepared to be told, among other things, what poetry to like and read.[38]

Many more artists and designers remained within the system. Some were genuinely committed to the system, some cynically exploited it and others worked in good faith, thinking they could improve things from within. They were in a privileged position, with a status the avant garde could only wish for in the West. They became the state-sponsored, but state-controlled, antennae of society. Artists lost their irrelevance. They were closer to power as part of a privileged political elite than they had ever been, with a new audience who were now responsible for government.[39] Conversely, the authorities depended, in part, upon the incorporation of a technical elite of professional poster designers within the state propaganda apparatuses for cultural legitimacy.

During most of the period the system was thought to be immutable and permanent. Simultaneously, the guarded optimism of post-war reconstruction, combined with the real or coerced compliance of the creative intelligentsia, encouraged by the betrayals of Munich and Yalta, slowly leaked away. The course of this drift is plotted particularly well in the ways in which poster production developed from a designed mass-produced utilitarian object with a clear agitational function to an expressive artefact rich in allusive words and imagery. Communism was axiomatic and, as in Eastern Orthodox thought, life and dogma are intimately related, so that individual actions are tolerated only as a denial of individuality in the name of a greater purpose. But, as Václav Havel pointed out, 'The way forward is not the mere construction of universal systematic solutions, to be applied to reality from the outside; it is also in seeking to get to the heart of reality through personal experience … Human uniqueness, human action and the human spirit must be rehabilitated.'[40] He set out to return to the subject on the basis of individual freedom. For the communist authorities such sentiments were a subjection to the nihilistic energies of the tyranny of freedom. But the problems of freedom, pluralism, individual emancipation and human rights were to remain.

The official political poster has always pictured ideological positions, whether in advertising or in socialist realism, and it is possible to narrow the epistemological and communicative horizons of the poster to the reproduction of the social order rather than its critique. In fact its function is more complex, and at times of crisis and change it has had a role in discursive argument, played out in the public cultural sphere.[41] The party was never able to establish a true hegemony. Most people expressed general contentment with their lot, but few believed in the official rhetoric which made equivalences of socialism, peace, unity, collectivity, internationalism and progress. The system was incapable of admitting the existence of crime, social deviance, dissent, alienation, exploitation, dissaffection or delinquency. The rhetoric was both denial and delusion, and the official political poster is the dual product of fakery and an unpleasant cognitive dissonance. As pictures of the self-deceptions and deceits masking a precarious grasp on reality, the posters conceal what Slavoj Žižek called the rupture that lies at the heart of the real. They are part of the facade which constitutes the coherent reality demanded by a belief in communism. But even when it has been demystified, people still act as if they believe, and the system is perpetuated:

> The cynical subject is quite aware of the distance between the ideological mask and the social reality, but he nonetheless still insists upon the mask … Cynical reason is no longer naive, but

1.5
Jindřich Štreit, *Dining room of state co-operative, Vajglov*, 1980, Czechoslovakia, the photographer.

1.6

1.7

1.9

1.8

1.10

1.11

1.6
Henryk Tomaszewski,
National Day, 1973, Poland,
private collection.

1.7
Miloš Slezák, *To all great
October Revolution
1917–1967*, 1967,
Czechoslovakia, Moravian
Gallery.

1.8
S. Balčiunas, *To All. Great
Power of the party in unity
with the people*, 1982, Soviet
Lithuania, Moravian Gallery,
Brno.

1.9
Piotr Młodożeniec,
Solidarność 1980–1990, 1990,
Poland, artist's edition, private
collection.

1.10
Pedrag Došen, *Osijek will
never be OCEK* (written in
cyrillic), 1991, Croatia,
Moravian Gallery, Brno.

1.11
Lex & Jadwiga Drewinski,
*Beware, you are now leaving
West Berlin!*, c. 1989,
GDR/Poland Moravian
Gallery, Brno.

it is a paradox of an enlightened false consciousness: one knows the falsehood very well, one is well aware of a particular interest behind an ideological universality, but still one does not renounce it.[42]

Marxist-Leninist ideology was not perceived to be true. Nobody trusted in it as a utopian political programme, any more than anybody took the exhortations of the posters seriously, but the lie was experienced as truth. The deceit, accompanied by persistent shifts in policy, took its psychological toll. In 1990 Estonia's Foreign Minister gave the predicament a dimension related to melancholic torpor:

> When you shut people's mouths so they cannot talk, when you close their eyes by forbidding them to travel, when you plug their ears by jamming airwaves, the population becomes very passive. In this condition, when people don't care, it seems as if nature herself reacts: fields produce less wheat, forests die of pollution, fouled rivers catch fire. The entire society degrades.[43]

By the middle to late 1960s politics had produced a profound boredom among the people. But the slogans, supported by the not inconsiderable powers of the state, elicited a conditioned response. Czesław Miłosz writes eloquently of what he called *Ketman* in Stalinist Poland, where individual public and private lives are divided, leading to a kind of social schizophrenia where dominant values are affirmed automatically and discontent is repressed.[44] Theodor Adorno defined the phenomenon as 'believing and not believing' in a characteristic he found in all modern societies.[45] Rational self-interest is pushed so far as to be irrational. Who could deny the value of the pursuit of international peace? But what is its validity in a militarized, policed and surveilled society occupied by a foreign power? There can be no personal basis for belief in the claims of the posters. The party slogans, just like Western advertising, address real anxieties and dislocations of which they appear to propose material resolutions. As the product of a conservative and retrogressive ideology they reproduce the *status quo* by demanding conformity for personal success. Generalized abstractions address each observer as a potentially active member of society, but at the same time anonymity is ensured in the collective. Fulfilment is found in service to the party and pleasure is divorced from the individual, to be realized in collective conformity.

THE POLITICS OF THE POSTER

The 'political' is defined by the officially produced poster designed for promoting communist aims, ideals, anniversaries and festivals. But the overtly and transparently political is complemented, according to shifting conditions, by what the audience perceives as political. Following the theoretical leads provided by Mikhail Bakhtin and Valentin Nikolaevich Voloshinov, the poster as a communicative act relies on the audience as its interpreter. Meanings are negotiated within specific geographical, historical and ideological positions. The audience reacts to various aspects of the political discourse explicitly represented in the pictures and slogans and engages in its own discursive practice through opposition or affirmation. Political posters are part of a fluctuating discursive structure, situated within the contexts of its exercise, as audiences and designers alike position themselves in relation to the official culture.

Posters emerging in the 1960s and 1970s often functioned on the fringes of the official public culture. They are more authentic in expression than their official counterparts and reveal inconsistencies and contradictions in the dominant ideology. But they are also determined by the dominant discourse. They are propagandist, or political, in the sense that they propagate the values of a particular fraction of the dominated. They are often hermetic or ambiguous in a postmodern manner and obvious, established meanings are obscured. At this juncture the language of the political poster shifts, in Bakhtinian terminology, from the monological to the dialogical. The original socialist-realist imperative was unitary, fixed and univocal. It was the epic discourse of the single subject providing 'definition', 'truth' and 'logical analysis'.

During the 1950s the art poster evolved as a visual register of a counter-public sphere which developed at different rates at various times in the states of the communist bloc: most notably in Poland throughout the period (apart for a short hiatus under martial law in the early 1980s); in Hungary before 1948 and after 1956; in Czechoslovakia up to 1968; in Yugoslavia from the 1960s; in the German Democratic Republic and Soviet Union after 1985; and in Romania not at all until the collapse in 1989. In contrast to the official poster, the art poster was defined by a polyvalent, multi-determined, multi-vocal, dialogical discourse. Its visual and verbal language involves doubling and indeterminacy, and it proceeds by analogy in the manner of a poetic language. In the monological official discourse the voice of the designer is deferred to the known narrative of communist ideology, regarding the audience as assumed and passive. Dialogical discourse is double-voiced to place designer and audience in a relationship of active understanding. Meaning is socially negotiated, not determined by authority or dogma.

To pursue the Bakhtinian analysis, posters bring with them internalized memories of previous usages and their reception is conditioned by the designer's and observer's previous knowledge in a pattern which constitutes an artistic act. The designer, the real and imagined audience and the communicative context together produce meaning. The art poster's multiplicity of incomplete meanings and unconcluded positions demands the active participation of the audience in the formulation of meaning. At this point the artistic or dialogical poster crosses over into the arena of the political poster. Precisely because of its nature as a dialogical cultural product, it is able to maintain the original agitational function of the political poster as a weapon in a social struggle for human emancipation. Through the deployment of national stylistic traditions and cultures, memories of pre-war and bohemian existences and contemporary Western graphic styles, the poster appropriates the role associated with the propaganda or monological posters of the 1940s and 1950s. Liberation is sought not from pre-war bourgeois capitalism but from post-war communist totalitarianism.

With the collapse of communism in the 1980s, the poster remained dialogical, but was tied to the languages of communism, religion and romantic nationalism. As the facade began to fall apart the poster took on a more aggressive posture, close to what Peter Sloterdijk calls *kynicism*: 'to confront the pathetic phrases of the ruling official ideology – its solemn, grave tonality – with everyday banality and to hold them up to ridicule, thus exposing behind the sublime noblesse of the ideological phrases the egotistical interests, the violence, the brutal claims to power.'[46] Authority is openly subverted by exposing it to ridicule and satire through the practice of revealing the paradoxes and contradictions at the heart of communist ideology and authority.

Just as there was a symbiotic dynamic in the field of politics between the *apparatchik* and the dissenter, so there was between the political and the art poster. The field of poster production was a site of confrontation between the values and subject matter of socialist realism and an emancipated democratic pluralism, distinct from the commercial pluralism of Western cultural production. The field was defined by the twin poles of the party and the individual. Progress, collectivism, harmony and singular meaning were set against alienation, subjectivity, desire, polysemy and ambiguity. There was a continual dynamic between a traditionalist aesthetic and the pursuit of the new; between prescribed ways of doing and knowing and the continual return of the repressed. The rhetorical imagery of the rearguard demands an avant garde. Under communism what would appear to be the exaggerated significance of avant-garde strategies comes from a continual dialectic of repression and revolt which constituted a legacy of distrust in the face of real rather than imaginary opposition, where the symbolic has the capacity

to subvert coercive organizations of public meaning.

Since the eighteenth century the European tradition has insisted on visionary privilege and the sufficiency of the unique psychology to experience and express its own subjectivity in authentic ways as a conceptual framework for the idea of the creative individual. Denied by the dialectical materialism of Stalin and Zhdanov, the sophist *diktat* of the party eliminates alienation and the existential predicament of the individual from socialist society and derides its expression as bourgeois formalism without proper party and national sentiment. The challenge to state authority came through the development of the political poster as an autonomous practice, independent of party directives. Significantly, this came about through a vision of the individual as a moral subject: 'The affirmation of individual dignity … The doctrine is wonderfully simple: live as if you were a free person. Precisely because totalitarianism depends for its success on spoiling individuals – on sowing mistrust and demoralization, or by outright killing – the refusal of a single individual to share these ways represents a decisive challenge to the regime.'[47]

EXHIBITIONS

In the communist bloc the poster had a status it rarely attained in post-war Western democracies. The poster's proximity to the policies of the state assured its status among the party faithful, while its freedom from commercial considerations gave it partial autonomy and wider political significance. Juri Kuuskemaa, the Estonian art historian, had a foretaste of the change in rank bestowed upon the medium with the first Soviet occupation in 1940, when he observed that the 'mudlark' of the arts suddenly became a sovereign member of the arts family.[48]

A permeable boundary existed between art and the poster, not least because socialist realist mastery is concerned with content. It was further served by the control the state exerted over every area of cultural production: from the nature of the product to the ways it was consumed by its audiences, especially in the display and exhibition of posters. Culture was theoretically unitary in practice, but the old pre-war cultural formations were never completely obliterated. Ironing out the boundaries only served to facilitate the re-establishment of a bourgeois cultural sphere in the medium of the art poster. This in turn served to obscure the traditional boundaries between a professional and commercial practice, aimed at popular markets, and an entrepreneurial and individualist practice aimed at an elite. The artist or designer was classified as a *grafik*, someone who deals with reproduced images. Western arguments over whether reproduced forms deserve the status of art were redundant. The poster had its own self-sustained status. Indeed, proceeding from the contested position that poster art grew from painting, the variety of techniques, imagery and expression found in posters had led many to suppose by the early 1950s that the divisions between the arts had been abolished.

Crucial to any understanding of political posters is an appreciation of the public spaces and galleries they inhabited. To gauge contemporary responses is extremely difficult, but it is in the sites of reception that readings can be suggested. At first, political posters were not designed for exhibition. They took their place on the streets as a 'democratic' art. This assertion was restated by the political scientist and economist Radoslav Selucký in the aftermath of the Prague Spring: 'Some people would be stunned in thinking that these posters should speak to us from our street corners and our walls … In short, I want these posters to become part of public life. They should be taken from the exhibition halls and moved to the cities and villages … .'[49]

After World War II the symbolic centres of cities were reconceived as a people's architecture. The ownership of public space was ideologically defined and its limits were marked by the political symbolism of the state. Typically, the 'democratic' was caught by the self-contradictory polemic of communist rhetoric, where space was articulated in a hierarchical manner through the physical disposition of political imagery. The star dominated the most elevated points of public buildings, followed in descending order of priority by the poster portraits of the fathers of the revolution, Marx, Engels, Lenin and Stalin; the leaders of the state; representations of the leading role of the party in home and world affairs; and finally by pictures of workers, peasants and enemies of the people, both domestic and foreign. The public spaces of the cities, articulated by monumental propaganda, mimicked the iconographical orders of a medieval altarpiece, a polyptych on a vast and monumental scale 'democratized' by its proximity to the people and its existence in the fabric of the city.

These orders were perpetuated into the 1970s and for increased effect posters were displayed in multiple arrangements in large-scale pictorial orchestrations of party policy. As Selucký had hinted, by the end of the 1960s the political poster as an effective tool of propaganda was all but exhausted, and its proliferation was nothing more than a measure of its invisibility.[50] Instead, it might be argued, the political poster came to the museum. Museums of the history of the working-class movement were established during the late 1960s and early 1970s in the culmination of a strategy begun by Lenin himself.[51] If the buildings were custom-built, their architecture was late modern. The architects of the Museum of the Working Class Movement of South Bohemia in České Budějovice, for example, aped the achievements of the modernist pioneers.[52] Late modernism, representative of scientific rationality and contemporaneity and a denial of Stalinist baroque monumentality, could provide a suitable showcase for a history determined by the precepts of dialectical materialism: 'to build up the museum of the revolutionary working-class movement, with its actual construction in ideology, technology, architecture and man-made respects, with the collection and selection of documents and materials, with the construction of the display itself, with the form of the surroundings of the museum … .'[53]

It was an important step for the reception and social meaning of the political poster. Collected by archivists, it was no longer a temporary artefact produced by the political needs of the moment and it became a record of party achievements. The status of the contemporary poster in the museum granted it the authority of evidence in a history of the communist party in a wider propaganda struggle for political legitimation, particularly in schools. Pertinently enough, Ernst Nehrlich of the Academy of Fine Arts, Berlin, defined exhibitions as 'extraordinarily persuasive political deeds'.[54] The poster had passed over into the world of curators and educators and it began to breed a pedigree independent of the Soviet-inspired instrumentalism of its origins.

The process paralleled contemporary developments in Poland, where poster art was a familiar part of a nationalist agenda. The poster played an important role in what was regarded as a cultural settling of accounts with the oppression the nation had suffered:

> Poland lost its independence and national existence, and
> during the period of violence and oppression it was graphic art,

1.12
Jindřich Štreit, *Portraits of decorated workers*, Prostějov, 1986, the photographer.

the most democratic of all arts, which filled its mission of documenting the spiritual endurance of the Polish nation. The poster became a herald of the Polish question, and residing in the streets it gave testimony to the dynamic public life, and kept our aspirations still alive and real in the realm of culture and science.[55]

The first exhibitions of Polish posters took place in the 1940s and were linked directly with the war effort (1.13).[56] After the communist take-over there were large national exhibitions of several hundred posters each in 1953, 1955 and 1961. Increasingly, posters acquired an exhibition value on a par with their ability to communicate political and propagandistic messages. Posters were included for the first time in the fourth German Art Exhibition in Dresden in 1958, largely as a result of the activities of Klaus Wittkugel, the pre-eminent designer and official of the Union of East German Graphic Artists (VGD). The exhibition *The Hundred Best Posters* began in 1966 under the auspices of the Union of Artists and the Ministry of Culture.[57] The first attempt to exhibit a history of the Hungarian poster took place at the Palace of Exhibitions in 1960: over a thousand posters which had appeared in the streets were shown. It was followed by a series of significant exhibitions in 1958, 1960, 1961, 1966, 1972 and 1975.[58]

By the mid-1960s national and international exhibitions had begun to be organized on a regular basis, assisted by generous official government support. In 1965 Tadeusz Grabowski organized the first General Polish Biennale of Posters in Katowice. Grabowski's purpose was to exhibit the cream of the Polish poster school in a showcase equivalent to the well established international art biennales. He sets out the discursive paradigms for the poster within the terms of an art practice, qualifying the contemporary poster as 'ideo-artistic'. Its role is determined not by the aesthetic terms of escape or the critical negation of dominant forms, but by the need to 'transfer information' in intellectual and metaphorical interventions in an antithesis of decorative art. He paraphrases the Polish poster designer Jan Lenica, describing the Polish poster as humane, romantic, poetic, lyrical, pathetic and heroic, distinguishing it from Western advertising and establishing it as an individualistic but educative medium, vital to the 'transformation of the world and the rebirth of man'.[59]

The tendency was by no means exclusive to Poland. In Czechoslovakia during the 1960s the Plakát group and in Hungary during the 1970s the Perspectivity group[60] pursued a similar agenda. Connections with the artistic avant garde reinforced dissenting readings and aesthetic status. During the period of *glasnost* and *perestroika* in the Soviet Union a few designers formed a subgroup within the Leningrad branch of the Artists' Union, where they used the language

of Aesop's fables to express their anxieties in exhibitions called Poster Fables. After the death of Stalin in a mutually reinforcing process the monologic language of the official poster was challenged by the dialogism of posters couched in poetry and metaphor. Possessed of a rich and grotesque allegorical language like their Polish and Hungarian contemporaries, they drew on a tradition of dissent more usually identified with literature and the work of Franz Kafka, Herman Wouk, Stanisław Lem and Mikhail Bulgakov. The poster was established as an artefact worthy of exhibition, with an aesthetic value found beyond the furtherance of Marxism-Leninism.

The poster biennales, part national celebration, part international relations exercise, were immensely important events. The year 1964 saw the first National Biennale and in 1966 the International Biennale of Graphic Design at the Moravian Gallery, Brno, in Czechoslovakia, under the presidency of Jan Rajlich, and the first joint exhibition of poster art from Estonia, Latvia and Lithuania in Tallinn (subsequently poster triennale, but not in existence today). In 1966 the first Warsaw International Poster Biennale under the direction of Józef Mroszczak was dedicated to 'applied graphic art ready to serve the prestige of the reborn Polish State in the realm of information, propaganda and representation'.[61] It was a genuinely international affair. Speakers were invited from the communist bloc, the United States, Italy and Switzerland, with a particularly strong contingent from France, a traditional cultural ally of Poland.[62] The second biennale in 1968 also featured a significant Japanese contribution to mark the beginning of a long association between Japanese and central and eastern

1.13
Stanisław Tomaszewski-Miedza, *In fighting. Revenge for the blood of thousands of Poles*, 1944, reprinted 1986, Poland, private collection.

European designers.[63] The biennales furnished unprecedented and privileged access to colleagues in the communist bloc and provided direct contacts with Western designers.[64]

Pierre Bernard, the French poster designer and future founder member of the socially oriented Grapus design group, had studied under Henryk Tomaszewski at the Warsaw Academy in 1964–65. It was a measure of the kind of international co-operation that designers were attempting to foster elsewhere through organizations like Icograda (International Council of Graphic Design Associations), founded in 1963, and the Alliance Graphique Internationale (AGI), established in 1952. Both organizations had been born of compensatory motives generated by the dislocations of war; their imperatives were international and extra-political. They set graphic design against advertising design in a late modernist belief in the efficacy of responsible quality design as an agent in improving people's lives, communications and international understanding in an 'act of protest against the old society'.[65] While these organizations were extremely important in fostering dialogue between designers, political conditions and restrictions on contacts with Westerners inhibited formal involvement by designers from the communist bloc.[66]

The biennales are late modern and are often devoted to humanitarian themes and the social role of the graphic arts. Even at the height of the tensions generated by Cold War politics, these prestigious events were regarded as significant contributions to the cause of international co-operation and they quickly took on symbolic importance. Jan Sawka's contribution from American exile to the Warsaw Biennale in 1978, La Voiture de l'année (6.141), in the context of the founding of the Committee of Free Trade Unions for the Baltic Coast in Gdansk, ominously featured a schematic Soviet tank, described by Mariusz Knorowski as a 'brutal disturbance of the pastoral idyll, so arduously staged by the propaganda of success'.[67] Unsurprisingly, it caused controversy and hostility in official circles when it won the gold medal. When martial law was declared in December 1981 Anna Rutkiewicz, a curator at Wilanow, commented on the national and political importance poster exhibitions had begun to accrue to themselves when she recalled soldiers tearing down posters for the exhibition Polish Social and Political Posters 1944–81. The exhibition was closed until it could be replaced with something less contentious.[68]

The degree to which the international stature of the biennales made them politically sensitive can be gauged by the relative freedom granted to the national biennale in Katowice.[69] As Zdzisław Schubert noted in 1981 when he featured a few Solidarity posters, the poster was 'a sensitive register of on-going change'. Schubert drew a distinction between the relatively arid field of orthodox political posters and independent 'socio-political' posters which engaged directly with the immediate post-August 1980 reality in Poland. The tenth national biennale in 1983, the first under martial law, had black covers for its catalogue, few illustrations, no political posters and no commentary. But by 1985 the organizers, and perhaps the nation, had recovered enough to publish the catalogue with covers in the national colours. The first prize was awarded to the exiled Polish designer Lex Drewinski, who sent from West Berlin the poster Untitled (1985). It features a projectile shaped like a boomerang, ready to return to its sender. By way of contrast, the ninth International Poster Biennale in Warsaw was cancelled in 1982: 'We wanted to avoid a showdown with the government. We were afraid of censorship.'[70]

The political poster is an illusion of escape into an area which reproduces the conditions of repression – what Ferenc Fehér has called the 'systems of dictatorship over needs'. Marx may have seen the 'dictatorship of the proletariat', in which the oppressive power of the state, the military and the bureaucracy would be abolished and replaced with a democratic system of universal suffrage. Lenin may have foreseen the 'withering away of the state', in which freedom of expression and organization were to become constituent factors in the establishment of a public sphere, defined as the fabric of media, educational, knowledge and opinion-forming institutions within civil society conducive to the emergence of public opinion as a political force. But the historical contradictions of communism made it useless as a tool of enlightened critical engagement. It saw itself as socialism in practice but required pre-socialist and pre-democratic forms closer to the feudalism of the Middle Ages than to any democratic socialist ideal to ensure its continued existence. Communist rhetoric was hung up on the fact of history. The vision of the socialist present and the communist future could never be anything more than delusion passed off as illusion. But there was always more than one sphere in communist societies, despite the Stalinist legal eradication of any kind of civil society. The communist public sphere served to introduce information in tune with the goals of the party, but at best it was a partial success only in the early 1950s. Ever since it has been a failure, and by the end of the era the never fully suppressed liberal space of the art gallery and the museum was to blossom in unpredictable ways to provide communities of resistance to the state and physical space for the opposition to organize.

As soon as the authority of the state begins to falter, official posters are among the first objects to be stamped under foot. The world over, the portraits of deposed dictators are habitually stripped from their places of honour and destroyed in a frenzy of release as each citizen wreaks individual revenge upon the figure in whose image the power of party and state had been inscribed. Archives like those of Plakát, the state publishing house in Moscow, were burned. Some archives and collections were absorbed by expanded state organizations like the Academy of Fine Art in Berlin with personnel and collections intact; others were unilaterally privatized and survive as independent organizations, such as the Museum of the History of the Working Class Movement in Prague. Horea Bernea, the director of the Museum of the Romanian Peasant, founded in 1990, commented:

> Before anything like this was inconceivable. ... The ideal of any museum was to begin with the neolithic and to end with Ceausescu ... Museums were instruments of ready-made communist indoctrination. Between 1953 and 1989 the building housed the Museum of the History of the Romanian Communist Party. It took us two years to dismantle it. Its contents were transferred to our history museums and state archives, where they belong. The less important items are in our basement, which is called – half jokingly – 'the chamber of horrors'.[71]

Official political posters, once the primary means for the regimes to picture themselves to themselves in a thoroughly modern and progressive vision, set out to define their subject peoples. Produced by party organizations, they repeated the slogans of the day and exhorted the people to comply with government policies as they responded to events. Their partial readings of history were intended to manufacture legitimation for the regimes with the people. Once ensconced in the museums of working-class history their value became evidential, giving support to communist readings of history and playing an important role in education through compulsory school visits and the communist youth organizations, socialist unions of youth and the Young Pioneers. In the satellite countries and, to a lesser extent, the Soviet Union, the discourse was always subject to challenge to fluctuating degrees at different times. Legitimation for the communist party poster was negotiated through the 'social and political' sections of international poster exhibitions. As propaganda the posters were the product of a hermetic cycle of censorship and control where only the single reading defined by the communist party was tolerable. But as part of an international showcase produced within a non-Soviet national agenda their imperatives became more flexible. National collections carefully stored poster designs which never found publication: exhibited for their aesthetic value, politically they could find no justification with the authorities. These have now become evidence of other kinds of histories, just as many of the former museums of working-class history, like that in Budapest, have become museums of contemporary history, the posters providing evidence not of communist triumph and the inevitable march of the working class in justification of the dictatorship of the proletariat but instead a story of foreign dominance and national struggle.

NOTES

1   A phrase coined by Winston Churchill in his speech at Fulton MO in 1946 to describe the communist bloc.

2   The Soviet Union had signed a non-aggression pact with Nazi Germany in 1939. On 17 September 1939 both countries invaded Poland. On 22 June 1941 the Germans invaded the Soviet Union. This period in Soviet history was excised from post-war Soviet history. As a member of the Allies the Soviet Union waged what became known as the Great Patriotic War, 1941–45, which led to their final triumph over fascism.

3   See Jan T. Gross, 'War as Revolution', in Norman Naimark and Leonard Gibanski (eds), *The Establishment of Communist Regimes in Eastern Europe 1944–1949* (Oxford, Westview Press), 1997.

4   See Jan T. Gross, *Revolution from Abroad. The Soviet Conquest of Poland's Western Ukraine and Western Belorussia* (Princeton NJ, Princeton University Press), 1988.

5   Pierre Bourdieu, quoted by Michael Brie, 'The Difficulty of Discussing the GDR', in Margy Gerber and Roger Woods (eds), *Understanding the Past – Managing the Future: The Integration of the Five New Länder into the FRG. Selected Papers from the Eighteenth New Hampshire Symposium on the GDR*, Studies in GDR Culture and Society 13 (Lanham MD, University Press of America), 1994, p. 10.

6   Michel Foucault, *Power/Knowledge: Selected Interviews and other Writings, 1972–1977* (New York, Pantheon Books), 1980, p. 93.

7   Invaluable discussions of these relationships can be found in Matthew Cullerne Bown and Brandon Taylor (eds), *Art of the Soviets. Painting, Sculpture and Architecture in a One-party State 1917–1992* (Manchester, Manchester University Press), 1993, and Susan E. Reid (ed.), *Journal of Design History special issue: Design, Stalin and the Thaw*, 10:2 (1997).

8   Szymon Bojko in Aleksander Wojciechowski, 'A Dyskusji Nad I Ogólnopolską Wystawą Plakatu' (From the Discussion at the First Polish Exhibition of Posters), *Przeglod Artystyceny (Arts Review)*, 3 (1953) 17.

9   *Ibid.*

10   J. A. C. Brown, *Techniques of Persuasion. From Propaganda to Brainwashing* (Baltimore MD, Penguin), 1963, p. 111.

11   Jerzy Bogusz, 'Niektóre Problemy Polskiego Plakatu Politycznego' (Some Problems of the Polish Political Poster), *Przeglod Artystyceny (Arts Review)*, 2 (1953) 24–40.

12   Florian Zieliński, 'Social and Political Frames of the Poster in the Polish People's Republic', in Krzysztof Dydo (ed.), *Hundredth Anniversary of Polish Poster Art* (Krakow, Biuro Wystaw Artystycznych), 1993, p. 39.

13   Directed by Jiří Menzel, it was not released until 1989.

14   Dagmar Finková and Sylva Petrová, *The Militant Poster 1936–1985* (Prague, International Organization of Journalists), 1986, p. 8.

15   G. Stokes, *The Walls Came Tumbling Down. The Collapse of Communism in Eastern Europe* (Oxford, Oxford University Press), 1993, p. 24, quoted in Robert Bideleux and Ian Jeffries, *A History of Eastern Europe. Crisis and Change* (London, Routledge), 1998, p. 563.

16 Katalin Bakos, *The Signs of Change. Posters 1988–1990* (Budapest, Hungarian National Gallery), 1990, p. 14.

17 See Marek Beylin, 'Language and Pluralism', *Krytyka*, 16 (1983), reprinted in Michael Bernhard and Henryk Szlajfer (eds), *From the Polish Underground. Selections from 'Krytyka' 1978–1993* (Philadelphia PA, Pennsylvania State University Press), 1995, pp. 93–9.

18 These elaborate structures of control had the potential effect of ensuring high production values and artistic standards. The Hungarian poster designer István Orosz described in an interview what it was like working for a state organization, Magyar Hirdeto: 'They were smart enough and generous enough to realize that you can't expect a creative person to produce on schedule every day from eight to five. The stipend wasn't much, but I didn't have to go in every day, and when I did go in, all the equipment I needed and couldn't afford was available to me. If they had no work for me to do, they still paid me. It was their way of saying, "You're on call."' Quoted in György Haiman and Carol Stevens, 'Smiting the Eye', *Print*, 18:1 (1991) 53.

19 Johannes R. Becher in Alexander Stephan, 'Johannes R. Becher and the Cultural Development of the GDR', *New German Critique,* 1:2 (1974) 84. Becher was the Minister of Culture in the GDR. The Ministry of Culture and the Union of Fine Arts with its Department of Graphic Arts were not created until after Stalin's death in 1954. In 1957 the designer and union official Klaus Wittkugel inspired the establishment of a Central Commission for Co-ordination of Poster Activities.

20 Wydawnictwo Artystyczno Graficzne (WAG).

21 Aleksander Wojciechowski, 'A Dyskusji nad i Ogólnopolska Wystawa Plakatu' (From the Discussion at the first Polish Exhibition of Posters), 1953.

22 Leonie ten Duis, Annelies Haase and Jan Noordhock (eds), 'Graphic Design in Eastern Europe 1981–1991', *Zee Zucht*, 5:5/6 (1992) 11. Bogusz points out that of five posters produced for 1 May 1953 four were for sale. Peter Zimmermann of the Archiv der Akademie der Kunst in Berlin remarked that many posters were ordered from brochures by the various party organizations, clubs and factories and were paid for before they were printed.

23 Irene Semenov-Tian-Chansky in Freddy Ghozland and Beatrice Laurans, *Moscou s'affiche* (Toulouse, Ghozland), 1991, p. 14.

24 In the West the Frankfurt school and other independents like Dwight MacDonald were careful to challenge any notion that mass culture was produced by the people. Theodor Adorno adopted the term 'culture industry' and MacDonald had written of a culture 'produced by technicians for businessmen' in critiques of commercially produced culture under capitalism. See Theodor W. Adorno and Max Horkheimer, *Dialectic of Enlightenment* (London and New York, Verso, [1944]), 1979; and Dwight MacDonald, *Against the American Grain. Essays on the Effect of Mass Culture* (New York, Vintage Books), 1962.

25 Czesław Miłosz, *The Captive Mind* (Harmondsworth, Penguin), 1980, p. 15.

26 Lenin, quoted in Richard Stites, *Revolutionary Dreams. Utopian Vision and Experimental Life in the Russian Revolution* (Oxford, Oxford University Press), 1989, p. 147.

27 Quoted by Margarita Tupitsyn, 'From the Politics of Montage to the Montage of Politics. Soviet Practice 1919 through 1937', in Matthew Teitelbaum (ed.), *Montage and Modern Life 1919–1942* (Cambridge MA and London, MIT Press), 1992.

28 *Zee Zucht*, 5:5/6 (1992) 63.

29 Václav Ševčík, 'In Memoriam. The Political Poster 1958–1991', partly published in Marta Sylvestrová and Dana Bartelt, *Art as Activist. Revolutionary Posters from Central and Eastern Europe* (London, Thames & Hudson), 1992, p. 46.

30 Ákos Róna-Tas, *The Great Surprise of the Small Transformation. The Demise of Communism and the Rise of the Private Sector in Hungary* (Ann Arbor MI, University of Michigan Press), 1997, p. 3.

31 See Claes Arvidsson and Lars Erik Blomqvist, *Symbols of Power. The Esthetics of Political Legitimation in the Soviet Union and Eastern Europe* (Stockholm, Almqvist & Wiksell International), 1987; Elena F. Hellberg, 'Folklore Might and Glory', *Nordic Journal of Soviet and East European Studies*, 3:2 (1986) 9–20 and 'The Hero in Popular Pictures: Russian Lubok and Soviet Poster', in Rolf Wilhelm Brednich and Andreas Hartmann (eds), *Populäre Bildmedien. Vorträge des 2. Symposiums für ethnologische Bildforschung Rheinhausen bei Göttingen* (Göttingen), 1989, pp. 171–91; and Victoria F. Bonnell, *Iconography of Power. Soviet Political Posters under Lenin and Stalin* (Berkeley CA, University of California Press), 1998.

32 Moisei Kagan, 'The Formation and Development of Socialist Art. The Logic of the Formation of Socialist Art in the Era of Capitalism', in *Socialist Realism in Literature and Art. A Collection of Articles* (Moscow, Progress Publishers), 1971, p. 163.

33 Alexander Solzhenitsyn wrote in a story concerning an old peasant woman with whom he had lodged during a journey he undertook in 1953: 'Matryona's house was nearby. It had a row of four windows along the side on which the sun never shone, a steep shingled roof with an elaborately ornamental dormer window. But the shingles were rotting away, the logs of the cottage walls and the once mighty gateposts had turned grey with age … I was fated to stay in this dark cottage with its tarnished mirror, in which it was completely impossible to see yourself, and its two cheap, brightly coloured posters hung on the wall for decoration, one advertising the book trade and the other campaigning for the harvest.' *Matryona's House and other Stories* (Harmondsworth, Penguin), 1975, pp. 12–13.

34 Socialist realism was established under the auspices of A. A. Zhdanov, Secretary of the Central Committee of the Communist Party of the Soviet Union. See Maxim Gorky, Karl Radek, Nikolai Bukharin, Andrei Zhdanov *et al.*, *Soviet Writers' Congress 1934. The Debate on Socialist Realism and Modernism* (London, Lawrence & Wishart), 1977.

35 A. Sutyagin (ed.), *The Bases of Marxist-Leninist Aesthetics* (Moscow, State Publishers of Political Literature, Institutes of Philosophy and History of Art of the Academy of Sciences of the USSR), 1960; and C. Vaughan James, *Soviet Socialist Realism. Origins and Theory* (London, Macmillan), 1973, p. 9.

36 Vera Dunham, *In Stalin's Time. Middle-class Values in Soviet Fiction* (Cambridge, Cambridge University Press), 1976, p. 19.

37 Herbert Marcuse, *Soviet Marxism. A Critical Analysis* (Harmondsworth, Penguin Books), 1971, p. 112.

38 Conversation with the authors, Mariusz Knorowski and René Wanner at Wilanow, Warsaw, May 1997.

39 Miklós Haraszti, *The Velvet Prison. Artists under State Socialism* (Harmondsworth, Penguin), 1987, p. 19.

40 Quoted by Nathan Stoltzfus, *Resistance of the Heart. Intermarriage and the Rosenstrasse Protest in Nazi Germany* (New York, Norton), 1997.

41 A process accompanied by breakdown of the social order and associated iconoclastic violence. See W. J. T. Mitchell, 'The Violence of Public Art', in W. J. T. Mitchell (ed.), *Art and the Public Sphere* (Chicago and London, University of Chicago Press), 1992.

42 Slavoj ižek, *The Sublime Object of Ideology* (London and New York, Verso), 1989, p. 29.

43 Pritt J. Vesilind, 'Estonia, Latvia and Lithuania Struggle toward Independence. The Baltic Nations', *National Geographic*, November (1990) 13.

44 Miłosz, *The Captive Mind*, pp. 54–81.

45 'The triumph of advertising in the culture industry is that consumers feel compelled to buy and use its products even though they see through them.' Adorno and Horkheimer, *Dialectic of Enlightenment*, p. 94.

46 Žižek, *The Sublime Object of Ideology*, p. 29.

47 Gross, *Revolution from Abroad,* pp. 235–6.

48 Juri Hain, *Estonian Contemporary Posters* (Tallinn, Eesti Raamat), 1987, unpag.

49 *Kulturní tvorba*, 15 October 1964, quoted by Václav Ševčík, 'In Memoriam. The Political Poster 1958–1991'.

50 A 1959 Mass Culture Research Unit at the Polish Academy of Sciences Institute of Philosophy and Sociology found that only one in ten cinema goers was found to be influenced by posters. See Jerzy Waśniewski, *The Polish Poster* (Warsaw, WAG), 1972.

51 '… the early extravagances of the artistic left were lost in a forest of mass-produced discs emblazoned with the new hammer and sickle. A typical Leninist touch was the order by the planning committee to preserve all decorative artefacts after the ceremonies as the basic collection of a new Museum of the October Revolution.' Stites, *Revolutionary Dreams*, p. 91.

52 Interestingly enough, the building became the object of an anti-communist terrorist bomb in the 1980s.

53 *Muzeum dělnického revolučního hnutí Jižních Čech* (Céské Budějovice), 1975, p. 174.

54 Ernst Nehrlich, 'Odborná škola pro užité umění v Berlíně' (College of Applied Arts in Berlin), *Tvar*, 12:3 (1962) 70.

55 Syzmon Bojko, *The Polish Poster Today* (Warsaw, WAG), 1972, unpag.

56 *Ibid.*: 'Posters addressing the soldiers of the Polish units fighting on the western battle fronts appeared in the West, where Jan Polinski, a soldier artist and a graduate of the Architecture Department of the Warsaw Polytechnic, did his best to maintain the union with his country. Posters were multiplied by hand, for lack of any other possibilities of reproduction. They were designed by painters in battledress as, for instance, Włodzimierz Zakrzewski … The losses and devastation suffered by Polish art during World War II were catastrophic indeed. The toll among our artists was shocking in extent: many of them perished, others were dispersed all over the world; almost all collections had been destroyed and printing facilities were simply non-existent.'

57 *Die Hundert Besten Plakate* foundered in 1991, but was restarted in 1996.

58 See *100+1 Years of Hungarian Poster Design 1885–1986* (Budapest, Mücsarnok), 1986.

59 He acknowledges a debt to an idea put forward by the Katowice District of the Union of Polish Plastic Artists in 1961, and places the biennale in the international history of such exhibitions. He mentions Venice (founded in 1895), São Paolo, Paris, Tokyo, Alexandria, Tehran, and graphics biennales in Lublau and Lugano. See *Ogolnopolska Biennale Plakatu* (Katowice), 1965.

60 The group included György Kemény, Tibor Helényi, Károly Schmal, Andras Felvidéki, Margit Balla, István Bakos and Kálmán Molnár.

61 Bojko, *The Polish Poster Today*. The year also saw the first post-war national retrospective of the Polish poster at Wilanow and a retrospective at the National Museum in Warsaw. Two years later a poster museum was established at Wilanow and the collection at the Museum of the History of the Polish Revolutionary Movement was founded in Warsaw.

62 See Mariusz Knorowski, *Muzeum Ulicy Plakat Polski w kolekcji Muzeum plakata w Wilanowie* (Warsaw, Muzeum Plakatu w Wilanowie), 1996. Alongside these contributions were psychedelic entertainment posters from Seymour Chwast and Martin Sharpe and an abundance of posters from Vietnam. Roman Cieślewicz's *Che Si* (1968) bridged the cultural and political gulf between them on visual and metaphorical levels. György

Kemény's psychedelic *Ho Chi Minh* performed a similar function at the Warsaw Biennale in 1970 as it played in psychedelic style to one of the political icons of those who opposed the Vietnam War in the West. Similarly, the straight political posters of Viktor Ivanov celebrating Soviet achievements and condemning Western imperialist ambition contrasted with the sexual licentiousness of designs by the Belgian Guy Paeellaert.

63 In the absence of significant Western influence and investment the Japanese have played an increasingly important role in the region. Their early involvement on the level of graphic design might be interpreted as the result of a dialogue between professional designers in the absence of similar events in Japan – the Toyama Triennale was not established until 1985 and the first poster museums were not established until that time. Graphic design was a fertile area of exchange because it has a comparable status in Japan – it is not regarded as a poor commercial cousin of fine art and is perceived as socially significant. Japanese designers shared an interest in international and universal graphic design language capable of communicating without the need for text. As early as 1964 a writer in the official Polish journal, *Projekt*, characterized Japanese design within broad socialist realist parameters when he described it as 'closely connected with the country's landscape, culture and traditions'. There is also an affinity between the sound of spoken Japanese and Polish which has helped to smooth the continuing good relations between the design communities in the two countries.

64 Jan Rajlich jun. listed the following exhibitions in 1988: IBA International Buchkunst-Austellung, Leipzig; Biennale of Graphic Design, Brno; BIB, The Biennale of Illustrations, Bratislava; Poster Biennale, Warsaw; BIO, Biennale of Industrial Design, Ljubljana; ZGRAF, The International Exhibition of Graphic Design, Zagreb; Zlatno pero Beograda, International Exhibition of Illustrations, Belgrade; International Festival of Humour and Satire, Gabrovo, Bulgaria. In addition the Toyama Poster Triennale, Japan, and the Colorado International Poster Exhibition, Fort Collins CO, were established in 1985. The Golden Bee Poster Biennale, Moscow, was established in 1990; Lahti Poster Biennale, Finland; Triennale européene de l'affiche politique, Mons; and the Festival d'Affiches de Chaumont, Paris, were established in the 1970s.

65 Colin Forbes in Jorge Frascara (ed.), *Graphic Design World Views. A Celebration of Icograda's Twenty-fifth Anniversary* (New York, ICOGRADA Kodansha International), 1990; see also F. H. K. Henrion, *AGI annals. Alliance Graphique Internationale 1952–1987* (Zurich, AGI), 1989.

66 In F. H. K. Henrion's history of the AGI, Poland and East Germany are featured only in the 1950s. This in spite of the personal friendship of Henrion and Henryk Tomaszewski and the involvement of Icograda and AGI in the biennales in Brno and Warsaw and the triennale in Zagreb. Annual general meetings of the AGI were held in Warsaw in 1974 and Prague in 1981. The only formal eastern European members of the admittedly elite organization were from Czechoslovakia and were elected between 1967 and 1981.

67 'A Kite in the Wind of History', 1998, unpublished ms.

68 Rutkiewicz in Susan Hornik, 'In Poland a Poster is a Fiery Art and a Way to Speak Out', *Smithsonian*, January (1993) 92.

69 Ministry of Culture and Art Society of Polish Graphic Designers Local Division and Art Gallery in Katowice.

70 Rutkiewicz, 'In Poland', p. 92.

71 ICOM Bulletin, Budapest, 1994, unpag.

CHAPTER TWO

GROUND ZERO AND THE AESTHETICS OF SOCIALIST REALISM 1945–56

CONSOLIDATION

On 23 November 1948 the Central Committee of the Communist Party of the Soviet Union adopted a resolution 'On the Shortcomings of and Measures to Improve Political Posters'. It spoke of the need to raise ideological and political content, to increase posters' agitational force and to diversify their subject matter to 'cover all the aspects of home and international affairs, and answer the most vital questions of the time'.[1]

The years 1945–49 were a period of consolidation, and a variety of styles operated simultaneously. Johannes R. Becher was one of the principal architects of cultural policy in the Soviet zone of occupation in Germany and he attempted to attract non-communists by demanding a *Kahlschlag* (clean sweep), starting from *Nullpunkt* (ground zero). There could be no return to Weimar and the conditions which had given rise to fascism: 'if we do not clear away the rubble, if we do not achieve a renewal in the spiritual realm and a moral rebirth of our people, then material reconstruction will sooner or later be doomed to failure.'[2] Becher's policy was opposed to Soviet aims and had little effect. But, for a while, it kept the field open for the revival of the pre-war forms he wished to avoid. Many posters aped expressionism, others combined innovative and modernist typography with figurative and abstract elements which might have led them to be compared unfavourably with more orthodox designs. The defeat of fascism had released energies suppressed since 1933 and the Soviets were wary of imposing Marxist-Leninist tenets too quickly for fear of rousing comparisons with the Nazis. Nevertheless, the proud and athletic figure as an embodiment of Nazi national and ethnic pride slipped effortlessly into Soviet dress to survive with very little modification across the whole area of former occupation.[3]

In Hungary abstraction and surrealism, suppressed under the pre-war regime of General Miklos Horthy (1920–44) were regarded positively.[4] Filo (Ilona Fischer) (9.34) and György Konecsni produced robustly optimistic posters tempered by a romantic sense of loss rather than the promise of the socialist future. In the Year of the Turning Point, 1948, when Stalin consolidated his power in the region, Konecsni and Gábor Papp made a series of posters dealing with the aftermath of war in an idiom derived from surrealism. As images of the night they were unstable and ambiguous, far removed from the certainties of the new dawn promised for communist Europe, and had far more in common with the sensibility of Arthur Koestler, the author of the political allegory *Darkness at Noon* (1948), than with Zhdanov's socialist-realist designs. Ultimately, they could not be tolerated:

> the poster had now to speak a language that should be distinct and accessible to all strata of the population. Abstract and surrealistic elements of surface art were energetically pushed aside so as to make room for harmonious, humanly vital realism. More and more the role of dispenser of commissions was taken over by the state and soon the poster painter had the reputation of the best situated of artists employed by the state.[5]

The position was similar in Czechoslovakia, where posters welcoming the Red Army or dedicated to Czech–Soviet friendship were loaded with residual memories of pre-war modernism and *la moderne* (6.138). Others were sombre and dark, drawing on indigenous expressionist and realist traditions which played on essentialist, poetic and pessimistic articulations of the human condition (6.154). The legacy and meaning of European romanticism and modernism were going to be hard for the communist party to eliminate.

Klement Gottwald, the first communist President of the Czechoslovak Republic, remarked in his inaugural speech in February 1948: 'We start today a great planned drive not only for the economic but also the cultural renewal of the people. In order to renew man spiritually and morally … it is not only a matter of making existing culture accessible, our people also need a new culture of today, living today and contributing today.'[6] A typically rhetorical statement, but, nevertheless, it reveals a very real sense of purpose. A similar story unfolded in the Soviet occupied zone in Germany. Relative aesthetic diversity was displaced by Stalinist *apparatchiks* such as Alexander Dymschitz, who, as the officer of the military administration responsible for cultural policy, mobilized the forces of socialist realism.

(detail of 2.7)

Dymschitz's response was symptomatic of moves throughout the region as he reacted to the directives of Stalin's aesthetic policy maker (and son-in-law), A. A. Zhdanov.

Czesław Miłosz described the process in Poland, where pre-war modernist aesthetic traditions persisted as strongly as anywhere else in the region. Socialist realism got a hostile reception:

> Usually, however, one daring artist would launch an attack, full of restrained sarcasm, with the silent but obvious support of the entire audience. He would invariably be crushed by superior reasoning plus practicable threats against the future of an undisciplined individual career. Given the conditions of convincing argument plus such threats, the necessary conversion will take place.[7]

Given the type of repressive control the communists were able to exert, and in combination with domestic desires to build something materially and socially and politically new, their influence was irresistible. Socialist realism was put forward as the true mirror of human life as it should be lived. In contrast, modern abstract and surrealist styles were regarded as warped and distorted reflections born of capitalist anti-humanism.[8]

Socialist realism is exemplified in the confident, sometimes 'baroque' and certainly 'classical' posters of Mikhail Abramovich Gordon and (6.143) Viktor Koretsky (6.12). Aesthetic innovation is divorced from progress and avant-garde experiment is identified with chaos: 'innovation reached its most insane point when a girl, for instance, would be portrayed with one head and forty legs, one eye looking at you and the other at the North Pole.'[9] Modernism and its less programmatic derivative *la moderne* were on borrowed time, and in an echo of the purges of the 1930s a campaign was launched to eliminate the last vestiges of bourgeois culture. Essentially it was an assault on the intelligentsia, carried out with a 'realist' and 'truthful' arsenal drawn from Russian and classical European traditions.

Zhdanov had first outlined his thinking at the First All Union Congress of Soviet Writers in 1934, and reasserted it in 1947 with attacks on the poetess Anna Akhmatova and the composer Dmitri Shostakovitch, culminating in the Conference of Soviet Music Workers in 1948. The crudity of the circular arguments is marked by the vulgarity and intemperance of his language. He called for a new art in the face of bourgeois degeneration: 'A riot of mysticism, religious mania and pornography is characteristic of the decline and decay of bourgeois culture. The "celebrities" of that bourgeois literature which has sold its pen to capital are today thieves, detectives, prostitutes, pimps and gangsters.'[10] Graphic interpretations abounded and

Konstantin Ivanov's visualization contrasts the clear-eyed vision of socialist realism with the fearful confusions of bourgeois culture (2.1). In an intuition fired by faith in the future and an idea of realism capable of addressing the party, the people and socialism, culture was given the task of 'socialist construction', of representing society in 'revolutionary development'. Stealing a lead from the legacy of the avant garde, culture had a role in the transformation of everyday life: 'our tomorrow is being prepared by planned and conscious work today'. Famously, Stalin had described artists as 'engineers of the human soul', and, as agents of socialist realism and the creative and technocratic intelligentsia, designers emphasized skill, craft and ideological content in their work. The aim was to be conservative and revolutionary: understandable but politically radical according to the tenets of proletarian revolution defined by 'the invincible teaching of Marx, Engels, Lenin and Stalin'.

At first socialist realism was uncritically optimistic, although later it was criticized for being unable to articulate lived experience. Art for art's sake was condemned outright because it had abandoned the people to a corrupted and difficult art obscured behind a mask of beauty. The programme was subject to direct political control through the party, and Zhdanov asserted the right of the Central Committee to act severely where ideological principles were transgressed. The threat of arrest and the actuality of institutional control, censorship and mutual self-criticism established its authority:

> Comrade Stalin teaches us that if we wish to conserve our human resources, to guide and teach the people, we must not be afraid of hurting the feelings of single individuals or fear bold, frank, objective criticism founded on principle. Any organization … is liable to degenerate without criticism … Only bold frank criticism can help our people and overcome any failings in their work. Where criticism is lacking, stagnation and inertia set in, leaving no room for progress.[11]

If class antagonisms and the crises of capitalism had been eliminated, so self-criticism was to become an essential component in the dialectic of communist society. Class struggle was replaced by the conflict between the old and the new, between the 'dying' and the 'rising' forms of consciousness. The individual, elitist and existential were condemned in favour of the popular, collective and socialist.

For Zhdanov formalism was anti-classical, individualistic and elitist, but it was also alien and foreign. In a policy underwritten by an unstated antisemitism, visible in the caricatured faces of the capitalist enemy found in Soviet posters, contact with the West and Western sympathies led to charges of 'cosmopolitanism'. As a product of the paranoia of the last years of Stalin's rule the campaign was halted only by his death. Charges of cosmopolitanism were usually linked with international modernism, its dislocations and ambiguities exemplifying the fragmentation of the bourgeois world.

In the name of the people Zhdanov lamented the lack of sensitivity to folk forms as collective products of the Russian nation, drawing a distinction between unrooted cosmopolitanism, identified with the European avant garde, and a national popular realism enriched by all that is 'progressive', popular and good from all cultures: 'To forget this is to lose one's individuality and become a cosmopolitan without a country.'[12] The post-war expansion of Soviet influence had necessitated a shift in cultural policy, involving on the one hand the promotion of an international subjection to Russian language and culture, but on the other promoting folk cultures under the umbrella of 'national communism' to fulfil the formula 'national in form but socialist in content'.

Socialist realism was a manifestation of reactionary modernity. In economics and technology it embraced radical progress, but in the aesthetic it looked to traditional and archaic forms as articulations of national identity. Latvian posters produced in the first half of the 1950s show how a simplified monumental and regional style was adapted to socialist-realist objectives. But the process was profoundly ambiguous: folk motifs such as national costume and emblems of outright national independence were appropriated to socialist realism as an affirmation and a challenge to Soviet dominance. *Long live great Stalin!* (6.9), for example, features Stalin within a niche of red flags arranged in the pattern of the traditional Latvian sunburst. He is imperially Napoleonic, but Latvian identity is not totally subsumed within a discourse of Russian manifest destiny and national repression.

For a brief period, socialist realism produced a highly codified, hierarchical, ideologically loaded form of narrative figurative expression. For the ideologues of culture it was neither God, Mammon nor Manifest Destiny but Marxism-Leninism which granted socialist realism its historically elevated optimism and the power to oppose decadent bourgeois individualism and indigenous romanticism. As such, it was resolutely middlebrow. Connotations of the aesthetic and the *chic* associated with constructivism, geometric abstraction and *la moderne* were banished in favour of an anti-aesthetic familiar from contemporary commercial utilitarian mass communications in the West.

In 1953, the year of Stalin's death, a conference was convened in Warsaw on the occasion of the first All Poland Poster Exhibition. It hosted delegates from the German Democratic Republic, Czechoslovakia and Hungary.

Preceding the relative thaw of 1955–57 by two years, it is possible from the published papers to set out the terms of the aesthetic debate as it emerged during the early 1950s. Against the Soviet example, which was both narrative and illustrational, the decorative use of line and colour was perceived as a negative legacy of the inter-war years; formalist compositions were criticized for being difficult to understand; social realism, as opposed to socialist realism, was seen to be too depressing; naturalism was identified with the *kitsch* taste of the workers and the peasants, and was denounced as deterministic and reactionary. The emblematic and metonymic were treated with the disdain deserving the clever visual conceits of the intelligentsia. Suspicion was heaped upon both humour and blind optimism for being both trivializing and insensitive to class struggle.

Józef Mroszczak emphasized the importance of idealism for the establishment of a new Marxist-Leninist order in Poland, calling for designers to grapple with the struggle for peace and socialism and to promote active engagement with politics.[13] Mroszczak establishes six main points in relation to the design and function of the poster. Firstly, it is to be experienced as part of daily life, attracting the attention of the people without distracting them from their tasks. Secondly, it must function as an ideological 'missile', capable of inspiring the translation of thought into action. Accordingly, it has to be succinct and accurate in its textual and visual expression: 'an abbreviation of a vast problem of ideological, economic or political nature'. Thirdly, the text and the image must work together. Fourthly, it must be topical, reacting quickly to the important events and issues of the day. The fifth point establishes the importance of realism and, finally, he asks for a certain truth to materials in the poster as a product of the printing process.

Older artists supported by the state because of their sincerity and their 'combative and generous natures' were criticized by Jerzy Bogusz for their close ties with pre-war modes and practices embodied in the 'formalistic burden' of the advertisement with its desire to shock and surprise.[14] For Bogusz, unlike the highly influential designer, Henryk Tomaszewski, who was committed to late modern international graphic design, these solutions were progressive only from an experimental point of view (5.10). To the committed communist they were unsuitable for the new reality of Poland. He also argued that many artists believed the public had been so thoroughly seduced by commercial *kitsch* that it was desensitized to any other kind of expression. Mroszczak concurred, making the comment that workers and peasants wanted neither photographic reproduction nor *kitsch* but a new kind of realism.[15]

Soviet socialist realism provided a benchmark for ideological and artistic quality, but it never imposed a uniform aesthetic on poster production. Orthodox socialist realism was nothing if not literal-minded in its approach. The scenes depicted in the posters make use of exaggerated perspectives and dislocations of scale, but to dramatic rather than graphic effect. Bogusz provided an explanation of socialist realism as 'art which is devoid of falsification but is a mirror of reality which serves to reform that reality'. Distinguished from 'slavish naturalism', it pursued the 'typical'. Anything which failed to demonstrate inevitable progress towards communism was less than 'typical' and, therefore, false. At the centre of this aesthetic lies the human figure, 'the psychological picture of a person': 'Artists as a measure of maturing of political consciousness realized that expression of humanistic character of our slogans without showing the human being is very difficult, does not allow for a full reference to the emotional relation between the idea expressed in the poster and millions of people for whom the poster is destined.'[16] Real character emerges from situations of struggle and achievement, and through

symbols and associations drawn from real life the artist finds an individuality of expression, defined, in part, through national traditions. But these were to be literally depicted; the programme could never be absolutely successful where the emphasis on communications had long since abandoned surface appearance as a qualification for effective design (6.12).

Many designers, Mroszczak and Tadeusz Trepkowski among them, were criticized in what was described by Bogusz as the 'battle for the realistic poster'. Their work was regarded as oblique in its use of symbols and abstract forms, succeeding only in creating posters illegible to everyone except for a narrow elite of *cognoscenti*. Visual eloquence and poetic association could only obscure the political message (5.13, 7.14). By the same token, posters which relied too heavily on symbols were criticized for carrying naturalistic tendencies into formal design; they stood doubly condemned for failing to address the typical and for subjugating content to form. Jerzy Bogusz censured Tomaszewski for his formalism, significantly taking as an example a poster dedicated to the centenary of Chopin's death in 1949:

> No fetishising of form could help here… what is important is not 'what' but 'how' this is nothing less than formalism. Deformed piano with dislocated keys (to attain pseudo-effect) cannot give the content which ought to be subordinate to the form, does not hit, does not address the mass audience for which in People's Poland the poster is made.[17]

He further lambasted the poster for being widely published and praised in the West. He contrasted it unfavourably with a Tadeusz Trepkowski poster, commemorating a play by Pushkin, as if only contact with Soviet culture could produce such 'warmth … thought and … feeling contained in it, and with what frugal means'. Ultimately the attempt was to extinguish the international language of graphic design in favour of a provincial Russian and subsequently Polish classical realism.

Polish posters were compared unfavourably with the Soviet examples of Dmitrii Moor, Viktor Koretsky (6.12) and Viktor Ivanov (8.76), and the importance of 'proper' guidance from Soviet artists and critics was established. Such criticisms were part of the process of mutual self-criticism.[18] But within this debate an important argument was slowly emerging which was to have long-term implications for the development of the poster. Western interpreters saw in the Polish poster, as a popular medium of expression, a justification for the belief some had in the emancipatory potential of modernism, freed from the elitist demands of high culture and the museum, and independent of the arbitrary demands of commerce and the market. This way of thinking in Poland opened up the possibilities of

2.1
Konstantin Ivanov, poetry A. Bezymensky, *Ours – art for the nation / Theirs – art of a kind / We build, aim / to serve our homeland, / aim of their art, / to deviate from reality*, 1956, Soviet Union silkscreen Agitplakat, Moscow, Academy of Fine Arts, Berlin.

individual expression without necessarily leaving designers open to charges of anti-communism.

Mroszczak, as a future director of the state publishing house in Warsaw, Wydawnictwa Artystyczno-Graficznego (WAG), was focusing his attack on the current director, Henryk Szemberg. WAG had taken an active role in making the work of the Polish poster school known abroad in international poster exhibitions and in the pages of propaganda magazines.[19] Szemberg encouraged, as far as possible, expressive, modernist individualism.[20] International modernism in poster design was condemned, but it did reach the walls of galleries in the West in the late 1940s and 1950s. In 1948, despite official criticism from cultural arbiters at home, Tomaszewski, whose debt to modernism and participation in the international graphics scene were well known, won five medals at the Vienna International Film Exhibition while the city was still under Soviet occupation. Furthermore, official publications promoted the posters with portrait photographs.[21] The photographs privilege the position of the designer and establish the value of the product in the artist, rather than the poster itself or any ideological values it may represent. By focusing on the artist, traditional authorial values are re-established and the poster is promoted as an art form rather than a utilitarian or commercial object.

Thousands of socialist-realist posters were widely disseminated in Poland but did not travel to the West and they remained virtually unknown beyond Poland's borders (6.14, 8.41). Beyond the Iron Curtain the regime needed a favourable image, particularly in relation to human rights. The artist, in particular, traditionally a figure of bourgeois individualism in Europe, had to be seen to be able to work according to the tenets of his or her individual conscience. Hence modernist modes could be tolerated for external consumption. Internally, the task remained that of propaganda, or, more accurately, visual agitation. Only the ideologically sound mode of expression could be deemed capable of carrying the socialist message to the masses.

Socialist cultural politics were not entirely new to the region in 1945, and the process of cultural transformation was built on residual cultural formations from the pre-war period. This was decisive in the German Democratic Republic, where political posters were generally more technically advanced in their use of photo-montage. Berlin had been the focus of modernist activity before the war, and designers could draw on traditions developed in exile which had flourished under the Weimar Republic. Important among these were the well known Der Malik Verlag, which had published *The Workers' Illustrated Magazine* (*AIZ*) and the photo-montages of John Heartfield, who had returned to East Berlin in 1950. There was also the lesser known but

no less important trade group NWG Ring neue Werbegestalter (Circle of New Advertising Designers), founded by Kurt Schwitters. Among its members were the artist Cesar Domela and the typographer Jan Tschichold. Many of these designers had direct contact with Soviet avant-gardists such as El Lissitsky and Alexander Rodchenko, both of whom had been involved in the production of foreign exhibitions and the Soviet foreign-language propaganda magazine *USSR in Construction*. Der Malik Verlag and NWG were associated with the radical politics of the left but were neither owned nor controlled by the German Communist Party (KPD). This situation changed in the post-war era and radical cultural politics were orchestrated by organizations belonging to the Socialist Unity Party (SED).[22]

The left-leaning, if liberal humanist, cultural elite, first ravaged by Hitler, was subjected to criticism at the Fifth Plenum of the SED in March 1951 under the slogans of 'partisanship' and 'accessibility to the masses'. The party published a declaration called *The Struggle against Formalism in Art and Literature, for a Progressive German Culture*. According to the party, formalist modernism and the legacies of the Bauhaus and German expressionism were seen to be grounded in classless cosmopolitanism and stood accused of indirectly supporting American cultural imperialism. Modernism in the West had been appropriated by capitalism, and little of its original utopianism remained. It was an important issue for the party as it struggled for legitimacy on a territory defined by claims for a specifically German Democratic and anti-fascist identity. On 12 July 1951 the State Commission on Art was founded to put these formulas into action, its tasks being the 'victory over formalism', 'the struggle against decadence' and 'the development of realistic art in continuity with the great classical masters'.

Between 1949 and 1955 the campaign against formalism and Americanism was interrupted for the short period from Stalin's death in March to October 1953 by the liberal demands of the New Course. Originally aimed at the economic, rather than the cultural, sphere, it was intended to stimulate growth at a time of increasing labour unrest provoked by price rises and shortages of consumer goods. The strategy failed on 17 June when the Federal Republic signed a treaty of friendship with the United States and Soviet tanks were sent into East Berlin to quell the unrest, killing 121 people: 1,200 arrests followed. Paradoxically, the repressive conditions which had led to the uprising made a gentle thaw necessary in the interests of stability. A series of discussions culminated on 27 May when Walter Ulbricht spoke in favour of open intellectual debate. The first open criticism of party cultural policy appeared in a ten-point declaration at the Academy of Arts in Berlin on 30 June 1953. It demanded the state should not meddle in matters of style, and called for the elimination of bureaucratic and jargon-filled language, and for criticism to be left to the public, not the party. The discussions got as far as allowing love, as well as labour, to be seen on film – but the willingness of the party to discuss cultural reform ended at that point.[23]

The failures of the *Aufbaujahre* precipitated a cultural revolution which drew not on the bourgeois traditions of classical high art but on modernism and the cultural ferment of Weimar. Focused on the circle around Bertolt Brecht and John Heartfield, it laid the foundations of the shift to more subjectivist and expressionist forms in the early 1960s. It is tempting to extrapolate Hans Eisler's and Brecht's designs for a new folk culture into the realm of the poster.[24] Formulated against the background of Konrad Adenauer's pro-American and fiercely anti-communist government in the Federal German Republic, *volkstumlich* made use of new media and materials. It was to be experimental and in tune with the mechanisms of the mass media. Conceived as a critical popular culture as a bastion against Western commercial popular entertainment and the culture industry, it would revolutionize and democratize cultural production in 'progressive' societies. Its ideal audience was to be the proletariat. Eisler, Brecht and Adorno shrewdly observed, but in reality criticized, directives coming from Moscow. Unlike Mroszczak in Poland, they credited the worker with intelligence, discrimination and a capacity for innovation within national traditions of international revolutionary class struggle:

New popular culture is the conversion of the new into the simple. Without becoming vulgar, it will establish community with a language that the inexperienced will also understand. … The historical contradiction between 'serious art' and 'light entertainment' will be sublated, and its elements will balance themselves out in a new unity. … The gap between art and the people will be closed.[25]

The project left a lasting legacy in the work of John Heartfield (until his death in 1969) (6.57) and Klaus Wittkugel, the most important of all the official poster designers in the GDR (8.77). These latter-day designers, such as Wittkugel, made use of photo-montage and photographic techniques in line with technological developments in the media, while repeating the formulaic content and slogans of the political posters of the period. As poster designs within a socialist-realist aesthetic they rely on the indexical character of the photograph, with its substantial popular and widely believed truth claims to realism, rather than the legacies of older bourgeois narrative forms derived from high art or more critical avant-gardist energies.

In Czechoslovakia designers also made frequent use of photo-montage. Despite their newly politicized subject matter, they owed their inspiration to the pre-war studios of Jindřich Štyrský, František Tichý, Ladislav Sutnar, Karel Teige, František Muzika, Zdeněk Rossmann, and others. Designers such as Bohumil Štěpán and the P5P group shared with them the combination of black-and-white photographic elements and exaggerated perspectives with more abstract and graphic compositional elements (8.34). Inter-war avant-garde traditions had been embodied in Czech functionalism and the politically inspired Left Front[26] with its connections with German and Russian modernism and the international style to provide designers with a sophisticated anti-Soviet visual vocabulary. These tendencies were compounded by memories of the SVU Mànes (Mànes Association of Fine Artists) and the 1934 International Exhibition of Political Cartoons featuring, most controversially, a selection of photo-montages by John Heartfield.[27] However, its legacies were not to be fully realized until the 1960s.

THE 1955–57 THAW

Following Stalin's death there was a period of aesthetic liberalization called the Thaw. It took its name from Ilya Ehrenburg's novel, published in 1954.[28] The revolutionary romanticism of socialist realism was spent, and Ehrenburg, among others, criticized culture for its bombast and lack of conviction,[29] calling for a more complex approach to the arts.[30] Condemned as illustrative, or photographic, and too optimistic and free of conflict, socialist realism was thought

2.2
Anon., *Flag burning*, Budapest, October 1956, Hungarian National Museum, Budapest, Department of Photography.

incapable of a 'historically concrete depiction of reality in its revolutionary development'. Jorn Gulberg has argued that socialist realism had effectively disappeared as a credible, practicable theory after the twentieth party congress in 1956 and Krushchev's 'secret speech'.[31] Even abstraction was tolerated, provided it functioned according to the aims of the party and conveyed the necessary political message.

Designs clearly inspired by the Polish poster school began to appear in the Soviet Union. In Poland the situation had changed since 1952, when, under the direction of Józef Mroszczak and Henryk Tomaszewski, the teaching of graphic design at the Academy of Fine Arts in Warsaw had taken a more independent turn, attracting many painting students. Designers were allowed to express their individuality through the autonomous demands of the design process. The new freedom was 'exemplified by the plastic decoration of the streets of Warsaw during the fifth International Youth and Students' Festival (1955), the work was monumental in size, and designed by Tomaszewski, Wojciech Fangor, Jan Młodoˇzeniec and others … it was a manifestation of avant-garde art, which affirmed abstraction and colour values, hitherto forbidden fruit'.[32] From that point on, designers in Poland were allowed a degree of autonomy. According to Mariusz Knorowski the expressive and metaphorical poster was dominant, and it aspired to the condition of art rather than applied graphic design (5.10, 6.125, 127). Significantly, the broadening of horizons was part of an already existing questioning of official culture which tolerated blue jeans, jazz and satire and deliberately promoted socialism with a Polish face.

Often dependent on indigenous ancient and modern traditions, designs became simpler and less dependent on surface detail and narrative. Mieczysław Berman's *Communism – it is the rule of the Soviets plus electrification* (1955) (7.20) unites schematized photographic elements with heroic imagery in a simple colour combination. Many other designs share a graphic clarity, even if the heroic aspirations of the figures remain. Roman Cieślewicz's *Create socialism …* (1955) and Zbigniew Waszewski's *1917–59* (1959) (6.73) use the abstract imagery of the hammer and sickle to give communism world significance. The anonymous *Today he does not care … but what about tomorrow?* (1955) (8.93) isolates the figure of a downcast alcoholic in an image of social ostracism and political alienation. The posters are not poetic but metonymic and emblematic, and the message remains clear.

The authoritarian old guard saw the Thaw as a revisionist threat, a foreign conspiracy contributing to civil unrest in Poland and to the uprising in Hungary.[33] József Révai, the Minister of Culture in Hungary, had pursued hard-line Stalinist policies, banning many artists and impoverishing the cultural and intellectual life of the country. But in the first years of Krushchev's and Malenkov's leadership the excesses of the regime came under review. In 1954 Révai noted in a report drafted by the Agitation and Propaganda Department that after 1948 it was justified to use 'administrative means' to combat 'bourgeois trash' and to promote Marxism-Leninism and socialist realism, but with the New Course after May 1954 it was possible to allow greater aesthetic freedom.[34]

Prominent poster designers took up a toast, proposed by

2.3
Anon., *No!*, Budapest, October–November 1956, Hungarian National Museum, Budapest, Department of Photography.

2.4
Jenö Virág, *Let me have your watch!*, Budapest, October–November 1956, Hungarian National Museum, Budapest, Department of Photography.

2.3

2.4

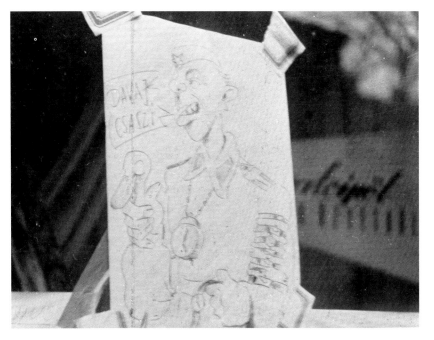

2.5
Tibor Szentpétery, *The battle continues. The government has not met our claims yet. The Soviet troops are still here. Do not surrender your weapons!*, 26 October 1956, the photographer.

2.6
Tibor Szentpétery, *Get out!*, 26 October 1956, the photographer.

2.7
Anon., *Go to the dogs!*, October 1956, Hungarian National Museum, Budapest, Department of Photography.

2.8
Tibor Szentpétery, *The strike is the workers' most effective weapon!*, 26 October 1956, the photographer.

2.5

2.6

2.7

2.8

Gábor Pál, to 'create only good works from now on, to wash off the shame of the graphic artists' output of the past seven years, the poster representations of this period of idolatry'.[35] The new forms were inspired by Western fellow-travellers, Italian neo-realist film posters, the communist artist Renato Guttuso, the legacy of inter-war modernism. A good example of this kind of post-Stalinist design is Filo's *No!* (1955) (9.34): conventional caricature is abandoned in favour of the metonymy of the iron heel. The meaning of military power is unambiguous, and with the Soviet invasion in 1956 it was an image as prophetic as it was a departure from socialist-realist convention (2.3).

During the uprising, traditional national emblems replaced those of the communist state, red flags were burnt and the streets were plastered with mocking and defiant hand-drawn and painted posters (2.3–8). The Soviet army had always been presented as morally correct liberators and protectors but, amazed by the relative wealth of Hungarian citizens, soldiers demanded watches and other personal possessions as they had in the aftermath of the occupation in 1945; consequently posters depicted them as criminals (2.4). Another more grotesque poster comments on the distortion of the aims of international socialism the invasion represented for the participants in the uprising and depicts Rákosi as a Red Army soldier in the act of self-castration (2.7). Others looked back to the revolution of 1918 and emulated the iconography of Mihály Bíró's world-famous poster *Red man with hammer* (2.8). On 23 October students toppled Stalin's statue in Budapest and five days later the security services withdrew or defected to the revolution, but on 4 November the Soviets launched a concerted attack backed by 200,000 troops and 2,000 tanks. Some eighteen months later, on 16 June 1958, Imre Nagy and several members of his government were executed after a short trial. In the aftermath up to 2,500 people were executed and 200,000 Hungarians fled to the West.

After the uprising the forces of repression consolidated. Artists' organizations inspired by revisionist pressures were closed. The reassessments of the role of the party in cultural life in the light of the wider history of aesthetic developments in Hungary and abroad were ended. Legal action was taken against those who had broken the law. Many, such as Pál Gábor, emigrated. György Aczél, a member of the Central Committee, who took an active role in the restoration of order, expressed the situation with characteristic authoritarian understatement:

> Besides giving far-reaching support to all forces which offered their help in restoring the people's power, the Party dealt patiently with those who had been misled, allowing them to be convinced of their error. It helped them to recognize their mistakes and to dissociate themselves from foreign and

domestic reaction. The Party did not encourage declarations of loyalty, it did not force anyone, even indirectly, to express views contrary to his convictions. Those who proved through their work that they did not oppose the system were granted working conditions that allowed them once again to take part in cultural life.[36]

Repression was followed by relative liberalization. The blame for the uprising was laid at the feet of both the westernizing liberal intelligentsia and Stalinist excess. Aczél felt the cultural had been subordinated to the political and its importance exaggerated, making it vulnerable to the same mistakes which had led to the uprising, when opposition had been ignored rather than defeated by argument. The authorities agreed repressive measures were counterproductive, and Aczél pursued a policy of accommodation and gentle persuasion. The state set out to court the liberal intelligentsia, asserting the partial autonomy of the cultural sphere, which, at times, may need assistance from the party in arriving at the sole correct Marxist solution. It was a significant, if loaded, concession and a major shift from the unitary vision proposed by Zhdanov: progress in the arts was no longer restricted to the domain of socialist realism.

The policy was couched within a communist model where creative artists and cultural workers, party members and non-party members carried out their work together. Eighteen months after the uprising, the Hungarian Communist Party published a paper, *Guiding Principles for Cultural Policy*. Typically it ensured, 'far reaching freedom for artists serving the people … we are convinced that artistic life, becoming cleansed of dogmatic distortions and revisionist damage, will offer possibilities for the creation of works which are worthy of the splendid efforts and achievements of our working people who are building socialism.'[37] The paper admitted that culture was not homogeneous and, while affirming the superiority of socialist culture over any other, it did not attempt an outright ban on other forms, provided they demonstrated 'honest intention'.[38] The policy laid the foundation of a relatively free aesthetic life, 'cleansed of dogmatic distortions and revisionist damage'.[39]

One interesting problem for the regimes focused on Pablo Picasso, his art and his communism. The painting *Massacre in Korea* (1951) and associated works formed the basis of a debate which took place in the pages of *Bildende Kunst* in the German Democratic Republic. Begun by the painter Heinz Ludecke in May 1955, the discussion turned on the concept of the limits of realism and the work of the Mexican muralists Siqueiros, Orozco and Rivera, and the Italian realist Renato Guttuso. They had been an inspiration to designers such as René Graetz who saw expressionism as the German national form of realism (6.112). In the issue of May 1956 the Hungarian, Endre Domanovsky, called for a more flexible approach to the 'classic heritage' of socialist realism and for the inclusion in the socialist canon of Western social realism, expressionism and constructivism. The debate took on international dimensions with contributions from authors in Zurich, Munich and Brno.

In the light of the 'events' in Poland and Hungary, the authorities in the German Democratic Republic attempted to establish a political and cultural quarantine against the 'capitalist decadence of West German culture'. From July 1957 the Socialist Unity Party started an intense campaign against modernism, abstractism and bourgeois decadence, at the same time recognizing that socialist realism was too bald and insufficiently engaging to be effective. Politically the regime was suffering from its geographical proximity to the Federal German Republic and many of its young people were fleeing across the border, a situation which led to the erection of the Berlin Wall in 1961. The regime called for greater participation from the people and a more creative and agitational *Kulturpolitik* under the slogan 'Cultural questions are questions of power'. The Ministry of Culture blamed the failures of its policies on Western influence. Popular music and fashions were proffered as evidence of the inroads made by Western imperialism and decadence. The regime compounded its lack of success by increasing censorship and repression just at the moment when the myth of party infallibility had been destroyed by the revelations concerning Stalin. Inevitable Marxist-Leninist historical progress was problematized and the image of the new socialist man was displaced by the picture of an alienated and powerless individual, utterly subject to the arbitrary authority of the state. Disillusion set in; the battle for the minds of the people had been lost (4.2).

NOTES

1 *We Follow the Road shown by Great Stalin. Lenin in the Arts of Soviet Ukraine. Political Posters*, Poetry (Kiev, Ukraine), 1985, p. 11.

2 Johannes R. Becher quoted in Alexander Stephan, 'Johannes R. Becher and the Cultural Development of the GDR', *New German Critique*, 1:2 (1974) 76.

3 The relationship between the Soviet and Nazi regimes up to 1941 had produced many examples of mutual if guarded co-operation, and propaganda was certainly one. See Igor Golomstock, *Totalitarian Art in the Soviet Union, Fascist Italy and the People's Republic of China* (London, Collins Harvill), 1990, for a comprehensive account of the relations established in the 1920s. Similar ground is also covered in *Berlin Moskau 1900–1950. Bildende, Kunst, Photographie, Architektur* (Munich and New York, Prestel), 1995. Material released from Soviet archives shows that in Belorussia, for example, anti-Nazi

communist poster designs were reused as anti-Soviet propaganda. See John Erikson, 'Nazi Posters in Wartime Russia', *History Today*, 44:9 (1994) 18–19.

4 See *Modern Art in Hungary* (Budapest, Corvina), 1969. It took a neo-romantic turn to create a late provincial modernism. See *International Poster Annual 1948–1949* (St Gall, Zollikofer Publishers), 1949. In the United Kingdom broad comparisons may be made with the work of Henry Moore, John Piper, Graham Sutherland and Paul Nash, while in the United States comparisons may be drawn with the work of Kurt Seligmann and Peter Blume, for example.

5 Eugen Bauer, in *International Poster Annual '48–'49* (St Gall, Zollikofer), 1949, p. 95.

6 Klement Gottwald quoted in Milan Šimek and Jaroslav Dewetter, *Cultural Policy in Czechoslovakia* (Paris, Unesco), 1981, p. 15n.

7 *The Captive Mind* (Harmondsworth, Penguin), 1953, pp. 12–13. Mariusz Knorowski commented, 'The method of socialist realism was accepted by a substantial part of the circle of artists not without enthusiasm – they believed in the postulate of revolutionary art.' *Forma i tresc w plakacie polskim 1944–1955* (Warsaw), undated, unpag.

8 Interestingly enough, similar criticisms of modernist styles had been made from Marxist and liberal humanist positions in Western Europe in the late 1950s and early 1960s. They were made in relation to the all-pervasive influence of American abstract expressionism by figures such as the art historians Anthony Blunt, whose communist sympathies even as Keeper of the Royal Collection are now well known, and Edgar Wind, a German-Jewish refugee from Nazism and the then editor of the scholarly periodical the *Journal of the Warburg and Courtauld Institutes*.

9 A. A. Zhdanov, *On Literature, Music and Philosophy* (London, Lawrence & Wishart), 1950, p. 65.

10 'On Literature. Speech at the First All Union Congress of Soviet Writers 1934', in Zhdanov, in *ibid.*, p. 13.

11 'Mistakes of Two Leningrad Journals. Report on the Journals *Zvezda* and *Leningrad*, 1947', in *ibid.*, p. 42.

12 *Ibid.*, p. 63.

13 Jószef Mroszczak, 'For the Furtherance of the Level of the Ideo-artistic Polish Poster', *Przeglod Artystyceny* (*Artistic Review*), 3 (1953) 5. Translations by Kazimierz Aulich.

14 Jerzy Bogusz, 'Some Problems of the Polish Political Poster', *Przeglod Artystyceny* (*Artistic Review*), 2 (1953) 27. Translations by Kazimierz Aulich.

15 Mroszczak, 'For the Furtherance of the Level of the Ideo-artistic Polish Poster'.

16 Bogusz, 'Some Problems of the Polish Political Poster'.

17 *Ibid.*

18 Mroszczak, 'For the Furtherance of the Level of the Ideo-artistic Polish Poster'.

19 Perhaps the best example is *USSR in Construction*, published as a monthly primarily for foreign consumption from 1930 to 1941. For a recent discussion see Victor Margolin, *The Struggle for Utopia. Rodchenko, Lissitsky, Moholy-Nagy 1917–1946* (Chicago and London, University of Chicago Press), 1997, pp. 163–214.

20 Krzysztof Dydo (ed.), *Hundredth Anniversary of Polish Poster Art* (Krakow, Biuro Wystaw Artystycznych), 1993, p. 26.

21 *Polish Film Poster*, produced for the Edinburgh Festival in 1956, an abbreviated version of the book *Plakat Polski* (Warsaw, WAG), 1956, in Polish and Russian-language editions.

22 The SED was founded in 1946 from an amalgamation of the Social Democratic Party (SPD) and the KPD.

23 See Stephan, 'Johannes R. Becher and the Cultural Development of the GDR'.

24 These ideas came out of direct encounters with Western popular cultural forms in the late 1940s when Hans Eisler, Bertolt

Brecht and Theodor W. Adorno were in Los Angeles with Thomas Mann, Heinrich Mann and Max Horkheimer.

25 Eisler quoted in Hans Meyer, 'An Aesthetic Debate of 1951. Comment on a Text by Hans Eisler', *New German Critique*, 1:2 (1974) 69–70. See also Bertolt Brecht, 'The Popular and the Realistic', *Sinn und Form*, 4 (1958) and 'Cultural Policy and the Academy of Arts', *Neues Deutschland*, East Berlin, 12 August 1953, in John Willett (ed.), *Brecht on Theatre. The Development of an Aesthetic* (New York, Hill & Wang), 1964, pp. 107–14, 266–9. Thomas Mann made a similar point in *Doktor Faustus* with the character Adrian Leverkuhn: 'Believe me, the entire character of art will change. It is unavoidable, and it is very fortunate. Art will shed a lot of melancholy ambition. We can only imagine it with difficulty, and yet it will happen, and it will be natural – art without suffering, spiritually healthy, an art which addresses humanity on the familiar basis of you and me.'

26 Including among their number Jindřich Štyrsky, Ladislav Sutnar, Miroslav Kouřil, Miroslav Novotný and Josef Raban.

27 See Jaroslav Anděl, *The Art of the Avant Garde in Czechoslovakia 1918–1938* (IVAM Centre Julio Gonzalez, Generalitat Valenciana Consellera de Cultura, Educació i Ciència), 1993.

28 The liberalizing trend in Soviet aesthetic policy did not begin as a result of Krushchev's partial denouncement of Stalin at the Twentieth Congress of the Soviet Communist Party in 1956, as is commonly thought, although the speech did have incalculable long-term effects, but when Georgi Malenkov, as Secretary of the Central Committee, called for new freedoms at the Nineteenth Party Congress some four months before Stalin's death in 1953.

29 Malenkov resigned in 1955, but the Thaw continued and reached something of a climax with his successor's 'secret speech'.

30 See the official address from the CPSU Central Committee to the First Congress of Soviet Artists in 1957.

31 'Social Realism as Institutional Practice. Observations on the Interpretation of the Works of Art of the Stalin Period', in Hans Gunther (ed.), *The Culture of the Stalin Period* (London, Macmillan), 1988, p. 151.

32 Mariusz Knorowski, 'A Kite in the Wind of History', 1998, unpublished ms. Young artists abandoned socialist-realist style in favour of more expressionist and subjective responses to the war in the exhibition at the Arsenal in Warsaw *Against Fascism, Against War*.

33 György Aczél, *Culture and Socialist Democracy* (Budapest, Corvina Press), 1975, p. 122.

34 'The Situation and Tasks of our Literature', quoted in *ibid.*, p. 111.

35 János Frank in *100+1 Éves a Magyar Plakát a Magyar Plakátmüvészet Története 1885–1986* (Budapest, Mücsarnok), 1986, p. 131.

36 Aczél, *Culture and Socialist Democracy*, p. 124.

37 *Ibid.*, pp. 20–1.

38 *Ibid.*, p. 21.

39 *Ibid.*, p. 20.

CHAPTER THREE

MODERNIZATION AND REBELLION 1956–68

The party still required a 'realist' art capable of providing a material analogue for figures placed in concrete situations in the society of the future. But the aesthetic only accentuated the divisions between the aspiration and the actuality. At the Third Writers' Congress in 1959 the Soviet leader Nikita Krushchev spoke of the party as supportive of artists who 'show the "pathos" of labour, … pointing the path to a new world. In their positive heroes they somehow epitomise all the best characteristics and qualities of man and contrast them with negative images, demonstrating the struggle of the new against the old, and the inevitable victory of the new.'[1]

The erection of the Berlin Wall in 1961 led to a shift in the terms of the Cold War.[2] NATO was within its rights to retaliate with armed force. But its inability to do so against the background of the failed rebellions in Germany and Poland in 1953 and the 1956 Hungarian uprising signalled that the West would respect the geopolitical integrity of the region. This was confirmed by the events in Czechoslovakia in 1968. It was also clear that struggles for autonomy would be met with armed intervention from the Warsaw Pact. John F. Kennedy's 'Ich bin ein Berliner' speech in 1962, combined with Krushchev's loss of face over the Sino-Soviet conflict and the Cuban missile crisis the preceding year, marked a mutually acceptable move from potential open conflict to a struggle of words in which culture played an important role. Internally the Thaw had led to conflict between sections of the intelligentsia and the party, while economic growth stimulated demands for self-determination, consumer goods, travel and basic human rights such as the freedom of expression. But as power slipped away from Krushchev there were a series of clampdowns. Matters of culture were increasingly debated, but politics were not up for discussion.

The relation between the applied and fine arts is difficult to determine, but poster designers often refer to the importance of developments in fine art. This was particularly true in the closed societies of the communist bloc, where it was difficult to acquire aesthetic information beyond the official. In this respect it is worth noting the aesthetic debate which marked the end of the Thaw. On 22 November 1962 a quasi-official exhibition of avant-garde work opened at the apartment of Eli Belyutin in Moscow. It was closed after only a few hours. Subsequently the work was summoned to the huge Manezh Gallery exhibition, *Thirty Years of Moscow Art*, where it was hung separately from the official pieces. Reportedly, Krushchev's words on seeing the material were 'Dog shit! Filth! Disgrace!'[3] The

organizers were rebuked for being too permissive and the aesthetic old guard were reinstated in a move symptomatic of the wider power struggles taking place in the party.[4]

The campaign for ideological purity was under way and again blame was heaped on the influence of the West. Paradoxically, the communists already looked to the West as a benchmark of achievement,[5] and, while artists stood accused of formalism, a large Fernand Leger exhibition opened to acclaim at the Pushkin Museum on 17 January 1963. Simultaneously *Pravda* published a statement praising the work of Picasso, Léger and Matisse and condemned the pomposity of Stalinist art, declaring 'new content does not always fit into old forms'.[6] In the autumn of 1962 Krushchev sanctioned the publication of Alexander Solzhenitsyn's *One Day in the Life of Ivan Denisovitch*, but international and domestic crises over consumer shortages further weakened his position. By the end of the year Krushchev had sacrificed the cultural intelligentsia:

> Some creative intellectuals have drawn incorrect conclusions from the Party's work to overcome the harmful consequences of the Stalin cult. They failed to grasp that struggle against the cult does not signify a weakening of leadership, a denial of authorities. Some have even begun to maintain that the time has come when everyone can determine his own line of conduct and the direction of his work, not reckoning with the interests of society and the state. This is nothing but an anarchist concept, hostile to Marxism-Leninism.[7]

The importance the party attached to the role of the arts in building socialism had succeeded in promoting interest in culture. As a result the main difference between the freeze of 1962 and those of 1954 and 1957 was the number of people involved. Signals were confused and warnings not to contact Westerners, for example, were undermined by the cessation of the jamming of the Voice of America. Often defined in relation to exposure in the West, dissident designers, artists and writers challenged the legitimacy of

(detail of 3.8)

official claims to cultural exclusivity. Dissident culture offered a critique without rejecting 'real existing socialism' and paradoxically kept alive the dream of a genuine socialist utopia. 'Dissident' and 'orthodox' values were mutually dependent but the liberals, however, were effectively silenced.

The Soviets accepted the difficulty of imposing the socialist and essentially Russian canon on the communist bloc countries. The effect was to produce an uneasy alliance between coercion and pragmatism. Official policy began to allow a more flexible approach to figures such as John Heartfield and Western communists such as Pablo Picasso, Fernand Léger and Renato Guttuso, whose attitudes towards realism and society could not be circumscribed by socialist-realist aesthetics. In the German Democratic Republic there had been various attempts to re-establish expressionism as a socially engaged and humane art precisely because of its formal inventiveness. In 1962 Ernst Fischer, the Austrian communist intellectual, published his paper 'Alienation, Decadence, Realism' in an effort to rescue modernist literature from capitalist and communist misinterpretation. For Fischer, literary modernism was capable of capturing objective reality and could be understood within the terms of socialist realism. Subsequently, in May 1963, a conference on Franz Kafka was convened at the castle of Liblice, near Prague. It is claimed that the ensuing debate initiated the road to the Prague Spring and the Polish August. Some intellectuals, Fischer among them, attempted to secure Kafka's expressions of existential alienation for communism, but orthodox communists identified such thinking with French

existentialism and bourgeois capitalism and denied alienation could persist in a socialist society. The controversy was linked with calls for what the sculptor Fritz Cremer described in 1964 as a 'socialist art without dogmas', unrestricted in form but answerable to the party in content.

In Czechoslovakia the magazine *Tvar* published an article about an exhibition of anti-war posters by the designer Bedřich Votruba. He was described as working independently of official commissions and therefore remained unpublished, with a unique personal graphic vision derived from socialist-realist convention, modern expressive abstraction and the devices of the caricaturist:

> there is chronic stagnation in our country, … cliché, orthodoxy, conformity to the committee … after an era of empty gestures … the irresponsible riff-raff of symbolic attributes covered in raspberry sauce, from the realist and the stereotypical we move to modernistically stylized contentlessness. … Into this unhappy situation comes Votruba with his posters, … he created the brief himself, he deformed the facts, discovered the connections and spoke to the audience … with a minimum of means.[8]

Votruba's stylistic heterogeneity was alien to official aesthetics. The habitual iconography of socialist realism is subjected to graphic, social and humanitarian reinterpretation. Severe modernist typography and geometry contrast with the melancholy of the death's head and the *memento mori*. Votruba's contribution to the development of the political poster is idiosyncratic, but his work does help to lay the foundations of more openly expressive and typographic posters, such as Josef Flejšar's exhibited but unpublished *Theresienstadt* (1969) (6.158).

Advanced designers in Hungary, Czechoslovakia and the GDR were looking to Poland, where they had to a large extent reoriented themselves to the international graphic design scene. In Czechoslovakia, as Marta Sylvestrová has pointed out, the grip of the artists' unions loosened, leading to the creation of various semi-autonomous design groups.[9] Groups such as Balance and Horizon fought to maintain the right to create new expressive means in line with advances in printing technology and modernist innovation. Designers glanced nostalgically at the functionalist and surrealist movements of the inter-war period and from about 1964 onwards engaged in the simultaneous appropriation of contemporary Western styles characterized by the hedonism of psychedelia, the playfulness of pop, the individual freedom represented by *art informel* and the anarchic energies of Lettrism.

Under censorship the truth is concealed: 'In Poland, we read every text as allusive; every situation described – even the most remote in time and space – is immediately applied

3.1
Miroslav Šimorda, *Twentieth anniversary of the road to socialism*, 1965, Czechoslovakia, Moravian Gallery, Brno.

3.2
Gábor Bükkösi, *Thirtieth anniversary of Association of the Hungarian–Soviet Defence*, 1978, Hungary, Hungarian National Gallery, Budapest.

3.3
Jānis Borgs, *Junta*, 1975, poster maquette, three sheets, Soviet Latvia, the artist.

3.4
Timotei Nădășan, *Marx is modern*, 1989, Romania, artist's edition, Moravian Gallery, Brno.

3.5
Zdeněk Chotěnovský, *Your contribution to socialism*, 1964, poster maquette, Moravian Gallery, Brno.

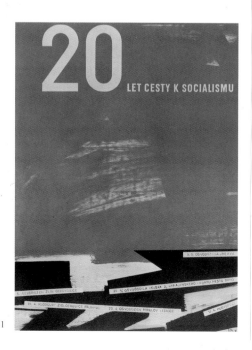

3.1

3.2

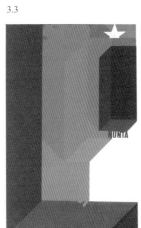

3.3

3.4

3.5

to Poland. Every text is a double text. Between the lines we look for the message written in invisible ink, and the hidden message we find is treated as the only true one.'[10] Many designers, especially in Poland, Hungary and Czechoslovakia, began to look to distant history as a place of refuge in strategies of avoidance. Cultural posters, in particular, are scattered with references via surrealist precedent to baroque emblematics and real or imagined hermetic meanings. They ape the look not so much of the polemically inspired photo-montages of John Heartfield as the avant-gardist work of Hannah Höch, Vladimir Mayakovsky, the Max Ernst of the 1920s and the work of Czech modernists such as Jindřich Štyrský.

Other designers looked to abstraction, producing posters indebted to international modernism and in the 1960s to contemporary Finnish design, which was also popular in the West. Polish periodicals published articles on El Lissitsky in the 1960s and similar Czechoslovak publications appeared even during the period of normalization in the 1970s. Miloslav Šimorda's *Twenty years of the path to socialism* (1965) (3.1), for example, was typical, inspired by the modernism of Zdeněk Rossmann and František Kalivoda, while Gábor Bükkösi's *Thirtieth anniversary of the Hungarian Soviet Republic* (1978) (3.2) looks to similar Hungarian modernist precedent. In Latvia designers such as Jānis Borgs took inspiration from Western minimalist and nonconformist art from Russia (3.3). Henryk Tomaszewski's National Day poster from 1960 looked to such apolitical hedonists as Henri Matisse. It was nothing if not high irony, intentional or not. In style, if not in content, many designs for the political poster enter a critique of socialist-realist practice and by implication the orthodoxies of totalitarian communism, as many designers were clearly aware by the time of the collapse (5.10).

One of the most effective and persistent motifs to emerge during the early 1960s was the image of a head with an open screaming mouth. Zdeněk Chotěnovský's *Your contribution to socialism* (1964) (3.5) made a strong political point by appropriating the primitivism of early twentieth-century modernism in a montage simultaneously expressive of individual angst and state interference. The image was largely confined to cultural and exhibition posters, yet they have political weight. Jan Lenica's *Wojcek* (1964) from Poland set the tone; Karel Teissig's *Free beast of prey* (1966) from Czechoslovakia and Nándor Szilvásy's *Sixth National Exhibition of Posters* (1972) and György Kemény's design for the exhibition *100+1 Years of the Hungarian Poster* (1986) from Hungary continued the theme. Lenica's aped the psychedelia of Western commercial forms. Teissig abandoned a coherent drawing style for a more fragmentary and dislocated composition

expressive of the fears, duplicities and contradictions of contemporary urban and political life. Towards the end of the decade posters such as Jan Rajlich's *Vietnam is bleeding – will you help?* (1966) (9.59), for all their ideological orthodoxy, touch on a darker side of contemporary existence through expressive imagery.

The party was nothing if not resilient, and following the fall of Krushchev in 1964 the Klement Gottwald Museum in Prague gave the orthodox communist Wolfgang A. Schlosser a retrospective exhibition. It plotted the course of his thirty-year career from communist and printer in Cologne and Leipzig in the 1930s and, after a sojourn in wartime London, to professional political poster designer in Prague in the 1940s and 1950s (9.45, 46, 48, 54). Described within an essentialist rhetoric of good and evil, his communist credentials are reaffirmed in the hyperbole of Zhdanovite orthodoxy. He is portrayed as rejecting the studio, and therefore his subjectivity, dedicating his work and aesthetic to the collectivity of the social, through which he served the people in the name of progress and the victory over fascism and capitalism.[11]

The question of Western influences was particularly vexed in the German Democratic Republic. In 1961 First Secretary Walter Ulbricht (1956–71) had warned against the dangers of bourgeois notions of creativity. On 22 February 1962 an article appeared in *Neues Deutschland* condemning 'late bourgeois modernism' in the graphic arts and the lack of class orientation in expressionism. Such official reactions gained impetus from Krushchev's outburst. Western elitism and artistic autonomy were a threat and had to be opposed for fear of undermining the ideological justification of the state itself. Ulbricht insisted on an unswerving partisanship and continued the campaign for a separate and unique culture.[12] The official press in the remaining years of Ulbricht's administration rarely deigned to mention, let alone condemn, West German culture. Even developments in Czechoslovakia in 1968 were met with silence. Only after the invasion was there any public discussion of the events, when modernist aesthetes were officially blamed for the revisionism of the Prague Spring. One of the consequences of the stiffening of ideological control was that the central Marxist-Leninist concept of manufacturing was widened to include the production and reproduction of socialist mankind. Art and culture were given a vital role in this process. Western pop music, once tolerated as the musical expression of the age of the technical revolution by the *Freie Deutsche Jugend*, was attacked by Ulbricht's heir apparent, Eric Honecker, as a Western conspiracy. Ulbricht warned: 'Those insipid and decadent products of light entertainment, as they are produced for the manipulation of the people by the monopolies dominating the field of culture in West Germany … [are] incompatible with socialist culture.'[13]

But despite the regime's best efforts Western consumer culture and narcissistic hedonism remained popular with the younger generation, to whom it was a form of anti-communism. To their official critics Western values offered no hope of social revolution, simply freedom as 'licence'. The 'alternative' was to be found in a cultural dynamic strung out somewhere between conservative traditionalism and *kitsch*: Ulbricht suggested that it was 'our highest duty to garner the riches of German art and culture for the treasure chamber of Socialism'.[14] The formula allowed two forms of bourgeois taste: one bad, decadent, formalist and capitalist; the other good, classical, progressive and humanist. The 'modern condition' was inauthentic in a socialist community where all conflicts had been overcome.[15]

If socialist-realist conventions and orthodoxies were undermined because of the desire to express national identity through the suppressed aesthetic histories of the 1920s and 1930s, and because of the inroads of Western popular culture, they were also undermined by the need to appear up-to-date and progressive. The poster had to subscribe to socialist-realist principles, but it was also a mass-produced utilitarian object manufactured for a mass market. Quality could not be maintained simply through application to craft, skill and ideological content, as in the fine arts, but attention had to be paid to issues raised by technology and manufacturing. An expression of this kind of aesthetic thinking can be found in Jan Moravec's *Yesterday, today and tomorrow* (1960) (6.115), where a hand provides the armature for an abstract vision of a technologically advanced future. The design was emulated by Vytautas Kaušinis's widely condemned *All in the name of man for the welfare of man* (1963) (6.116).

Despite the best efforts of the old guard there was a shift towards a more consumer-oriented culture. It was a pragmatic response by the authorities, who could not prevent knowledge of the West percolating their borders: and if jazz, jeans and consumer durables subverted communist cultural meaning, they had to be countered.[16] Correspondingly, a sense of change crept into design, mirrored by a need to compete with the West, but not by imitation or subjection to the unfettered demands of consumption, commerce and industry. The former emphasis on heavy industry had been necessary for defence and reconstruction, but now attention was focused on questions of 'art' and 'aesthetics' in everyday mass-produced objects where socialist realism was a mechanism through which the whole of life might be aestheticized.[17] Exhibitions of design promoted high-quality aesthetics in tacit admission of the inadequacies of industrial production: the task was to improve design, finish, function, beauty and 'truth to materials'. Decoration was frowned upon as a legacy of

petty-bourgeois taste and, implicitly, Stalinist excess. Just as architectural projects had been shorn of their embellishments and monumentalism, so graphic design was stripped of its grandiose stylistic pretensions.

Claims were made for the socially transformative capacities of advanced materials, technology and the impact of automation on production. The promise of a harmonious and leisured future as a legitimation of Marxism-Leninism was encouraged by mythologized Soviet successes in reconstruction and the space race. Paradoxically, the cant echoed the demands of the revolutionary Russian constructivists and the pre-war modernists. In posters, abstraction may have been impossible because of its inability to bear a direct message, but function and beauty were essential: 'The more beautiful, the better; the cheaper the means of production, the more revolutionary is the effect of production on the easing of the life of the people, making our living environment and our forms of life more beautiful.'[18] Aesthetic beauty was politically, socially and morally affirmative, and resided in the quality of manufacture and design. Manufactured objects, such as posters, were produced not for the sake of consumption for consumption's sake but to enhance the quality of life.

The Soviet Exhibition in Paris in 1961 was one of the most impressive manifestations of the New Creative Process, as it was called by László Juhász, Secretary of the Hungarian Committee on Applied Art. Communist museology saw exhibitions as primarily didactic. Considered by its organizers as rational, logical and harmonious, in a throwback to high socialist realism the exhibition was also gigantic in scale. It was effective through force of spectacle. Erected in the glare of Krushchev's brave new world of technological revolution, announced at the twenty-first Soviet party congress, it told the story of the reconstruction of Russia, its pursuit of peace, and its industrial and technological prowess. Images of war damage were juxtaposed with photographs of the new cities rising from the ruins of Kiev, Stalingrad and Novgorod. Industrial development – smelters, oil refineries, gas installations, hydro-electric stations and the like – featured as the emblems of the new Russia. Intended for foreign consumption but widely reported in the communist specialist press, the exhibition was radical by Soviet standards. A display featured a most unsocialist-realist piece of free-standing sculpture made from 'rusted metal twisted like snakes',[19] combined with montaged elements of bricks, images of fascist destruction and an expressive wide-mouthed, staring-eyed face. Broadly comparable to much western European art produced in the aftermath of World War II, it lacked any sense of the existential, the sexual or the psychological. It was like talking about society without talking about people.[20] The phenomenon was emphasized in the photo-displays commemorating the 'hero cities', where in the space between the 'logical' and the 'emotional' the exhibition polemicized for communism. In another part, a window literally opened on to wonderful landscapes of the Russian motherland as 'an apotheosis on the theme of leisure' and a promise of the socialist future. Aesthetics married to technology dramatized contrasts between the past, the present and the future.

Dominated by an installation featuring the first Soviet cosmonaut, Yuri Gagarin, and accompanied by large-scale models of atomic structures and planetary orbits, the whole was worthy of El Lissitisky's work under the influence of Gustav Klutsis and S. Senkin for the 1928 *Pressa Exhibition* in Cologne. In many respects it was a return to the iconographies of the 1920s, combining radical montage with contemporary technological forms: 'Industrial art is the collective art of our age, it is a demanding and responsible creative process, the aim of which is not simply making beautiful and decorating, but also in feeding through the special demands of contemporary culture to ensure a synthesis of beauty in manufacture and economy at a high level.'[21] Karel Langer, for example, to whom style was 'a fast spreading preference for certain objects, acts and ways of seeing',[22] found justification in the modern and simplified look of posters in the 1960s. Following the pattern already established by Polish designers, they cease to emulate painting, they are less illusionistic, more explicitly graphic, more posterlike, 'functional' and 'true' to their medium, with flat, unmodulated tones, clean edges, planar constructions, schematic figuration and simplified formalized compositions (6.73, 7.47). Abstraction, previously condemned, becomes increasingly important and is combined with photographic and drawn lithographic components (6.40, 9.46). The decorative and 'modern' are juxtaposed with expressive 'realism'. The posters have the appearance of the mass-produced and machine-made, and many are formalist rather than formulaic.

In all the discussions of the New Creative Process from Soviet, Czechoslovak and Hungarian cultural critics there is no mention of 'formalism', or the visual consequences of this new attention to 'purity' in design. Modernist tendencies were condemned as long as they threatened to enable individual expression and criticism of the party. Most often posters emulated the anonymity of commercial Western and international graphic and typographical styles without deviating from serious didactic and explicitly political purposes.

Socialist realism was losing its grip on the medium in an uncomfortable liaison between the conservative and contemporary. The contemporary was signified in the grafting of decorative aspects of high and late modernism on to established figurative and political iconographies. The liaison also marked a gravitation towards applied aesthetics, where concepts of the rational, logical, harmonious and functional were adopted as stylistic effects for ideological purposes. The attempt was to affirm the legitimacy of progressive Marxism-Leninism, and to offer subject populations a meaningful answer to the inroads of Western culture. The aestheticization of life and the leisured future was to be achieved not so much in social utopian as in technological scientific terms, expressed in official media through affective modern-looking surfaces.

Within the circular terms of the discourse of socialist realism, mass communication media were 'progressive', technologically efficient, collective and 'popular'. C. Vaughan James finds a definition of the popular as that which gives best expression to social awareness, reflecting true social conditions and man's most humane aspirations.[23] Works are popular in so far as they are progressive, and progressive in so far as they reflect man's universal and collective aspirations. But thousands of poster designs mimicked Western commercial popular culture and indigenous *kitsch*. Some designers such as the Plakát group in Prague took a more independent position. Frustrated with the monotony and meaninglessness of official propaganda, they claimed, 'If a "political poster" must exist, then let it speak to somebody, let it make people think,' and they set out to 'stage the renaissance of the political poster, a poster in the spirit of humanism'.[24] Admired by western Europeans, the posters were never seen in the streets. On the occasion of the first Plakát exhibition, which took place at the Czechoslovakian Writers' Salon in Prague, the political scientist, economist and spokesman of the group, Radoslav Selucký, commented:

> Some people would be stunned in thinking that these posters should speak to us from our street corners and walls. I personally would like them to speak to hundreds of thousands. I want them inexorably to pursue the self-satisfied, unmindful citizen so that he can no longer walk nonchalantly through our society and through our lives. Only then will he ponder and think and critically evaluate matters of concern, only then will he form his own opinion ... so that they can shake, if only a little bit, the heavy burden of our overcautiousness and opportunism, the burden which hinders the creative energies of our society.[25]

Like the posters themselves, Selucký's comments are aimed at the authorities, those 'unmindful citizens'. The group wanted the poster to engage with the social and political on more critical territory, away from the infelicitous dogma of party doctrine. There is a degree of freedom already familiar from Polish experiments in these posters, but their messages are not mediated by the function of advertising a film or a theatre performance. As autonomous posters they are not aesthetic objects in the manner of fine art, but are socially and critically engaged from a position outside party ideology. Zdeněk Chotěnovský's *Authority* displays the bloated head of a king with slit eyes looking in two directions. In another Chotěnovský poster, *When they proclaim 'Long live progress!' always ask, 'Progress in what?'* (1968) (8.13), a crowd is weighed down, almost oppressed, by a banner carrying the words 'Long live progress'. Plakát was symptomatic of a growing and subterranean liberal humanist shift towards consideration of the individual and private life. The posters were produced for a small audience of *cognoscenti* for exhibition rather than for general public display independent of party organizations. Conforming to the concept of social-political poster, they have made the transition to the status of the art poster. This not only says something about a change in the nature of poster production but also points to the appropriation of a particular kind of space previously the preserve of fine book producers and fine artists. A 'popular' medium was making inroads into the territory of surviving, but suppressed, vestigial 'elitist' and liberal humanist forms.

Plakát found its most vigorous precedent in the tradition of poster production in Poland. The main producer of posters in Poland until 1974 was the specialist publishing house Wydawnictwo Artystyczno-Graficzne (WAG) which, along with the Film Distribution Office (CWF), played a considerable role in the development of the art poster. Both Schubert and Hornik pinpoint its origins to the CWF and the relative freedom granted to designers. There were a number of insitutional factors which contributed to this development, not least the fact that designers could work freelance with small cultural organizations such as galleries, theatres and film organizations, with which they often built up long-standing relationships. According to Florian Zieliński, public space had become partially depoliticized and cultural posters were far more common than political posters.[26] This was in stark contrast to the GDR and Czechoslovakia after normalization. The change had a marked effect on the tenor of public space: the grand international claims for supremacy were relinquished for localized and elaborately double-coded expressions of discontent. In Hungary a similar process was under way: the ninth Congress of the Socialist Workers' Party in 1966 concluded that they had 'increased the independence of the various creative workshops, publishers, film studios and editorial boards'.[27]

By the middle 1960s to speak of the errors of the past with reference to Stalinist culture was normal, but what was proffered instead by cultural polemicists such as

Lesnodorski[28] was a vision of a complex weave of history and modernity: a socialist system rooted in specific traditions of the past and directed towards the future. Within the Polish context, the art poster engaged with life under communism in the present through the agency of the individual artist, a notion which sits comfortably with traditional humanist definitions of a work of art as the record of a time and a place interpreted through an individual psychology. The poster was no longer simply a mass communication medium but one which would bear comparison with the art film in the West: 'Polish artists demonstrated that the poster, despite its natural limitations, can be as sensitive, elastic and deep a way of expressing the author's attitude to reality as any other branch of art ... showing a preference for subjective vision, irrationalism, freedom of association and creative intuition.'[29] The poster compared itself with painting, and realism was abandoned in favour of the subjective, the idiosyncratic and the individual. The art poster denoted a move from a patron-driven situation to one where the individual perceptions and experiences of the designer come to the fore. The poster weakens its links with party polemics and ceases to be reading matter for the masses to become, instead, a conversation piece for the intelligentsia. No longer a reactive medium, it created its own market and represented the potential for a genuine public sphere and the beginnings of incipient market economics in Poland.

According to Zieliński, 'an index of this change is the controversy between the publisher (CWF) and poster designers over whether the author's signature can be put in letters of the same size as the leading actor'.[30] The poster was further asserting itself as an authorial rather than party medium. Under Władysław Gomułka's leadership (1956–70) Poland had gained a certain amount of autonomy from Moscow, and the Polish Way maintained some kind of legitimacy in the eyes of Polish society until the expulsion of Leszek Kołakowski and other relatively independently minded intellectuals in 1965. This relative independence led to the unbelievable situation where the state financed and published posters but had very little control over them. Provided they did not pose a direct threat to the state or the party, designers had a great deal of freedom.

Officially, these tendencies were promoted as 'conspicuous individualism', an acceptable, if stereotypically romantic, 'attribute of the Polish national character'.[31] Tadeusz Galinski, writing on the eve of the Congress of Polish Culture in the final year of the celebrations marking the thousandth anniversary of the Polish state,[32] felt that much had been achieved to weave the national culture into an interrelationship with its historical struggles for sovereignty. Indigenous traditions of romantic poetry personified in the work of Adam Mickiewicz, for example, were co-opted to the socialist cultural revolution. Culture had the task of carrying socially transformative traditions from one generation to the next, but the principal point was that the traditions were national in character and were perceived by the Polish authorities to be independent of Soviet influence. National characteristics combined with the liberalization of culture led to a situation in which artists were constantly testing the limits of state control and, in turn, the state tested its independence from Moscow.

The political poster became increasingly marginalized as designers abandoned the problems of socialism for principles of design and authorship which took their measure from the West. Vladimir Shlapentokh has argued that 'A distinctive feature of the 1970s and, to an even greater extent, the 1980s, was the emergence of the West as the ultimate judge of the quality of intellectual work.'[33] This change in orientation implicitly entails a largely covert, but nevertheless substantial, shift towards Western modes of expression. György Aczél, the Hungarian ideologist, expressed it this way:

> Freedom, as we interpret it, is not manifest first and foremost in the fact that writers and artists who have preserved their essentially bourgeois world outlook are writing and creating in our country. True, it is important to give them scope, because it is impossible to join ideological battle with trends which are silent … when we speak of freedom, we understand first of all by this greater scope for socialist art … the principle and practice of freedom also mean that our public should become familiar not only with classical art but also with the real values of contemporary bourgeois art, and find its bearings among the best cultural products of the Western countries … .[34]

Aesthetic forms which did not conform to socialist principles were accommodated because out in the open they could be subjected to criticism. Marxist-Leninist aesthetics were broadened to accept the desire for individual human progress and liberal humanism, rather than being dedicated exclusively to socialism. The regimes were keen to present a positive image to the West, to secure loans and to stimulate trade, but it is difficult not to read these breakthroughs as an admission of the *status quo*. According to Florian Zieliński, the Polish poster took part in a dream about the freedom of art and disinterested state patronage to represent Poland as a country of modernity and culture. As such it was a legitimation of the regime and in due course Western forms and practices in other countries met with qualified acceptance. In Hungary, Aczél condemned the actions of liberals and the demands for freedoms by identifying them with market values. He called for non-Marxist views to 'be overcome with ideological weapons'.[35] But Aczél continued to search for an accommodation with the creative intelligentsia and provided a programme of coexistence

within socialist parameters. Culture was an extremely important site of struggle and he welcomed contact with bourgeois forms in order to expose their inferiority:

> It is scarcely necessary for me to explain to you the inhumanity of the capitalist system. I would only mention the single fact that the aggressive leaders of imperialism have hardly been able to find a single poet, dramatist or film director to glorify the Vietnam war, which has been going on for years, to hire himself out as their Kipling to be an apologist for imperialism. We know that in the West there are official artists of the imperialist system, and a supportive entertainment industry, but there is also significant humanist, and indeed a socialist communist literature and art.[36]

Following the general Act of Amnesty in 1962, the Hungarian authorities permitted a relaxation of cultural policies and allowed an alternative network to establish itself among the intelligentsia. This was a move inspired and perhaps fuelled by internal contacts with Czechoslovakia and Poland. Aczél rationalized the tendency as a period of transition from capitalism to socialism, naturalizing what he called 'transitory ideological formulas'. They might be non-Marxist and therefore necessarily bourgeois, yet they were not anti-Marxist. Nevertheless, he warned of the dangers of the ever present potential of the third way: the much discussed, never to be realized, compromise of the best in socialism with the best in capitalism.[37] The liberal intelligentsia was curtailed by the intervention of the Warsaw Pact in Czechoslovakia in August 1968, but its after-life continued in Poland until 1981, and in Hungary until 1974, when the relatively relaxed regime was ousted from power.

The most important event of the period was the Prague Spring. Between 1963 and 1968 the Czechoslovak reform movement sought to establish 'communism with a human face'. In January 1968 the leader of the Czechoslovak Communist Party, Antonín Novotný, was deposed by Alexander Dubček, who instituted a number of reforms to stimulate the ailing economy. The Action Programme published in April 1968 promised far more than economic measures: it advocated the freedom to travel and live abroad, freedom of expression and the rehabilitation of the victims of Stalin. The aim was to bring about a decentralized, liberalized and democratic form of state socialism. The mass media suddenly filled with open discussions about the country's problems and future.

As a year of crisis, 1968 was preceded by a series of protests by students and intellectuals. In the East, anger was directed at state capitalism and its impact on human rights and freedoms; in the West, the nature of market capitalism and its relation to the war in Vietnam and the nuclear arms race came under scrutiny. They shared deep suspicion of repressive state apparatuses and fears relating to free speech.

In June 1967 Milan Kundera told the fourth Congress of Czechoslovak Writers: 'I am sometimes frightened that our present civilization is losing that European character which lay so close to the hearts of the Czech humanists and revivalists … in our case, the guarding of frontiers is still regarded as a greater virtue than crossing them.'[38]

The civil disturbances on the streets of European cities in 1968 began in Warsaw in January. Demonstrations took place when Adam Michnik and Henryk Szlaifer, among others, were arrested and subsequently expelled from Warsaw University following a protest after the forced closure of Adam Mickiewicz's play *The Forefathers*. Interestingly enough, the poster for the play, designed the year before by Roman Cieślewicz, featured a shattered golem-like figure, easily read as a comment on Soviet giganticism, but also as a representation of the 'Polish soul and mentality' as 'hot inside and frozen on the surface, just like volcanic lava' (8.18).[39] In March students at Warsaw Polytechnic passed a resolution in solidarity with the Warsaw writers, who were under pressure following calls for curbs on censorship. The resolution was presented to the offices of the government newspaper, *Życie Warszawy*:

(1) Article 71 of the Constitution guaranteed freedom of speech, of assembly, and of the press; (2) all students arrested should be listed and released; (3) those responsible for police brutality should be punished; (4) workers should not be set against students; (5) the press, radio and television should provide a true account of student demands and actions; (6) no measures should be taken against 'academic workers' [teachers] who had supported the students; (7) the Citizens' Militia should be withdrawn from campuses; (8) dissociation from both antisemitism and Zionism.[40]

Protests spread to Katowice, Poznań and Wrocław to the chant of 'Long live Czechoslovakia'. The academics Zygmunt Bauman, Leszek Kołakowski and Bronislaw Baczko were dismissed from their posts at Warsaw University; as a measure of Czech liberal opinion the Philosophy Faculty at Charles University in Prague immediately invited them to speak.

Poster production in Czechoslovakia at the time of the Prague Spring is difficult to assess. State collections and the portfolios published by the former Klement Gottwald Museum from the period of liberalization feature few political posters aside from the painfully orthodox.[41] Mainstream production reproduced formulaic blandishments (3.14). The Prague Spring did, however, give the opportunity for collective groups such as Plakát to develop their art. The group's second exhibition, *Angažovaný Plakát*, sponsored by the Czech Artists' Union, was held at the Writers' Union in Prague during the March and April of 1969 but was closed by the authorities.[42] The introduction to the catalogue provides coded criticism of communist rule by way of memories of the atrocities of World War II, the realities of the Cold War and the threat of a new war, all of which inspired feelings of disillusionment: 'Wisdom was achieved through the experience of life and painful disenchantment.'[43] The group affirmed the vital role of art in the struggle to re-establish humanitarian and social values in fulfilment of the romantic ideals of youth and student rebellion, which after the Warsaw Pact invasion, in contrition, they saw as naive. Their work had progressed, they felt, from the private confession of the studio poster to something which had its primary existence in the public domain. As Jan Baleka reported, it had been impossible to make a truly engaged political poster: 'In fact the doctrine of socialist realism and the practices of political life reclaimed part of the critical political graphic, but at the same time you could not have it.'[44]

Socialist realism was described as limited because, once it had expounded its anti-war and anti-imperialist themes, it was incapable of entering into a dialogue with its own practices except in the most obvious and affirmative of ways. Plakát offered a solution in so far as their work was not circumscribed by party doctrine either aesthetically or rhetorically. Furthermore, it questioned the nature of socialism, authority, progress and latterly 'normalization'. The events of 1968 had stimulated challenges to the basic premises of the system: 'there is nothing better than to have a confident search for truth as a means of regenerating content, and perhaps the supreme ethical effort. … The last internal metamorphosis of the posters of our group addressed the whole of humanity.'[45] The polemic of the catalogue was careful to situate the work within the

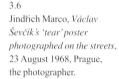

3.6
Jindřich Marco, *Václav Ševčík's 'tear' poster photographed on the streets*, 23 August 1968, Prague, the photographer.

ideologically acceptable parameters of a collective practice driven by humanitarian ideals and new materials and techniques in the interests of social progress. Nevertheless they were expelled from the art union.

Václav Ševčík, a member of the Plakát group, remembers another aspect of poster production at the time of the Warsaw Pact invasion. Many of the posters produced by the demonstrators, he observed, were anonymously produced and their lack of regard for artistic quality gave them all the more authority. His own designs were worked on in the print shops without any heed of official approval and were distributed under the noses of the Russian troops (3.6).[46] One journalist made the observation that Prague was just like one huge poster (3.7–13).[47] The photographer and design historian Jindřich Marco made a similar point:

from the very beginning when the nation entered the fight against a modern army empty handed, there has been another factor more powerful than the spoken word and more effective than machine gun fire and grenades from cannons and tanks. It was the written word, the countless posters, newspapers, bulletins and slogans in Czech as well as Russian, small and large. And all, or almost all, used the most powerful weapon which from the time of the French Revolution was known to all who fought against violence, mockery. Witty cartoons of the occupying forces appeared on wrapping paper; with the speed of lightning Prague was transformed into a huge newspaper. The shop windows in the centre of town, and not only the centre, were one next to the other papered with posters. The inhabitants of Prague stood in front of them and bitterly amused themselves.[48]

Despite the presence of the Russian, Bulgarian, Hungarian, East German and Polish troops on the streets, the Czechoslovak people demonstrated and plastered the walls, windows and monuments of their cities with handbills, posters and graffiti. It was not possible to make many posters because the printing shops were soon occupied by Warsaw Pact troops, although some posters such as Václav Ševčík's *Tear* (1968) did appear during the occupation (3.6).[49] Art students, professional designers and willing amateurs had to improvise with what was available. The protestors were forced to use direct forms of communication once they were excluded from the media and had lost possession of the art academies and the premises of the Artists' and Writers' Unions. To decorate the cities with hand-made posters, bills and placards was to claim them back in a symbolic war of possession (3.10). It was a demonstration of power and non-violent resistance against impossible odds: a gestural politics. In posters, banners and graffiti, rebellion found itself preserved in photographs. Constructed by observers in the tradition of the European avant garde, the protestors were perceived within a counter-myth to the collective, bureaucratic and ritualized ideologies of communism. It was as if the romantic myth of expression where everyone becomes an artist in communal, free and unalienated labour had finally been fulfilled. Childlike drawing defied the sophistication of dissembling official media. Leaders' portraits and official political posters were despoiled. The vernacular of the cartoon, the atavistic and the comic surfaced in a denial of authority. As posters of resistance they are the record of the extremes of a disrupted but authentically experienced everyday life.

The emblems of communist rule and Soviet influence are subverted by gallows humour: 'Joking with a rope around

3.7
Jindřich Marco, *Dove of peace*, 21–23 August 1968, Prague, the photographer.

3.8
Jindřich Marco, *Posters commemorating Jan Palach*, 20 January 1969, Prague, the photographer.

3.9
Jindřich Marco, *Blindfolded cameraman*, 21–23 August 1968, Prague, the photographer.

3.7

3.8

3.9

your neck is a feeble way of transcending your oppressors, but it is a sort of transcendance all the same … .'[50] The Red Army soldier, heroic protector and friend; the tank driver, liberator and ally incarnate; the party leaders, father figures and political inspiration to the people, are mocked. Posters show bleeding, defecating doves of peace and mothers with dead children. Emblems and iconographies of anti-fascist propaganda are identified with the actions of the invaders. Warsaw Pact soldiers are depicted as traitors; the Bolshevik poster by Dimitri Moor *Have you enlisted with the Red Army?* (1920) is transformed with the caption 'You too are guilty for occupying Czechoslovakia'. One, in a parody of the high socialist realism of designers such as Viktor Ivanov, shows a charging Red Army soldier and is captioned with the words 'Go and kill!' while, behind, the customary figure of the leader, Brezhnev in this case, rips the mask from his face to reveal Hitler. Another poster shows the heads of a Nazi soldier and a Red Army soldier as equivalent, with the caption '1939 = 1968' (3.11). Another makes the point that the Red Army was brought flowers by children in 1945, but in 1968 murders them. Others show Lenin in tears or covering his face as tanks roll on to Prague. The map of Czechoslovakia sheds the hammer-and-sickle symbol of the communist party and is bayoneted or flattened by tank tracks.[51] In Bratislava the story was similar. Red stars were inscribed with swastikas; tanks were decorated with chalk swastikas; an official portrait of Alexander Dubček in a shop window was tilted and modified with a cartoon arm to clobber the head of a Red Army soldier. The bleeding heart of Czechoslovakia was impaled by the knives of the invading Warsaw Pact countries. National flags and symbols appeared devoid of party emblems.[52]

Images are loosened from the authority they represent and in this context it is useful to consider Bakhtin's notions of carnival, thought out under the shadow of Stalin. Terry Eagleton has remarked on the riot of semiosis which is produced in carnival as all transcendental symbols are rendered relative through ridicule and the 'radicalism of humour'. Power structures are made strange and grotesque through parody, and necessity is travestied in a process of inversion where the protector becomes the violator and all is subsumed into the ambiguity of deconstructed, misread and collapsing binary oppositions: 'Absolutely nothing escapes this great spasm of satire: no signifier is too solemn to be blasphemously invaded, dismantled and turned against itself. The grotesque is intrinsically double-faced, an immense semiotic switchboard through which codes are read backwards and messages scrambled into their antitheses.'[53]

Simultaneously, in other countries of the Warsaw Pact there were protests and anti-state graffiti, but these tended to be dissipated, individual, negative acts, sharing only in

an identification of communism with national socialism. Such gestures, especially in the GDR, were a register of the widespread dissatisfaction and the failure of the state to gain any true legitimacy outside the circles of the privileged: 'increased daubing of swastikas, S.S. runes, graffiti in toilets, factories, on buildings, streets and squares. Mostly this graffiti consisted of slogans such as "Long live Dubček" – "Freedom for Czechoslovakia" – "Russians and Germans get out of Czechoslovakia" – "It is just like thirty years ago" and Soviet soldiers were described as "pigs and pig-Russians". There were such graffiti as "Long live Dubček, down with Ulbricht", "Dubček has got more people supporting him than Ulbricht has in the GDR", "Ulbricht is Hitler No. 2".'[54]

Anti-fascism was a foundational myth of the communist states and under the circumstances of the Prague Spring it was subjected to mocking interrogation. As if to compensate for the loss of the illegitimate mythologies of communism, older forms of authority began to reassert themselves in national and religious forms. In towns and cities across the country makeshift shrines were dedicated to those who had been killed: made from bricks, wooden crosses, candles, flowers and photographs of the martyred citizens, they shared the same strength of feeling and power of the chalked and daubed graffiti. Like them, they relied on a sense of the present and a hope for the future configured around an absence: the loss of a putative revolutionary and socially transformative order pictured in the trope of the grave.

Unlike carnival, the Prague Spring was not a licensed rupture of the dominant order. The invasion and the

3.10
Jindřich Marco, *Students making posters at the foot of the Josef Jungmann monument, Jungmann Square*, 21–23 August 1968, Prague, the photographer.

3.11
Jindřich Marco, *1939 = 1968*,
21–23 August 1968, Prague,
the photographer.

3.12
Jindřich Marco, *Brezhnev
expiring on a stretcher*, 21–23
August 1968, Prague,
the photographer.

3.13
Jindřich Marco, *A line of
posters*, 21–23 August 1968,
Prague, the photographer.

3.11

3.12

3.13

inevitable repression that was to follow were no fiction. In Prague the hand-made poster of a blindfolded news cameraman, as a symbol of the official media, speaks for the new-found status of the political poster free of the constraints of party dogma and the platitudes of party rhetoric. As cries in the streets these posters are exiles from the domain of aesthetics. One large hand-made poster carried nothing but the words 'Reward, $100,000,000, Brezhnev & Kosygin and Novotný, Dead or Alive, $10,000 reward for Ulbricht, Gomułka, Kádár & Živkov, Wanted for Treason, Morders [sic] and Krádež slobody (Stolen Freedom) (Federal Polizei)'. Partly in English, partly in Czech, it was clearly meant to be seen not just by the people of Bratislava but by Western tourists and journalists. It was made to be filmed and photographed by the press; it was a broadcast to the free world.

At the end of June 1968 a group of writers and intellectuals including Jaroslav Seifert, Jiří Menzel and Miroslav Holub signed Ludvík Vaculík's public statement '2,000 Words which belong to the Workers, Farmers, Officials, Scientists, Artists and to All'. The document was published in the national daily press and condemned the isolation of the party from the people for creating conditions which stimulated self-interest in the context of absolute power. Part of it contained the following words: 'This spring like after the war great possibilities returned. Again we have got the chance to take into our hands our common cause, it has got the working title socialism. … This spring is gone and will never come back. In winter we will know everything.'[55] In retrospect it reads like a coded warning of what the future might bring, rather than a criticism of the chauvinism and incompetence of the communists in power, and a rallying call to all those who might support the process of socialist democratization both inside and outside the party.

On 22 August *Rudé právo* reported: 'Our determination to create a highly humane and democratic socialist society, to return to socialism its human face, was not understood. In fact it could not be understood … out of fear that the nations of socialist states might perceive in the Czechoslovak example a course worthy of imitation.'[56] The Prague Spring of 1968 was the culmination of the conflict between the intellectuals and the party and it marked the high point of the political influence of the intelligentsia until the Polish August in 1980. Acting, as it were, as a link between the party and the people, the intelligentsia expressed democratic socialist aspirations and the wider public's concern for national sovereignty. The party blamed the counter-revolutionary demagoguery of the media in promoting through disinformation 'the impression of an all-national patriotic movement'.

On 24 April 1969 Alexander Dubček was replaced by Gustáv Husák, a former political prisoner of the regime. Under his leadership all organizations which had displayed liberal tendencies in 1968 were dissolved and in the Czechoslovak Communist Party the purges began. In December 1970 during the thirteenth Congress of the Communist Party the document 'Instruction from the Crisis Evolution in the Party and Society' was accepted as the bible for normalization. It is worth quoting a short passage to illustrate the political tenor of the times:

> The effort of anti-communist circles was to revive bourgeois opinion, to evoke illusions about capitalism, to develop nationalism and anti-Soviet feeling, to query the leading role of the party and also the leading position of the working class, the class origins of the revolutionary struggle and the principles of socialism.
>
> … The newly established Marxist-Leninist left wing [Husák] emphasized the aim to purify the party and all social life of all residues of revisionism, opportunism, nationalism, and to deprive anti-socialist powers of their influence, to completely restore and further develop the power of our socialist establishment.[57]

The policies of the new government were aimed at the liberal intelligentsia, who were identified with 'Zionism, international imperialism and anti-communism' and named many who had taken an active part in the Prague Spring. Ivan Klíma recalled:

> It would be hard to find, in the history of modern totalitarian systems, such a stark polarity, such a concerted attack on a national culture and such a clear decision on the part of the elite to accept any fate rather than co-operate with the powers-that-be. In a single year, practically all the faculties of arts in the universities were destroyed, scientific and scholarly institutes were scattered to the winds, all magazines and journals dealing with the arts and culture were forbidden.[58]

A poster by Jiří Figer, *Unified in the construction of socialism–unified in the elections* (3.14), promoting the elections of 1971 which signalled the consolidation of normalization, epitomizes the hold of the party on life in Czechoslovakia. The word 'elections' is set out in a simple geometric pattern across the five sheets. The top half of each letter is embellished with photographs of cheering workers, agricultural machinery, people in national costume, members of the technical intelligentsia and manual workers. Its controlled banality is striking.

In contrast and in private, and for small numbers of initiates, artists such as Václav Ševčík continued to produce unique maquettes as designs for political posters highly critical of the regime and the process of normalization. Some poster-sized photographs modified in tempera take the image of the cobbled surface of Wenceslas Square with all its revolutionary associations to commemorate Jan Palach, the student who committed suicide in protest at the invasion in January 1969. Others take the image of Josef Myslbek's statue of St Václav to express Czech nationalism in the cause of liberalization. These posters are not street graphics; their true significance lies in the institutional contexts of their private consumption, although Ševčík's well known poster *21.8.1968* (3.6) did find illegal distribution on the streets in A2 format.[59]

NOTES

1   C. Vaughan James, *Soviet Socialist Realism. Origins and Theory* (London, Macmillan), 1973, p. 92.
2   Dubbed the 'anti-fascist wall of protection' by the communist authorities.
3   John Berger, *Art and Revolution. Ernst Neizvestny and the Role of the Artist in the USSR* (Harmondsworth, Penguin Books), 1969, p. 82.
4   Vladimir Serov was restored to his position as President of the Academy of Fine Arts. Alexander Gerasimov was elected head of the Union of Artists and another extreme conservative, Alexander Laktiniov, became head of Moscow's Surikov Institute of Art. See Priscilla Johnson, *Krushchev and the Arts. The Politics of Soviet Culture 1962–1964* (Cambridge MA, MIT Press), 1965, p. 8.

3.14
Jiří Figer, *Elections 26–7 November 1971. Unified in the construction of socialism – unified in the elections*, 1971, five sheets, Czechoslovakia, Historical Archive of the Czech Army, Prague.

5 'Ilya Ehrenburg countered with the examples of Picasso and Mayakovsky as modernists who were not political reactionaries. He cited the tolerance Lenin showed to art. An interesting exchange took place between Yevtushenko and Krushchev. Yevtushenko said, "We must have great patience with this abstract trend in our art and not rush to suppress it. … I am convinced that formalist tendencies in their work will be straightened out in time." To which Krushchev replied, "The grave straightens out the hunchback." Yevtushenko countered, to even Krushchev's applause, "Nikita Sergeivich, we have come a long way since the time when only the grave straightened out hunchbacks, there are other ways."' Johnson, *Khrushchev and the Arts*, p. 11. Shostakovitch's Thirteenth Symphony, on the theme of Yevtushenko's *Babi Yar*, was performed at the Moscow Conservatory on 18 December to silence from the political bureaucracy, the critics and the media. After two performances it was cancelled.

6 Johnson, *Khrushchev and the Arts*, p. 17.

7 *Ibid.*, p. 48.

8 M. L., 'Politický plakát Bedřicha Votruby', *Tvar*, 13:3 (1963) 68.

9 Marta Sylvestrová, *Český plakát 60.let* (*Czech Posters of the '60s*) (Brno, Department of Applied Arts of the Moravian Gallery), 1997, p. 12.

10 Ryszard Kapuscinski quoted by Jacques Rupnik, *The Other Europe* (London, Weidenfeld & Nicolson), 1989, p. 201.

11 See Josef Raban, 'Politická grafika W. A. Schlosser', *Tvar*, 14:4 (1964) 106–15. In conversation Dr Ivan Leudar felt that the hyperbole of the polemic might, at least in part, be ironic, signifying not so much the glorious career of a dedicated communist as the identification for the reader of 'one of them'.

12 The Bitterfeld Conference in 1965 signalled the end of the Thaw in the GDR which had begun with the Twentieth Congress of the CPSU.

13 Walter Ulbricht, *Social Development in the German Democratic Republic up to the Completion of Socialism* (Dresden, Verlag), 1967, p. 259.

14 Jost Hermand, 'The "Good New" and the "Bad New": Metamorphoses of the Modernism Debate in the GDR since 1956', *New German Critique*, 1:3 (1974) 88.

15 Ulbricht quoted in Hermand, 'The "Good New" and the "Bad New"', 80.

16 See S. Frederick Starr, *Red and Hot. The Fate of Jazz in the Soviet Union 1917–1991* (New York, Limelight Editions), 1994.

17 One of the criticisms from the West of communist production was a lack of variety which resulted in a dull uniformity: but this was answered by a kind of 'diversity by genre' under socialism. According to the logic, if you did not want to make political posters, then you could always make public information or cultural posters.

18 László Juhász, 'Rada pro průmyslové výtvarnictví v Mad'arsku', *Tvar*, 12:2 (1961) 45.

19 Boris Brodsky, 'Úspžšný debut sovětskèho výstavniho projektanta', *Tvar*, 12:10 (1961) 320.

20 Dr Ivan Leudar made this shrewd observation in Manchester, April 1998.

21 Juhász, 'Rada pro průmyslové výtvarnictví v Mad'arsku', p. 46.

22 In 'Móda a socialistický životní sloh' (Fashion and Socialist Life Style), *Tvar*, 12:3 (1961) 65.

23 A. Sutyagin (ed.), *Bases of Marxist-Leninist Aesthetics* (Moscow, State Publishers of Political Literature, Institutes of Philosophy and History of Art of the Academy of Sciences of the USSR), 1960; see James, *Soviet Socialist Realism*, p. 4.

24 Václav Ševčík, 'Is there a Future for the Czech Political Poster?', quoted in Marta Sylvestrová and Dana Bartelt, *Art as Activist. Revolutionary Posters in Central and Eastern Europe* (London, Thames & Hudson), 1992, p. 46.

25 Radoslav Selucký, *Kulturní tvorba*,15 October 1964, quoted in 'In Memoriam. The Political Poster 1958–1991', partly published in Sylvestrová and Bartelt, *Art as Activist*, p. 46. The exhibition subsequently travelled to West Berlin and the Federal Republic of Germany, Holland and the United States.

26 Krzysztof Dydo (ed.), *Hundredth Anniversary of Polish Poster Art* (Krakow, Biuro Wystaw Artystycznych), 1993, p. 40.

27 *Minutes of the Ninth Congress of the Hungarian Socialist Workers' Party* (Budapest, Kossuth Publishers), 1967, p. 474, quoted in György Aczél, *Culture and Socialist Democracy* (Budapest, Corvina), 1975, p. 22.

28 Tadeusz Galinski (ed.), *Culture in People's Poland* (Warsaw, Interpress), 1966, p. 32.

29 Zdzislaw Schubert, *The Polish Poster 1970–1978* (Warsaw, Kralowa Agencja Wydawnicza), 1979, unpag.

30 Dydo, *Hundredth Anniversary of Polish Poster Art*, p. 40.

31 Schubert, *The Polish Poster 1970–1978*.

32 The Polish Workers' Party was superseded by the Polish Committee of National Liberation. Set up in 1944, it acknowledged the Treaties of Yalta and Potsdam which returned Poland's borders to ancestral Piast lands on the River Oder and the coast of the Baltic. The present map of Europe shows the return of twentieth-century Poland to its borders of the tenth century. No mention is made of the Soviet occupation of 1939–41 and 1944 and the subsequent loss of Silesia and West Pomerania, nor is there any mention of the Forest Army and the indigenous resistance to the Soviet occupiers.

33 Viktor Shlapentokh, *Soviet Intellectuals and Political Power. The Post-Stalin Era* (Princeton NJ, Princeton University Press), 1990, p. 37.

34 Aczél, *Culture and Socialist Democracy*, pp. 23–5.

35 *Ibid.*, p. 29.

36 *Ibid.*, p. 32.

37 *Ibid.*, pp. 136–7.

38 Quoted in David Caute, *Sixty-eight. The Year of the Barricades* (London, Hamish Hamilton), 1988, p. 161.

39 Mariusz Knorowski, 'A Kite in the Wind of History', unpublished ms, 1998.

40 Caute, *Sixty-eight*, p. 54. It is worth noting that antisemitism was regarded as Stalinist, and Zionism as imperialist.

41 *Politický plakát proti fašismu a válce za mír a socialismus 1945–1985* (Prague, Vydalo Oddēleni propagandy, agitace ÚV KSČ and Muzeum Klementa Gottwalda), 1985; *Politický Plakát 1960–1970* (Prague, Vydaldo Odděleni propagandy, agitace Úv KSČ and Muzeum Klementa Gottwalda), 1970.

42 The 'normalization' process took some eighteen months to two years before it had any real effect.

43 Jan Baleka, *Angažovaný Plakát. Druhá výstava tvůrčí skupiny Plakát* (Prague, Svaz čs výtvrných umělců nakladatelství Svoboda, Výstavní síň Čs spisovatele), 1969, unpag.

44 *Ibid.*

45 *Ibid.*

46 Václav Ševčík in Sylvestrová and Bartelt, *Art as Activist*, p. 46. 'Two decades later, 17 November 1989, the massacre on Nàrodní třída in Prague again produced an immediate reaction. Prague was flooded with witty home-made leaflets and signs. Before creating new posters I dusted off some of my 1968 "Eye with a bloody tear" posters, wrote in a new date by hand, and took them to where the opposition was being born, to Prague theatres and universities.'

47 Caute, *Sixty-eight*, p. 296. As each of the state broadcasting and newspaper offices was taken over by Warsaw Pact forces and closed down, so numerous illegal radio stations started up all over the city, and as soon as one was discovered another would spring up to replace it.

48 Jindřich Marco, *Soudruh Agresor* (*Comrade Aggressor*) (Prague, Mladá fronta), 1990. Originally published by Europa

Verlag, in September 1968 under the pseudonym Václav Svoboda (Freedom). It was published in 1990 in Prague under the author's real name with the dedication, 'To all known and unknown courageous and honourable people, who for forty-one years endeavoured to keep alight the torch of truth.'

49 Under Antonín Novotný's regime (1962–68), as under Ulbricht, even the most rudimentary forms of reproduction equipment had been tightly controlled, although between March and September 1968 censorship laws were briefly relaxed.

50 Terry Eagleton, *Walter Benjamin, or, Towards a Revolutionary Criticism* (London, Verso), 1981, p. 145.

51 Photographs of many of these posters are reproduced in Gary Yanker, *Prop Art* (New York, Darien House), 1972, pp. 161–3.

52 See OKO (Pavel Meluš and Juraj Králik), *August '68 … in Slovakia* (Bratislava, Bratislava Editorial Series Slovakia in Photography I), 1990.

53 Eagleton, *Walter Benjamin*, p. 145.

54 Quoted from the GDR Trade Union Archive in Mary Fulbrook, *Anatomy of a Dictatorship. Inside the GDR 1949–1989* (Oxford, Oxford University Press), 1995, p. 197.

55 Published on 27 June 1968 in the national dailies *Mláda fronta, Práce, Zemždžlské noviny* and in the weekly *Literàrní noviny*. Translation by Marta Sylvestrová.

56 Caute, *Sixty-eight*, p. 295.

57 Translation by Marta Sylvestrová.

58 Ivan Klíma, 'Culture v. Totalitarianism', in *The Spirit of Prague and other Essays* (Cambridge, Granta Books), 1994, pp. 111–12.

59 These posters are well illustrated in Petr Pithart, Marta Sylvestrová and Jarmila Vacková, *České reflexe, Politický plakát Václava Ševčíka 1959–1994* (Prague, Narodní galerie v Praze), 1998.

Wir sind doch keine Affen

WOHLSTAND
NOTSTAND

CHAPTER FOUR

STAGNATION 1968–85

The period of stagnation in the communist bloc was ushered in by the Kosygin and Brezhnev administration in Moscow. But Soviet expansionism in Africa and the Middle and Far East and the perception of a weakened West produced a new confidence (9.63–68). A sense of mission and eternal vigilance was encouraged by the victory of the socialists in Portugal in 1974, and in 1973 the US-sponsored overthrow of President Salvador Allende's socialist regime in Chile (9.69, 70). Essentially the Soviet Union saw itself at the head of a large group of 'progressive' countries as history itself gave substance to the abstractions of Marxism-Leninism (9.71–78). Progress and stagnation were inextricably linked and Brezhnev's revival of the 'cult of personality' served only to stultify the visual rhetoric of the party and the state.

Beyond the aesthetic, the Prague Spring had notified the dangers of liberalization. On 21 September 1968 the Moscow propaganda centre published the so-called White Book in response to the events in Czechoslovakia. It set out to find justification for the occupation and the period of 'normalization' in the face of counter-revolutionary forces. In March 1971 Brezhnev criticized culture under Krushchev in a report of the Central Committee warning of the dangers of playing up shortcomings and dwelling on problems of the past because of the threat they posed to contemporary achievements. An attempt was made to re-establish the cult of Lenin and his image was given a high profile in celebrations of his birthday on 22 January and on the anniversary of the October Revolution on 7 November (6.41). In Poland hard-line policies in the face of widespread public disaffection led to the permanent installation of red flags on party buildings, and every printed artefact, even bus tickets, had to be subject to direct party control.[1] Repression and neo-Stalinist measures led to increased apathy but stimulated *samizdat* activity and the production of independent posters.

A second generation was coming of age for whom systems of repression were no longer imposed from without by a foreign power. Censorship was in the nature of life under communism and it functioned much as market restraints in capitalist societies. State sponsorship ensured self-regulation:

> In the past, censors never dreamed of justifying their acts of suppression by boasting of the many battles that had been fought for cultural freedom. … Of course, the joke only works where it is not funny, where the ideology of censorship has absorbed the ideology of the censored, where tyranny has learned the language of its victims, where the existence of censorship is based on a lasting identity of interests between censor and censored, where censorship … is not the simple oppressor of those who create culture but is their natural home.[2]

The system was no less brutal, but it was more sophisticated, relying more upon surveillance, domestic ostracism, exile and judicial repression. Those who opposed the system in Czechoslovakia would find themselves accused and imprisoned for disrupting the socialist system, engaging in private enterprise or sponging, for example. In the Soviet Union dissidence and opposition were often treated as mental illnesses rather than as crimes against the state meriting imprisonment, physical torture or worse. However, one result of this process was the decimation of the cultural intelligentsia, forcing most prominent creative individuals to emigrate, willingly or unwillingly, to the West; the other related result was the rise of the incompetent and cynical to prominent positions in the cultural bureaucracy.

If this were true of the Soviet Union, it was also true in some degree of the German Democratic Republic, Hungary, Poland and Czechoslovakia. But, while many left, many more stayed. For the latter, as the Hungarian artist Miklós Haraszti points out, complicity guaranteed authority. Artists were at the centre of the cultural apparatus and their function was to disseminate the official knowledge and to embellish the environs of the powerful and the people. So, for example, factory workers could see themselves in ideal pictures sustaining the illusion of communist progress. With the help of the creative intelligentsia, official culture was intended to fill the lives of the citizens so that they had no time for hostility or discontent and the workers would supposedly increase output with enthusiasm.[3] In return, the state guaranteed privileges, foreign travel and better housing for its cultural *apparatchiks*.

Throughout the region official designers adhered to the principles of high socialist realism in their iconography, draughtsmanship and attention to surface detail. To great visual effect they adapted the exaggerated perspectives and sweeping dynamics of Stalinist precedent to simpler, more

(detail of 4.2)

bombastic monumental statements (6.30, 31). Many featured square-jawed, resolute heroes in dramatic contexts, but there is nothing of the richly textured surfaces of their models. Low viewpoints make the figures appear monumental, and, combined with deformations of linear perspective, fragmentary figurative elements stand out from the surface in unnatural ways. The posters can be emblematic and echo many of the stylistic and compositional techniques of the Polish poster school. Drawing on modernistic conventions, many have a simple, flattened and residually photographic appearance which lent itself to cheap reproduction. But the visual rhetoric, like the nonsensical slogans, was vacuous to the point of invisibility, it was banal and few people paid it any real attention (6.23). Other designers resisted monumentalism in an atmosphere of illustrational and easy domestic familiarity, depicting optimistic workers hard at work in conventional compositions (8.6). Designs were formulaic (8.7) and frequently quite openly decorative (7.26, 8.12). By way of contrast, photo-montage, a tradition partially repressed in the Soviet Union, produced some of the most effective propaganda designs. V. Solokov and Viktor Koretsky, working in the manner of Gustav Klutsis and Alexander Zhitomirsky, struck at American imperialism, the arms race, the military industrial complex, and American domestic problems relating to race, poverty and the social meaning of the dollar (9.64–69). But these posters were published in relatively small editions.[4]

Official political posters in Poland, driven by Gierek's propaganda of success, were iconographically conservative and formally mannered. Building on national patterns established by the Polish poster school, older stereotypes were updated with exaggerated perspective and self-consciously graphic styles (8.22). Monumentalized body parts gained preference over half- and three-quarter-length figures; silhouette and overlay blended with photographic imagery. Designers' vocabularies were fundamentally expanded but, combined with a preference for emblematic imagery, they produced a strangely neutral effect. Few designers created their own style. Strong jawlines and distant gazes were replaced by the flattened shadows of an iconography devoid of human expression. The posters' deadened and unmodulated appearance was exaggerated by the low quality of the paper and the printing. Similarly, in Czechoslovakia official poster designers emulated socialist-realist precedent while subjecting it to graphic simplification, but without any of the self-conscious modernizing of the 1960s, echoing instead the styles of pre-war popular realism associated with the left (4.1). Normalization saw little in the way of innovation except a tendency towards decorative embellishments which lightened the political message. Zdeněk Filip, Wolfgang A. Schlosser and others simply repeated the empty, well established formulas.

To outside observers, bureaucracy, economic stagnation, alcoholism and inertia were symptoms of a society in decay. But according to party rhetoric everything was well, despite vigorous official anti-alcohol campaigns (8.91, 92). Weaknesses were covered up with falsified statistics guaranteeing social and economic progress: 'Happily babbling to itself, the Soviet colossus was slowly sinking into a morass of waste, inefficiency and indifference that almost defeats credulity.'[5] Under such delusional circumstances, it was sufficient for the state security apparatus to control public, not private, life, and posters played a significant role in orchestrating ritual commitment to party aims and projected public desires while masking the reality of the situation. The dual thinking demanded of the individual under totalitarian communism stepped over from the psychological, to become a structural element in everyday life. The chimerical imagery of the posters finds significance only in the denial of family breakdown, substandard accommodation, poor food, shoddy consumer goods and the vacuous ritualization of public life: there is little sense of commitment behind their blandishments: 'The language of the official press which is filled with clichés and stereotypes is a dead language.'[6] In the late 1970s in Poland, for example, many first-rate designers took up political commissions only because of the very high financial rewards: Henryk Tomaszewski's and Maciej Urbaniec's May Day posters are particularly fine examples and they are without political commitment (6.127, 132).

In the context of *détente* the suppression of the 'bulldozer' exhibition of avant-garde art in Moscow produced such a fierce reaction abroad that the authorities took a step back. As a result, Gorkom (Municipal Committee of Graphic Artists) and the Artists' Union began to tolerate contemporary and international modernist styles, and Brezhnev, with an eye to the West, called for a Soviet culture which would be 'socialist in content but international in form, spirit and character'.[7] International Marxism-Leninism had become strangely plural. Both reformist and official, it had liberal dissident and orthodox strains, its nationalism embracing independence movements and communism:

> A sound knowledge of the culture of other peoples helps us to overcome moribund and obsolete elements of culture, language, forms of intercourse and forms of individual and social consciousness, and makes the established forms and stereotypes of culture more dynamic, mobile, dialectic, profound and universal. In a word, our multinational culture attains international status, becomes international culture.[8]

The culture was dependent not on national diversity but on the well established rhetorical categories of 'progressive', 'democratic', 'humanist' and 'socialist': pluralism was tolerated only in so far as it could contribute to the 'new communist society'. Echoing Soviet policy, leader of the GDR Erich Honecker (1971–89) declared, 'In the area of art and literature there are no taboos!'[9] Tolerance was to be a new weapon of the state: 'a vast range of creative possibilities and a rich variety of subjects, themes, styles, forms, means of expression and individual artistry. The creative endeavour to match new artistic content with forms which are both appropriate and convincing is an important element in artistic progress.'[10] Taking Imre Nagy's maxim, János Kádár, leader of the Hungarian communists (1956–88), had concluded, 'Those who are not against us are with us.'[11] The official position in most communist states, apart from Czechoslovakia and Romania, was in line with that proposed by György Aczél's three 'f's' (or 't's' in Hungarian): 'to further or support, to exercise forbearance or tolerance and, if the case demands it, to forbid'.[12] Aczél echoes Kádár's sentiments on the necessity for vigilance against 'right-wing' and 'left-wing' while being careful to accommodate non-communists who were 'honest and talented enough to reach or return to the people and to socialism, even if there were bitter struggles for a time'.[13] Official histories of socialist realism redefined the canon and included fellow-travellers from the nineteenth century as diverse as Adolf Menzel, Honoré Daumier, Vincent Van Gogh, Edgar Dégas, Gustav Courbet; and from the pre-war period Renato Guttuso, Pablo Picasso, David Siqueiros, El Lissitsky, Käthe Kollwitz, Otto Dix, Diego Rivera, George Grosz, Frans Masereel, John Heartfield, Paul Nash, Fernand Léger and José Clemente Orozco.[14]

In the Soviet Union elements of the pre-Stalinist Russian avant garde underwent qualified rehabilitation, especially those who could be plainly identified with the Russian people and their revolutionary past. In the absence of Stalin and his excesses from the contemporary discourse (mention of Stalin was considered in bad taste and was more or less forbidden), constructivism was identified with Stalin's debasement of the machine aesthetic in the image of the screw in the machine. An important aesthetic

ideologue, Mikhail Lifshitz, for example, as an opponent of modernism, denounced the work of Malevich, the Vkhutemas, Rodchenko and Tatlin as a distortion of humanism which had brought about Stalinism; just as surely as Picasso, the Bauhaus and the expressionists had prepared the way for National Socialism.[15] If, however, as some historians like Boris Groys have argued, the state took over the unitary and utopian desires of the avant garde, then socialist realism, as an extension of political life into the cultural sphere, must be considered as a form of socially engaged modernism. Regionalist tendencies, therefore, with their focus on locality could be interpreted as a form of postmodernism. As a product of normalization Zdeněk Filip's *Fifty years of Rudé právo, 1920–70* (1970) (4.1), celebrating the half-century of the Czech national communist newspaper, apes the appearance of pre-war forms of popular illustration associated with leftist, if not socialist and communist, aims. As such it is a rehabilitation of certain expressive aspects of central European modernism. Filip's poster quotes from the styles of the past, not as part of a wider synthesis, as in orthodox socialist realism, but in a nostalgic gesture towards the memory of certain aspects of an independent and culturally advanced Czechoslovakia (4.1). Communist aesthetics demanded provincialism in permitted national styles partially inspired by indigenous folk art forms.[16] Broadly speaking, acceptable aesthetic parameters remained middlebrow, imitative and comparable to popular Western commercial graphic styles (5.20).

In a policy which contributed to the internal contradictions and ultimate demise of communist cultural policy as a workable orthodoxy, the 'nation' was again proposed in the renewed effort to establish legitimacy. The state was given new sanction to develop national 'popular' and 'folk' culture. Individual countries and republics could now bring their distinct voices to totalitarian socialism. President Nicolai Ceausescu (1965–89) in Romania, for example, had resisted direct Soviet domination but rejected Westernization. As a result, political posters dropped most of their socialist-realist pretensions for striking and lavish designs in a distinctively heraldic and national style. If the iconography comes straight from the socialist-realist arsenal, the emblems of the state and socialism are

4.1
Zdeněk Filip, *Fiftieth Anniversary of Rudé právo 1920–1970*, 1970, Czechoslovakia, Museum of Working Class Movement, Prague.

embellished in the national colours of red, blue and gold (6.74). Numerals and letters are dominant design elements, there are few if any figures, perhaps as a measure of the regime's scant regard for ordinary people, however hyperbolic its rhetoric to the contrary. Formulaic schemes like these were only occasionally disrupted by designs with a contemporary 'modern' Western look.

The graphic arts in the Baltic States had established clear national identities which looked forward to the struggles of national independence at the end of the decade.[17] In Latvia anything which was not expressly forbidden was allowed, although the stencilled flyers 'Sakharov our conscience' found in trains and at Riga railway station probably produced little satisfaction for the authorities.[18] Closer than the other Soviet republics to the West, vigorous national cultures in the Baltic States had never really been successfully suppressed. Lithuania was open to influences from Poland, and Estonia had good relations with Finland. In Latvia, for example, the former hyperrealist artist Juris Dimiters began to produce simple but monumental posters influenced by Western absurdist and surrealist idioms. Dimiters readily admits to admiration for the work of René Magritte, Paul Davis and Push Pin studios of the late 1960s (6.10, 9.62). Typically, Western influences reinforced national idioms to subvert stereotypical Soviet solutions.[19]

Allegiances to indigenous folk forms and traditions took unsuspected turns and many demonstrated a clear political intent. Among the most interesting is Dimiters's *Welcome to Chile* (1979) (9.62). A couple tango on the beach to give it all the appearance of a tourist poster. But it is shot through with a number of bullet holes, drawing attention to the American-orchestrated anti-socialist *coup*. Other designers favoured simple, strong graphic solutions with the bare minimum of words. Jānis Borg's poster triptych, *Junta, Chile, Venceremos* (1975) (3.3), shows a clear affiliation with Western Op and Minimal precedents, but it also shares geometric tendencies found in contemporary Soviet nonconformist art.[20] Similarly, Laimonis Šēnberg's *1 May* (1979) (6.133) relies on geometric conceit to conflate the images of the date, forward-looking profile and dove of peace into a single monochromatic motif.

As we have already seen, the German Democratic Republic followed a path of *Abgrenzung*, or the politics of separate development. It demanded increased dependence on Soviet models while simultaneously developing indigenous traditions of photo-montage. Murza and Panndorf's *Our party is the party of unity* (1971) (8.10) is a particularly good product of this policy. Iconographically it presents a 'typical' crowd, literally inundated by a sea of red

flags and sentimentalized goodwill. But formally it is forged of a spectacularly banal kind of double-bonded *kitsch* in a single rose-tinted photographic image of mass adulation which fails to understand the principles of socialist realism as surely as it misunderstands the classical tradition.

Walter Ulbricht's (1956–71) course of separate development stimulated theoretical discussion of the principles of montage and estrangement among the creative intelligentsia. Ultimately the debates carrying over from the previous decade surrounding Walter Benjamin had the potential to subvert the aims of *Abgrenzung*. His theories of mechanical reproduction placed the materials and structures of industrialization in the cultural sphere which would define the poster, as a mass-produced functional object, in relation to the process of democratization.[21] Official designers such as Klaus Wittkugel (1.3, 8.77), and, later, more radical spirits like Manfred Butzmann (7.27), Joseph W. Huber (4.2) and Wolfgang Janisch made use of photo-montage. Within Marxist-Leninist ideology photo-montage was a model of rational, industrial efficiency and technological achievement, its currency further guaranteed because of its links with national and socialist culture.

But Benjamin's theories were potentially threatening to official rhetoric. They undermined the Marxist-Leninist base–superstructure model by integrating artistic with more general forces of production. In turn, they subverted the idea of representation as the reflection of established and socialist ways of knowing and being. The certainty of the outcome of socialist history in the collapse of capitalism and the socialist future is no longer guaranteed. As a result, the justification of the one-party state as the mediator of the whole process disappears. Benjamin's idea of the author as producer makes of the designer an active participator in history. Furthermore the whole audience, not just the party, achieves an active role in the construction of consciousness.[22] Volker Braun, for example, asserted in a denial of the universalized, objective party view upon which censorship had staked its rationale: 'Historical consciousness is consciousness of self. The reality with which we live is working history, and what we usually call history is the "object of construction" which is loaded with "now-time".'[23] Despite its self-avowed role as a mediator of official policy, the cultural public sphere could now provide a modicum of space for critical discussion. The connection between a theory of production and a theory of history which was the theoretical cornerstone of Marxism-Leninism for the legitimation of existing socialist societies had now been undermined.

Manfred Butzmann, for example, pitched a critique aimed at the public sphere. In the GDR public spaces were assiduously zoned, controlled and surveilled by the authorities, but they appear in Butzmann's posters as neglected places, scoured of humanity and nature: 'Butzmann realized that apparently everyday details and the dereliction and brutalization of public spaces held significant information on the condition of society in East Germany with all its unattainable goals. ... Butzmann began to loosen the straitjacket of propaganda by setting its false slogans against reality.'[24] The sites in the designs are places where the rhetoric of the official dream has no purchase, but where life is lived by the majority. Butzmann sought relief from the tedium through the fragile inroads of nature and an ecological consciousness which was beginning to capture the imagination of the radical left on both sides of the Iron Curtain. His environmental concerns were coloured by the history of the locality and its unwritten and inconvenient pasts. These intensely moral pictures appeared in small editions of less than 100; avoiding censorship, they existed outside the official discourse.[25] As posters, or postcards, they are but small interruptions in the homogeneity of the party gloss which refused anything but the most optimistic interpretation of contemporary life. Butzmann's posters challenge the authority of the single declamatory party image. They are constructed as multiples from unmodified photographs of forgotten but recognizable corners of Berlin and are restricted to sombre monochromes, in contrast to the predominant reds of the party propaganda (7.27). Joseph W. Huber engaged the official discourse in similar ways, weaving commentaries on contemporary life by placing traditional and well known images and iconographies important to German Democratic identity into telling juxtapositions. A long series of postcards found irony and contradiction in unmodified photographs of road signs whose declamatory innocence parodies the duplicity of official rhetoric (7.28).

According to Marxism-Leninism, the lessons of history, truth and science remained at the helm of the ship taking socialist societies towards communism. But the regimes had to admit that the new society could not be brought about merely by command. Membership of the communist party was rarely more than 10 per cent of the population, a number almost equivalent to the numbers imprisoned in the 1950s. The authorities had to accommodate a much broader range of opinion if their goal was finally to be achieved. At least, that was the way the rhetoric framed the problem for communist parties desperately manoeuvring for legitimacy in an increasingly difficult climate. The 1960s had opened a Pandora's box of 'anarchist' and 'nihilist' energies among a post-war generation which needed a voice. Nevertheless, the dominant rhetoric blamed the sins of the fathers on the sons, looking back to the 'golden age' of the 1950s: 'We do not wish to deny that we have forbidden the publication of

works and will do so in future cases where ideas of fascism are promoted or incitement is given to war or chauvinism, where the foundations of our people's system are attacked, where lack of humanism, purblindness or spiteful nationalism are found.'[26]

Western influence grew because of increasing tourist, business and diplomatic contact.[27] In 1970 only 8 per cent of the Soviet population could gain access to foreign broadcasts, but by the middle 1970s the figure was 50 per cent. Visits of West Germans to the GDR doubled in the decade 1970–80, and telephone calls rose from 700,000 to 24 million.[28] Relations between Poland and the Federal Republic of Germany were 'normalized', contacts between the two countries were improved and 130,000 Poles visited the Bundesrepublik.[29] Rudolf Bahro, the German Democratic intellectual, argued that 'really existing socialism' had achieved only a superficial transformation of capitalism, reflected in the desire to catch up and surpass the West.[30] And there were substantial but not universal gains in personal income, the ownership of consumer durables and social welfare. Many posters were commissioned to advertise improvements in housing, in long-standing partial fulfilment of party aims, often in the face of a less than ideal reality (7.21, 22). But the people wanted more. Modernization bred discontent more than disaffection, encouraging the desire for consumer goods and freedom of expression and movement but not necessarily for wholesale conversion to Western capitalism: in 1981, Solidarity, for example, demanded free trade unions, not democracy. Poland, like the GDR, Hungary and Yugoslavia, continued to promote a hybrid of socialist mass culture and Western commercial popular culture in the attempt to breathe new life into state culture:

> Our social base is too weak to induce a renaissance of autochthonous individualism. We select from the pre-packaged expressions of individualism concocted in the West. ... As in industry, so too in art: we have no technology of our 'own'. Our colleges of art teach the methods of, and justification for, this aesthetic parasitism.

> Why shouldn't I utilize the style of Robbe-Grillet or Andy Warhol when our police use French tear gas and our citizens are registered on American computers?[31]

Lenin appeared in psychedelic colours (6.29), 1 May posters aped the look of pop (6.129), and surrealist devices familiar from Western popular commercial culture decorated cultural and political posters alike. In Poland this aesthetic dependence echoed policies of openness to the West and the propaganda of success:[32] 'the authorities were clearly aware that today they [could not] shape the views of society through repetition of direct orders and slogans, which cause nausea in the average recipient, but only indirectly: through smuggling directives, pressures, ideological schemes, and value systems wrapped as attractive products of mass culture … .'[33] The adaptation of commercial imagery was paralleled by inroads from conceptual and performance art. Designers with close contacts with the contemporary avant garde produced unofficial political posters for exhibition. Boris Bučan in Yugoslavia made clear, if coded, political statements of an independent nature in *Admittance forbidden to the unvocational* (1976) (6.86); Sándor Pinczehélyi in Hungary used cobblestones and other revolutionary symbols, with all their historical and contemporary associations with the Paris of 1789 and 1968, to design posters as part of his conceptual interrogation of political symbolism (6.85).

Official events and culture had little appeal; television and 'illicit' Western forms of entertainment were much more popular. Even in prison, the dissident, playwright and future President of the Czech Republic, Václav Havel, would ask his wife to provide him with tapes of the latest rock music. The official culture looked crude and dated and could not hold the attention of its audience. Meaningful cultural activities became more private, taking place in apartments and in new informal institutional structures which grew up around particular theatres, private salons and the like rather than in the official ceremonies, Parks of Culture and Rest, Houses of Culture, trade unions and the numerous other party-sponsored organizations.

The emergence of this semi-autonomous public sphere offered the young an alternative. In response, youth organizations, traditionally the recruiting grounds of the party, turned to popular culture rather than ideology. In a mirror image of the extra-parliamentary opposition in the Federal Republic of Germany, the phenomenon was exaggerated in the GDR by a reaction to the complicity of the older generation in World War II. Growing out of a complex mesh of official and unofficial sentiments, a new discursive space began to open up. Based in notions of national independence and civil rights activities, it offered the hope of individual as well as national self-determination. The romanticism of socialism blended perfectly into the universalism of national and human rights ideology.

The 'talk across the Wall' between the dissidents in the GDR and the extra-parliamentary opposition in the FRG fuelled the propaganda war of words as official constructions of 'East' and 'West' were undermined from within and without. They shared many values in relation to peace, the arms race, democratic socialism, ecology and feminism, although in the East human rights issues were less easily articulated. In posters, the examples of Klaus Staeck from the Federal Republic and of Joseph W. Huber (4.2), Martin Hoffmann (9.29) and Manfred Butzmann

(9.23) from the GDR give us, on the margins, a blurring of the cultural and political lines between the two systems. The year 1971 saw the Protestant Church proclaim itself not against but parallel with socialism, to give the Church a lever with the state. But as pastors aligned themselves with the peace movement and the campaign for civil rights, and against military conscription, so the Church provided a platform for views not tolerated in the official media. In 1979 Wolfgang Janisch exhibited his photo-montages critical of state apparatuses and in the cause of peace at the first exhibition of the Art Service of the Evangelical Church in the Castle Church in Cottbus.

Radical designers began to see themselves and their pens and brushes as weapons in the battle for freedom of expression. The work of Janisch, Butzmann, Huber, Feliks Büttner and others, such as Klaus Lemke, challenged communist conventions. If Butzmann and Huber had developed a kind of laconic, photographic realism shot through with a wry humour, Büttner and Lemke were resolutely graphic, dependent for effect on a schematic directness of vision, communicating their messages without the aid of supporting texts (5.15). Their language was that of international graphic design. It was a relatively liberal time, but immense difficulties remained before anything was printed: arbitrary authority remained. A key event in this process lay outside the field of the visual arts and occurred on 27 November 1976 when the dissident poet and balladeer Wolf Biermann had his citizenship revoked. Reform from within, it seemed to many, was impossible.

The politics of reform gave way to the '"anti-politics" of the self-emancipation of civil society'.[34] Encouraged by the Helsinki accords in 1975, many designers were inspired by the counter-culture and the ethics of spiritual resistance. Slowly the counter-sphere became a structural feature of life and its visual trace can be found in the changing nature and status of the unofficial political poster: sometimes tolerated but usually suppressed, it existed in the vacuum left by the collapse of official ideology, a fact recognized by the authorities:[35]

A large number of people who are very active in the field of culture have not yet adopted the ideas of socialism. … Those envisaging such a weighty decision stand in need of skilful and tactful guidance. Particular importance is attached to the contribution made by artists, educators, directors of cultural establishments, etc., who, without being out-and-out supporters of scientific communism, uphold the social order and the efforts made by the GDR in the field of culture, whether because they are sincere humanists, democrats opposed to imperialism, or in deference to a religious ethic. Many citizens who are professing Christians take part in cultural activities, their rights and duties being the same as other citizens'.[36]

The key year was 1976. Strikes in Poland acted as the catalyst of a process which ended with the collapse of communism. It was a war without blood, a war of symbols. The controversy surrounding the exhibition *The Four from Wilanow* was symptomatic. The exhibitors, Eugeniusz Get-Stankiewicz, Jan Sawka, Jerzy Czerniawski and Jan Jaromir Aleksiun, had graduated from the Academy of Fine Arts in Wrocław.[37] The work was not political in a direct sense, but addressed moral, social and ethical problems. As a product of the New Culture[38] it was youth-oriented and broadly comparable with Western alternative culture. But it was necessarily more political in the aftermath of the Prague Spring and the reality of living under communism at a time of civil strife. Like the posters produced for the Grotowski Theatre in Wrocław, the Oder jazz festival and several literary cabarets at the centre of the New Culture, the four were characterized by 'private vision, moral concern and social commitment'.[39] The notions were in tune with party aims, but they were far removed from the political fervour demanded by the authorities.[40] Other posters produced in association with the experimental theatre group STU or Theatre 100 in Cracow demonstrate a critical position. The poster for the stage production *Exodus* (1975) (8.20) shows a hooded figure represented as a spent match standing in a deep red field, combining allegory and politics in the image of the individual; in *Patients* (1976) (8.14) a group huddled as if standing in a tram are isolated in a barren landscape. Another for Teatre in Opole, *Canterbury Tales* (1976), shows a prostrate and psychedelically rendered fat prostitute accompanied by diminutive caricatures of identifiable public figures encumbered with images of excess and corruption.

These posters attracted official criticism because they represented the individual in ways which could not be circumscribed by the state ideology. As official political posters plied an exhausted rhetoric, their role as a critical tool of engagement passed into the realm of the art poster. Symbolic cultural posters were commonplace in Poland and were highly influential even among designers in the West. Their influence can be seen most easily in the work of Grapus, founded and based in Paris in 1970 as a socially oriented co-operative.[41] Despite the material and technological difficulties facing artists working at the margins of official culture, hundreds of designs were produced. For designers of an essentially leftist persuasion, on both sides of the Iron Curtain, the philosophy was to produce designs which offered the public an intellectual and critical challenge, rather than simple entertainment or an exhortation to action, political or commercial.

Jan Sawka's *Jazz on the River Oder* (1978) (4.3) is particularly revealing. A black man, face obscured, lost in the darkness which surrounds him, sits listless, slumped in a chair. Beside him, but out of reach, lies a trumpet with a flower growing from its mouthpiece. It is an allegory, it has no single meaning and relies upon the viewer to produce meaning. Neither the imagery nor the text directs the spectator to the already known. Meaning, it seems, has become 'poetic', perhaps discovered by the artist only in the act of designing itself. The figure is melancholic; he has abandoned the tools of his trade and is resigned to a kind of listless torpor. He stands in for the artist, who finds his dialectical opposite in the political intriguer who is as clear about the futility of his actions as the artist is sure of his inability to affect the course of events. Saturnine esotericism takes precedence over the need to communicate simple political messages.

Sawka, Aleksiun, Get-Stankiewicz and others such as Franciszek Starowieyski make posters which often appear fragmentary or unfinished: skulls, geometric shapes, architectural mouldings, shells, all-seeing eyes, snakes, annotated drawings, staircases, ladders, body parts in arbitrary but encrypted combinations pass oblique comment on temporal conditions: 'this fragmentation in the graphic aspects is a principle of the allegorical approach. ... The allegorical personification can be seen to give way in favour of the emblems, which mostly offer themselves to view in desolate, sorrowful dispersal. ... It is as something incomplete and imperfect that the objects stare out from allegorical structure.'[42] Image and meaning are presented as discontinuous and the posters reject the false unities of socialist realism:

> Allegory was 'the mundane exposition of history as the history of world suffering'. Classical art portrayed a harmonious totality ... using nature symbolically for the ahistorical representation of the ideal. Its beautiful appearance covered up the antagonisms and contradictions of reality. But the contemplative mode of the allegorist was dialectically opposed to classicism. To quote Benjamin: 'the false appearance of reality withers away'. In its place was a critical representation of history as the 'unfreedom, the imperfection and brokenness of the sensual'. The allegorical mode of portraying truth was meaningful only in times of historical decay ...[43]

The posters make reference to the existential plight of the individual and are antagonistic towards communist aesthetic orthodoxies. In the West, the human condition is born of the anxiety of total freedom of choice, where any act seeks a premium on meaning. Under totalitarianism articulations of the human condition have less to do with individual angst than the psychological pressures of living with *Ketman* and the lack of individual freedoms and basic human rights. Under these conditions, any assertion of the individual became a political act in the denial of the collective aspirations of the state. Allegorical forms, in the

4.2a
Joseph W. Huber, *Seeing does not protect against being blind*, c. 1985, postcard, GDR, private collection.

4.2b
Joseph W. Huber, *We are no monkeys*, c. 1985, postcard, GDR, private collection.

4.2c
Joseph W. Huber, *Something is WRONG*, c. 1985, postcard, GDR, private collection.

4.2d
Joseph W. Huber, *Affluence – crisis*, c. 1985, postcard, GDR, private collection.

4.3
Jan Sawka, *Jazz on the River Oder*, 1978, Poland, offset, the artist.

hands of the designer or the *apparatchik*, had become essential under the *ersatz* conditions of life:

> Communication between the lines already dominates our directed culture. This technique is not the speciality of the artist only. Bureaucrats, too, speak between the lines: they, too, apply self-censorship. Even the most loyal subject must wear bifocals to read between the lines: this is in fact the only way to decipher the real structure of our culture. Real communication takes place only between the lines. And it is public life itself that is the space between the lines.[44]

Bureaucracy demands obfuscation, dissembling and inauthenticity.

Allegorical ruminations are not revolutionary, but act as the state's conscience as it provides relative freedom without risk either to itself or to the designer. Political protest leads to arrest. The ability to write between the lines, to separate words and objects from their meanings, is therefore a skill and a test of professionalism for the *nomenklatura* as much as for dissenting members of the cultural intelligentsia:

> Our messages between the lines are suggestions sent to the same state and the same public that our official lines continue to serve. Debates between the lines are an acceptable launching ground for trial balloons, a laboratory of consensus, a chamber for the expression of manageable new interests, an archive of weather reports. The opinions expressed there are not alien to the state but are perhaps simply premature. This is the true function of this space: it is the repository of loyal digressions that, for one reason or another, cannot now be openly expressed.[45]

The power of allegory, the play of sense, lay in their ability to convert objects into signs which could be endlessly combined. 'Every person, every thing, every relation can signify any other.'

The true force of allegory lies not in its diversions into irony and the subversion of objects and their meanings in the dominant discourse but rather in the deep melancholy produced by the destruction of the natural (communist) language of existence. This manifested itself in poster design in a reassessment of romanticism and its insights into the suffering and alienation generated by instrumental reason and collective values. The language of authority may have become vacuous, but the systems of repression were intact. Fantasy was proposed as an expansion of realist possibilities, representing a shift from class to individual struggle and inner conflict. Rich illustrative styles became the resting place of sublimated histories even within the socialist canon and held the silences of the repressed histories of Stalinism. Starowieyski, identified by Cyprian Koscielniak[46] as one of the principal fathers of the art poster in Poland, established a territory in the field of cultural posters where he could give relatively free rein to his own ideas in metaphors and symbols (6.18). Individual expression found its own political currency as the expression of the dark corners of the subconscious inevitably drew parallels with social realities during times of repression. Grotesque reversals explore the dark underbelly of contemporary existence: the figure of new socialist man is cut, drilled, crushed, metamorphosed and recombined. In these posters the body revolts against the abstraction of ideas which links material progress with the improvement of the human condition (4.3, 8.14, 18–21, 23, 24).

4.2

4.3

In the official ideology there was no place for social strife, nor for the use of public space by the people for anything other than official ritual and organized leisure. The means of communication were in the hands of the state. Telephones in Czechoslovakia, for example, were notoriously unreliable and the waiting list might be ten years; in the GDR they were also extensively tapped. In these circumstances the leaflet and the poster came into their own. Easily made and distributed, they carried the messages of the day. As Jan Kubik has recounted, when Stanisław Pyjas, a student of Polish literature and an associate of KOR,[47] was found murdered in Kraków, leaflets and posters calling for attendance at the funeral were constantly removed by the police. In 1978 posters for banned commemorations of those killed during the strikes of December 1970 in Gdańsk, Gdynia and Sopot saw the process continue. The 11 November 1978 was also the sixtieth anniversary of Polish independence; the fiftieth anniversary had been ignored by Edward Gierek and the party leadership in the wake of the Prague Spring, but now there was no holding back. Posters showing two Polish white eagles, one with legs chained with the date 1978 underneath, the other with the chains broken and the date 1918, were distributed throughout Warsaw in a demonstration of the strength of national feeling. The following year the visit of the 'Polish Pope', John Paul II, displayed before the television cameras the authority of the Church and exposed the inauthenticity of party power.[48] This is not the place to go into the history of Solidarity and the complexities of the issues leading up to General Wojciech Jaruzelski's (1980–89) declaration of martial law in 1981, but what had started as protests over hikes in food prices and

demands for a memorial to strikers killed in Gdańsk in 1970 soon developed into a major political crisis for the communist party.

The most famous graphic design to emerge from the Polish August of 1980 was the Solidarity logo. It was created during the strike by the Gdańsk designer Jerzy Janiszewski:

> I saw how solidarity appeared among the people, how a social movement was being born out of that and how institutions joined in. This all had a great effect on my spirit and I decided I wanted to join the strike.

> I chose the word solidarity because it best described what was happening to people. The concept came out of the similarity to people in dense crowds leaning on one another – that was characteristic of the crowds in front of the gate. They did not press or push each other. … Finally I added the flag because I was aware that this is not a regional group question but is a universal movement. The letters have a disordered look because this is their strike attribute.[49]

The iconography of the crowd has been manipulated by poster designers, popular illustrators and artists since the French Revolution. In communist posters the crowd was always led by the heroic worker, militia man, Lenin or Stalin. The Solidarity logo adopted this motif, subjected it to typographical interpretation and substituted the national flag for the socialist hero. In the national colours of red on white, it sustains the use of red as a colour vital to revolutionary causes. Janiszewski and the Solidarity committee responsible for the design took elements of the dominant discursive language of politics, but turned them to their own purposes. This had the dual effect of

4.4
Erazm Ciołek, *By the wall of the Gdańsk shipyard*, August 1980, Poland, the photographer.

challenging the *status quo* while simultaneously appropriating the rhetoric of the ruling elite. Whether deliberate or not, the strategy was extremely effective in helping to situate Solidarity in such a way as to minimize the risk of open conflict (4.6).

The Lenin shipyard strike of August 1980 was the focus of the largest spontaneous social and national movement the Soviet bloc had ever seen. A single powerful discourse was constructed from a complex weave of national identity found in the political legacies of romanticism, the Catholic Church, the inter-war republic and a new tradition of workers' martyrdom. At its centre stood Lech Wałęsa. For the media and for the Polish people the struggle found its symbolic focus at Gate Two of Gdańsk Lenin shipyards, where among the Solidarity posters were flowers, crosses and a large white Polish eagle (4.4). As Jan Kubik has pointed out, there were two other pictures: one of Pope John Paul II, and another of the Black Madonna of Częstochowa. The first made visible allegiance to the 'Polish Pope' and to Polish Catholic nationalism. The second made reference to the partially suppressed celebrations of the millennium of Polish nationhood and Christianity which had taken place between 1957 and 1966.[50] In 1981, on the declaration of martial law, a poster by Wiesław Strebejko for a concert (6.98), featuring a schematic representation of the Madonna, suddenly appeared in apartment windows in Warsaw as a gesture of defiance. The people regarded the poster as an effective medium of political communication under a regime where the mainstream media were directly controlled by the state. It was a graphic demonstration of the breakdown of the boundaries between the political and

the cultural outside the limits of the official discourse.

The Polish people paid official culture little attention. In ways hard to understand for Western observers, for whom cultural freedom is not an obvious issue, and where culture is politically marginal, unofficial poetry, music and the visual arts flourished. Millions saw Andrzej Wajda's film *Man of Iron* in July 1981, often screened with its predecessor, *Man of Marble*: no one could deny any longer the brutality and inhumanity of the regime (4.5). Andrzej Pągowski's design for the film emulated the Solidarity logo in the typography of the title, and demonstrated a strain of martyrological opposition in a red-stained white shirt spreadeagled in the manner of a crucifix (6.99). Small handbills and postcards by designers such as Jan Bokiewicz have the simplicity and directness of the hand-made gesture to become under the pressures of active opposition an expression of a political position on behalf of the artist and his audience (4.7). They are an example of what the art historian Mieczysław Porebski described as the articulation of 'philosophical concepts, historical controversies and political arguments in tangible form'.[51]

There was conflict between the established political, economic and cultural class and an emergent class made up of all those who subscribed to counter-hegemonic, alternative, unofficial and independent principles and values. The ethos of the emergent culture was revolutionary and romantic. Marxism-Leninism and its dependence on modernization and the scientific-technological revolution was under pressure. The role of the individual was open to question in the face of bureaucratic inertia, inefficient and outdated production techniques and the power of the state.

4.5

4.6

4.5
Erazm Ciołek, *Advertisements for the films* Man of Iron *by Andrzej Wajda and* The Charge *by Krzysztof Wojciechowski in Defiliad Square in Warsaw*, 1981, Poland, the photographer.

4.6
Erazm Ciołek, *Warsaw University (Museum of Astronomy), election day, 4 June 1989*, Poland, the photographer.

4.7a

4.7b

śmigus

'81

MILICJA

WSZYSTKIEGO

4.7c

GRU+
DZIEŃ

Pamiętajmy

4.7d

4.7e

HAPPY
1984
ORWELL

W ROCZNICĘ SIERPNIA '80

SOLIDARNOŚĆ

4.7f

GDAŃSK '84

4.7g

Światło w tunelu   '82

4.7a
Jan Bokiewicz, *Smigus militia*,
1983, postcard, the artist.

4.7b
Jan Bokiewicz, *Everything*,
1981, New Year card,
the artist.

4.7c
Jan Bokiewicz, *We remember
October*, 1984, card
commemorating Father
Popiełuszko's kidnap and
murder, the artist.

4.7d
Jan Bokiewicz, *Solidarity*,
1981, postcard, the artist.

4.7e
Jan Bokiewicz, *1984 Happy
Orwell*, 1984, postcard,
the artist.

4.7f
Jan Bokiewicz, *Anniversary of
the Polish August 1980,
Gdańsk '84*, 1984,
A4 poster, the artist.

4.7g
Jan Bokiewicz, *A light at the
end of the tunnel*, 1982, New
Year card, the artist.

Communist rhetoric had emptied itself of authority and meaning. The role of the artist shifts from 'engineer of human soul' to 'seer' – the consequence of the dialectic of melancholy which Benjamin identifies at the heart of allegory. From out of the collapse of the communist discourse of rational progress emerged the self-image of the designer as a free spirit possessed of penetrating intelligence and the profoundest gloom, genius and madness. The 1970s saw the applied arts develop powers of self-expression; they saw designers insinuate into their work idiolectic visual vocabularies. Posters produced outside the institutional structures of the political organizations of the state were allegorical, coded, private things. What messages they did carry were not those of the political masters. Their audiences were circles of initiates from the liberal intelligentsia where personal friendships bound together relatively small, close circles of writers, artists and intellectuals in a field of cultural production symbiotically related to the organizations of the state. Paradoxically, it was a field made the more fertile because the various party organizations brought individuals together who might otherwise have remained relatively isolated. Some would call this art.[52] But it was a necessary political tactic: as the institutional structure of the poster altered so the position and the role of the designer changed, to be drawn into a position of moral defiance. The poster excluded itself from the social contracts between totalitarian power or consumerist models offered by the West. The position of the unofficial designer paralleled that of the socially engaged Russian *intelligent*:[53] 'Their imagination is flooded with romantic utopias. They are obsessed with the former independence of the individual and want to plunge society back into the fecund chaos of unfettered personal passions; they wish to split apart the interlocking domains of economy, culture and political power.'[54]

Poster production was less well policed than radio, television or high art, and enabled designers to make a living in a freelance, entrepreneurial way. The independence it offered attracted individuals of an anarchic persuasion, such as Felix Büttner, who adopts an aristocratic and nostalgic position, or Joseph W. Huber, who refuses both communist and capitalist models in his tiny flat in Berlin: or 'the now middle aged *enfant terrible* of Polish posters, Franciszek Starowieyski. … Gone is his headband: his long black hair has been shorn. … But he still cultivates outrageousness. He calls the late Senator Joseph McCarthy "an American hero", did not support Solidarity "communism with a more human face", and once reputedly dubbed Warsaw's "Stalinist Gothic" Palace of Culture the most beautiful building in the city.'[55]

In Poland graphic artists became celebrities whose opinion was sought on a myriad of matters. A Poster of the Month competition was run by the daily *Życie Warszawy* (*Warsaw Life*). All that was required was that it must admit of an officially acceptable interpretation. Simultaneously, graphic designers addressed different audiences. The monolithic and homogeneous mass audience of the Stalinist era was forgotten.

NOTES

1 Censorship was orchestrated through the main office for the Control of the Press, Publications and Public Performances (GUKPPiW). In the 1970s the main authority for posters, Wydawnictwo Artystyczno-Graficzne (WAG), was superseded by Krajowa Agencja Wydawnicza (KAW), which almost entirely controlled the production of political and social posters.
2 Miklós Haraszti, *The Velvet Prison. Artists under State Socialism* (Harmondsworth, Penguin), 1987, p. 8.
3 *Ibid.*, p. 93.
4 Editions were usually in the region of 8,000–12, 000, unlike posters which addressed internal affairs, which ran from 60,000 to 500,000 or more.
5 Kristian Gerner and Stefan Hedlund, *Ideology and Rationality in the Soviet Model. A Legacy for Gorbachev* (London and New York, Routledge), 1989, p. 337.
6 'Interview with Robert Havemann', *New German Critique*, 15:3 (1978) 42.
7 Margarita Tupitsyn, 'Avant Garde and Kitsch', in *No! – and the Conformists. Faces of Soviet Art of 50s to 80s* (Warsaw, Fundacja Polskiej Sztuki Nowoczesnej Wydawnictwa Artystyczne i Filmowe Warszawa), 1994, p. 40.
8 K. M. Dolgov, 'Culture and Social Progress', in *Marxist-Leninist Aesthetics and the Arts* (Moscow, Progress Publishers), 1980, pp. 23–4.
9 At the Eighth GDR Party Congress in 1971.
10 Hans Koch, *Cultural Policy in the German Democratic Republic* (Paris, Unesco), 1975, p. 35.
11 Kádár had been part of the Imre Nagy administration but had returned to Hungary as the Soviet-nominated prime minister. He was responsible for the repression and judicial murders which had continued into the 1960s after the suppression of the uprising.
12 György Aczél, *Socialism and the Freedom of Culture* (Budapest, Corviana Kiado), 1984, p. 406.
13 *Ibid.*, p. 390.
14 Nóra Aradi, *A szocialialista képzömüvészet jelképei* (Budapest, Kossuth Könyvkiadó/Corvina Kiadó), 1974.
15 See Mikhail Lifshitz, *The Philosophy of Art of Karl Marx* (London, Pluto Press), 1976.
16 Particularly good examples are Yuri Mokhor and Oleg Ternetyev's design *The All Union Young Communist League* (1968) and L. Nepomnyashchy's *5 May – National Press Day* (1966) (Nina Baburina, *The Soviet Political Poster 1917–1980* (Harmondsworth, Penguin Books), 1985, pp. 134, 143); both ape the cubo-futurist figuration of early Tatlin and Malevich.
17 *Sovremennyi Plakat Latvii* (Moscow, Sovetskii Khudozhik), 1989.
18 Ronald Misiunas and Rein Taagepera, *The Baltic States. Years of Dependence 1940–1990* (London, Hurst), 1993, p. 251 and plate between pp. 132–3.
19 James Fraser and Sandra Basens, 'Remarkable Posters from Latvia', *Print*, March/April (1985) 60–6.
20 'Geometric' was the word used in preference to 'abstract' in artistic circles to help avoid accusations of cosmopolitanism and formalism.

21   Walter Benjamin was being discussed in the GDR as early as 1973 in the literary contexts of the seventh Writers' Congress. See David Bathrick, *The Powers of Speech. The Politics of Culture in the GDR* (Lincoln NE and London, University of Nebraska Press), 1995, p. 40.

22   Here are the origins of Stalin's dictum of artists and writers as 'engineers of the human soul'.

23   Bathrick, *The Powers of Speech*, p. 40.

24   Matthias Flügge, 'Signs of the Times. Some Views on East German Art and the Artist Manfred Butzmann', in James Aulich and Tim Wilcox (eds), *Europe without Walls. Art, Posters and Revolution 1989–1993* (Manchester, Manchester City Art Galleries), 1993, p. 81.

25   See Flügge, 'Signs of the Times'.

26   Aczél, *Socialism and the Freedom of Culture*, p. 406.

27   Stephen White, *Political Culture and Soviet Politics* (London, Macmillan), 1979, pp. 182–3.

28   David Childs, *The GDR. Moscow's German Ally* (London, Unwin Hyman), 1988, pp. 88–92.

29   Jerzy Topolski, *An Outline History of Poland* (Warsaw, Interpress Publishers), 1986, p. 271.

30   'The functionaries in the middle and at the base represent the unbridgeable gulf between the apparatus as a whole and the masses or, more exactly, the so far unorganized sum of emancipatory and compensatory interests.' *The Alternative in Eastern Europe* (London and New York, Verso), 1981, was written as a response to the 1968 invasion of Czechoslovakia. Bahro's book was first published in the Federal Republic of Germany. Subsequently, despite his credentials as a party member, he was arrested and charged with being a West German spy. Sentenced to eight years in prison, he was released in 1979.

31   Haraszti, *The Velvet Prison*, pp. 113–14.

32   Alan Aldridge, Martin Sharpe and Terry Gilliam.

33   Stanisław Barańczak, quoted in Jan Kubik, *The Power of Symbols against the Symbols of Power. The Rise of Solidarity and the Fall of State Socialism in Poland* (Philadelphia PA, Pennsylvania State University Press), 1994, p. 72, n. 99.

34   Jacques Rupnik, *The Other Europe* (London, Weidenfeld & Nicolson), 1989, p. 218.

35   What cultural reputation Marxism sustained was through the work of Georg Lukács and Leszek Kołakowski, for example.

36   Koch, *Cultural Policy in the German Democratic Republic*, p. 12.

37   See Janina Fijalkowska, 'The Four from Wilanow', *Projekt*, 4 (1976) 113–17.

38   See Tadeusz Nyczek, 'Jan Sawka. A Total Self-portrait', *Projekt*, 4 (1975) 26–31.

39   Theatre companies such as STU which toured in the West grew out of the student movement. Jan Sawka was the visual director in a collaborating forum of artists from different disciplines. Indirectly companies such as STU provided the model for other similar avant-garde arts organizations on the fringes of official culture like Brotherhood in Czechoslovakia and Neue Slovenische Kunst in Yugoslavia.

40   See Tadeusz Galinski, *Culture in People's Poland* (Warsaw, Interpress), 1966.

41   Among its leading members were Pierre Bernard and Gerard Paris-Clavel, both of whom had studied under Tomaszewski at the Warsaw Academy of Fine Art in 1964–65.

42   Charles Rosen, 'The Ruins of Walter Benjamin', in Gary Smith (ed.), *On Walter Benjamin. Critical Essays and Recollections* (Cambridge MA, MIT Press), 1988, p. 150.

43   Susan Buck-Morss, *The Origin of Negative Dialectics. Theodor W. Adorno, Walter Benjamin and the Frankfurt Institute* (Hassocks, Harvester Press), 1979, p. 56.

44   Haraszti, *The Velvet Prison*, pp. 144–5.

45   *Ibid.*, p. 145.

46   Leonie ten Duis, Annelies Haase and Jan Noordhoeck (eds), 'Graphic Design in Eastern Europe. Posters 1981–1991', *Zee Zucht*, 5:5/6 (1992) 45. Franciszek Starowieyski was exceeded in numbers of posters in the publication *The Polish Poster 1970–1977* (Warsaw, KAW), 1979, only by his contemporary Waldemar Świerzy.

47   In 1968, when the intellectuals and the students protested, the workers did not join in. In 1970, when workers protested against price rises, the intellectuals and students looked on. In 1976 the intellectuals quickly organized to provide support networks which led to the foundation of the Workers' Defence Committee (KOR) to co-ordinate both workers and intellectuals.

48   See Kubik, *The Power of Symbols against the Symbols of Power*. I am indebted to Kubik's book for this part of the chapter.

49   *Ibid.*, p. 195.

50   *Ibid.*

51   *Ibid.*, p. 75.

52   Susan Hornik, 'In Poland a Poster is a Fiery Art and a Way to Speak Out', *Smithsonian*, January (1983) 92, quoting the curator of the Poster Museum in Wilanow, Anna Rutkiewicz.

53   See Boris Kagarlitsky, *The Thinking Reed. Intellectuals and the Soviet State from 1917 to the Present* (London and New York, Verso), 1989.

54   Haraszti, *The Velvet Prison*, p. 154.

55   Hornik, 'In Poland', p. 92. Starowieyski's liking for Senator McCarthy is not such an absurd proposition from where he sits as a subject of communist totalitarianism.

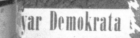

CHAPTER FIVE

THE COLLAPSE OF COMMUNISM 1985–95

In 1985 President Mikhail Gorbachev (1985–91) introduced the policies of *glasnost* and *perestroika*
which indirectly led to the divestment of empire and the internal disintegration of the Soviet Union.
Gorbachev had set out to reform the communist party and to bring the Soviet bloc into line with
global economic and social developments, but the reforms were imposed on an environment and
economy weakened by the grandiose modernization programmes of the past. Bureaucracy and a
self-reproducing, inept, corrupt and opportunistic *nomenklatura* exacerbated the problem.[1]
People were increasingly, if cautiously and fearfully, critical of the party and the state.
Slowly, democratic movements took shape, each feeding off the achievements of the other.
By 1989 there was little the regimes could do in the face of imminent collapse.

As the political poster loosened its ties with state-controlled media it played a minor and significant role in the wider historical process. Ideologically, it reappropriated national histories and subverted party iconographies to emancipatory ends. Materially, it defied the official mainstream media to disseminate the news of demonstrations and democratic successes. Politically, it issued from communities of resistance and, institutionally, it laid claim to spaces for the opposition to organize and to constitute itself into democratic reform movements.

During 1989 posters of democratic revolution reclaimed symbolic public spaces. In acts of defiance, unofficial propaganda plastered the statue of St. Wenseslas in Wenceslas Square in Prague, the Berlin Wall, the unmarked grave of Imre Nagy. By 1991 opposition had reached the ideological centre of the former empire and the statue of Felix Dzerzhinsky outside the Lubyanka in Moscow. Hand-made posters adorned the offices of the unions of artists, the universities and academies, the foyers of theatres, and galleries. These actions embodied the rising confidence of the national independence movements in the struggle against communist tyranny to provide a material index of the 'changes' which saw the end of Soviet supremacy and party authority, democratic reforms, national and nationalist revivals and the unleashing of market forces.

The impact on the institutional structures of the political poster was profound. The independently produced and often unique poster of *glasnost* and *perestroika* emerged in the middle 1980s to grapple with the absurdities of official rhetoric. It helped create a publicly consumed and openly critical discourse which for a brief period contributed to the iconographical, rhetorical and institutional frameworks of the political campaigns of the newly formed opposition parties. The parties, without the benefit of democratic traditions, were internally motivated by imperatives ranging from the liberal and democratic, the religious and

nationalist to the demagogic and the self-interested.

Representations of Václav Havel track the metamorphosis from idealism in opposition to pragmatism in power. Black-and-white photographs of Havel widely circulated in cheaply produced pamphlets during and immediately after the Velvet Revolution show him in the Činoherní klub, or at the base of the Wenceslas monument, as a harassed figure carrying the chain-smoking and world-weary expression of the bohemian dissident.[2] Later, Civic Forum posters depict him in colour, wearing a sweater and swathed in smiles, arms outstretched in a gesture of welcome. But by the time of the elections he wears a jacket and tie and his expression is statesmanlike. Revolutionary fervour has evaporated. The public sphere has been replaced by modern publicity.[3] Momentarily, as people took to the streets, the liberal bourgeois public sphere was re-established. Liberated from the pressures of the state and commerce, it was driven by the will for the free exchange of ideas. Artefacts circulated and value accrued on the basis of 'communicative action' in a primitive, possibly authentic public sphere: a market place, not so much of commodities as ideas.

Relying on well established formulas, the official political poster struggled to keep alive the old certainties. Polls taken by the authorities in the Soviet Union revealed that only 15 per cent of respondents who walked past a political poster paid it any attention, and only 7 per cent were able to recollect its content.[4] As communism collapsed the poster lost its authority. Since the 1970s there had been quantitative compensation, posters being pasted over ever larger areas. But as circulation increased, so the more they were despoiled by graffiti as a measure of the hollowness of the rhetoric which echoed the desire of the *nomenklatura*'s need for a 'Soviet way of life'. What was required was total obedience to a cult of authority, without revolutionary pretensions, and coloured by the self-interest of the privileged and xenophobic.[5]

(detail of 5.28)

In the Soviet Union these attitudes were influenced by Alexander Solzhenitsyn's Russian fundamentalism, which promoted a vision of Russia as the country of a great God-inspired people with a vitally important role to play in the world. Such Christian and historically inspired notions of manifest destiny were exhibited in hierarchical and formulaic compositions, compared by scholars such as Ulf Abel to Byzantine precedent.[6] The decline in communist authority generated nostalgia for pre-revolutionary Russian forms which were vaunted in 1985 at the fortieth anniversary celebrations of the end of World War II.[7] Brave Bolsheviks, heroic fighters, red stars and flags established under Stalin were repeated in updated graphic styles. Emblems and figures were framed by silhouette, or montaged within figurative compositions displaying, for example, the Kremlin, an eternal flame or an obelisk commemorating the Red Army, to create what Mariusz Knorowski has called 'monumental ideograms'.

Leonid Mikhailovich Nepomnyashchy's large-scale *Moscow: victory, 1945–85* (1985) (5.1), repeats the formula, with the added distinction of punctuating the design to spell 'Moscow', the name of the greatest of all the 'hero cities'. Reading from left to right, searchlights and blimps protect the Kremlin walls, in whose shadow the Red Army marches. Under an unfurling red banner, munitions workers, partisans, workers' militias, and the women workers who sustained the city under siege, accompany the standards of the vanquished Nazis. This part of the composition derives directly from photographs of the official Victory Day celebrations in 1945 to bear comparison with heroic paintings such as Mikhail

Khmelko's *The triumph of the conquering people* (1949). Similarly, fireworks explode in imagery familiar from posters by designers such as Mikhail Abramovich Gordon (6.143). A victorious Red Army soldier stands at the centre, arms outstretched in triumph. After Brezhnev's attempts to revive the cult of personality, he is emblematic of the sacrifice and solidarity of the common man.[8]

Such grandiose gestures of military ascendancy were augmented by officially sponsored poster competitions and exhibitions promoting international peace and nuclear disarmament. Nepomnyashchy's poster was used as the cover of the portfolio accompanying the exhibition *Great Victorious Way: Poster Collection from the International Competition in Moscow*, exhibited in Prague and Bratislava in 1985. But, as a whole, the poster designs were less nostalgic than the cover suggested, relying on photographic and montage techniques and other graphic devices to convey a broadly pro-peace and anti-American message (5.18–20).[9] The competition *The Poster in the Struggle for Peace, Security and Co-operation* attracted over 3,500 posters from fifty countries and its political tenor can be measured in Mustafa Misoko's statement: 'Peace is love! We are peace. … Peace fighters are our heroes. Glory to them! … The correctness of the ideas of Lenin … is confirmed by the entire course of history. … I want to take part in the contest as an ordinary person, … simply as a supporter of the peace movement.'[10] Such motives echoed the rhetoric of the anti-nuclear peace movement, augmented by habitual invocations of anti-Americanism:

All those who participated in the contest, both professionals and amateurs, showed they were very much aware of the

5.1
Leonid Mikhailovich
Nepomniashchy, *Victory:
1945–1985 Moscow*, 1985,
Soviet Union, Historical
Archive of the Czech Army,
Prague.

terrible danger which the current U.S. administration poses for the whole of mankind. The posters, while exposing the criminal activities of imperialism, of its aggressive circles, warn of the grave consequences of nuclear insanity, brand the criminals and condemn their crimes, both past and present, and remind us of what political adventurism leads to.[11]

The regimes had always defined themselves as peace movements, at first in the name of anti-fascism and, later, in the name of opposition to Western imperialism and the nuclear arms race (5.2). Despite its original genuinely international aspirations, evidenced in Tadeusz Trepkowski's design for the poster, the Wrocław International Congress in Defence of Culture in September 1948 established a pattern for all events propagandizing peace in the war against Western imperialism (5.3).[12]

The peace poster was one of the most popular themes in communist posters and its iconographies had long since been established. The exhibited posters tend towards simple emblematic designs, making repetitive use of the symbolism of the dove, children and the globe (5.4–12).[13] The globe had been one of the most popular emblems of the cause of the international working class from early socialist history, but since photographed from space it had become a symbol of a fragile ecosystem vulnerable to nuclear and environmental catastrophe. The exhibitions were dominated by the colour blue as demonstrations of peaceful rather than revolutionary intent. Slogans such as 'The peoples are united in their will for peace' and 'US nuclear adventurism – insanity of the century', or 'The Earth is our home! Peace to children throughout the world' were staples of the official rhetoric. They masked the arms race in the name of the 'world revolutionary process' and the 'worldwide victory of communism'. Peace was the aim, but there could be none until 'Western aggression' was contained. The scale and prestige of these events reaffirmed the efficacy of the political poster for the authorities as an instrument of instruction: 'the political poster is struggling for man's sacred right to live and work in peace, for the sake of peace. No greedy desires of those who are whipping up a military psychosis can overshadow mankind's determination to save the world, to prevent a nuclear catastrophe.'[14]

The exhibitions were part of an international propaganda campaign designed to exploit the revived anti-nuclear protest movements in the West and were a reaction to President Reagan's agitated anti-communist rhetoric, characterized in the unforgettable announcement of 8 March 1983, when he accused the Soviets of 'the aggressive impulses of an evil empire'. Soon afterwards he launched his celebrated Star Wars initiative as an umbrella for a hostile anti-communist military and economic strategy. Simultaneously, the Soviet deployment of SS-20 missiles

5.2

5.3

5.4

5.2
Anon., May Day parade. The dove of peace acts as a herald for the banner *'Long live Klement Gottwald'*, First Worker of the Republic, 1951, Czechoslovakia, Museum of the Working Class Movement, Prague.

5.3
Tadeusz Trepkowski, *World Congress of Intellectuals for Peace, Poland, Wrocław, 25–8 August 1948*, 1948, Poland, Museum of Independence, Warsaw.

5.4
Anon., *Peace, friendship, strength*, 1957, Soviet Union, Andrei Sheliuto Collection, Minsk, Belorussia.

stimulated the domestic and foreign crises generated in western Europe by the NATO counter-deployment of cruise missiles. In the German Democratic Republic the crisis generated an explosion of posters dedicated to the anti-nuclear movement. Often original in their interrogations of the iconography of war and peace, they were rigorously graphic in design. The fear was real enough, even if the response was often state-sponsored (5.15–17).

For the Soviets there was a lot to play for in this discourse free of the outdated rhetoric of class struggle. Reaganite accusations of world communist conspiracy were tempered by a growing awareness, encouraged by recollections of the Vietnam War, of less than benign American involvement in the affairs of Iran, Mozambique, Afghanistan, Angola and its 'back yard', El Salvador, Nicaragua, Grenada, Panama and Cuba. American foreign policy was subjected to criticism by Western anti-nuclear movements which generated an oppositional culture capable of producing political posters on a scale hitherto unknown in the West outside established party political boundaries.[15] Criticism spread to mainstream popular culture in films with liberal agendas like Oliver Stone's *Salvador* (1985) and in the affective appeal of the Sandinistas to youth culture.[16]

American polity in the Western democracies was severely dented, and, as if to emphasize the point, the International Organization of Journalists in Prague organized the exhibition *The Militant Poster*. Conceived in 1985 to commemorate both the fortieth anniversary of the IOJ and the Year of International Peace, 1986, it was part of the official response to the UN General Assembly's appeal 'for the international community to mark in a dignified way the fortieth anniversary of victory over fascism in the Second World War'.[17] The organization was controlled in Prague by the central committee of the Czechoslovak Communist Party (KSČ) and with many KGB agents on its staff it was known as 'the long hand of Moscow'. The IOJ's mission was to export communism to developing countries and the exhibition was a self-serving tribute to the political poster 'devoted to the wartime, national liberation and anti-war struggle of nations of the world'.[18] The posters trace an historical narrative from the struggles of pre-war European communism and the triumph over fascism in the Great Patriotic War (there are no posters from the period of the Hitler–Stalin pact (1939–41)) to the Cold War and the fight for world peace. (According to the official rhetoric, America has the bomb for the purposes of imperialism and war, the Soviet Union for progress and peace.) The twenty-fifth anniversary of the Holocaust is commemorated as a tribute to the anti-fascism of the victims of the Nazis rather than anything specifically Jewish. Support is pledged for

Marxist-Leninist national liberation movements in the Third World, which had had a modicum of success in the 1970s. Proletarian emancipation, human rights, the Hungarian uprising, the Prague Spring, Charter 77 and Solidarity are not part of this history of national liberation, anti-fascism and socialist peace and security in the service of the 'peaceful coexistence of two antagonistic social systems'.

Ten years later the exhibition commemorating the fiftieth anniversary of the end of World War II, *Moscow Plakat/Adres Moscow* was without triumphalism. Anti-militarist posters virtually without text focus on a history which had failed to fulfil its Marxist-Leninist promise (5.21). Posters by Andrei Logvin concentrate on the city of Moscow, its Russian legacy and the love–hate relationship Muscovites have with the New Russia. As a whole the exhibition may be regarded as the fulfilment of the policies of *glasnost* and *perestroika* which had been directed at the falsification of history, authoritarianism and the denial of contemporary social problems.

Glasnost, or openness, involves making things available to public scrutiny and has implications for basic human rights and the freedom of speech, information and the press. *Perestroika* proposes a solution to the problems which *glasnost* reveals. It asks for a fundamental restructuring, reforming, reshaping and reorganizing:

> There is no alternative. Socialism must present the world with a model of a dignified human existence that begins with a genuine ennoblement of the individual and ends with a far-sighted concern for the world around us, preserving it for our descendants. The goal is clear and firmly dictated by history. At the same time, advance towards this goal is extremely difficult, and it is easy to foresee obstruction, setbacks and even defeats here. The inertia of bureaucratic methods, cliques and dogmatism is still too great.[19]

The April 1985 plenum of the Communist Party Central Committee rescued Lenin from the legacies of Stalin and stagnation. Gorbachev increasingly identified himself with an original and blameless Lenin. As if to emphasize the point, a collection of poetry and posters, *We follow the Road shown by Great Lenin*, was published in commemoration of the 115th anniversary of Lenin's birth. The hagiographic introduction places him at the centre of the success of communism in the Soviet Union, but it was also a swan song for the official political poster as an ideologically engaged object designed for mass consumption:

> Naturally, while depicting the image of Lenin, masters of poster art use documentary photos, painted, graphic, sculptural portraits, made from life by other artists. This is one of the prerequisites of its authenticity. Documentary photos are interpreted by print graphic (engraving, etching) as well as by usual printing methods, screen printing, for instance. Sometimes, the photos are introduced in a so to speak

untouched, 'pure' form, which imparts a specific naturalness to posters, fills them with the unique atmosphere of the October Revolution and first post-revolutionary years.[20]

The art of poster making acquires authenticity by virtue of its referentiality to painting, sculpture and photography. Realism is assured by virtue of reference to well established discourses capable of guaranteeing historical authenticity. The reference assures legitimacy within a socialist-realist orthodoxy and grants the medium the status of art by proxy: an increasingly important fact for the consumption and reception of the poster.

After 1985 the political poster in the Soviet Union took a more individual and less controlled turn. Igor Maistrovski remarked that having a poster with its 'own face' was a kind of 'victory': 'The battle against bureaucracy, against Soviet bosses, was fun, a kind of gamble – and a great risk.'[21] Even before 1985 the structures and institutions controlling poster production were not monolithic, and this was particularly true in Hungary, which had already begun to develop a more plural system: 'It wasn't allowed for graphic artists to print posters, only if they had a firm order from a customer … the director of a museum, who hated the communists, always gave me a so-called order, a falsification of an order. In that way he [the designer] could print all his posters.'[22] Compliant and sympathetic bureaucrats created conditions where the boundaries of censorship were permeable and, in the case of Péter Pócs, led to paradoxical situations where a design might be rejected by one committee only to be approved by another: 'Ironically some very creative things were being done in that "repressed" society.'[23]

The political was suppressed. But officially sanctioned cultural posters shared the symbolism of the Polish poster with their clawed and unseeing eyes, open, agonized mouths and distorted, fragmentary bodies. Expressive and existential, they oppose the healthy, beautiful body which was the communist ideal. Darkness and shadows prevail, as we can see in the representative piece *Macbeth*, by Sadowski (1986) (5.23). Starowieyski, a resolutely apolitical artist, defies the official ideology. His posters beckon an aristocratic past to conjure up a surrealistic and savagely erotic world worthy of de Sade. But his anxieties are displaced in a strategy of avoidance. Communism, martial law, shortages and queues are simply not part of his universe. Similarly, the film maker Ferenc Daniel observed in the work of the Hungarian designer István Orosz 'a weaving of dreams suffused in myth and central European distress. It bears the print of both our ravaged history and the pitiful materialism of our culture … .'[24] This sensibility is at the heart of a surviving *déclassé* bourgeois residue of the pre-war world to express political ideas in coded form for an educated and culturally sophisticated audience.

In Hungary the DOPP Group represented by Krzysztof Ducki (6.20, 135), István Orosz (5.28, 29), Péter Pócs (5.24, 25) and Sándor Pinczehélyi established a way of working which allowed more personal and immanently political expression. Trips to Poland in the 1970s had made Pócs aware of the expressive potential of an otherwise applied and utilitarian art: 'all so-called cultural posters which appeared before 1987 had somewhere a hidden political background or undertone.'[25] One of the most public manifestations of this new spirit in poster making in Hungary occurred in 1983 when Pócs's design for the film *Lucky Daniel*, premiered on 15 March, appeared on the streets in Budapest (5.22). Against a black ground the Hungarian flag metamorphoses into a tragic mask. Its mouth is the hole which remains after the communist emblem has been cut out. This 'cutting out' was a practice established during the 1956 uprising in Budapest and nothing like it had been seen on the streets since then.[26] The national flag was controversial enough without the wilful removal of its communist heart. The date was also significant, corresponding to the official communist commemoration of the republic of 1919:

> they [the Hungarian National Film Company] were afraid to print this poster in 1983. In spite of that it was printed in a huge number and in a large format. … He went to Budapest on 10 March and he saw his poster everywhere on the streets … at nine o'clock in the morning he went to take part in a meeting of young artists. … That afternoon he went back on the streets and there were no posters there at all. … Was it a dream, or was he crazy?
>
> … Finally, he found out what the problem was. Another very similar poster with a French flag with a face on it was stuck on his poster … when he went home he took all the posters he had left over and put them in a hiding place because the police came after that, trying to collect all the posters.[27]

György Aczél played a part in this act of censorship and, if the poster under discussion and others like it were banned in Hungary, they were exhibited in the West as a measure of the liberal accommodation the Kádár regime sought with the cultural intelligentsia at home and abroad.

Three other posters by Pócs from 1983 advertising one-man exhibitions form a series. One shows chickens behind a wire fence with small insets containing a camera (illegally imported), arrest warrant and negatives of photographs taken for police records (5.24); another shows Pócs against a wall, as a condemned man waiting to be shot, except that his eyes penetrate the blindfold; the last projects the artist as a pariah, a stray dog, as if to affirm his status as persecuted outsider and visionary.[28] Though clearly political, they constitute a personal testament. Unlike the literary example of Solzhenitsyn's *A Day in the Life of Ivan Denisovich* they do not condemn a Stalinist past, but a lived

5.5

5.6

5.7

5.8

5.9

5.10

5.5
Anon., *Peace to the children of the world*, 1951, Czechoslovakia, All Trade Union Archive, Prague.

5.6
A. Krasitskaya, *Peace, work, freedom, equality, brotherhood, happiness*, 1964, Soviet Union, Academy of Fine Art, Berlin.

5.7
Juozas Galkus, *Peace, friendship, happiness!*, 1978, Soviet Lithuania, Moravian Gallery, Brno.

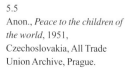

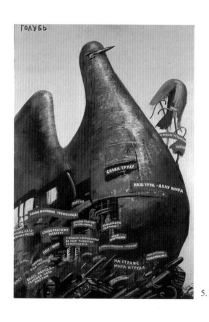

5.11

5.12

5.13

5.14

5.15

5.16

5.8
Anon., *World peace front against fascism and war. International Thanks and Peace Day. September 1950*, 1950, GDR, Thomas Hill.

5.9
Tadeusz Gronowski, *First Polish Peace Congress*, 1950, Poland, private collection.

5.10
Henryk Tomaszewski, *22 July. Constitution Day*, 1960, Poland, National Museum, Poznań.

5.11
Alexander Lozenko, *Dove*, 1989, poster maquette, the artist.

5.12
Nijole Jurgelioniene, *The October for all mankind, for all times!*, 1967, Soviet Lithuania, Juozas Galkus.

5.13
Tadeusz Trepkowski, *No!*, 1952, Poland, private collection.

5.14
Vytautas Kaušinis, *No!*, 1960, Soviet Lithuania, Moravian Gallery, Brno.

5.15
Feliks Büttner, *Peace poster*, 1988, GDR, Moravian Gallery, Brno.

5.16
Ingrid Stitte, *Stop NATO missile plans*, 1981, GDR, Thomas Hill.

5.17
Alexander Schiel, *The way with NATO. Missile launch! STOP!*, 1981, GDR, Thomas Hill.

5.18
Mikhail Avvakumov, *Peace is the common will of all people!*, 1984, Soviet Union, Moravian Gallery, Brno.

5.19
Anatoly Bondarak, *Peace poster*, 1985, Soviet Union, Moravian Gallery, Brno.

communist present and echo writers in exile such as Ivan Klíma and the grotesqueries of Mikhail Bulgakov. The posters are not drawn but are carefully constructed from photographic and photographed elements to demonstrate faith in the objectivity of a scientifically rational process. Consequently they profess to be the product of the ideological legacy of the Enlightenment, but on terms different from those of official communist culture.

Uniquely, these Hungarian poster designs were often not hand-drawn or photographic in the orthodox sense and relied instead on the photography of models and tableaux made in the studio. *Does it not irritate you?* (1987) (5.25), commissioned by the city council in Kecskemét, relies in part on the pun of the title, meaning either 'Does rubbish irritate your eyes?' or 'Does anything irritate your eyes?' It points to a position commonly adopted by the intelligentsia and reflects critically on prevalent political conditions. A screwed-up newspaper article which had attempted to define human rights comments on the limited democratic freedoms in Hungary. But the Fuji film boxes, Marlboro cigarette packets and empty Schweppes cans articulate a critical attitude to westernization and the pressures of commercialization. The reluctance to undertake advertising briefs was almost as strong as the desire to avoid state propaganda. The 'third way', as it was known, was a common ideological position among designers like Pócs who worked in groups and preserved elements of socialist ideology and collective ways of working, usually remote from commercial demands.[29]

As we have already seen in Poland and Hungary, cultural organizations in the Soviet Union were crucial to the

development of a critical discourse. The film agency Reklamfilm in Moscow was decisive in the development of the poster of *glasnost* and *perestroika*. The artists Yuri Boxer (6.45, 79), Alexander Chantsev, Konstantin Geraymovich, Tatyana Nemkova, Georgii Kamenskich (6.161, 8.66) and Igor Maistrovski carried out 'a little revolution' as they subjected official iconographies to deconstructive interrogation. Together with these artists and with the addition of Mikhail Zlatkovski, Andrei Kolosov and his wife Valeria Kovrigina formed the Plackard group. Its first exhibition of poster maquettes and private silk-screen editions opened on 6 July 1988. The posters abandon narrative structures and text is marginal, liberating the image from anchored monological meanings. The aesthetic combines with typography and emblematic imagery to produce a rich semiotic structure in an object which is granted artistic autonomy:

the Soviet poster has long ceased to be the only medium combining artistic information, political agitation, and advertisement, its approach to the depicted event has changed as well. That is why the Soviet political poster of today is 'anti-narrational'; it no longer needs to tell about events in detail … because it is now directed to the sensibilities of the viewer living in the same informational stream as the artist.[30]

The visual and verbal language of the state had already been subjected to the same kind of deconstruction in the field of fine art and the poster of *perestroika* drew on the work of the 'nonconformist' avant garde.[31] The search was on for a socially engaged but 'liberal' practice remote from the avant garde of the Bolshevik period, because it too, like the visual language of socialist realism, was contaminated

5.17

5.18

5.19

by the experience of history. Boris Groys has explained, likening Soviet avant-garde art in Russia to the fate of fascist art in the West:

> When members of today's Russian intelligentsia read those avant-garde manifestos full of Communist rhetoric or detect symbols of Soviet propaganda in avant-garde art … it is hard for them to have a purely esthetic reaction. This symbolism is inevitably associated in their minds with a period of quite real terror and repression, which they themselves partly experienced. … One of the requirements for full appreciation of this art was the viewer's recognition of the real possibility of being shot.[32]

With the collapse of communism, fine artists pursued various kinds of internationalism to achieve recognition in the West. The question of success in this sense for the political poster designer was not on the agenda, particularly because the political poster never severed its commitment to societal transformation. But the conflicts between artistic, moral and political integrity, and the desire to remain professional, were always present. Alexander Faldin and Svetlana Faldina, whose poster *Bravo!* (6.42) features on the front of the book *The Posters of* Glasnost *and* Perestroika, published in the West by Penguin in 1989, was virtually unknown at home: within the communist bloc this work was regarded with caution. *Bravo!* was chosen as the design for the invitation to an exhibition of posters of *glasnost* and *perestroika* organized by Marta Sylvestrová at the Moravian Gallery in Brno in November 1988: 'The title, "Perestroika", was not permitted and I had to use the title "Soviet Poster". I was not allowed to reproduce for the exhibition invitation Faldin's poster *Bravo!* … I was not allowed to exhibit some of the rare posters I had collected.

How dangerous art can be!'[33]

Marta Sylvestrová played an important role in the history of the medium in the region. *The Soviet Poster* as an exhibition of independently produced political posters from the Baltic States and Leningrad sat uncomfortably close to the radical tenor of the times for the authorities.[34] On her own initiative she had travelled to Riga in August 1988 and had taken part in the first mass demonstrations against the Ribbentrop–Molotov pact of August 1939. While there and *en route* she collected posters in Cesis, Talinn and Leningrad:

> [I] did not collect them for posterity, but to organize the exhibition, which would encourage the people to do something against totalitarianism. … I wore a large metal hammer and sickle ear-rings to denigrate those hated symbols. Black dress and red scarf. I invited Jaromír Nohavica, a singer of protest songs, who at that time was forbidden to give public performances, to sing at the opening of my exhibition. … I decided to collect these poster originals (poster-size photographs, hand painted and drawn posters) in the hope I could exhibit them in Czechoslovakia, where fear of the consequences still silenced many citizens. (Artists were already active, but not most of the people who were still afraid of repressions as a result of the events of 1968.) (5.27)[35]

By comparison conditions in the Soviet Union were more liberal. Interestingly enough, Alexander Faldin, who as a communist party member had sent to the 1982 Brno Biennale a poster depicting Solidarity as a politically blind figure, had formed a subgroup within the Leningrad branch of the Artists' Union to organize a series of exhibitions between 1986 and 1988 dealing with the effects of Gorbachev's policies of *glasnost* and *perestroika*. They used

5.20

5.21

5.20
Bogdana Janowska-Novašek, *For peace. Humanism against danger of nuclear war*, 1985, Poland, Moravian Gallery, Brno.

5.21
Sergei Voychenko and Vladimir Tsesler, *Fifty 1945–1995*, Russia, Moravian Gallery, Brno.

5.22
Péter Pócs, *Lucky Daniel
1983–1989*, 1989, Hungary,
Moravian Gallery, Brno.

5.23
Wiktor Sadowski, *Verdi,
Macbeth*, Poland, 1985,
Poland, private collection.

5.24
Péter Pócs, *Péter Pócs posters*,
1984, the artist.

the language of Aesop's fables to express subjects excluded from the mainstream media in exhibitions called Poster Fables. None of the group was a poster designer as such and they avoided working for the official poster agency, Plakat. Coincidentally, their success corresponded with Gorbachev's decision to remove the red banners and political posters published by the party from the cities of the Soviet Union. Subsequently Vladimir Fillipov, together with ten other artists, founded Interplakat in 1988 as an independent organization to encourage artists who were addressing Gorbachev's reforms. The aim was to exhibit posters declared too 'political' and 'individual'. Most of these posters were unique because of the shortage of materials and the unwillingness of the authorities to allow significant print runs, although Interplakat organized limited circulation of some of the designs in postcard form.[36]

According to Faldin, 'They were published in newspapers and magazines and shown on television. But even in that form they attracted a great deal of interest. People wanted to know where they could get hold of them, who was printing them, when they would be printed. I think it is now reasonably safe to answer that with never.'[37] Poster production decouples from state organizations as the state begins to go into free fall. It loosens its ties with the mass media to become its subject, simultaneously finding the freedom to give expression to individual, regional and national sentiments:[38]

> Whereas the social and political value of the poster has always been recognized, it has not been easy to prove that the poster also represents an independent sphere of art reflecting characteristic national features … the essentially international art which

transcends the barriers of different cultures and languages and aims at imparting information, nonetheless contains national features which must be retained and developed.[39]

As Marta Sylvestrová had realized, there were striking correspondences between the poster designer's quest for autonomy from state organizations and the wider struggle for autonomy from the party and Moscow. Since the early 1980s poster designers in Latvia had been addressing themes related to the environment and bureaucracy while celebrating national identity (7.50, 52, 53). Criticism of the system was giving rise to increased demands for national sovereignty and a return to the pre-war *status quo*.[40]

> Original 'artists' posters' created during the period of *glasnost* and *perestroika* in the Soviet Union constitute a very specific phenomenon … in the Poster Fest at Cesis, near Riga, Latvia. Printed posters were installed on panels in the streets of the town. … Most of the posters were either political or ecological in nature and openly criticized the defects of the Communist system. This was the real *glasnost*, and yet one could still be punished for it in my native Czechoslovakia.

> Increasing national pride was evident at the festival in Cesis. Latvian national symbols, forbidden for decades, appeared in the streets as well as on original posters.[41]

The crucial year was 1988. After a visit to Warsaw, a number of students from the Poster Studio at the Kiev Art Institution (now the Academy of Arts) in the Ukraine set up their own union as a counter to what they perceived as the conservative and pompous Union of Artists. They called themselves the SLAP group; the members were Andrei Budnik, Alexander Orlovsky, Igor Prokofiev (6.166) and Viktor Pishii (7.29).[42] They were inspired by the

5.22

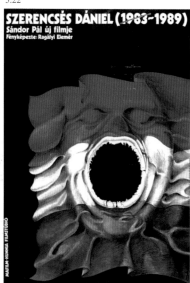

5.23

5.24

Peredvizhniki, the nineteenth-century realists who exhibited throughout Russia had been one of the major historical and programmatic precursors of socialist realism. As unique maquettes or designs for posters they are unrestricted by the technical difficulties or costs of printing. They are painterly and rich in colour. Text is absent and they have a dreamlike quality encouraged by dislocations of scale and elements of the grotesque: 'Their aim was to revive the poster as a polemical art form and rescue it from a period of stagnation and stereotyping … to respond quickly, in a creative and original way to political, ecological and social developments in the Soviet Union as they occur.'[43] They addressed the legacy of Stalin, the *nomenklatura*, the emblems of Soviet and party power, prostitution, AIDS, safe sex, the environment, and the path to democracy and national independence. These were subjects which until very recently had been considered taboo. Prostitution, for example, could not be confronted because it was not admitted that it existed in socialist countries (8.67). Later, as a measure of the group's success as political conditions changed, Alexander Orlovsky's *Use condoms as an individual means of AIDS protection* was used by the Ukrainian Ministry of Health.

Andrei Budnik considered SLAP to be part of the struggle for Ukrainian independence from Moscow. In Kiev the exhibitions were placed in a semi-derelict but functioning theatre, Na Padole, at the behest of the director Vitaly Molochov. *The Nude Socrealism* exhibitions featured 'the worker with working woman naked, they have got nothing on at all'. The first exhibition travelled all over the Ukraine, staying in some places for two or three weeks, or,

as happened in Cherkasy on the Dnieper, was banned by the mayor and the local communist party. At the first exhibition in Kiev in 1989 the mayor 'began to stamp his feet, talk and shout'. Wider acceptance came when the exhibitions were picked up by the media, but even then they attracted controversy and were received with suspicion by the members of the 'Stalin generation'.[44]

Gorbachev's star rose and, as he charmed government leaders and beguiled the Western media, so the cultural manifestations of *glasnost* and *perestroika* found a market in the West and stimulated poster production for external rather than internal consumption. The collection *The Posters of Glasnost and Perestroika* was published by Penguin Books in conjunction with Sovietsky Khudozhnik Publishers, Moscow, in 1989. Exhibitions were promoted in London by Andrei Budnik,[45] by Fillipov in Manchester[46] and by James Fraser in Rutherford NJ.[47] Marta Sylvestrová's exhibition in Brno in 1988 formed the basis of *Art as Activist*, which toured the United States in 1992–94 and provided the core of the poster section in the exhibition *Europe without Walls and Art Posters and Revolution 1989–93* at Manchester City Art Galleries in 1993.[48] Plakat changed its name to Panorama and ceased to promote Marxism-Leninism in favour of ecology, environmentalism, the human rights abuses of the past, the Gulag and the legacy of Soviet history.[49] The shift in emphasis can be found in Mikhail Avvakumov's portfolio *Is Stalin with us?* (1990). Stalinist posters are juxtaposed with posters of *glasnost* and *perestroika* to comment on the legacy of communism, and Lenin's so-called 'last will' warning of fatal weaknesses in Stalin's character. Published

5.25
Péter Pócs, photo Péter Walter, *Does it not irritate you?*, 1987, Hungary, Moravian Gallery, Brno.

5.26
Poster Festival in Cesis, 1981, Soviet Latvia, Laimonis Šēnbergs.

5.25

5.26

in Moscow as a portfolio, the format is a measure of the retreat of state communism, its consumption circumscribed within a private, rather than public, sphere.

The retreat of the authorities can be seen in the Berlin exhibition *State Propaganda in the U-Bahn Station Alexanderplatz. Thinking about Revolution*, held in 1989. As a state-sponsored activity it functioned within established power structures. Billboard exhibitions had been taking place on the site since the 1950s under the auspices of the Union of Artists. During the 1980s they variously campaigned for human rights, against censorship and the bureaucracy. Envisaged as a commemoration of the bicentennial of the French Revolution, *State Propaganda* was conceived in October 1988 by a group of thirty-three artists, including Manfred Butzmann and Joseph W. Huber. Blocked by the authorities until October 1989, it opened only weeks before the fall of the Berlin Wall. With each passing day not even the authorities could miss the implications of the anti-militaristic, anti-Stalinist and anti-capitalist imagery as political pressures gave the French Revolution a new meaning outside official communist history.

By the early 1990s revolutionary optimism had given way to listless acceptance of the changing significance of the medium. Previously, because they were illegal, political parties and counter-cultural expressions had little recourse to anything other than the poster. This was given no more fitting expression than in the exhibition of Hungarian posters including designs by the DOPP group organized by Marta Sylvestrová in Prague during the spring of 1989 at what was then known as the Julius Fučik Park of Culture and Rest (the Prague Trade Fair Centre). In Hungary a slow process of liberalization known as 'goulash communism' had precipitated what had become by the second half of the 1980s a crisis which stimulated reform. In September 1988 no action had been taken to counter the emergence of the Hungarian Democratic Forum (MDF) or the Alliance of Free Democrats in November 1988. The Hungarians were moving towards a form of political pluralism and its actions in opening Hungary's borders precipitated the collapse of the Berlin Wall in November 1989. In other words the Hungarian designers were becoming accustomed to democratic reform, and the DOPP group played an important role in the promotion of a new kind of political culture which was, as yet, virtually unknown in Czechoslovakia. Four posters by Péter Pócs were removed by the StB, the Czech secret police, or stolen by admirers from the exhibition on May Day. Following a meeting between Pócs and Sylvestrová in Berlin during the official fortieth anniversary celebrations of the German Democratic Republic, Pócs agreed to travel with DOPP to Brno in

November. By chance they arrived during the heat of the Velvet Revolution but were considered too radical by the gallery authorities to take part in the open discussion taking place at the Moravian Gallery. Instead they met Brno designers and went with them to a gymnasium to meet striking students where overnight, fuelled by revolutionary fervour and vodka, the students reproduced designs by DOPP. In the morning they plastered them around the city on walls and shop windows. As a measure of the success of their designs, resonant with the political tenor of the times, DOPP exhibited in Prague and Warsaw the following summer.

In Hungary, even during the elections of spring 1990, political parties did not have the money for television campaigns and István Orosz's *Farewell, comrades* (1989) (5.28)[50] was adopted by the MDF with the new caption 'Comrades, it's over'. Many wrote the poster off as too expensive and obsolete in the age of television. If Orosz saw the end of the traditions of double meaning and irony in the poster in central Europe with the departure of the Red Army, it did not stop him executing a reprise on the theme when the communists were voted back into power in Hungary in 1995 (5.30).

According to Michel Foucault, the exercise of surveillance and control in the interests of progress began within the walls of prisons and lunatic asylums before proceeding to medical institutions and the spaces of art galleries and libraries. Culture, understood as the manners, morals and beliefs of the nation, had the responsibility for spiritual health and it became the object of government. Communism in its desire to improve and edify, had at its centre the legacy of the liberal nineteenth-century institutions of the gallery and the museum the party wanted to replace. Galleries and museums provided a space of observation and regulation where the visitor might be moulded in accordance with new norms in the service of the transcendant sovereignty of the party. A. A. Zhdanov had called for the incursion of socialist culture into every walk of life as part of an historical mission and 'the attainment of cultural wealth as a chief task of socialism':

> The young Soviet generation will be called upon to consolidate the strength and power of the socialist Soviet order, to make full use of the motive forces of Soviet society to promote our material and cultural progress. ... Our people must be educated people of high ideals, tastes and moral and cultural demands ... the Party and the people [should] ... educate our young people in the spirit of supreme devotion to the Soviet order and service in the interests of the people.[51]

Under pre-democratic systems of government, art and culture were concerned with exhibiting power before courtly society and indirectly before the populace.[52] The formation of the bourgeois public sphere saw the separation of culture from repressive power; instead, it was used for progressive social and political criticism. Through the academies, art galleries and private salons bourgeois citizens acquired self-consciousness in a process which continued under communism. It simultaneously fulfilled and undermined party aims as it furnished the contemporary exhibitionary culture communist policies demanded while at the same time drawing attention to older national high cultural traditions and identities. The aesthetic was joined to the state and its objectives, but the environment of the museum and the gallery preserved pre-war liberal avant-garde and traditional formations of cultural sophistication and taste antagonistic to the values of the party.

Communism relied on education for social mobility, but quality education was restricted to party members and their children. The museum audience was largely located, therefore, in the lap of an aspirant managerial class identified by Vera Dunham.[53] There was, therefore, a paradox at the core of state communist cultural policy. Pierre Bourdieu and Alain Darbel have pointed out that the physical and intellectual experience of art galleries and museums is dependent on education. They have shown that the frequency of visits declines once full-time education is complete. The proportion of young people visiting galleries in Poland was found to be greater than in any of the Western countries analysed: 'The high rate [must] be ascribed … to a transformation of the social meaning of museums and above all to the direct and particularly intense action of schooling …'[54] The new socialist culture was transmitted primarily through schools and the decline in visits after education has been completed corresponds with the lack of 'ancient culture'. But the family remains the most important source for the acquisition of values, motivation and ambition in communist society[55] and was the source of cultural values at odds with those of the party.[56]

The decline in museum attendance could, therefore, reflect dissatisfaction with an officially orchestrated and unchallenging middlebrow culture. This was especially true of those who opposed communism and those who had their class origins in the pre-war intelligentsia. For the latter, state culture would sit uncomfortably within national and traditional cultures embodied in its museological and exhibiting institutions. As a measure of the depth of the cultural resistance inherent in those 'ancient' institutions, universities, churches, theatres, museums, galleries, art schools and academies provided spiritual and material sustenance for the embryonic democratic movements. Photographs taken in 1989 of theatre foyers and galleries from Berlin to Kiev show posters, caricatures, banners and art objects critical of the state. They bear witness to those in communist society who had not forgotten the language of the poets. The intelligentsia established a public sphere which was characterized by the DOPP group in Brno during the November demonstrations when they worked through the night with the striking students to produce posters attacking the communist regime. However, their moment was brief and they were to be outrun by events and the will of the people.

Under communism, public display fashioned a figure of 'man' within hierarchies prescribed by the party. As Bourdieu has indicated, the capacity of the art gallery to confer social distinction depends on the fact that only those with sufficient and appropriate cultural capital can perceive the controlling exhibitionary order. Under totalitarian communism, and particularly in the client states, this cuts two ways: for the Soviets the exhibitionary order

5.27
Ladislav Lasťůvka, *Jaromír Nohavica at the opening of the 'perestroika' poster exhibition,* Moravian Gallery, Brno, 1988.

5.28
István Orosz, *Farewell,
comrades!*, Budapest, March
1989, Hungarian National
Museum, Budapest.

5.29
István Orosz, *I am back
again!*, 1995, Hungary, artists
edition, private collection.

5.30
Anon., *Plastic People of the
Universe – psychedelic band
of Prague*, c. 1971, Moravian
Gallery, Brno.

5.28

5.29

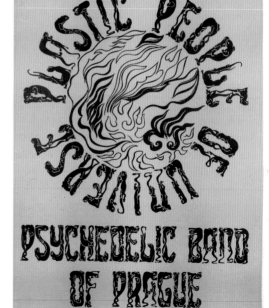

5.30

5.31
Jindřich Štreit, *John Lennon's unofficial memorial, Prague – Kampa*, 1981, the photographer.

5.32
György Soós, *Extreme music '85*, 1985, Hungary, Hungarian National Gallery, Budapest.

represented the natural order after the heroic sacrifices of the Great Patriotic War; for those under effective occupation it revealed the alien character of a foreign and imposed ideology. By association with established national and traditional institutions of culture, poster exhibitions made powerful inroads on behalf of official culture into the domain of popular culture and entertainment.[57] Posters' ideological power, however, was determined by the audience's relationship to the subject matter and their connection with the museum and its legitimating power. In the museum or gallery, power is rendered visible to the people and represented as their own. The public can see, but it can also be seen, and is thereby restrained in its modes of behaviour; but it also recognizes itself. The public sphere was severely inhibited under communism but it found sustenance in fine publishing, certain forms of literature, theatre and film and the cultural poster.

For the communist authorities, 'No better ally could be found than the young woman craving marriage, polka-dotted tea cups, orange lampshades, and the status of the first lady of the district'.[58] But for the independently minded and the remnants of the *déclassé* bourgeoisie the new order was alien, middlebrow and utilitarian, a product of what Kant had called 'barbarous taste'.[59] The museum and gallery became a site of contestation for the displaced intelligentsia who were accustomed to wider European cultural *mores* and whose familial ease with indigenous pre-Soviet forms of expression signified a subterranean moral superiority over the newly established party elites and their Soviet masters. Natural privilege provided psychological resistance.[60]

The appropriation of the applied art of poster making to a subcategory of fine art is a political act. Society was never totally communized. Many areas such as the national museums and art academies were ideologically immune from the inroads of dictatorship. As a result the development of a related counter-sphere modified and undermined official culture. In Honecker's GDR, for example, the systems of repression, surveillance and state control were expanded, while in the field of aesthetics experimentalism and a market were tolerated. A complex system of exchange developed and informal contracts existed, even in opposition, between artists, designers, intellectuals and the party leadership. Each had something to offer the other. By the middle 1980s in East Germany, Poland and Hungary these forms had managed to assume a relatively independent existence.

The counter-society, or liberal space of the alternative public sphere, was largely unseen, but its protagonists evolved structures to ensure their continued existence as designers. They consolidated their positions in existing institutions of exhibitions and commissioning committees. Combined with a growing market place, resources and control were redistributed away from the centre to establish a social space with a diverse set of participants with different interests and aims. Cultural producers were substantially integrated into the official power structures and tightly bound together in small groups. They cut out new discursive spaces which became increasingly public.

In the late 1980s the poster as an institution in Poland was dominated by the market: commercial galleries, private publishers and dealers created new conditions.[61] Decentralization, combined with the rapid westernization of public space, produced a set of parameters governed by international popular culture which reduced the public for 'art' as theatre commissions and the like dried up.[62] Designers had become minor celebrities, opinion makers unleashing visual interpretations of cultural and political life in a 'paper Tower of Babel'.[63] But at the beginning of the 1990s the art poster was criticized for a loss of direction. Fantasy displaced typography, caprice superseded the message, and, as a visual conceit produced for pleasure, poster art became detached from its roots as a medium of criticism and social engagement as the state appropriated formerly taboo bourgeois individualist subjects.[64]

The state had been unable to prevent the accelerating alienation of the young and their identification with Western counter-cultural and commercial forms. One force of conformity was exchanged for another. The appeal of consumer-oriented, hedonistic international youth culture with its delusional anti-establishment credentials was strong. By way of contrast with the fundamental political upheavals experienced in Poland, people in Czechoslovakia, the GDR and Hungary saw new developments in poster design associated with popular music. The music was iconoclastic, and, like the posters advertising the concerts and records, it represented a challenge to established authority, though it had no particular political agenda. Originating at the end of the 1970s, punk and new wave music attracted a semi-illicit following as a focus of youthful resistance to the regimes. The movement had been preceded in Poland by New Culture and in Czechoslovakia by the Plastic People of the Universe, the arrest of some of whose members in 1976 had stimulated the establishment of the human rights group Charter 77.[65]

Until the advent of new wave and punk the focus on Western popular culture was linked with the attempt to carve out an alternative cultural space allied to the artistic avant garde, where the approach was intellectual rather than nihilistic. The appeal was to a younger section of the intelligentsia, rather than to the disaffected young at large.

Their attitudes reflected opposition to everything communist, of necessity their revolution was of the spirit, not the body politic: as far as it is possible to tell from the posters the Plastic People refused engagement with the dominant rhetoric altogether (5.30). Long hair, for example, was prohibited in school and on the television and acquired a significance as a symbolic protest against normalization. Unlike the ironic identification with the icons of a failed communist revolution which characterized the youth culture of the 1980s, psychedelia and the transformation of consciousness offered a hedonistic and spiritual challenge to the authorities. The counter-culture was subject to various degrees of disapproval and suppression, resulting in arrest, imprisonment, unemployment, lost educational opportunities, intimidation in the mass media and police surveillance.[66]

By the early 1980s independent cultural activities were beginning to get out of control for the authorities and many previously approved plays, rock and jazz groups were banned. One result was the formation of the Jazz Section of the Musicians' Union, an independent semi-official group and focus of nonconformist culture from 1971. Václav Havel was among the membership. In an interview in 1983 with the French journalist Antoine Spire, Havel summed up the attitude of his generation:

> If I serve anything, then it is only my own conscience. I am neither a Communist nor an anti-Communist, and if I criticise my government, then it is not because it happens to be a Communist government but because it is bad. I am not on the side of any establishment, nor am I a professional campaigner against my establishment. I merely take the side of truth against lies, the side of sense against nonsense, the side of justice against injustice.[67]

John Lennon was widely adopted as a martyr to the cause of just such an apoliticized freedom after his murder in 1980. An unofficial memorial to his memory in Prague became the focus of many confrontations between the young and the police, who eventually fenced it off (5.31). The publication of Jan Krýzl's infamous article '"New" Wave with the Old Subject' immediately preceded the banning of music groups such as Prague Selection in 1983. Josef Vlček, a member of Jazz Section, wryly observed how the authorities who had previously described John Lennon as 'only a cynical eccentric millionaire' now saw him as 'almost a victim of the CIA' in their desperation to halt the slide of young people away from communist values and into the kind of apolitical nihilism represented by punk.[68] The authorities in the shape of Krýzl claimed that popular music derivative of Western commercial forms acted as a drug, leading the young 'away from the class struggle, from everyday problems' and to 'passivity, to the

escape from reality into the imagination and the empire of dreams'. Its true purpose was to secure profit for Western business, but in the past, unlike today, it had campaigned against social injustice:

> mainly against mass oppression and the war in Vietnam. … In the middle 1960s the world applauded the Beatles and Rolling Stones for their songs against the war in Vietnam and barbarousness [sic], the lead in this was taken by the U.S.A., in songs which supported the fight of black Americans in the ghettoes and slums of New York, Miami and other cities of the U.S.A. … the great October march to the White House was begun by a rock concert. At that time one fighting song appeared after another. … Such militant rock, music and texts, inspired thousands of boys and girls to the struggle – even if undisciplined, unrestrained – against the politics of the capitalist states, to the discomfort of the ruling class.[69]

Retrospectively the authorities tried to gain the acquiescence of disaffected youth by garnering aspects of popular culture to their cause. Unfortunately for them, as Vlček was quick to point out, most knew the Beatles and the Rolling Stones wrote no such songs, and many knew that the moratorium in Washington had little to do with 'Great October'. According to the authorities, punk and new wave were orchestrated through the mechanisms of the broadcasts and illicit tapes of the Western 'diversionist centrals' to breed not so much passivity as negativity. 'No future' as a rallying call for the young presented the communists with a direct threat because without a future there could be no communism. Krýzl saw it as a Western conspiracy aimed:

> first to affect our youth directly through this trashy music and second through slogans about 'new' wave world music to provoke through the rise of groups which would produce this music opposed to all moral and aesthetic norms … through deafening racket, monotonous melodies and primitive, often vulgar texts to give to our youth a proven and certified music narcotic, which would also inculcate in our young people the life philosophy 'No Future' and such postures, activities and opinions which are foreign to socialism. Through this music our youth shall be led into indifference, passivity and opposition to society.[70]

Such activities were driven underground but were defended by turning the dominant rhetoric against itself. In his reply Vlček wrote, 'in contradiction to your theory about smuggled tapes which … damage the true direction of Czech rock, we have to say that Czech punk appeared in isolation from world activities, … Czech punk appeared in isolation, … they used original Czech texts. Their contribution is in their sense of parody, irony, satire, black humour, travesty.'[71] The defence was based on an argument for a national culture, founded in indigenous forms in accordance with communist cultural policy.

In Hungary technical resources were limited and posters associated with youth culture and popular music were small and crude in execution by comparison with officially sponsored products and privately produced art posters, like those of the DOPP group discussed above. Their iconographies drew variously on the taboos of violating official emblems, the mockery of communist youth, heroic labour and images of a sexual and fascist nature (5.32, 33). These posters defined the psychological location of a marketplace where ideas could be exchanged. As the products of an entrepreneurial culture they were reliant on market success among a financially constrained section of the community which occupied alternative cultural and geographical spaces. In Budapest official institutions such as the National Office of Events, the Petöfi Hall and the Laser Theatre adopted these styles and iconographies and even made use of many of the same artists. But what was really significant about the phenomenon was not so much the ways in which the State Advertising Company appropriated these potentially destabilizing iconographies, as the way the entrepreneurs of this youthful and affective apolitical culture moved into new spaces, colonizing, as László Beke has pointed out, 'the entrance halls of universities, the staircases of student hostels, the underground passageways, the construction sites and the elevators of office buildings. They are not afraid to stick their posters on top of official ones. The authorities cannot fight them.'[72] Sometimes the young people effaced official posters.[73] As Beke asserts, such strategies were adopted for the election campaign of 1990 in Hungary, but they also signalled the recapture of the spaces of the city for its citizens in the lead-up to the collapse of 1989, when the communist authorities were forced out of power in Hungary, the German Democratic Republic, Poland, Czechoslovakia and Romania. In Hungary, as the new political parties jostled for position in the run-up to the elections, so the vocabularies of the underground and those associated with the youth styles surrounding new wave music were taken up, particularly by the League of Young Democrats (FIDESZ): 'Graffiti, mocking verse, horrible little rhymes, puns, careless montages, typesetting that defied the rules of typography and caricature came back to life …'[74]

In Slovenia, then a republic of Yugoslavia, Neue Slovenische Kunst (NSK), a multi-media art group working in the tradition of the Plastic People of the Universe and the Jazz Section from Czechoslovakia, had taken up a less directly political or, indeed, oppositional stance (5.33). Their position was deconstructive, based on an understanding of communications as a weapon of the powerful rather than the oppressed. They subjected to critique the iconographies of totalitarianism *and* consumer capitalism: 'The level of mastery of the information system depends on the determination and possibilities of those in power to master the entire social structure. Thus, any given social system approaches information from the angle of exercising power.'[75] Intellectuals such as Stanisław Barańczak had long since identified a contradiction in the hopes of scientific rationalism if mass culture reflected the interests of the ruling class but did not have the trust of the populace.[76] In Czechoslovakia another multi-media experimental arts group, Brotherhood, exploited similar ground. Their iconographies are ambiguous and it is unclear, perhaps deliberately so, whether their proclamations and actions are ironic or celebratory, divided as they are between ultra-nationalism and a deep engagement with the rapidly changing mass media. Ivan Novak of Laibach, the pop music wing of NSK, remarked:

> Pop culture is the social realism of the West. It is the social theatre. Why we deal with social realism and Nazi *kunst* so much is because the relationship between art and ideology was so clear. The basic problem is that Westerners believed that they were – in contrast to those in the East – free, and that they alone were doing pure art and pure music whereas Easterners had to make ideological art. It's not true. It's basically the same model, except it's more sophisticated in the West.[77]

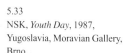

5.33
NSK, *Youth Day*, 1987, Yugoslavia, Moravian Gallery, Brno.

Slovenia declared independence in 1991 and managed to avoid direct involvement in the civil war in Yugoslavia. This is a fact which comments on the unique conditions prevalent in Slovenia, where life was relatively prosperous and political oppression was not a part of daily experience: 'Dissidence is about shouting against a regime and we never dealt directly with any political regime. We never dealt with any concrete political programmes. We were always defining the relationship between art and ideology, or, if you like, between individual and collective. ... We had no need to act as dissidents.'[78]

During the Brno Biennale in 1992 the design group Trio Sarajevo exhibited at the Gallery Ambrosiana. Two members of the group, Dalida and Bojan Hadžihalilovič, had brought the work out of the city with great difficulty while still suffering the ill effects of the siege. As graphic designers they saw themselves working within the tradition of the political poster in the region: the work was a direct and immediate reaction to the folly of the war in Bosnia-Herzegovina, the siege of Sarajevo, the shelling and the snipers. Produced in the form of unique poster maquettes and postcards, the work was restricted in scale and the size of print runs by the severe shortage and expense of materials. But, more significantly, their iconographies were drawn from Western popular culture. The imagery of Coca-cola, Uncle Sam, Marilyn Monroe, Hollywood, punk and the Beatles was subjected to reinterpretation in a manner which implicated the Western media as it transformed the war into spectacle and implicitly condemned the impotence of the European liberal democracies and the indecision of the international community as Sarajevo suffered at the hands of Bosnian Serb nationalism (6.105). The terms of engagement for the political poster had shifted from state communism to international capitalism. Politically controlled public space was replaced by the territory of the private commercial gallery as the site of the self-recognition of a newly emancipated liberal intelligentsia.

NOTES

1   See Milovan Djilas, *The New Class. An Analysis of the Communist System* (London, Thames & Hudson), 1957, and Michael Voslensky, *Nomenklatura. Anatomy of the Soviet Ruling Class* (London, Bodley Head), 1984.
2   *Československo '89* (Prague, Panorama), 1990.
3   'Intelligent criticism of publicly discussed affairs gives way before a mood of conformity with publicly presented persons or personifications; consent coincides with the good will evoked by publicity. Publicity once meant the exposure of political domination before the public use of reason; publicity now adds up the reactions of an uncommitted friendly disposition. In the measure that is shaped by public relations, the public sphere of civil society again takes on feudal features. ... Publicity imitates the kind of aura proper to the personal prestige and supernatural authority once bestowed by the kind of publicity involved in representation.' Jürgen Habermas, *The Structural Transformation of the Public Sphere. An Inquiry into a Category of Bourgeois Society* (Cambridge, Polity Press), 1992, p. 195.
4   Stephen White, 'Posters Mark a Soviet Turning Point', in Sue Causey (ed.), *Tradition and Revolution in Russian Art* (Manchester, Cornerhouse Publications), 1990, p. 157.
5   This was tempered in official rhetoric by overt antisemitism.
6   'Icons and Soviet Art', in Claes Arvidsson and Lars Erik Blomqvist (eds), *Symbols of Power. The Esthetics of Political Legitimation in the Soviet Union and Eastern Europe* (Stockholm, Almqvist & Wiskell International), 1987.
7   Initiated in the 1960s, it found its largest expression in multi-volume works dealing with the painting and architecture of early Russia, or 'Rus', and its most profound expression in Andrei Tarkovsky's film *Andrei Rublev*, dealing with the life and work of the fourteenth-century monk and icon painter.
8   Ubel makes the point that the historically important *The Church Militant*, commissioned by Ivan the Terrible after his victory over Kazan in 1552, is directly comparable, both compositionally and ideologically, as an assertion of Russia as the defender of the true faith. The figure of the saint familiar from Christian iconography is replaced by a Soviet hero.
9   The national origins of the posters are revealing: eight are from the Soviet Union; three are from the GDR; one each from Poland, Hungary, Cuba, Vietnam, North Korea, Czechoslovakia, Mongolia, Bulgaria and France; and three are from Japan. Their geopolitical disposition makes a vivid picture of the communist world and provides an index of its internal and external relationships. The Western economies of France and Japan had for different reasons maintained their distance from the NATO alliance and the United States. France, suspicious of American influence in Europe, always preferred its own independent nuclear capability. Japan, which had been the subject of US atomic attacks, had been prevented from developing its armed forces since the end of World War II.
10   Mustafa Misoko was the delegate from Mali. Quoted in *The Poster in the Struggle for Peace, Security and Co-operation* (Moscow, Plakat), 1985, p. 7.
11   *Ibid.*, p. 9.
12   The Soviets projected themselves as the liberators of Europe from fascism. The British historian A. J. P. Taylor, however, gave a speech describing them as opportunists who had entered the war only when directly attacked, and that men of culture should be suspicious of politics and the great powers. The Poles treated him as a hero. Alexander Fadeyev had led the attack on Western writers like T. S. Eliot and Jean Paul Sartre. Following the revelations concerning Stalin, Fadeyev committed suicide. Others present included Fernand Léger, Andre Malraux, Julien Benda, Paul Eluard, Renato Guttuso, J. B. S. Haldane, Georg Lukács, Ernst Fischer, Hans Eisler, Sholokhov, Pudovkin, Ilya Ehrenberg, Julian Huxley and Lubetkin.
13   Pablo Picasso's *Dove of peace* became Wrocław's emblem and provided the model for one of the most popular icons in the design of peace posters.
14   'The poster *The peace programme in action*, by the Soviet artist [Oleg Maslyakov] tells how the consolidation of peace became a nation-wide and state concern, and how this Programme is being strictly implemented ... this poster of vast ideological content ... depicts the entire history of the Soviet Union's desire for peace – from the Decree of Peace passed after the revolution to the Leninist course for peace construction. Peace concerns each and every one of us! The artist, together with all people of good will, demands peace and security for planet Earth. Today the political poster is struggling for man's sacred right to live and work in peace, for the sake of peace. No greedy desires of those who are whipping up a military psychosis can overshadow mankind's determination

to save the world, to prevent a nuclear catastrophe.' *The Poster in the Struggle for Peace, Security and Co-operation*, pp. 7–9.

15 See Liz McQuiston, *Graphic Agitation. Social and Political Graphics since the Sixties* (London, Phaidon Press), 1993, pp. 100–5 and probably emulated only by the anti-Vietnam War protest movement of the late 1960s; see Gary Yanker, *Prop Art* (New York, Darien House), 1972, pp. 171–85, and David Kunzle, 'Killingly Funny. US Posters of the Vietnam Era', in Jeff Walsh and James Aulich (eds), *Vietnam Images. War and Representation* (London, Macmillan), 1989, pp. 112–22.

16 The Clash issued a triple LP *Sandinista!* in 1980 as an indication of the attraction of Marxist-Leninist revolutionaries for essentially apolitical but style-conscious and rebellious Western youth cultures.

17 Jiří Kubka, Secretary General of the International Organization of Journalists, 'Introduction', in Dagmar Finková and Sylva Petrová, *The Militant Poster 1936–1985* (Prague, International Organization of Journalists), 1986. The IOJ owned travel agencies, a lottery, a translators' and interpreters' service, and had access to otherwise inaccessible computer technology and an extensive business network. The financial profit funded communist-backed organizations in Angola, Vietnam, Afghanistan and other countries.

18 Finková and Petrová, *The Militant Poster*, p. 7.

19 Alexander Yegorov, 'Perestroika', in *The Posters of Glasnost and Perestroika* (Harmondsworth, Penguin), 1989, unpag.

20 V. Vladich and I. M. Blyumina, *We Follow the Road shown by Great Lenin. Lenin in the Arts of Soviet Ukraine. Political Posters, Poetry* (Kiev, Goligrafkhiga), 1985, p. 13.

21 'Graphic Design in Eastern Europe 1981–1991', *Zee Zucht*, 5/6 March (1992) 11.

22 Péter Pócs speaking through István Orosz to Marta Sylvestrová in Kecskemét on 23 April 1995.

23 István Orosz quoted in György Haiman and Carol Stevens, 'Smiting the Eye', *Print*, 48:1 (1994) 14.

24 Ferenc Daniel, Films, *Orosz István. OYTIZ* (Budapest, Balssi Kiadó), 1994, p. 65.

25 Interview with Péter Pócs in Kecskemét, Hungary on 23 April 1995, conducted by Marta Sylvestrová. The quotation is from the transliteration of the translator's interpretation of Pócs's words.

26 Widely emulated throughout the region in 1989.

27 Péter Pócs in Kecskemét, Hungary, on 23 April 1995.

28 'This poster has a lot of messages … it started with the camera he bought with money he had received from work he had done abroad. … He paid no import duty on the camera. Some of his "friends" went to the police and told them that they knew somebody who had a camera, so the police came … to his home, took the camera. … The police knew what he had on his bookshelves, … the books that were forbidden to read and to have, here you can see the warrant, he was on trial because of the books, there is the copy of the final decision of the courts, he was given a six-month suspended sentence. He made some pictures, like the police use for criminals and murderers … you can see three teeth, three words in Hungarian, "accepted", "helped" and the third one, "in between", three types of somebody: we accept what that guy is doing, we don't accept it, OK we don't accept it, but we let him work somehow; the third one is art with an "s" in front, which means shit. The chickens behind the wire, in jail, looking out somewhere.' Péter Pócs in Kecskemét, Hungary, on 23 April 1995.

29 This was certainly the case with GRAPPA in Berlin: Kerstin Baarmann, Dieter Fehsecke, Detlef Fielder, Thomas Franke, Ralf Kurzel and Andreas Trogisch, subsequently joined by Heike Grebin and Daniela Haufe.

30 Anna Suvorova, 'An Observation on Soviet Posters in the Era of Glasnost', *Perestroika/Glasnost/Demokratika. A Catalog of an Exhibition of Printed Posters and Poster Maquettes from 1986 to 1989* (Rutherford NJ, Fairleigh Dickinson University), 1989, p. 3.

31 See SOTS art and the work of Erik Bulatov and Komar and Melamid.

32 Boris Groys, 'On the Ethics of the Avant Garde', *Art in America*, May (1993) 111–13.

33 Marta Sylvestrová, 'The Art of the Street', in *Art as Activist. Revolutionary Posters from Central and Eastern Europe* (London, Thames & Hudson), 1992, pp. 14–15.

34 The exhibition was wrongly dated in James Aulich, 'Through the Looking Glass'. These posters formed the basis of the exhibition *Art as Activist*, which with the help of Dana Bartelt subsequently toured widely in the United States under the auspices of the Smithsonian Institution Travelling Exhibition Service (SITES) from January 1992.

35 Letter to James Aulich from Marta Sylvestrová, 15 October 1996.

36 Interplakat's first competitive exhibition was put on at the Leningrad Museum of Ethnography, where it was an immense success with the public. Seventy thousand roubles were raised in support of the Leningrad rehabilitation centre for disabled Afghan war veterans. The proceeds of the second exhibition, which travelled to Moscow, Sverdlovsk and Izhevsk in the Urals, also went to help those whose existence had barely been recognized by the state: orphans and disabled children of drug addicts and AIDS victims, and the mothers of soldiers missing in Afghanistan. In 1990 an exhibition held in France entitled *The Ten Commandments* drew attention to contemporary national and ethnic conflict in the Soviet Union. See Vladimir Fillipov in Freddy Ghozland and Beatrice Laurans, *Moscou s'affiche* (Toulouse, Ghozland), 1991, p. 8. Fillipov defined Interplakat's philosophy: 'Interplakat members emphasize the importance of the individual point of view, the need for the designer to appeal to human beings in the name of other human beings. The artists receive no payment for their work for the exhibitions. So far, none of the designs has been officially endorsed for publication, although all those chosen for the first exhibition were donated free to the Leningrad branch of the Soviet Culture Fund: some have received limited circulation in postcard form.' Vladimir Fillipov, 'Glasnost and the Graphic Conscience', in Sue Causey (ed.), *Tradition and Revolution in Russian Art* (Manchester, Cornerhouse Publications), 1991, p. 156.

37 *Zee Zucht*, 5:5/6 March (1992) 15.

38 Officially sanctioned posters appeared in *Reklama*. Mass circulation periodicals such as *Ogonyok*, *Sputnik* and *Kino* have all published unofficial as well as official posters. In Poland in the early 1990s, for example, a major outlet for satirical posters could be found in magazines such as *Nie*.

39 Juri Hain, *Estonian Contemporary Poster* (Tallinn, Eestii Raamat), 1987, p. 13.

40 Cutting edge of poster design found in some of the publishing houses of the republics – Mintis in Vilnius; Avots in Riga; Eestii Raamat in Tallinn.

41 Sylvestrová, 'The Art of the Street', pp. 14–15.

42 In Ukrainian the name was the Youth Poster, or LYAPAS, meaning SLAP. Andrei Budnik subsequently became an important collector of posters.

43 Xeroxed catalogue produced for exhibition seen in London, Wells, Cardiff and Manhattan in 1991. Published by SLAP, unpag.

44 'Several exhibitions were banned, nerves shook – a very serious situation developed during the 1991 *putsch*, when Gorbachev was deposed. At that moment our posters were supposed to go abroad. We went to the theatre to see Vitaly Molochov. He put on the radio and a reporter's voice said: "Close all airports of the Soviet Union, stop foreigners from entering, declare a state of emergency … ." The director said: "I will be imprisoned, you as well… ." So we were afraid, we sat around all day feeling terrible, we were nailed to the radio for three days, listening to what was happening in Moscow – strikes, a small war

... .' Unpublished interview with Andrei Budnik by Marta Sylvestrová, June 1995. The threat to return to the old order was held off in the Ukraine by Kravchuk.

45 Molochov was a well known director with contacts in the West. It was these contacts that led to a SLAP group exhibition reaching Britain in 1989 at the height of the Western fascination with Gorbachev and what was, by that time, a fast receding Soviet empire.

46 *Posters of Perestroika* formed part of *Tradition and Revolution in Russian Art* organized by Susan Causey as part of the Leningrad in Manchester Olympic Festival in 1990. See Sue Causey, *Tradition and Revolution in Russian Art*.

47 See James Fraser, *Perestroika/Glasnost/Demokratika*, 1989, an exhibition which coincided with the collapse of communism in central and eastern Europe.

48 Under the auspices of SITES *Art as Activist. Revolutionary Posters from Central and Eastern Europe* was published by Universe Books, New York, 1992. The exhibition was completed with other revolutionary posters collected by Marta Sylvestrová from Hungary, Germany, Poland, Czechoslovakia, Ukraine, Lithuania, Russia and Romania.

49 In 1990 Panorama received half the income it had in previous years, while Agitplakat, a publishing house attached to the Artists' Union in Moscow, produces only about sixteen posters per month; more daring than those of Panorama they are limited in the size of their screen-print editions to 2,000. Shortage of paper has guaranteed most designs are never published. They remain as poster maquettes, primarily for exhibition rather than reproduction.

50 He regarded the poster as a measure of political events. When he saw it on the streets he felt there could be no turning back. Signed with his pseudonym, Oytiz, meaning 'nobody' in Greek, it was produced in reaction to the collapse of Soviet authority: 'I felt as Ulysses must have felt when he was fighting the giant. I, too, was fighting a dangerous giant – the Russian army – and I hoped I knew that, like the giant in the story, he had to lose. I hoped he hadn't been absent from school the day Homer was taught.' István Orosz quoted in Haiman and Stevens, 'Smiting the Eye'.

51 'Mistakes of Two Leningrad Journals. Report on the Journals *Zvezda* and *Leningrad*', 1947; A. A. Zhdanov, *On Literature, Music and Philosophy* (London, Lawrence & Wishart), 1950, p. 50.

52 See Norbert Elias, *The Court Society* (Oxford, Blackwell), 1983.

53 See Vera Dunham, *In Stalin's Time. Middle-class Values in Soviet Fiction* (Cambridge, Cambridge University Press), 1976.

54 *The Love of Art. European Art Museums and their Public* (London, Polity Press), 1991, p. 35.

55 See 'Youth and Youth Policy in GDR Society', in Mary Gerber (ed.), *Studies in GDR Culture and Society III* (Lanham MD, University of America Press), 1983.

56 See David K. Shipler, *Russia. Broken Idols, Solemn Dreams* (Harmondsworth, Penguin Books), 1989.

57 Until the final collapse when posters took to the streets again on a large scale the major outlets for the poster during the 1980s were the large international poster exhibitions. The twelfth Brno Biennale in 1986 revealed little of what was to come, and the 1988 Warsaw Biennale was as staid. It found 'safe', more hospitable territory as it plied a course within the commercial framework of graphic design, leaving the political largely to one side. There were a few notable exceptions, such as Sadowski's *Macbeth* (1987) (5.23), mentioned above; Krzysztof Ducki, Vladimir Tsesler and Andrei Sheliuto's profile of Stalin as a spade (6.20); Piotr Młodożeniec's *Oblicza Socrealizmu* (1987), displaying a portrait of Stalin sliced in half horizontally and then printed looking both ways; and Slawomir Witkowski's *Liberators* (1987) which comments on the ostentation and materialism of Western values in strident graphic style; but they were very much in the minority.

Similarly, in Brno in 1988 there was little to be seen within the containment of the mainstream organization of the biennale, which, in any case, focused on book and editorial design and typography. The Poster Biennale alternates with the Book and Editorial Design Biennale in Brno.

58 Dunham, *In Stalin's Time*, p. 104. See also Stephen Kotkin, *Magnetic Mountain. Stalinism as a Civilization* (Berkeley and Los Angeles CA, University of California Press), 1995.

59 See Bourdieu and Darbel, *The Love of Art*, p. 40.

60 *Ibid.*, p. 110.

61 W. Serwatowski (Warsaw), K. Dydo (Cracow), F. Zieliński (Poznań), J. Gunia (Warsaw), A. Mieczynska and B. Cybulski (Theatre in Opole and Nowy Theatre in Warsaw).

62 Henning Wagenbreth, Feliks Büttner and István Orosz all regaled the authors at various times with tales of falling commissions from theatres as they adapted to market conditions following the collapse.

63 Susan Hornik, 'In Poland a Poster is a Fiery Art and a Way to Speak Out', *Smithsonian*, January (1993) 88.

64 Miklós Haraszti, *The Velvet Prison. Artists under State Socialism* (Harmondsworth, Penguin), 1987, p. 112.

65 Throughout the 1970s the Plastic People of the Universe refused to kow-tow to the pressures of 'normalization'. Their lyrics became more politicized – the song '100 points' listed 100 things of which the communists were afraid such as freedom, democracy and truth and asked the question, 'So why are we afraid?'. As a result they lost their professional status and were forced underground where they and their audiences suffered imprisonment, interrogation, intimidation and the loss of civil rights.

66 Marta Sylvestrová, letter, 19 February 1999. Hungary, GDR and Poland were more 'liberal' than Czech Republic and the Soviet Union.

67 Václav Havel quoted in Michael Simmons, *The Reluctant President. A Political Life of Václav Havel* (London, Methuen), 1991, p. 151.

68 Josef Vlček, 'Rock on the Left Wing', translated by Marta Sylvestrová, in *Documents of the Jazz Section No. 1*, published by Jazz Section with the Music Board of Unesco and the International Society for Research in Popular Music, *Jazz Bulletin*, 8445/69 July (1983) 11.

69 Jan Krýzl, '"New" Wave with Old Subject', reprinted from *Tribuna* 12 (1985) 5, translated by Marta Sylvestrová, in *ibid.*, pp.19–23.

70 *Ibid.*

71 Vlček, 'Rock on the Left Wing', p. 11.

72 'Politics – Arts – Posters. Hungary 1988–1990', in Katalin Bakos, *The Signs of Change. Posters 1988–1990* (Budapest, Magyar Nemzeti Galéria), 1990, p. 12.

73 *Ibid.*

74 *Ibid.*, p. 10.

75 New Collectivism (ed.), *Neue Slovenische Kunst* (Los Angeles, CA, Amok Books), 1991, p. 44.

76 Stanisław Barańczak quoted in Anne White, *De-Stalinization and the House of Culture. Declining State Control over Leisure in the USSR, Poland and Hungary 1953–1989* (London, Routledge), 1990, p. 45.

77 Louise Gray, 'Faith in the State and the Power of Rock', *Wire*, 115 (1997) 29.

78 'Yugoslavia was a liberal communism and Slovenia a rich state, perhaps the only state where communism worked. But we did define the paradox of the relationship between art and politics and there were lots of conflicts.' *Ibid.*, 30.

CHAPTER SIX

GREAT LEADERS, POLITICAL SYMBOLS AND COMMUNIST CEREMONIES

Historically, divinely sanctioned autocracy, absolutism and centralization have been part of the political culture of eastern Europe. The personality cult grew out of this tradition. Beginning with Lenin and reaching its apotheosis with Stalin, the cult had its origins in the symbolic power structures of tsardom and it defined the relations between the leader, the state and the ruled.[1] In the 1960s and 1970s the authority of the cult declined and was replaced by an emphasis on public ceremonial and communist ritual, bolstered by emblems and symbols and based on the memorialization and calendrical cycles of revolutionary and communist history (6.1). The purpose of communist ritual and ceremony was to emphasize hierarchies of power and to recognize officially individual achievement in the arts, sciences, industry, agriculture and the military.

THE GREAT LEADERS

In public ceremonial portraits of the leader had pride of place. Mounted high on podiums, carried by participants, or held aloft as banners, they gave the processions a religious air. For major national communist festivals, gargantuan portraits were the focus of parades and indoor ceremonials. Garlanded with flowers, the portraits were paraded through the streets as if they were the pictures of annointed saints (6.2). But these secular saints were temporal and subject to the vicissitudes of political intrigue and ambition: with shifts in the leadership, familiar faces disappeared from public display to be replaced with the new.

Processional routes proceeded from outlying working-class districts, factories, unions and clubs to the symbolic centres of the cities, towns and villages. The intention was to make the distribution of posters relate to the political control of the spaces they inhabited, marking out the lines of the face of communism in the streets through the figures of the leaders and their political and ideological ancestors. The processions and the ceremonies were a spectacular dramatization of communism which effectively pictured itself to itself in the effort to build a facade of legitimacy: but the shows were little more than a hall of mirrors.

The ideology of the great leader had found fertile ground in the legacies of romantic nationalism. The philosopher of history and German nationalist Oswald Spengler defined the worship of the heroic as a catalyst of national identity; simultaneously, Marxist-Leninists drew on Hegel and the memory of the great men of history. Stalinists, inspired by pan-Slavist thought, shared with the nationalisms of the area the irrationalist myth of spiritual greatness ultimately derived from Herder's definition of the *Volksgeist* (folk spirit). These often contradictory ideologies encouraged, through folklorist and neo-pagan tendencies of

symbolic identification, the heroicization of the leader as a symbol of the nation. During the inter-war period, with the exception of Czechoslovakia, the countries in the region had thrown up just such militarist heroic national leaders. After the war, in the wake of the defeat of fascism, the Stalinist cult of personality was reproduced throughout the region (6.3, 4). Effectively, the new regimes aped forms of government from the inter-war period to give communism a kind of legitimacy by partially satisfying indigenous national feeling. But the party guaranteed subjection to the will of the Kremlin. The process was, therefore, a product of the fulfilment of Russian manifest destiny, rather than of Marxist-Leninist revolution or of national independence. Allied victory was a liberation from fascism, not national liberation.

In 1956, at the twentieth Congress of the Communist Party of the Soviet Union, the Soviet leader, Nikita Krushchev, condemned the cult of personality in an ill-concealed attack on his predecessor Josef Stalin.[2] Before the speech, leaders throughout the communist bloc had imitated Stalin and made themselves the objects of manufactured charismatic personality cults, and some, such as Walter Ulbricht (1956–71) and Erich Hönecker (1971–89) in the German Democratic Republic and Nicolae Ceausescu (1965–89) in Romania, continued to do so afterwards.[3] To achieve this, the material and ceremonial resources of the state were marshalled to the task and designers gave the cults visual form. Posters from Czechoslovakia, Poland and Hungary position Klement Gottwald, Bolesław Bierut and Mátyás Rákosi next to Stalin in tributes of friendship and in celebration of the October Revolution. Three-quarter-length, they have all the dignity ascribed to eighteenth-century formal portraits and owe a debt to high-status official portrait painting rather than any specifically graphic precedent. That they are by different artists from different countries and are almost indistinguishable in style is a measure of the success

(detail of 6.15)

OVER PAGE

6.1
V. Runova, *Military parade, Moscow*, 7 November 1990, Novosti Agency (TASS). The parade was followed by an anti-communist demonstration which caused Mikhail Gorbachev and his fellow leaders to leave the podium on top of the Lenin Mausoleum in disarray.

6.2
'With President Gottwald, forward for peace and socialism', *May Day, Wenceslas Square, Prague*, 1951, Czechoslovakia, Museum of the Working Class Movement, Prague.

6.3
K. Skála, *Our country will be beautiful and rich*, 1951, Czechoslovakia, All Trade Union Archive, Prague.

6.4
Tibor Bánhegyi, *Forward with the Congress of the Young Fighters for Peace and Socialism*, 1950, Hungary, Museum of Contemporary History, Budapest.

6.1

6.2

6.3

6.4

6.5

6.6

6.7

6.5
A. Kossov, *Long live the great undefeatable flag of Marx, Engels, Lenin, Stalin!*, 1953, Soviet Union, Museum of the Working Class Movement, Prague.

6.6
Anon., *Belorussian Soviet Socialist Republic. Proletarians of all countries. 'Through storms a son of freedom shone and great Lenin illuminated our way, Stalin brought us up for loyalty to nation for hard and enthusiastic labour'*, c. 1950, Soviet Belorussia, Sheliuto, Minsk.

6.8

86

LAI DZĪVO PADOMJU TAUTAS VADONIS –
LIELAIS STAĻINS!

6.9

6.10

6.11

ВЕЛИКИЙ СТАЛИН–ЗНАМЯ ДРУЖБЫ НАРОДОВ СССР!

6.12

ВПЕРЕД, К ПОБЕДЕ КОММУНИЗМА!

6.13

6.7
Mikhail Gordon, *Long live the thirty-first anniversary of Great October 1948. Under the flag of Lenin, led by Stalin, forward to communism! All power to the Soviets*, 1948, Soviet Union, the artist.

6.8
Anon., *May Day, Wenceslas Square, Prague*, 1951, Czechoslovakia, Museum of the Working Class Movement, Prague.

6.9
Anon., *Long live the hero of the Soviet people – great Stalin!*, 1949, Soviet Latvia, National Library, Riga, Latvia.

6.10
Juris Dimiters, *untitled*, 1981, Soviet Latvia, the artist.

6.11
B. Muchin, *Forward to communism! Stalin*, 1949, Soviet Union, Museum of the Working Class Movement, Prague.

6.12
Viktor Koretsky, *Great Stalin. Flag of friendship of Soviet nations*, 1950, Soviet Union, Academy of Fine Art, Berlin.

NIEŚMIERTELNE IMIĘ STALINA SZTANDAREM LUDZKOŚCI
W WALCE O POKÓJ, DEMOKRACJĘ I SOCJALIZM

6.14

PREVIOUS PAGE

6.13
Leonid Fedorovich
Golovanov, *Forward with the
victory of communism!*, 1952,
Soviet Union, Academy of
Fine Arts, Berlin.

6.14
Waldemar Świerzy, *The
immortal name of Stalin is a
banner for mankind in the
struggle for peace, democracy
and socialism*, 1953, Soviet
Union, private collection.

of the programme of socialist realism within the realm of widely disseminated official portraiture. The posters stress the subordinate status of the national leader to Stalin, but the portrait of the leader became the material mechanism through which it was hoped that the people might identify with the party and the nation.

The bust was the most common form of the portrait of the leader. But while Stalin was in power another very popular scheme was the multiple portrait of the contemporary leader in the company of the founders of the revolution: Karl Marx, Frederick Engels and the father of the Russian Revolution, Lenin. They are placed in linear juxtaposition, with Stalin as the most prominent figure (6.8). Depicted on placards and banners in parades, or suspended above the peoples of the Soviet republics and the communist bloc, the pictures were an iconographical and formulaic demonstration of the surrender of national, for supposedly transnational, socialist culture (6.5). They are found throughout the region and were talismanic of subject relationships to the Soviet Union. Before 1941 and the Nazi invasion of the Soviet Union, Stalin commonly placed himself in such august circumstances to boost his revolutionary credentials. He had been careful to emulate the Lenin cult, and made sure his hagiographers stressed the unsupported fact that he was Lenin's right-hand man. The closeness of the two men in life was a central iconographical motif of Soviet culture in the 1930s and it continued into the post-war era. For example, a Byelorussian poster in gold and red of a statue of the two men carries the poetic lines

Through storms a son of freedom shone
and great Lenin illuminated our way
Stalin brought us up for loyalty to nation
For hard and enthusiastic labour

(*c.* 1950) (6.6): it depicts Lenin showing the true path to Stalin. Iconographically the sculpture may have been inspired by Evgenii Kibrik's graphic falsification of history, *Lenin arrives in Smolny during the night of 24 October* (1947.). Lenin embraces Stalin as he brings him into the headquarters of the revolution in Petrograd, but Stalin was never there.[4]

After the war the strategy was redundant, because Stalin was the proven victor in a war of national survival. He had vanquished the fascist beast and his place was assured in communist mythology. A Soviet poster designed by Mikhail Gordon commemorating the *Thirty-first anniversary of Great October, 1917–48* (1948) (6.7) places under the ubiquitous red flag a naturalistic and humanized portrait bust of Stalin next to the graphically simplified and spectral features of Lenin.[5] Stalin is in the centre of the poster and, although his head is smaller, he is marginally higher than Lenin and is pictured as the living heir to the dead Lenin.[6]

Stalin's seventieth birthday in 1949 saw his stature reach its peak and during the celebrations his portrait was projected into the night sky on to a barrage balloon above Red Square. Despite his poor record as a war commander, his lack of regard for the lives of his soldiers, the terrible human cost of the collectivization programme and the Terror, most of the population were ignorant of his mistakes. He had become 'the still point of the turning world', 'appearing to be kind, wise, moderating and correcting his foolish and wicked ministers and officials'.[7] Memoirs confirm that he inspired a despairing faith, even among the inmates of the Gulag. Contemporaries granted his likeness spiritual authority:

> I approached Stalin's portrait, took it off the wall, placed it on the table and, resting my head on my hands, I gazed and meditated. What should I do? The Leader's face, as always so serene, his eyes so clear-sighted, they penetrate into the distance. It seems his penetrating look pierces my little room and goes out to embrace the entire globe. I do not know how I would appear to anyone looking at me at this moment. But with my every fibre, every nerve, every drop of blood I feel that, at this moment, nothing exists in this entire world but this dear and beloved face. What should I do?
>
> The Soviet government handles the enemies of the people with a firm hand …
>
> These are my words, comrade Stalin. I believe them sacredly. Now I know how to act.[8]

A Latvian poster of Stalin with the caption *Long live the hero of the Soviet people – great Stalin* (1949) (6.9) places him in a niche-like space as he steps forward to bless his people. His surroundings sanctify him as Christ himself. Above, the spiritual presence of God the Father appears in the portrait of Lenin. But Lenin's likeness is fixed in the pictured medallion, he is safely consigned to history; not active but memorialized. Elena Hellberg has discussed the mythic dimensions of these iconographies. She assigns structural roles to the depiction of horizontal 'earthly' space and the vertical line connecting it with 'celestial' space in an iconographical scheme familiar from traditional folklore, Russian heroic epics and pre-Stalinist images of proletarian revolutionaries. But the figure of the great leader has entirely replaced generic representations of revolutionary heroes from the early part of the century.[9] Instead, the hero Stalin looks down on the world from his pedestal and, as the mediator between the profane and the divine, he has magical and superhuman powers.[10] Stalin's scale naturalizes his status to provide a gloss of historical and popular legitimacy. As the Latvian critic Vlaga Melngaile remarked: 'For many … song stands for history.'[11] The poster is paradigmatic within socialist-realist discourse.[12]

A diminutive procession of workers brandishing red flags to establish Latvia's revolutionary history and future parade pass the House of Collective Farmers, a building barely begun in 1949 and not completed until 1957.[13] The building was made in the image of Rudnev's Moscow University and the Palace of Culture and Science in Warsaw, 'Stalin's gift'. Outwardly it represents Stalinist munificence and beneficence while implicitly signifying Russian imperialism,[14] and the image of the port of Riga pictures the historical significance of the city to Russia as an outlet to the Baltic Sea. The red flags surrounding Stalin at first seem to assert the revolutionary pedigree of the Soviets. They are in the pattern of a sunburst and embody the party's promise of a radiant future. But the sunburst is also the traditional national emblem of Latvia. The symbolism may conform to Zhdanov's desire to make socialist realism national in form and socialist in content, but at this point the poster as a representation of the Soviet nation splits.

The poster displays recognizably Latvian traits and the representation of Stalin makes an interesting contrast with Juris Dimiters's celestial ecological poster from the 1980s (6.10). It partakes of what the art historian Vaira Vikis Freibergs identified in Latvian art as a 'certain coolness': 'a strong reserve and reticence towards the direct expression of deep emotions'.[15] Until 1940 Latvia had been a sovereign and neutral state and, contrary to communist histories, many Latvians had sided with the Nazi occupiers after 1941.[16] Armed resistance to the Soviets persisted until 1949, by which time collectivization had enveloped 80 per cent of the farms, internal passports were required for travel and living standards had collapsed for most of the population. New Russian settlement had begun in 1945, and in the decade which followed the population rose from 1.4 million to pre-war levels of 2 million, with ethnic Russians making up over a quarter of the total population.[17] Of the thirteen members of the Central Committee of the Latvian Communist Party, six were Russian: 'The process of russification was far more intense and thorough than it had ever been under the old Tsarist regime. The general rule was: everything Russian must be extolled, everything Western European discredited.'[18] To be Russian was to be 'more glamorous, more glorious, more true-to-life'.[19] Unlike most of communist Europe, Latvia was Lutheran, but the poster's formal, almost Byzantine, character identifies it with a subordinate, if thriving, Catholic culture more closely associated with a newly aspirant and largely Russian communist ruling class. Riga attracted a high proportion of educated Russians who dominated the industrial working class and managerial positions.[20] It was this class of people at the top of the professions and active

within party circles who provided the majority audience for these posters.

The connection with status persists in the cultural as well as the political economy. Posters are exhibited in national institutions as a measure of both the privileged position of designers as members of the creative and technical intelligentsia and the cultural aspirations of what Vera Dunham called the middle class. According to Sheila Fitzpatrick, a central concept in the discourse of socialist realism was *kulturnost*, the attribute of being cultured.[21] Rooted in the traditional high culture and national folk forms, *kulturnost* was steeped in nostalgia, but the continuity of the tradition had been broken and in practice it was little more than an affectation, reduced to a code for correct communist behaviour. Socialist realism may have been *ersatz*, derivative and *kitsch* but, as Fitzpatrick notes, the upwardly mobile sons and daughters of the Stalinist peasant cadres of the 1930s realized that the only kinds of superiority which could be acknowledged were culture and education. Communist cultural policy gave birth to a populism found, on the one hand, in A. A. Zhdanov's advice to the composers to learn from the simple folk songs of the people and, on the other, in the authority of the old conservative cultural intelligentsia; ironically enough, this was a class of people the revolution had been determined to displace but whose distorted values had survived in the legacy of the inter-war petty bourgeoisie in Europe.

Stalinism inherited from the avant garde the desire to transform the world through aesthetics: 'Socialist realism, the art of the winners, wanted to take all of reality inside itself, change it all, and "bless" it with Socialist ideals.'[22] B. Muchin's poster is a good example. In the centre Stalin's portrait is supported on a laurel wreath, the whole surrounded by an *ersatz* baroque frame (6.11). Below, there are historical allusions to the people's history of the revolution: the storming of the Winter Palace and the final triumph of the revolution. Above, caught between the silver birch trees which are vital attributes of Russian national identity there is a naturalistic scene of the communist 'future in the present'. It shows a land of plenty and advanced technology on a par with Western representations of post-war affluence. It is an updated image of Stalin as the Father and Russia as the Motherland, and encourages traditional memories of a matriarchal, egalitarian, peace-loving and pagan golden age familiar from romantic reinventions of folk history. The heraldic form of the poster links it with the iconography of pre-revolutionary imperial and religious posters and establishes a sense of continuity between the past and the present, stressing Russian national tendencies in Stalinist culture.[23] The aesthetic is communist and Russian, modernist and traditional.

6.15
Otakar Švec, *Stalin's
monument, Prague, summer
1959*, 1959, Museum of the
Working Class Movement,
Prague.

6.16
Anon., *'We will overcome
droughts, too!' May Day 1953,
Wenceslas Square, Prague*,
1953, Museum of the Working
Class Movement, Prague.

6.17
NSK, *The death of ideology.
Laibach*, 1982, Yugoslavia,
Moravian Gallery, Brno.

6.18
Franciszek Starowieyski, *Tym
okret. Theatre in Osterwy,
Lublin*, 1985, Poland, private
collection.

6.19
Manfred Butzmann, *The
poster 'Chinese souvenir' at a
demonstration against the
amnesty for Stasi members,
Berlin, 29 March*, 1990, GDR,
the artist.

6.20
Krzysztof Ducki, Wojczenko,
Andrei Sheliuto and Vladimir
Tsesler, *Stalin*, 1988, Hungary
and Soviet Belorussia, Poster
Museum, Wilanow.

6.21
Efim Tsvik, *'We swear to you,
comrade Lenin, that we will
accomplish your commands
with credit.' Stalin*, 1990,
Soviet Union, Moravian
Gallery, Brno.

6.22
Jindřich Štreit, *Celebration of
the Great October Revolution,
Jiříkov*, 1981, Czechoslovakia,
the photographer.

6.23
Jindřich Štreit, *Great October
Revolution, Husova Street, in
front of the Moravian Gallery,
Brno*, 1981, Czechslovakia,
the photographer.

6.24
Jindřich Štreit, *Celebration of
the Great October Revolution*,
1981, Czechoslovakia, the
photographer.

Rarely seen in public even during the war, Stalin increasingly distanced himself from the people and government. Simultaneously the party enshrined him as the deity. The historical mission of the Soviet people in the figure of Stalin was destined to bring socialist culture to the world. He is pictured in military uniform by Viktor Koretsky (6.12) and Leonid Fedorovich Golovanov (6.13) as the sole leader of the unified Soviet people. Every nation is in national costume and they stand behind and below him, receiving flowers, or in the presence of his great works. The iconographic scheme was a familiar one repeated throughout the region. It found its most gargantuan expression in Stalin's monument in Prague (6.15).[24] It is tempting to read into the poster by the Polish designer, Waldemar Świerzy, an unconscious irony: Stalin's likeness accompanies the other flags of the communist bloc, but there are no people (6.14).

Few men since Napoleon have been the object of such widespread and passionate adulation. For Władisław Gomułka, leader of the communist regime in Poland (1956–70), Stalin 'was an expert in everything, knew everything, decided everything, ran everything. … Whatever his actual knowledge, his talents, his personal qualities might be, he was the wisest of men.'[25] Viktor Govorkov's *We beat the drought!* (1949) portrays Stalin as the 'great architect'. Pipe and pencil in hand, he pores over a map of a vast afforestation scheme stretching from Moscow to the Black Sea. It was printed in an edition of hundreds of thousands and was even paraded in a hand-made version in Wenceslas Square during the May Day celebrations of 1953, a full month after the dictator's death (6.16).

The public image projected by Stalin was paternal and serene. As a master narrative it inflicts a certain kind of reading and an ideological reality. Retrospectively, it imposes a meaning on the present, tradition and the past. But the narration is structured by what it cannot depict. The Soviet occupation of the Baltic States, Poland and Byelorussia in 1940 and the drive to Berlin in 1945 had precipitated mass deportations of the professional and landed classes, the politically unreliable and the ethnically 'inappropriate'. Typically, NKVD[26] instructions demanded the separation of the father from the family, and in this sense the rhetorical and iconographical role of Stalin the father is especially interesting.[27] Likewise, the purges throughout the communist bloc which had taken place at various times throughout the late 1940s and 1950s divided families and fractured communities in an atmosphere of distrust and fear. Political posters are the shape of the public face of communism and in them the repression at the heart of the regimes resists communication and interpretation. Slavoj Žižek described the process as 'a stain that cannot be included in the circuit of discourse … but is at the same time a positive condition of it'.[28] The threat of imprisonment, deportation and execution binds the audience; it is the unspoken thing against which the whole reality is utterly defenceless. The repression cannot be represented, but at the same time it is the only thing which gives the regime its consistency, and, paradoxically, destroys its legitimacy. The leader is the absent, all-powerful and beneficent father who provides where mortal kin fails. As a surrogate he is both heavenly and profane. The necessary and unspoken condition of his presence

6.15

6.16

6.17

6.18

6.19

6.20

6.21

6.22

6.23

6.24

divides and separates the people from themselves.

If that which cannot be spoken is represented, the forces of repression are brought to bear, as an account of an anti-Stalinist demonstration on the anniversary of his ninetieth birthday in Red Square on 21 December 1969 reveals:

> We stood there, hemmed in by a crowd of KGB men. Convinced that in these conditions any unauthorized activity was inconceivable, and hence that any open demonstration by the Stalinists would be impossible, we decided to leave. At that moment one of our comrades dropped on the ground a portrait of Stalin with a black cross painted over it. (We had decided to hold this portrait up above our heads as a protest, should the Stalinists appear on Red Square, as expected, with pictures of their idol.) The dropped portrait fell by A. Yakobson's feet. Yakobson was instantly seized by KGB agents, bundled into a car … and driven away.[29]

At the time of martial law in Poland in 1981 there were posters critical of the cult of the leader and the meaning of military prowess for the people. In the figure of General Jaruzelski, leader of the regime (1980–89), artists could find an easy target, with his large sunglasses and sharp bird-like features. Published in Paris, posters show Jaruzelski presiding vulture-like over the coffins and graves of his people.[30] As early as 1982 NSK in Yugoslavia juxtaposed the heads of Marx, Engels and Lenin with the heads of the victims of communism and a version of Malevich's black cross on a white ground to speak for the fate of the utopian hopes of the revolution (6.17); while in Poland a theatre poster such as Starowieyski's *Tym okret* showing a row of monkey-like heads from 1985 could be read only in one way (6.18). Inversions of the socialist-realist scheme are unusual outside the Soviet Union until after 1989 (6.19, 21), but the Ducki/Tsesler/Wojczenko/ Sheliuto contribution to the 1988 Warsaw Biennale was an early public condemnation of Stalin's record (6.20).

THE LENIN CULT

In 1955 Krushchev switched the commemoration of Lenin from the day of his death on 21 January to his birthday on 22 April.[31] The shift from winter to spring altered Lenin's commemorative significance. Formerly a memorialization of the past through the cult of death, his memory became a celebration of new life. The parades were optimistic and were closely associated with the Young Pioneers, 'Lenin's grandchildren', who would lead the Soviet people to future glory. Millions of portraits and hagiographies of Stalin were replaced by posters, books, badges, paintings, busts and statues dedicated to Lenin, who is portrayed as grand, imposing and humane. As Nina Tumarkin has pointed out, the Lenin cult of the 1960s simply took over from where the Stalin cult had left off (6.26).

Lenin's memory was sentimentalized in the attempt to engineer a bridge between the party, its Marxist-Leninist orthodoxies and the people. Photographs by Jindřich Štreit taken in the 1980s of street decorations and Young Pioneers reciting poetry in celebration of the October Revolution at local party meetings in Czechoslovakia show a profound lack of interest on the part of the people (6.22–24).[32] In contradistinction Antonín Pelc's commemoration of the fortieth anniversary of the revolution shows Lenin in civilian clothes, imperiously but benignly presiding over a loyal and enthusiastic procession of the peoples of the communist bloc (6.25). The image of Lenin standing and addressing his people below, with his arm outstretched towards the future, repeats an iconography established in 1920 and repeated by artists such as A. I. Strakhov and Gustav Klutsis in the poster *Towards the Leninist days* (1930).[33] However, attempts were made to update the iconography. Miron Lukianov, for example, in a denial of the cult of personality, places Lenin on a level with the ordinary workers – but he is the only figure to be fully rendered, to be fully alive, as it were (6.26). Another extraordinary Soviet poster by Efim Tsvik, rejected by Soviet censors in 1969, was only published in 1989; sporting the caption *Power to the Soviets! Peace to nations! Land to peasants! Factories to workers! Bread to hungry people* (1969/89) (6.27) in red on black, it apes Western psychedelia in a formulation echoed in György Kemény's poster of *Ho Chi Minh* (6.28) and again almost ten years later by Anton Cetnarowski's poster *Lenin* (1977) (6.29). These three posters emphasize the desire of the communist authorities to appeal to youth through the appropriation of Western counter-cultural styles in the aftermath of the Prague Spring and dissaffection in Poland. It was a dangerous strategy because the attempt to accommodate the anti-establishment and anti-capitalist credentials of Western counter-culture implicitly promoted consumerist and hedonistic values.

The cult of Lenin was not a cult of personality but a declaration of devotion to sacred party aims and ideology. Something of the bombast of the anniversaries and party conferences can be registered in the grandiosity of the designs for posters produced to commemorate the occasions (6.30–34). Nina Tumarkin remarked on the tenor of the Lenin centennial celebrations in 1970: '[it] had been intended to saturate political, civic and cultural life with Lenin. But the celebration was a disaster for the credibility of Communist propaganda and political ritual. The barrage of Leniniana was so vast and unrelenting that the jubilee took on the appearance of a burlesque performance.'[34] Large in scale, sweeping and visually effective, the posters were a small part of the anniversary celebrations. But the scale of the centennial backfired and people began to make jokes about Lenin's omnipresence. An officially approved design from Hungary in 1983 demonstrates how far the cult had retreated from the high seriousness of the 1960s and 1970s (6.35), while in Poland Eugeniusz Get-Stankiewicz could risk near open parody by the late 1980s (6.36). Get-Stankiewicz's almost entire *oeuvre* engages with communist and Christian iconography and the iconic heads of Lenin and Christ. The profile portrait is variously placed against a red ground or stuck with a crown of thorns; we see the features of the artist depicted as the hero. A figure not of secular or spiritual power, but the embodiment of individual freedom and its existential consequences.[35]

One of the more enthusiastic celebrants was Walter Ulbricht's German Democratic Republic. Ernst Thälmann, the pre-war leader of the German Communist Party, had perished in the Nazi death camps and was something of a genuine socialist hero in the fight against fascism. In 1955 a film poster portrayed him as a Lenin figure and another poster did the same for Karl Liebknecht in 1958 (6.37, 38). In the 1950s the iconography of Lenin was identical with communist leadership. Later the revolutionary legacy of heroic struggle, intentionally or not, becomes distorted, and the centennial poster by Harry Pflaum *Lenin, 1870–1924* (1970) (6.39) shows a sinister Lenin, a man of the shadows rather than the light.

Even Leonid Brezhnev, the Soviet leader (1964–82), could not halt the process. He struggled and failed to step into Lenin's shoes in the effort to build a personality cult to bolster his own authority. One poster has him lecturing from a podium exactly in the manner of Lenin addressing the troops outside the Bolshoi Theatre in Moscow on 5 May 1920 (6.41). The original photograph was iconic of the revolution worldwide, and provided the inspiration for countless posters and paintings of Lenin.[36] Brezhnev capitalized on a revival of the Stalin cult. Mention of Krushchev, for example, was more or less forbidden because of his role in undermining the authority of the party apparatus. Stagnation produced nostalgia for a golden age of revolution and victory in war which can be seen in the popularity of eulogistic novels, memoirs and films.[37]

Mikhail Gorbachev's rise in 1985 coincided with the fortieth anniversary of the victory over fascism and his speech on that occasion did not fail to mention Stalin to great applause. But Gorbachev's administration was to oversee a gradual relaxation of censorship, and in 1987, on the seventieth anniversary of the revolution, he promoted a measured reconsideration of the 'blank spots of Soviet history'. Marxism-Leninism had generated class-based historical narratives focused on the motivating figures of revolutionary socialist history. They had effectively ignored

wider social forces and contexts, with the result that the heroes of the revolution from Lenin to Brezhnev formed the *dramatis personae* of historical understanding who embodied the spirit of their times. Such genealogies provided the backbone of the discourse of Marxist-Leninist history and generated personalized narratives which leant themselves to visual articulation in the likenesses of the leaders. If the Lenin cult had exhausted itself under Brezhnev, it was revitalized under Gorbachev and his reform programme. The Lenin of 1920–21 and the national economic plan was literally seen as the grandfather of *glasnost* and *perestroika*, and Faldin and Faldina's *Bravo!* (1988) (6.42), for example, depicts Gorbachev conducting from the text of Lenin.

As the truth of the history of the Russian Revolution and the post-war occupation of eastern and central Europe was revealed, so the official public language of the party became vulnerable to subversion and satire. The monuments to the Brezhnev era were swept aside, and poster artists such as Faldin could openly mock the hollowness of Brezhnev's claims. Brezhnev had identified with Stalin and, as his reputation sank, so testimonies to the evils of Stalin and the weaknesses of subsequent regimes began to fill the television and newspapers. Even Krushchev, who had been responsible for the first attacks on the 'cult of personality' and whose own profile in political posters had been relatively low key (6.40), was subject to criticism because of his agricultural policies and his historical role as an ally of Stalin in the famine of the 1920s.

There are many poster designs which bear witness to a process of historical re-evaluation. According to Nina Tumarkin, who has plotted its trace, at first the focus was on 1937, the worst year of the Great Terror. Other critiques of Soviet history were to follow from both inside and outside the Soviet Union: the collaborative poster *Stalin* (1988) (6.20) was exhibited at the Warsaw Biennale in June 1988. As time wore on the emphasis shifted to consideration of the famine created by collectivization, and by 1989 Soviet revisionism looked to 1939 and the Nazi–Soviet pact and the Red Army incursions into eastern Poland, the Baltic States and Finland. Visual analogies between Hitler and Stalin are frequent, especially after the final collapse.[38]

Lenin's reputation was slow to sink and Stalin was regarded as the leader who had corrupted the former's idealism. But in 1988 Lenin was implicated in the Terror state by Vasily Seliunin in an article published in the influential *Novy mir* which connected Lenin with the famine of 1917 and the liquidation of the Kulaks in 1918–21.[39] Such was the potency of the Lenin myth that, even at the time of the Warsaw Pact invasion of

6.25
Antonín Pelc, *1917–1957*,
1957, Czechoslovakia, Central
Committee of the Communist
Party, Moravian Museum,
Brno.

6.26
Miron Lukianov, *The unity of
the working people and the
Communist Party.
Indestructible!*, 1968, Soviet
Union, Mikhail Avvakumov,
Moscow.

6.27
Efim Tsvik, *Power to the
Soviets! Peace to nations!
Land to peasants! Factories to
workers! Bread to hungry
people! Lenin*, 1967/1989,
Soviet Union, private edition
by Andrei Kolosov, Moravian
Gallery, Brno.

6.28
György Kemény, *Ho*, 1970,
Hungary, Poster Museum,
Wilanow.

6.29
Anton Cetnarowski, *Lenin*,
1977, Poland, private
collection.

6.30
Eduard Artsrunian, *Glory to
the Great October. Twenty-
fourth Congress of the
Communist Party of the Soviet
Union*, 1973, Soviet Union,
Mikhail Avvakumov, Moscow.

6.25

6.27

6.26

6.28

6.29

6.30

6.31
Viktor Ivanov, *Lenin lived,
Lenin lives, Lenin will live!
V. I. Mayakovsky 1917*, 1975,
Soviet Union, four sheets,
Mikhail Avvakumov, Moscow.

6.32

6.33

6.34

6.35

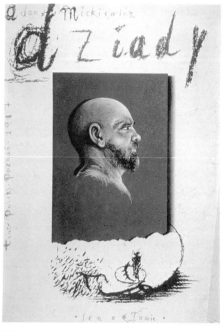

6.36

6.38

6.39

6.32
Vladimir Sachkov, *Time works for communism! V. I. Lenin*, 1982, three sheets, Andrei Budnik, Kiev.

6.33
Vladimir Kononov, *Pravda. At the beginning of communist civilization stands the figure of Lenin, philosopher and revolutionary*, 1983, Soviet Union, three sheets, Andrei Budnik, Kiev.

6.34
György Kemény, *7 November (Revolution Day)*, 1967, Hungary, Hungarian National Gallery, Budapest.

6.37

Czechoslovakia in 1968, spontaneous street graphics opposing the invasion depicted Lenin as grief-stricken, his ideals betrayed. But by 1989 Lenin's portrait was being utilized as a warning from the past in Hungary by the League of Young Democrats (FIDESZ) in the first free democratic elections (6.43). In the early 1990s the official Soviet historian General Dmitri Volkogonov published a vitriolic and sustained demolition: 'Lenin was an evil man. And he had the eyes of a wolf.'[40] And the Russian designer Vladimir Chaika could simply put his image up for rent in a deeply ambiguous image which speaks for his legacy (6.44).

Analysis establishes the pseudo-religious and spuriously mythological, traditional and folkloric content of the rhetoric and iconography. The great leader is depicted as godlike and, as in Christian theology, there is an implicit reference to death through the sacrifice despotism demands. As the show trials of the 1930s and the purges of the 1950s demonstrated, the believer admits his shortcomings and sacrifices his life for the cause. The non-believer dies as a victim. The revolution finds irrational justification in brutality.[41] In the 1930s Bahktin wrote of the underlying liberating anti-totalitarian force of laughter, of carnival as opposed to what Christopher Binns characterized as regimented and militarized ceremonial. Slavoj Žižek, on the other hand, writing in 1989, speaks of distance, where laughter and irony are part of the game and the ruling ideology is not meant to be taken seriously: 'Perhaps the greatest danger for totalitarianism are people who take its ideology literally.'[42] Or, as the following well known joke reveals, both the people and the state understand the

meaning and reach of totalitarianism: 'It's 4.00 a.m. There is a knock at the door. "Who's there?" "NKVD. Open up!" is the reply. "No, no," the residents respond. "You've got the wrong apartment. The communists live upstairs."'[43] Those caught within the logic of the police state are subject to its excesses, as the events of 1989 were to show. The participants are aware of the distance between the ideological mask and the social reality, but they insist on the mask. Illusion is the artist's *forte*: 'one knows the falsehood very well, one is well aware of a particular interest hidden behind an ideological universality, but still one does not renounce it.'[44] The artist portrays a lie experienced as truth; the lie is purely instrumental and is secured by violence and the assurance of advancement.

To pursue warlike aims and the defeat of your enemies in the name of peace is a shocking revelation because it shows how ideology structures social reality. The official political poster masks forms of exploitation and repression in a 'rose-tinted' and distorted expression of the political order. But the hyperbole of the poster is part of a colossal and intricate repression of the social, political and linguistic forces which brought it into being. The great leader's universe is not a fantasy: it is the place where the fantasy is at work in social reality. The great leader is excluded from the everyday and the ordinary cycle of the natural. His representation is the symbolic and sublime body of the leader. It is known he is not a god, but behaviour in his presence is determined by belief in his omniscience. The construction of social reality represented in these posters of the great leaders is supported by a series of assumptions, as if the leader is the incarnation of the 'will of the people', or

6.35
Imre Halmos, *Karl Marx 1883–1983*, 1983, GDR, Thomas Hill.

6.36
Eugeniusz Get-Stankiewicz, *Forefathers' Eve. Adam Mickiewicz. Dream of a Gilead*, 1987, Poland, Moravian Gallery, Brno.

6.37
C. H., *Ernst Thälmann, leader of our class*, 1955, GDR, Moravian Gallery, Brno.

6.38
Carl Sauer, *November Revolution in Germany 1918. Struggle for peace, democracy and socialism*, 1958, GDR, Thomas Hill.

6.39
Harry Pflaum, *Lenin 1870–1924. Peace is the reality, the all-persuading question*, 1970, GDR, Academy of Fine Art, Berlin.

6.40
Arno Fleischer, *Friendship*, 1959, GDR, Moravian Gallery, Brno.

6.41
Juri Tzhakevich and S. N. Shkolnik, *Peace. The flag of peace and co-operation between nations was raised by Lenin. We will be faithful to that flag*, 1980, Soviet Ukraine, Andrei Budnik, Kiev.

6.40

6.41

6.42

6.42
Alexander Faldin and Svetlana Faldina, *Bravo!*, 1988, artist's edition, Moravian Gallery, Brno.

6.43
Anon., *Backwards on the Lenin road*, 1989, Hungary, Museum of Contemporary History, Budapest.

6.44
Vladimír Chaika, *For rent (Lenin)*, 1994, Russia, Moravian Gallery, Brno.

6.45
Juri Boxer, *Gorbachev calendar*, 1989, Soviet Union, the artist.

6.46
Alexander Faldin, *Grosny ... 10 December 1994*, 1994, Russia artist's edition, Moravian Gallery, Brno.

6.43

6.44

6.45

6.46

6.47

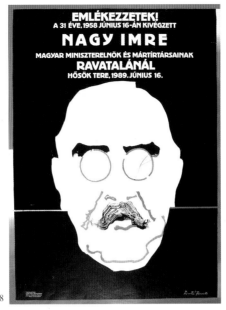

6.48

6.49

6.50

6.51

6.47
Piotr Młodożeniec, *Lech Wałęsa. He destroyed the wall already, which was the limit of freedom*, 1989, Poland, hand-printed private edition, Moravian Gallery, Brno.

6.48
Ferenc Pinter, *Remember at the bier of Imre Nagy*, 1989, Hungary, Moravian Gallery, Brno.

6.49
No kiss without Smint, Czech Republic, 1996, Irena Armutidisová.

6.50
Daniel Hovorka, Vítězslav Kopřiva (director of Mars advertising agency), *Václavka a Dášenka: Wear Raveli – Fuck the World*, 1997, Czech Republic, Irena Armutidisová.

6.51
Anon., *Sixty-fifth anniversary of the founding of the Romanian Communist Party*, c. 1970, Romania, private collection.

as if the party represents the interests of the working class. But the emperor has no clothes and the whole empire of signs comes tumbling down (6.43–6, 52–4).

Not only are the historical leaders of communism subject to ridicule, but the portraits of the new leaders are made more humane as censorship controls are relaxed and designers appropriate iconographies and stylistic formulations from outside the established discourse. The Solidarity leader in Poland, Lech Wałęsa, was depicted behind bars in a poster published in Paris. At home in 1989, Piotr Młodożeniec, in a hand-printed private edition, attempted to wring new life from the iconography of the great leader through application to surface and the limits of reproducibility (6.47). Imre Nagy reappears as a ghostly presence, his meaning refusing the constraints of realism (6.48). Other designers looked West. Gorbachev is portrayed in the manner of a 'smiley badge' familiar from Western youth culture in a poster by Lex Drewinski. Brezhnev and Honecker are seen to engage in a passionate kiss with the caption *The deadly kiss* (1989–90) in a poster by Dmitri Vrübel advertising the East Side Gallery in Berlin. Its grotesque hedonism is a vicious transgression of socialist-realist manners, but the image was subsequently appropriated in the Czech Republic by an advertisement for Smint pastilles in a reversal of the process already described (6.49). Later still, in 1997, a sculptural image by the artist Milan Knížák of the President of the Czech Republic, Václav Havel (1989–), originally entitled *Czech landscape No. 1* (1990), was used in an advertisement for Raveli footwear, *Václavka a Dášenka. Wear Raveli, fuck the world* (1997) (6.50). It was an elaborate punning joke making fun of the much criticized relationship between Václav Havel and his new wife.[45] The East gazes West, and the East looks

to itself to assert that which it is no longer, to see itself as a participant in the reinvention of democracy in images distorted by the institutional forces of international corporate capitalism.

Gorbachev's reforms had led in unforeseen ways to the collapse of the communist bloc. The vested interests of the party old guard and the military soon plotted their revenge. In August 1991 the *putsch* ended Gorbachev's power in the Kremlin. President Boris Yeltsin emerged as the victor, but the struggle for power still continues in the government and among the people. Posters litter the byways of the struggle for history in a process revealed in the survival of the old iconographies existing alongside the new. On Revolution Day in 1991 Working Moscow and the Union of Workers resuscitated the image of Lenin (6.53). The communists who had been legislated out of existence between August 1991 and summer 1993 began to parade regularly with portraits of Stalin and Lenin (6.55). Popular history credits Mikhail Gorbachev with the dissolution of the Soviet Union, although Boris Yeltsin was actually responsible – and on Paris Commune Day Gorbachev was charged, as it were, with what the Nazis failed to achieve in World War II in an appropriation of the anti-Stalinist iconography of the late 1980s (6.54).

Christopher Binns and Stephen White have argued that the colossal propaganda machine established by the regimes in central and eastern Europe with the express purpose of introducing Marxist-Leninist values and ideologies into the practices of everyday life was a substantive failure. The festivals and rituals attached to the regimes were institutionalized and had a permanent and large-scale administrative infrastructure of dedicated buildings, staff and equipment. Enormous creative effort and the skill of

6.52

6.53

6.54

6.55
Uldis Briēdis, *7 November.
Revolution Day*, 1997, Latvia,
the photographer.

6.56
Grohman Schuman, *Rubbish on the path!*, c. 1950, GDR, Thomas Hill.

6.57
John Heartfield, *Fortieth anniversary of the Great October socialist revolution*, 1957, GDR, Academy of Fine Art, Berlin.

6.58
H. P., *This is the reality of anti-fascist fighters in the GDR* (the montage is a photograph of the Fritz Cremer Buchenwald Memorial), 1960, GDR, Academy of Fine Art, Berlin.

6.59
Ivo Lovrenčić, *Spring sowing, sowing of victory*, 1945, Yugoslavia, Croatian Historical Museum, Zagreb.

6.60
Hölter, *1946. The Future lies with you*, 1946, GDR, Berlinische Galerie, Berlin.

6.61
Guenter Mickwausch, *Chemnitz. Forge a unified Germany*, 1946, GDR, Academy of Fine Art, Berlin.

6.62
Jerzy Srokowski, *We forge the foundation of socialism. Six Year Plan. Seventh Congress of Workers' Unions*, 1949, Poland, Museum of Independence, Warsaw.

6.63
János Macskássy, *The core of heavy industry – firm foundation of the Three Year Plan*, 1945, Hungary, Hungarian National Gallery, Budapest.

6.64
Hanuš, *Instead of promises – machinery to our country*, 1948, Czechoslovakia, All Trade Union Archive, Prague.

6.65
Josef Burjanek, *Next year we quicken the step! Forward with socialism*, 1950, Czechoslovakia, All Trade Union Archive, Prague.

6.56

6.57

6.58

6.59

6.62

6.60

6.61

6.63

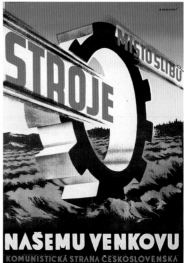

6.64

6.65

6.66

6.67

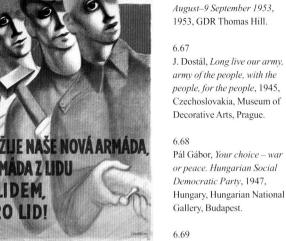

6.66
Arno Drescher, *Leipzig Trade and Technical Fair, 30 August–9 September 1953*, 1953, GDR Thomas Hill.

6.67
J. Dostál, *Long live our army, army of the people, with the people, for the people*, 1945, Czechoslovakia, Museum of Decorative Arts, Prague.

6.68
Pál Gábor, *Your choice – war or peace. Hungarian Social Democratic Party*, 1947, Hungary, Hungarian National Gallery, Budapest.

6.69
Rudolf Bedö, *Social Democratic Party*, 1945, Hungary, Hungarian National Gallery, Budapest.

6.70
Tadeusz Trepkowski, *Welfare of our homeland – from the work of our hands*, 1954, Poland, private collection.

6.71
Zoltán Tamássi, *Hungarian Youth Industrial and Trade Fair for new apprentice hostels, 27 April–7 May*, 1947, Hungary, Hungarian National Gallery, Budapest.

6.72
György Konecsni, *The bread starts here*, 1945, Hungary, Hungarian Museum of Contemporary History, Budapest.

6.68

6.69

6.70

6.71

6.72

6.73

PREVIOUS PAGE

6.73
Zbygniew Waszewski,
1917–1959, 1959, Poland,
Moravian Gallery, Brno.

6.74

6.75

6.74
T. Ispas, *Conference of the
Romanian Communist Party*,
1977, Romania, Museum of
Fine Arts, Bucharest.

6.75
Miloš Pirdek, *With comrade
Gottwald forward to socialism.
Ninth Conference of the KSČ
25–9 May 1948*, 1948,
Czechoslovakia, private
collection.

6.76
Viktor Koretsky, *All power in
the USSR belongs to the
workers of the cities and
villages in their deputies –
soviets – workers –
constitution*, 1947, Soviet
Union, Academy of Fine Art,
Berlin.

6.77
Andor Bánhidi, *Read the
monthly 'New World', the
organ of the Society of the
Hungarian–Socialist
Friendship*, 1949, Hungary,
Hungarian National Gallery,
Budapest.

6.78
Kestutis Gvalda, *With the
Great October way*, 1966,
Soviet Lithuania, Moravian
Gallery, Brno.

6.79
Juri Boxer, *East side story*,
1990, Soviet Union, the artist.

6.76

6.77

6.78

6.79

countless of thousands of artists and designers were dedicated to the task. Yet the ceremonies, festivals and posters are empty of real political and ideological content. They are icons without a god.

COMMUNIST EMBLEMS

National coats of arms were a prominent part of the material culture of communist political life. They were emblematic of a grandiose and imperial ambition meted out from the Kremlin and reproduced by national leaders. As the regimes fashioned their iconographies of power, old national and state emblems were appropriated or discarded according to their worth within communist and revolutionary histories (6.56). The old was augmented with communist symbols: the colour red, the rising sun in gold, red stars and flags, sheaves of corn, hammers and sickles, cogwheels (6.57–78). In the Russian language the word 'red' is etymologically linked in a punning relationship with the word for beautiful, but the immediate ancestry of its use lies in the red banners, scarves and armbands of the French Revolution. The rising sun, often associated with Stalin, was one of the principal iconographic motifs of socialist-realist art, literature, poetry, architecture and popular culture and represented the new dawn of socialism (6.58–60).[46] The red star was introduced as a symbol of the Red Army by Leon Trotsky in 1918.[47] The hammer and the sickle, symbolic of the working class and the peasantry, came to Soviet heraldry in 1918 by way of the imagery of the forge, the hammer and the anvil and nineteenth-century European emblems of working-class struggle (6.61, 62).[48] Many of these elements are brought together in the Soviet seal of government, where, in front of the rising sun, the hammer and the sickle are cupped in a wreath of corn.[49] Justified within the discourse of Marxism-Leninism, these components provided the basis for the development of the national coats of arms for the communist bloc.

In the early days of occupation the communists were careful not to impose Soviet symbolism too overtly for fear of antagonizing the population and associating the national party with the Kremlin. Born of necessity, this approach encouraged innovation. With the addition of red and gold, national colours were integrated into the seals. The former Axis ally, Romania, developed a coat of arms with a socialist landscape of industrial, domestic and rural well-being against a blazing sunrise, framed by sheaves of corn and crowned by a star. Likewise, Hungary combined a ribbon of national colours with ears of corn, a hammer and a rising star. The German Democratic Republic incorporated a set of compasses to replace the sickle and introduced a symbol of scientific and industrial prowess more fitting for a country with only a small peasant base (6.58).[50] Communist parties, as distinct from the national governments in Czechoslovakia and the German Democratic Republic, adopted the cogwheel as an emblem of technological progress (6.64–66). This was both a reference to revolutionary Leninism and to Stalin's invocation of the new socialist man as a 'screw in the machine'. The cog was an iconographic theme with a modernizing impulse absent from contemporary Soviet political symbolism.

The iconographies of these national and party emblems crept into posters in marked contrast to the homogeneity of the socialist realism of Soviet posters, which clung to narrative and painterly designs. Exceptionally, when designers dropped naturalistic realism to mimic other art forms such as sculpture and architectural decoration, emblems were more common (6.76). The rising sun, the hammer and the anvil were popular motifs because they could be associated with the practical and political tasks of rebuilding the physical and ideological fabric of societies shattered by war. The imagery of the forge prominent in early European socialist iconography had been largely abandoned by the Bolsheviks at the end of the 1920s and was therefore free of immediate connections with Soviet communism. Its revival and visual power associate it with a youthful and heartfelt desire for a new beginning (6.61, 62). The hammer was a favourite image of Hungarian designers. Pál Gábor, for example, made modernist use of the motif (6.68), while Rudolf Bedö, in his poster commemorating the role of the Social Democratic Party in the defeat of fascism, reused Mihalý Biró's internationally known and revolutionary 'red man with hammer' of 1918 (6.69). Biró's image also appeared unmodified on the streets in 1945 as the communists appropriated the history of the Social Democratic Party and the founding of the republic during the 'Chrysanthemum Revolution'.

In Poland and Hungary early attempts at a more humorous, humanized and international approach can be found where the hammer literally provides nurture for the young or gives fruit to an apple (of temptation) against a surrealist sky (6.70, 71). But these idiosyncratic approaches soon gave way to strident designs and the reintroduction of the sickle. György Konecsni's The bread starts here (1945) (6.72) and Zbygniew Waszewski's 1917–59 (1959) (6.73) assign 'cosmic' significance to the power of the revolution. The latter signals the Soviet lead over the West in the space race and envisages what Victor Buchli has described as de-artefactualization and the creation of an objectless world capable of overcoming the social and material contradictions of industrialization and commodity fetishism in the white heat of Krushchev's scientific and technical revolution.[51]

6.80
István Orosz, *untitled*, 1989, Hungary, Moravian Gallery, Brno.

6.81
Mikhail Soloviev, *Time works for communism*, 1990, Soviet Union, poster maquette, Alexander Lozenko.

6.82
Uldis Briēdis, *Russian National Front meeting in Riga*, 14 May 1998, Latvia, the photographer.

6.83
Andor Bánhidi, *Welcome to the thirty-second anniversary of the Great October*, 1949, Hungary, Hungarian Museum of Contemporary History, Budapest.

6.84
Anon., *Hungarocarrot*, 1990, Hungary, Moravian Gallery, Brno.

6.85
Sándor Pinczehélyi, *Sickle and hammer* (from original photograph taken in 1973), 1993, Hungary, Moravian Gallery, Brno.

6.80

6.81

6.82

6.83

6.84

6.85

6.86

6.87

6.88

6.89

6.90

6.91

6.86
Boris Bučan, *No admittance to the unvocational*, 1976, Yugoslavia, Moravian Gallery, Brno.

6.87
Boris Bučan, *Croatian Faust*, 1983, Yugoslavia, Moravian Gallery, Brno.

6.88
Karel Haloun, *Jasná páka (Clear Control Lever)*, 1983, Czechoslovakia, private collection.

6.89
István Orosz, *Concert for the victims of communism*, 1990, Hungary, Moravian Gallery, Brno.

6.90
József Szurcsik, *Art Reaktor*, 1987, Hungary, Hungarian National Gallery, Budapest.

6.91
Venyamin Markovich Briskin, *1917. Peace, democracy, socialism*, 1970, Soviet Union, Mikhail Avvakumov, Moscow.

When held aloft, the hammer and sickle invariably denoted communist progress and unity, and provided the inspiration of thousands of posters in almost infinite variety.

Vera Mukhina's sculpture *Industrial worker and collective farm girl*, which was originally installed in the Soviet pavilion at the International Exhibition in Paris in 1937, provided a useful vehicle for the motif. It also formed the basis of Andor Bánhidi's hymn to the glories of the communist press (6.77). The scheme was widely emulated (6.78), and was revived with satirical verve at the end of the 1980s (6.79–81), only to be adapted as a swastika by the extreme right in Russia during the 1990s (6.82). Likewise the Soviet memorial by Kisfaudy Strobl erected in 1947 in Budapest known as the Liberty statue was an emblem of that country's socialism: 'The piquancy of the thing is that that figure was originally designed by the artist as a memorial in honour of Horthy's son, who died in an air crash. The woman in the antique robe was then holding a propellor in her hands.'[52] It was repeated endlessly in badges, posters and political ephemera until it became an object of ridicule (6.83, 84). Since the 1970s the more liberal regimes in Hungary and Yugoslavia had produced a steady interrogation of communist emblematics in cultural fields associated with the avant garde and youth culture which were able to provide value systems independent of communism (6.84, 88–90). The Prague rock group Jasná páka, for example, mocked communist rhetoric in its name and used the image of the corkscrew as a reference to scientific rationalism and the hedonism the communists deplored (6.88). The hammer, once the breaker of chains (6.91), in Romania became a symbol of reaction as Ion Iliescu's regime used the miners to repress democratic reform (6.92–94).

Political symbols do not, and indeed cannot, operate in a vacuum. They form an important part of a geographical and rhetorical discourse of power and control. Continuously displayed as a background visual noise to the comings and goings of everyday life on hoardings and in the streets, political symbols provided the seal of legitimation for government and the party. They sanctified with Soviet-ordained authority trade union buildings, clubs, collective farms and factories, and public institutions such as hospitals, universities, schools and libraries. More important, these symbols played a role in the numerous communist festivals spread throughout the year. Officially organized festivities were intended to help establish a normative and natural framework of essential common sense for the supremacy of the communist party, loyalty to the Kremlin and the totalitarian rule of the leader. Authority is not wholly dependent on coercion, but depends on links with moral symbols and sacred emblems which have what

seems to be a natural currency with the population. Therefore it was vital for the regimes to establish cogent and meaningful symbolic systems to reproduce the *status quo* and affirm the political order. However, there was a divide between state and existing discourses. The regimes needed congruent readings of history, national identity, community and the people to claim legitimacy. But the regimes were caught in a dialectic with forces which ultimately had the power to change them, and from time to time these forces broke out into public space.

Much of the opposition to the state under communism took symbolic form. The 1956 uprising in Budapest saw the destruction and capture of Soviet tanks, accompanied by rebels singing the national anthem and posting hand-made traditional Kossuth emblems. Famously, the national flag was reclaimed by removing the communist hammer and sickle emblem. Similarly, in Czechoslovakia in 1968 and 1989, protesters salvaged national symbols on behalf of the people, gathering at the St. Wenceslas monument in Wenceslas Square and wearing national tricolours to awake national consciousness and pride. In 1969 Jan Palach had immolated himself close to this site of national significance, to shake the conscience of the politicians and the people who had begun to collaborate with the occupying power and the beginnings of the process of 'normalization' and the moral devastation of the nation. His gesture of peaceful, if mortal, resistance emulated the Reverend Quange Duc's protest against the Saigon regime in South Vietnam in 1963, which had been made known to the world in a widely published photograph. Consequently, Palach's act in close proximity to a public and national symbol ensured the attention of the international media to tie the predicament of the Czechoslovak people to a supranational discourse of non-violent struggle against foreign occupation, oppression and war.

In the late 1940s, before the communists had established cultural control, it was not uncommon for politically inspired artists to adopt traditional religious and national symbols. This was particularly true of Poland, where national identity is closely linked with the Catholic Church. Stefan Gałkowski and Jerzy Karolak produced a poster for a fund-raising exhibition, *Polonia* (1946) (6.95), picturing a personification of the prostrate country as a *pièta*. Indigenous pre-communist religious and national symbolisms of this kind were never very far from the surface. Solidarity posters by Jacek Ćwikła (6.97) and Eugeniusz Get-Stankiewicz (6.96) transform the ear of corn and the hammer into Christian crosses in designs executed in national colours, in affirmation of Polish Catholicism and worker solidarity. Wiesław Strebejko's cultural poster *Sixth Festival of Ancient Music from Eastern Europe* (1981) (6.98), featuring the Black Madonna of Częstochowa,

6.92

6.93

6.94

6.95

6.96

6.97

6.98

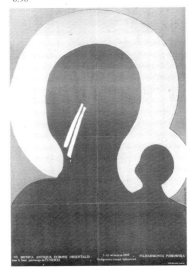

6.92
Stasys Eidrigevičius, *Have your own politics*, *c.* 1985, Poland, private collection.

6.93
Ilie Bumbac, *Miners in the Palatul Cotroceni*, Bucharest, 27 September 1991, Romania.

6.94
Timotei Nădăşan, *Bucharest, 14–15 June 1990. How dark the gold has become, how the pure gold has changed! The sacred stones are poured out of the corner of every street. Lamentations of Jeremiah 4.1*, 1990, Romania, Moravian Gallery, Brno.

6.95
Stanislaw Gałkowski and Jerzy Karolak, *Polonia. An exhibition of the Polish Artists' Professional Union*, 1946, Poland, Poster Museum, Wilanow.

6.96
Eugeniusz Get-Stankiewicz, *Independent Autonomous Union of Farmers 'Solidarity'*, 1981, Poland, private collection.

6.97
Jacek Čwikła, *Twenty-fifth anniversary of Poznan riots, 28 June 1981*, 1981, Poland, private collection.

6.98
Wiesław Strebejko, *Sixth Festival of Ancient Music from Eastern Europe*, 1981, Poland, private collection.

6.99
Andrzej Pągowski, *Andrzej Wajda. Man of Iron*, 1987, Poland, private collection.

6.100
Manfred Butzmann, *And I will live for you … 700 years of the Church in Berlin*, 1985, GDR, the artist.

6.101
Péter Pócs and László Haris, *301 SzDSz (Alliance of Free Democrats)*, 1989, Hungary, Moravian Gallery, Brno.

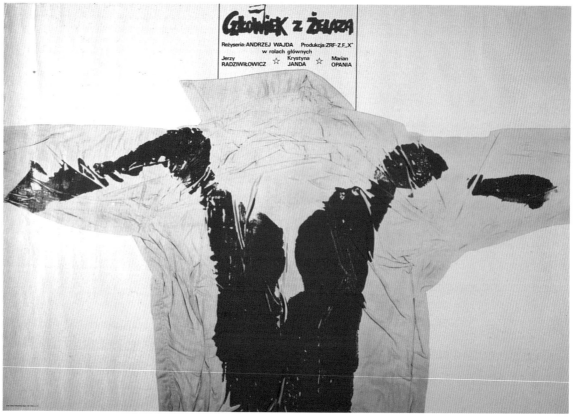

6.99

6.102
Sándor Pinczehélyi, *Posters 1971–1991*, 1991, Hungary, Moravian Gallery, Brno.

6.103
Feliks Büttner, *Human rights!*, 1989, GDR, Moravian Gallery, Brno.

6.104
Jindřich Štreit, *T-shirt stall in Buriatsko, Russia, 1997*, the photographer.

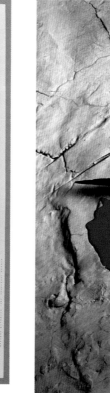

6.100

6.101

6.102

6.103

6.105
Trio, *Sara-Jevo*, December 1993, Sarajevo, Bosnia-Herzegovina, Moravian Gallery, Brno.

6.106
Ivar Sakk, *New Russia*, 1995, Estonia, silkscreen artist's edition, Moravian Gallery, Brno.

6.107
Andrei Logvin, *Hold on, Gregory!*, 1995, Russia, Moravian Gallery, Brno.

6.108
Visvaldis Asaris, *Latvia's way*, (on the occasion of elections), 1995, Latvia, poster maquette, the artist.

6.104

6.105

6.106

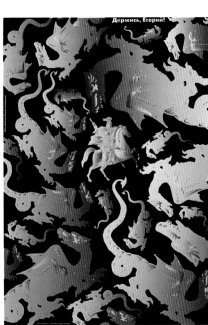

6.107

6.108

Zachvátí-li tě zahyneš!

6.109

6.110

6.111

6.112

6.113

6.114

6.115

6.116

6.117

6.118

6.119

6.120

6.109
U.R. Umělecká Reklama (Art Advertising Agency), *You'll perish if it gets hold of you*, 1941–43, Czechoslovakia, Museum of Decorative Arts, Prague.

6.110
Anon., *American way of life*, 1953, Czechoslovakia All Trade Union Archive, Prague.

6.111
G. M. King, *Get out!*, 1946, GDR, Academy of Fine Art, Berlin.

6.112
René Graetz, *Fight for peace*, 1950, GDR, Academy of Fine Art, Berlin.

6.113
Anon., *Battle ready!*, 1957, GDR, Thomas Hill.

6.114
Andrei Kolosov and Valeria Kovrigina, *Party. Communist Party of the Soviet Union*, c. 1989, Soviet Union, the artists.

6.115
Jan Moravec, *Exhibition. Yesterday, today, tomorrow*, 1960, Czechoslovakia, Moravian Gallery, Brno.

6.116
Vytautas Kaušinis, *All in the name of man for the welfare of man*, 1963, Soviet Lithuania, Juozas Galkus, Vilnius.

6.117
Zdeněk Chotěnovský, *Unanimously*, 1964, Czechoslovakia, poster maquette, Moravian Gallery, Brno.

6.118
Klaus Wittkugel, *We have fulfilled our pledge. Twenty years free of fascism*, 1965, GDR, Academy of Fine Art, Berlin.

6.119
Fritzsche, *Venceremos!*, 1974, GDR, Academy of Fine Art, Berlin.

6.120
Péter Pócs, *Pócs (P)art Forum*, 1990, Hungary, Moravian Gallery, Brno.

6.121
Lucian Tudose, *Commemoration of the seventh month after the revolution*, 21 July 1990, Romania.

6.122
Piotr Młodożeniec, *11 November 1918/1981*, 1981, Poland, Moravian Gallery, Brno.

6.123
Aleš Najbrt, *Spring 1968. Autumn 1989*, November 1989, Czechoslovakia, Moravian Gallery, Brno.

6.122

6.123

6.121

6.124
Anon., *Long live 1 May*, 1953,
Soviet Belorussia, Andrei
Sheliuto, Minsk.

6.125
Henryk Tomaszewski, *1 May.
Long live the workers' and
peasants' alliance*, 1954,
Poland, Museum of
Independence, Warsaw.

6.126
Vytautas Kaušinis, *1 May*,
1957, Soviet Lithuania,
Moravian Gallery, Brno.

6.127
Henryk Tomaszewski, *1 May*,
1960, Poland, private
collection.

6.128
Waldemar Świerzy, *1 May*,
1956, Poland, private
collection.

6.129
György Kemény, *1 May*, 1971,
Hungary, Hungarian National
Gallery, Budapest.

6.124

6.125

6.126

6.128

6.127

6.129

6.130
Andrzej Krajewski, *1 May
1972*, 1972, Poland, private
collection.

found itself posted in the windows of apartments in Warsaw on the eve of martial law. Mariusz Knorowski observed: 'According to the legend, the two scars on the Madonna's face occurred at the moment of foreign invasion of Poland. Presenting the outlines of the figure, the author did not forget about the golden aureole which he marked with national colours, that is, red and white. ... The identical motif can be found in the graphic work of Piotr Młodożeniec. ... It might as well be considered a *signum temporis*.'[53] As a suppressed discourse – it was forbidden to publicize religious meetings, for example – religious imagery provided a symbolic vocabulary at the time of the final collapse. In the German Democratic Republic the Church was also a focus of resistance, and Manfred Butzmann was derided by the authorities for his poster commemorating the dual seventh centenary of Berlin and the Church (6.100). Religion did not play a large part in public life in Hungary, but Christian symbolism was widely used. Péter Pócs and László Haris's election poster *301-SzDSz* (1989) (6.101), for the Alliance of Free Democrats, commemorated the reburial of Imre Nagy, the leader of the Hungarian Communist Party at the time of the 1956 uprising. The image made use of nails and blood familiar from the symbolism of the Passion. But religious symbolism was now one among many. As a result, a redundant state symbolism also had to compete with that of corporate capitalism. Many designers maintained a healthy scepticism of any totalizing symbolic vocabulary, capitalist, communist or national (6.102, 105–108).

The essential ambiguity and polysemy of the use of visual emblems can be caught in the series of posters presented here which include the human hand. The hand is a sign of human agency: it is the red-handed communist menace, the claw of capitalist corruption, the protector of the people from exploitation and war, the defiant fist of the struggle of the oppressed and the open palm of beneficent surplus. It votes and signals victory, and it is also a sign of betrayed hopes and lost ambition (6.109–121).

COMMUNIST CEREMONY

The regimes were the representatives of an occupying force, and public ceremonial was vital in the attempt to establish the foundational myths of the regimes, which had fresh loyalties and new geographical borders. Cyclical, repetitive, stylized, ordered and state-sponsored, the ceremonies presented an ideological message on a cosmological level, as if they were permanent, legitimate and authentic rather than cultural products with a specific political aim.[54] Ceremony was important because it gives form to belief by playing on the sentiments of the participants, but its meanings are complex. Communist parades were indebted to traditional religious processions and to mass gatherings held for political expression such as those on May Day which had traditional folk connotations as a celebration of spring. Under communism May Day was a formal occasion headed by a military parade, but it was never completely stable in its meaning. Many communist ceremonies were deliberately timed to coincide with religious and national festivals to make the new appear traditional, but the strategy simply kept memories alive. In Poland, for example, May Day replaced the commemoration of the 1791 constitution.[55]

6.131

6.132

6.133

The temporal juxtaposition increased emotional identification but failed to immerse the old totally in the new: under martial law in 1982 Solidarity reinstated National Day. For designers with an oppositional stance numerological patterns offered a challenge to the communist obsession with calendrical cycles and anniversaries (6.122, 123). Piotr Młodożeniec, for example, celebrated the founding of the Second Republic in a design which conflated that event with the Polish August. Executed in a stripped-down hand-made calligraphic style, it refused incorporation into the dominant aesthetic which had reduced political posters to a bland and banal repetition of socialist-realist convention, albeit fragmented, emblematic and often national in sentiment.

The essential ambiguity of communist ceremony can be observed in the heterogeneity, not to say the beauty, of May Day poster designs (6.124–136). The iconographies of socialist hegemony, solidarity, prosperity, harmony and peace are expressed in the imagery of the red flag, comradeship, dance, technological advance, flowers and the dove. Dance allowed the expression of national feelings, while the giving of flowers speaks of spring and is a gesture of friendship at a personal level. After the formal parades, people played music, danced, read poetry aloud, ate and drank alcohol. Public ceremonial was communist in content but formally traditional; the tension between official and personal meanings could engender identification with the regime only as an incidental by-product.

Abner Cohen has discussed the importance of symbolic rituals. For him, they work on ideological and sensory levels to mystify power relations while instilling moral

obligation. If rituals did not inspire political loyalty, they ensured apparent commitment and compliance. The former Vice-president of Yugoslavia and dissident, Milovan Djilas, gives a revealing account of a May Day festival to indicate just how important it was to the leadership:

> The issue of how to celebrate May Day caused the members of the Agitprop of the Central Committee, and particularly me, its director, no end of grief.
>
> As the organizational structure of celebrations grew, so did complaints, right there on the grandstand and later at Politburo meetings. … The criticism, however, was petty. Why did you have a poster of this leader and not that one? Why are some posters smaller than others? … Why is Stalin's picture smaller (or bigger) than Tito's? Tito complained the least, perhaps because every unit in the parade cheered him and carried his picture – bigger and better than the rest, except for Stalin's! … I made a proposal … specifying the number of posters to be used in the May Day celebration, of which leaders and how large, how many thousands of citizens should attend (the figure did not have to be exact), how many floats, how many, how much, all down the line. That brought an end to both criticism and spontaneity, from the top and from the bottom.[56]

In the 1960s and 1970s communist ceremonies became increasingly formal and militarized, the relatively spontaneous parades of the immediate post-war period giving way to meticulously planned and carefully choreographed festivals. May Day and other public ceremonials associated with communist supremacy, such as Victory Day, Revolution Day and (after 1955) Lenin's birthday, were ritualized symbolic displays which served to objectify communist power to 'politically numb' populations, who progressively paid them less and less

6.134
Vitalii Shostia, *1 May*, c.1980, Soviet Ukraine, private collection.

6.135
Krzysztof Ducki, *1 May SzDSz (Alliance of Free Democrats)*, 1989, Hungary, Moravian Gallery, Brno.

6.136
Andrei Logvin, *Welcome, festival of 1 May*, 1995, Russia, Moravian Gallery, Brno.

6.134

6.135

6.136

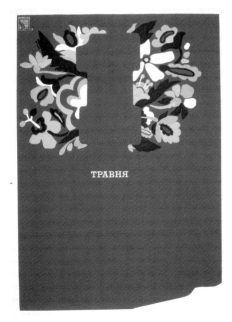

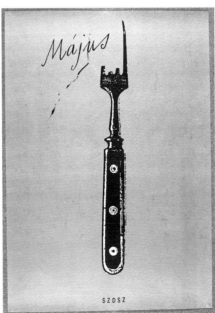

6.137
Irakly Moiseyevich Toidze,
*Fiftieth anniversary of the
October Revolution. Our
common festival*, 1967, Soviet
Union, Academy of Fine Art,
Berlin.

6.138
Karel Šourek, *Welcome, Red
Army*, 1945, Czechoslovakia,
Museum of Decorative Arts,
Prague.

6.139
A. Haase, *Never Munich*,
1948, Czechoslovakia, All
Trade Union Archive, Prague.

6.140
Wolfgang Frobus and Martin
Friedrich, *Weapons in the
service of the people*, 1989,
GDR, Academy of Fine Arts,
Berlin.

6.141
Jan Sawka, *Car of the year*,
1978, Poland, the artist.

6.142
David Černý and the
Neostunners, *Pink tank*, 1991,
Czechoslovakia, postcard,
private collection.

6.137

6.138

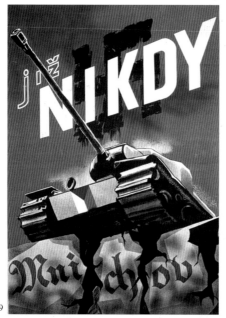

6.139

6.140

6.141

6.142

118

6.143

6.144

6.145

6.146

6.147

6.148

6.149

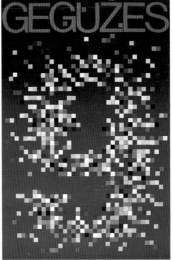

6.150

6.143
Mikhail Abramovich Gordon, *Onward to new victories*, 1945, Soviet Union, Leningrad, the artist.

6.144
Mikhail Abramovich Gordon, *Glory to the victors!*, 1969, Soviet Union, Mikhail Avvakumov, Moscow.

6.145
Tibor Gönczi (Gebhardt), *4 April 1945* (National Liberation Day), 1945, Hungary, Hungarian National Gallery, Budapest.

6.146
Nándor Szilvásy, *4 April*, 1972, Hungary, Hungarian National Gallery, Budapest.

6.147
Leonid Mikhailovich Nepomniashchy, *Victory Day*, 1975, Soviet Union, Mikhail Avvakumov, Moscow.

6.148
Nazarie Pavlin, *Thirty-fifth anniversary of 23 August. 1944–1979*, 1979, Romania, Museum of Fine Arts, Bucharest.

6.149
Hirth, photo. Yevgony Khaldei, *Thank you, our Soviet soldiers. Day of thirtieth anniversary of the Liberation*, 1975, GDR, Thomas Hill.

6.150
A. Kovelinas, *9 May. With the victory day*, 1988, Soviet Lithuania, Moravian Gallery, Brno.

6.151
Tadeusz Trepkowski, *1939.*
The war campaign will never
be repeated!, 1945, Poland,
Poster Museum, Wilanow.

6.152
Lex Drewinski, *1939–1989.*
For a mutual future learn from
the past, 1989, Poland,
Moravian Gallery, Brno.

attention.[57] Victory Day embodied what was, perhaps, the most important of the foundational myths for the new governments. Each country marked its anti-fascist credentials with the Nazi surrender to the Red Army. It was a highly potent moment, celebrating liberation from the Nazi yoke and the triumph of a new communist nationhood, but it was caught by the profound ambiguity of the guidance necessarily provided by the Red Army and the Kremlin. Nevertheless, to varying degrees, Victory Day parades, celebrations of the October Revolution on 7 November and the revolutionary heritage of Lenin were capable of generating a considerable impact, particularly for those who had opposed fascism. The sheer weight of the visual rhetoric, the months spent in preparation for major anniversaries of the victory in World War II, in particular, produced a complex weave of reaction. For the young it was yet another round of dutiful exercises and self-conscious, conditioned and superficial patriotic responses. For those who had direct experience of the war, it was a time of family remembrance: according to Nina Tumarkin the overstatement of official ceremony and the cant of the rhetoric produced offence and a sense of betrayal.[58] In affirmation or denial, the national and individual meaning of the defeat of fascism and of personal survival combined with the sheer force of spectacle: 'Norms and values become saturated with emotion, while the gross and basic emotions aroused by the sensory pole become ennobled through contact with values. The irksomeness of moral restraint is transformed into the love of goodness. Ritual symbolism is thus a mechanism which periodically converts the obligatory into the desirable.'[59]

May Day, Revolution Day, Lenin's birthday and Victory Day were but four of a multitude of communist ceremonials. Other annual events included International Women's Day on 8 March; Press Day and various festivals associated with communist youth, the armed forces and Soviet friendship. Quinquennial events celebrated the founding of the various national communist parties and the establishment of the Soviet Union. Tenth and fiftieth anniversaries were treated particularly seriously. The festivities had the express purpose of providing the regimes with an autonomous anti-fascist and anti-capitalist legitimacy, and paradoxically confirmed their subject status within the revolutionary cosmology of the Russian Revolution. Immutability, repeatability and exclusivity were of their essence.

The commemoration of founding events such as Victory Day or Revolution Day gave a temporal direction to the new regimes and stressed important themes such as the solidarity of the international working class (6.137). Historical time is framed within the cosmological time of revolution and the struggle against fascism. Events and personal experience are given meaning in the context of the overall narrative of the inevitable march of history. But, with the decline of the personality cult, death in the service of the country became almost an obsession and might be interpreted as a state attempt to produce an alternative to religion. The 1970s saw the major building programme of large-scale memorials to the sacrifices of the Great Patriotic War, and in Irkutsk, for instance, the giant memorial stands adjacent to the Polish Catholic church.[60]

One of the major iconographical motifs of the Great

6.151

6.152

6.153

6.154

6.155

6.156

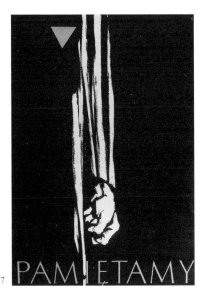

6.157

6.158

6.153
Schaumann, *Robert Ley. Without baggage one travels lighter. Anti-fascists, never forget that. Nuremburg, May 1945*, 1945, GDR, Academy of Fine Arts, Berlin.

6.154
T. Hanuš, *Do not forget Lidice – Ležáky*, 1945, Czechoslovakia, Moravian Museum, Brno.

6.155
R. Barnick, *International Buchenwald Meeting 10–16 April, Weimar*, 1952, GDR, Thomas Hill.

6.156
Juozas Galkus, *This must not be repeated*, 1957, Soviet Lithuania, artist's proof, Moravian Gallery, Brno.

6.157
Zbigniew Kaja, *We remember*, 1962, Poland, private collection.

6.158
Josef Flejšar, *Theresienstadt*, 1969, printed 1979, Czechoslovakia, artist's edition, Moravian Gallery, Brno.

6.159
Boris Mysliveček, *Auschwitz*,
1984, Czechoslovakia, artist's
edition, Moravian Gallery,
Brno.

6.160
Tadeusz Piechura, *The month
of national memory dedicated
to the victims of World War II*,
1981, Poland, Moravian
Gallery, Brno.

6.161
Gosha Kamenskich and
Tatyana Nemkova, *Trials of
the thirties*, 1988, Soviet,
poster maquette, Alexander
Lozenko.

6.162
József Árendás, *The Baldhead
and the Camp Whore. A drama
by Solzhenitsyn*, 1989,
Hungary, Hungarian National
Gallery.

6.159

6.160

6.161

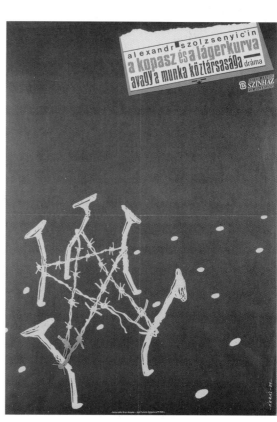

6.162

6.163

6.164

6.165

6.166

6.163
Krzysztof Ducki, *Hungary 12,000 km. Hungarian prisoners in Stalin's camps*, c. 1989, Hungary, Moravian Gallery, Brno.

6.164
Bator, *Katyń 1940*, 1990, Poland, Moravian Gallery, Brno.

6.165
Galina Tereshonok, *Transformation*, 1995, St Petersburg, Russia, the artist.

6.166
Igor Prokofiev (SLAP group), *Dedicated to the soldiers of the Great Patriotic War who died in the Hitlerite and Stalinist death camps*, 1991, Soviet Ukraine, poster maquette, Andre Budnik, Kiev.

6.167
Zoran Filipović, *Diary of a death*, 1992, Bosnia, Moravian Gallery, Brno.

6.168
Vasile Moldovan, *Timișoara! 27 December 1989*, Romania.

6.169
Sorin Lupța, *Rehearsal for May Day*, Bucharest, 1982.

6.167

6.168

Patriotic War and Victory Day is the Soviet T-34 tank. The tank was established in Soviet poster art by Gustav Klutsis as early as 1935, and after Stalingrad the T-34 soon became an important part of the Soviet symbolic arsenal. Celebrated on postcards and literally used as memorials, it attained mythological status. Widely credited as the most effective battle tank of World War II, its meaning lay less with military efficacy than its status as an emblem of the Promethean struggle of the Soviet people, who from their transported factories beyond the Ural mountains laboured and sacrificed to vanquish the Nazis. As a physical symbol instrumental in the defeat of fascism, it bestowed a moral authority on Soviet post-war claims to an empire in eastern and central Europe. These are claims testified to in the brutality of A. Haase's *Never Munich* (1948) (6.139), and in the optimism and residual modernism of Karel Šourek's *Welcome, Red Army* (1945) (6.138). But the tank is as emblematic of tyranny as of liberation. Soviet tanks crushed the Berlin uprising in 1953 and the Hungarian rebellion of 1956, and the tanks of the 'five brotherly armies' (Romania did not take part) rolled into Prague in the night of 20–21 August 1968. A lone protestor halted a line of tanks in Tiananmen Square, Peking, in June 1989.[61] Tanks had turned against the Ceausescu dictatorship in Romania, and Boris Yeltsin had harangued the military and the Russian people from the turret of a tank in August 1991, to neutralize the attempted *coup*, before turning tank guns on the parliament building in Moscow in November 1993. Nearly two years earlier, tanks had killed civilians in January 1991 on the streets of Vilnius in Lithuania as the country had struggled for independence. That event was

6.169

commemorated in the anonymous poster *Vilnius, 1991.01.13* (1991). It used all the techniques of the communist political posters of being direct and up-to-the-minute but pointed to a sad legacy of brutal oppression in the region. Though, as Antonin J. Liehm has argued, 'tanks don't usually have the last word in arguments about ideas'.[62]

In Czechoslovakia tank No. 23 was placed on a plinth in the Smíchov area of Prague. It was dedicated to the memory of Soviet troops who had died in the liberation of the city in May 1945. But, as Patrick Wright has pointed out, the first T-34s to enter Prague were not the Red Army's. The tanks had come with General Andrei Vlasov, who had raised maverick anti-Stalinist battalions from the ranks of Germany's Soviet prisoners before the Axis defeat at Stalingrad. The memorial was placed in a part of Prague which had fallen into the hands of the Czech resistance as the Wehrmacht fell back, but as a working-class area it was one the authorities wished to claim for communism. In the early hours of 28 April 1991, just over a week after the 121st anniversary of Lenin's birthday, David Černý and the Neostunners painted the memorial bright pink, and modified it with a vertical finger in emulation of the well known American gesture (6.142). It was a credible move: Václav Havel was President but the Red Army had not yet left Czech soil.[63] People were still very nervous, and not at all convinced that events might not take a turn for the worse. Needless to say, uproar ensued. The Minister of National Defence, Mr Dobrowsky, denounced it as an act of vandalism and offered hasty apologies to the Soviet embassy. The event provoked communist supporters to smear white paint on the memorial to Jan Palach at the Philosophy Faculty building of Charles University, and the memorial in West Bohemia dedicated to US soldiers who had lost their lives in liberating that part of Czechoslovakia was similarly desecrated. Soldiers were despatched to cover the tank and paint it green again. The memorial became the focus of agitprop activity and rock bands played in the square. The name of John Lennon was invoked. Postcards were distributed. Toy replicas of the pink tank were sold. Eventually the tank was quietly removed at dead of night to the city museum.[64] As an exemplar this struggle tells us that the use of the tank as an emblem is about different tellings of history, the control over histories and their physical articulation in the geography of cities and their public spaces. In 1989 a poster produced for the celebrations of the fortieth anniversary of the founding of the German Democratic Republic and featuring the photographic image of a contemporary tank as an index of the threat and protective might of the armed forces never saw the light of day (6.140).

Memorialization was a major tool in the state's arsenal but (6.143–50), as the story of tank No. 23 illustrates, it was a risky business. The year 1989 was the sixtieth anniversary of the beginning of World War II and, because of the hole in Soviet history covering the period of the Nazi–Soviet pact between 1939 and 1941, posters were produced commemorating the millions who died (6.152). Much was made of the legacy of the Nazi regime: the forced labour, the destruction brought about as the result of military aggression and the ingress of homeless ethnic German people into the GDR from other parts of the region such as Hungary, Poland and Czechoslovakia. A principal focus of re-education was the Nuremburg trials and many posters were produced in the Soviet zone of occupation which concentrated on the human cost of the war and Nazi guilt (6.153). Throughout the communist bloc, posters were produced on a regular basis as a testament to Nazi atrocities in Lidice, Theresienstadt and Auschwitz, as well as to the heroism of anti-fascist resistance and the dangers of militarism (6.154–160).

Poster artists did not cease to memorialize as the political ground began to shift (6.161). But the agendas subtly changed. In the Soviet Union the Pamyat (Memorial) group campaigned to publish and restore the names of those who had perished in the Gulag. In Hungary posters advertising plays which portrayed the human cost of Stalinism began to appear (6.162, 163). The communist government in Poland had been ousted from office in the first democratic elections in July 1989, and Gorbachev finally admitted the Soviet massacre of Polish officers in Katyń forest in 1940 (6.164). The hammer and the sickle were transformed into death's scythe and the graveyard cross, but they were also a reference to the sickle moon of the Muslim red crescent and the war in Afghanistan (6.165). Igor Prokofiev, a member of the SLAP group from Kiev, took the red star pinned to the gatepost or doorway of every household which had lost a relative in the armed forces, coloured it white, and supplied it with the caption 'Dedicated to the soldiers of the Great Patriotic War who died in the Hitlerite and Stalinist death camps' (6.166).[65] The tradition of commemoration in the political poster continues to this day, with many examples lamenting the loss of life in Romania in 1989 and the war in the former Yugoslavia (6. 167).

The regimes had created structures of memorialization and commemoration in the attempt to furnish themselves with a degree of legitimation and the poster played an important part in giving them visual form. In so doing the regimes successfully established patterns of public behaviour which in the end provided frameworks for other kinds of historical truth to be articulated in the political poster and the spontaneous street graphic (6.168). The emblems of national communism (6.169) are abandoned in favour of those of nationalism. The myths to which they had originally given support are subjected to interrogation, reinterpretation and deconstruction in a carnivalesque atmosphere generated by Gorbachev's reforms and the subsequent withdrawal of communist influence from public life.

NOTES

1   The Russian empire looked back to Hellenic traditions of deified Roman emperors and Constantinian Christendom: one God, one emperor, one empire. God's temporal representative on earth was the Holy Christian Emperor, who ruled, protected and nurtured the Christian Roman empire. Early medieval Constantinople had established a divinely sanctioned framework of strong, highly centralized, autocratic political authority. The leader was the mediator between the material and ideological worlds, a practice emulated by the Tsars. After the fall of Constantinople to the Turks, Moscow saw itself as the natural inheritor of its legacy. Tsar Alexander III (1881–94) defined this political ideology in the late nineteenth century in an official slogan to which all subjects of the Russian empire were expected to subscribe: 'Autocracy (absolute political authority vested in the Tsar and his governing bureaucracy), Orthodoxy (the official state Church, which validated the Tsar's supreme authority), and Nationalism (loyalty to the Russian Empire, ruled by the tsar).' See Dennis P. Hupchick, *Culture and History in Eastern Europe* (New York, St Martin's Press), 1994, p. 117.

2   Krushchev's so-called secret speech is quoted in full in *Krushchev Remembers*, translated by Strobe Talbot (London, Sphere Books), 1971, pp. 503–62.

3   'The East European Communist leaders imitated his every move and gesture. They made themselves the object of personality cults, and employed all the police methods appropriate to this oriental brand of despotism.' François Fejtö, *A History of the People's Democracies. Eastern Europe since Stalin* (Harmondsworth, Pelican Books), 1977, p. 11.

4   David King, *The Commissar Vanishes. The Falsification of Photographs and Art in Stalin's Russia* (Edinburgh, Canongate Books), 1997, pp. 28–30.

5   Lenin was deprived of his customary cap between 1929 and 1953, perhaps because it was considered too informal, or possibly bohemian in conjunction with his suit and tie. For further discussion see Victoria E. Bonnell, *Iconography of Power. Soviet Political Posters under Lenin and Stalin* (Berkeley, Los Angeles CA and London, University of California Press), 1997, p. 143.

6   Since 1945 Lenin's memory had been installed in communist ritual as a death cult with the building of the tribunal on top of the Lenin Mausoleum in Red Square. As Nina Tumarkin put it, 'The dead Lenin was a stepping stone for the living Stalin.' Nina Tumarkin, *Lenin Lives. The Lenin Cult in Soviet Russia*, enlarged edition (Cambridge, MA, and London, Harvard University Press), 1997, p. 255.

7   Christopher A. P. Binns, 'The Changing Face of Power: Revolution and Accommodation in the Development of the Soviet Ceremonial' I, *Man. The Journal of the Royal Anthropological Institute*, 14: 4 (1979) 602.

8   *Pergale (Victory)*, 4 April 1950, p. 52 (organ of the Soviet Writers of the Lithuanian SSR), quoted by Czesław Miłosz, *The Captive Mind* (Harmondsworth, Penguin Books), 1980, p. 231.

9   Posters from the 1920s typically pictured the hopes of the proletariat not in the figure of the great leader but in one of their number.

10   He is like Ilya Muromets, the giant of Russian folklore, picking old oaks from the forest, or Bogatyr Svyatogor lifting the earth. Elena Hellberg, 'Folklore, Might and Glory. On the Symbolism of Power Legitimation', *Nordic Journal of Soviet and East European Studies*, 3:2 (1986) 12.

11   Anatol Lieven, *The Baltic Revolution. Estonia, Latvia, Lithuania and the Path to Independence* (New Haven CT and London, Yale University Press), 1993, p. 122. In Latvia folkoric heroes had been revived in the nineteenth century in Ossian-type epics. Andrejs Pumpurs's Lacplesis (the Bear Tearer) was the most famous. For Pumpurs he was the emblem of a democratic Latvian future, for the communists he was the symbol of a sometimes misguided proletariat.

12   In late 1949 and early 1950 the Soviet Latvian Artists' Association expelled fifty members, a very high proportion of its total membership, for bourgeois, liberal, national and Western tendencies.

13   Latvia's revolutionary tradition goes back at least as far as the 1905 uprising against the Tsar. Latvia's independence of Russia was established only as late as 1920.

14   For a discussion of the symbolism and reception of the Palace of Culture and Science in Warsaw see David Crowley, 'People's Warsaw/Popular Warsaw', *Journal of Design History*, 10:2 (1997) 212–14.

15   Lieven, *The Baltic Revolution*, p. 114.

16   Arnolds Spekke describes the scenes after the Soviet expulsion in July 1941: 'The National Anthem and other patriotic songs were broadcast over the Riga radio. Latvian flags were flying all over the city. Soviet emblems were burnt in a multitude of small fires which were kindled in the streets which were crowded with people who felt an intense joy at being freed from the Bolshevik nightmare: they congratulated themselves on having escaped the Red Terror.' *History of Latvia. An Outline* (Stockholm, Goppers), 1951, p. 397.

17   Roughly 60 per cent of the population shortfall can be attributed to Soviet actions.

18   Spekke, *History of Latvia*, p. 392.

19   Lieven, *The Baltic Revolution*, p. 291.

20   Arnolds Spekke recounted what conditions were like under the first Soviet occupation in 1940 in his admittedly nationalist history: 'The feelings among the Latvians ... cannot be understood by anyone who has not himself lived under Soviet rule, subject to its domination ... the constant fear of being awakened at night by NKVD agents and taken away to an unknown destination without any reason being given, the constant necessity of professing love and admiration for a system which is actually loathed and feared, the impossibility of trusting one's friends or even members of one's own family, confinement to Soviet information and propaganda, an extremely low standard of living and similar things made people long for any change, since anything, it was argued, was better than life under this oppressive omnipresent regime which had a thousand eyes and ears and a multitude of suspicions.' *History of Latvia*, p. 397.

21   *The Cultural Front. Power and Culture in Revolutionary Russia* (Ithaca NY and London, Cornell University Press), 1992, p. 218. *Kulturnost* was implicitly contrasted with being uncultured, uncivilized, 'dark' and 'backward' like a peasant.

22   Boris Groys, 'Stalinism as an Aesthetic Phenomenon', in Alla Efimova and Lev Manovich (eds), *Tekstura. Russian Essays on Visual Culture* (Chicago and London, University of Chicago Press), 1993, p. 122.

23   See Nina I. Baburina, *The Soviet Political Poster 1917–1980* (Harmondsworth, Penguin Books), 1985.

24   It was the last Stalin monument to be completed in Europe and it stood the longest. Designed and executed by Otakar Švec, it was 13 m high. Inaugurated in 1955, the year of the sculptor's suicide, it was demolished in 1962.

25   Fejtö, *A History of the People's Democracies*, p. 10.

26 Forerunner of the KGB.

27 'Considering that a great number of people, marked out for displacement, have to be arrested and accommodated in special camps, and their families to proceed to places of special settlement in distant regions, it is necessary to initiate the operation of separation of the families from the fathers simultaneously without their being informed of their impending separation.' Spekke, *History of Latvia*, p. 392.

28 *The Sublime Object of Ideology* (London and New York, Verso), 1989, p. 75.

29 Peter Reddaway, *Uncensored Russia. The Human Rights Movement in the Soviet Union. The Annotated Text of the Unofficial Moscow Journal 'A Chronicle of Current Events' (Nos 1–11)* (London, Jonathan Cape), 1972, p. 425.

30 Mariusz Knorowski drew the attention of the authors to these posters.

31 In 1961 Krushchev ordered Stalin's body to be removed from the Lenin Mausoleum.

32 Jindřich Štreit was imprisoned in 1982 for defamation of the regime and these photographs are illustrated in Antonin Dufek, *Forbidden Photographs*, exhibition catalogue (Brno, Moranian Gallery), 1999.

33 See Barburina, *The Soviet Political Poster 1917–1980*, plate 44; Stephen White, *The Bolshevik Poster* (New Haven CT and London, Yale University Press, 1988), plates 6.1–2; and Bonnell, *Iconography of Power*, pp. 143–4.

34 Tumarkin, *Lenin Lives*, pp. 262–3.

35 This play indirectly contributed to the riots in Warsaw in early 1968.

36 See King, *The Commissar Vanishes*, pp. 66–73, for a full account of the uses of this particular photograph. See Bonnell, *Iconography of Power*, and Tumarkin, *Lenin Lives*, for further discussion of pre-war iconographies of Lenin.

37 See Viktor Zaslavsky, 'The Rebirth of the Stalin Cult in the USSR', *Telos. A Journal of Radical Thought*, 40 (1979) 5–18.

38 See Nina Tumarkin, *The Living and the Dead. The Rise and Fall of the Cult of World War II in Russia* (New York, Basic Books), 1994, for a fuller discussion of the course of the historical debates surrounding the legacy of communism which emerged in the late 1980s. Posters covering these topics are well illustrated in Marta Sylvestrová and Dana Bartelt, *Art as Activist. Revolutionary Posters from Central and Eastern Europe* (London, Thames & Hudson), 1992; and James Aulich and Tim Wilcox (eds), *Europe without Walls. Art, Posters and Revolution 1989–1993* (Manchester, Manchester City Art Galleries), 1993.

39 Tumarkin, *Lenin Lives*, p. 262.

40 Aradna Tyrkova quoted in *Lenin: A New Biography* (New York, Harold Shukman), 1994, p. xxxvii.

41 In Žižek's terms the revolution finds *jouissance*. For Anatoly Lunacharsky the Marxist religion was to overcome death through its link with the future, through man's perception of the 'universal connectedness of life, of the all-life, which triumphs even in death'.

42 Slavoj Žižek, *The Sublime Object of Ideology* (London and New York, Verso), 1989, p. 27.

43 Robert W. Thurston, 'Social Dimensions of Stalinist Rule. Humor and Terror in the USSR 1939–1941', *Social Dimensions*, 24:3 (1990–91) 547.

44 Žižek, *The Sublime Object of Ideology*, p. 29.

45 Dagmar/Dášenka in the caption puns on her name, Dagmar, and draws on associations with the children's novel *Dášenka* (Life of a Puppy) by Karel Čapek. Václavka is the name given to a mushroom which grows around the time of Václav's name day.

46 It was also an important part of the iconography of Tomasso Capanelli's city of the sun (1602) which had provided Lenin with inspiration for a 'monumental plan of propaganda', a conception which lay at the heart of all socialist decorative propaganda schemes. Capanella was a fanatic Catholic whose vision was that of a papal world state, 'an ideal city state which turned religion into science and the urban landscape into a museum and outdoor school … Lenin wanted cities that talked'. Richard Stites, *Revolutionary Dreams. Utopian Vision and Experimental Life in the Russian Revolution* (Oxford, Oxford University Press), 1989, p. 88.

47 Richard Stites suggests it may have been inspired by A. A. Bogdanov's *Red Star*. Bogdanov was one of the principal theorists of the prolecult.

48 The hammer is usually associated with masculine industrial labour and armaments work, while the sickle is regarded as more feminine and passive and is associated with agricultural work and the land.

49 The design was the result of a competition organized by Lenin and Anatoly Lunacharsky, the Minister of Culture.

50 It is tempting to see a reference to Durer's *Melancolia I* where the discarded compasses of her humanistic and rational heritage have been abandoned for a more assertive and bombastic vision founded in the vision of scientific Marxism-Leninism.

51 Unpublished paper, 'The De-artefactualisation of Post-war Soviet Society. Design and the Battle against Commodity Fetishism' given at *Socialist Artefacts, Places and Identities*, a research seminar at the Victoria and Albert Museum, London, 11 November 1998. See also *An Archaeology of Socialism* (Partidge Green, Berg Publishers), forthcoming.

52 Katalin Bakos, letter to the authors, 27 August 1998.

53 'A Kite in the Wind of History', unpublished ms, 1998.

54 Abner Cohen, 'Political Symbolism', *Annual Review of Anthropology*, 8 (1979) 100–1.

55 Ended in 1793 by a joint Russian and Prussian invasion leading to the second partition of Poland.

56 Milovan Djilas, *Tito. The Story from Inside*, translated by Vasilije Kojic and Richard Hayes (London, Weidenfeld & Nicolson), 1981, p. 112.

57 See Robert Rotenberg, 'May Day Parades in Prague and Vienna. A Comparison of Socialist Ritual', *Anthropological Quarterly*, 56:2 (1983) 62–8.

58 See Tumarkin, *The Living and the Dead*.

59 Cohen, 'Political Symbolism', 100.

60 Christopher A. P. Binns, 'The Changing Face of Power. Revolution and Accommodation in the Development of the Soviet Ceremonial System' II, *Man. The Journal of the Royal Anthropological Society*, 15:1 (1980) 178. Death in the service of one's country had been a major theme since 1965. Between 1965 and 1970, 6,000 memorials and obelisks, 38 parks and 600 gardens were built in memory of the World War II dead in Belorussia alone.

61 Tiananmen had figured as a touchstone for the democracy movements in the Eastern bloc in the months leading up to the collapse in November 1989.

62 'Franz Kafka in Eastern Europe', *Telos*, 23 (1975) 81.

63 The agreement to end the twenty-three-year-old occupation of Czechoslovakia by the Red Army was signed on 25 June 1991 and four days later the last troops left the country. In September 1990 the four powers gave up occupation rights to Germany, Soviet withdrawal from Poland began on 4 April 1991 and the last troops left Hungary in June 1991.

64 Patrick Wright, 'Why a Pink Tank made Prague see Red', *Guardian Review*, 25 July 1991, pp. 23–4.

65 Soviet soldiers who had been captured by Axis forces were sent to the Gulag on their return by the NKVD. Recent research has shown that large numbers of Russian nationals fought with the Wehrmacht as auxiliaries in what was to all intents and purposes a reignition of Civil War conflicts. There were up to 50,000 at Stalingrad, with an unknown but possibly significant proportion in arms.

На совість зроблено ремонт
хоч завтра на весняний фронт

CHAPTER SEVEN

THE COMMUNIST FUTURE

Political posters gave the party an image of how it wished itself and the nation to be.
They created a romantic and utopian fantasy supported by coercion and brutal party self-interest.
Marxist-Leninist philosophical faith in the ideals of the Enlightenment and in technological
and industrial progress, and the historical role of class conflict were based in the efficacy of
scientific rationalism (7.1). Logically, Marxism-Leninism could not understand itself as myth,
and it unleashed dystopian repressive political power, the careless exploitation of natural
resources and justified surveillance of its people, and denied people basic human rights of
freedom of movement and expression.

Inspired by the myth of revolution, the communist idyll was projected on to physically ruptured and psychologically traumatized communities. The unpopular drive for the collectivization of agriculture, for example, was carried out under a rhetorical umbrella of a rustic utopia of nurturing contentment and national sentiment. In contrast to the evil empire of the West, the subject states were populated with well provided, happy, enthusiastic, virtuous and moral people. It was an imaginary, unitary and ultimately global construction of a cornucopia based on the perfection of agriculture, heavy industry and giant civil engineering projects. Dedicated, egalitarian workers of the new ruling class would rise up out of the social injustice, inequality and the historical contradictions of capitalism. The new people were the natural product of the inevitable march of history. Capitalism in the body of European fascism had been destroyed by the might of the Red Army and the political power of the communist party: the new age had dawned. Exceptionally, in Hungary the imagery was not exclusively of labour but pictured people at leisure (7.2). Richard Stites and Vera Tumarkin have each pointed out that much of the inspiration for these visions can be found in the final pages of Leon Trotsky's *Literature and Revolution*, where: "'Man would rebuild the earth to his own taste by re-registering mountains, rivers, meadows, fields and steppes through technology" … it would be subjected to a "general industrial and artistic plan" where "Physiological experiments of science would transform the body, balance metabolic growth, and reduce morbid fear of death." The resultant "superman" would "rise to the heights of Aristotle, a Goethe or a Marx. And above this ridge new peaks will rise".[1] Tadeusz Gronowski gave the vision a unique neoclassical allegorical expression in a neoclassical style redolent of the 1930s (7.1). Unsurprisingly, the Trotskyite origin of this communist vision was a constant source of muted embarrassment to the authorities.

The era of post-war reconstruction was impossibly hard. According to official statistics, in the Soviet Union alone 70,000 villages and 1,700 towns and cities had been destroyed from 1941 to 1945. Population shifts took place on an unimaginable scale as borders and spheres of influence were redrawn. The infrastructure was badly damaged; able-bodied men were few and much of the work had to be done by hand, often by women. Conditions were very bad, as economic recovery was given priority over human welfare.[2] At first, volunteer labour was given happily enough and, as David Crowley has observed, the days designated for unpaid work were viewed by the people as a form of patriotic and meaningful recreation.[3] But later the state realized the political potential of the phenomenon and designated labour days to appropriate this collective altruism as spectacle, in the end forcing workers to give up a day's paid work for the benefit of the state (7.3). Labour days paralleled official ceremonial and the other new festivities of the communist state.

Designers involved with parties dedicated to the democratic reconstruction of the region and, later, to the creation of 'national communism' generated relative independence of form and iconography, while at the same time maintaining a clear generic relationship with Stalinist iconographies of giant civil engineering schemes and Stakhanovite labour. As Mariusz Knorowski has pointed out, there was reliance on metonymy, later to become a vital characteristic of the most advanced poster design in the region.[4] The imagery was often fragmentary and denied explicit narrative readings. It owed clear debts to European modernism or, more particularly, to *la moderne* in its numerous immanent and national classical and radical forms (7.4).

Such deviations could be easily tolerated within A. A. Zhdanov's edict of 'national in form and socialist in content', but there was more to it than that. Even under the

(detail of 7.42)

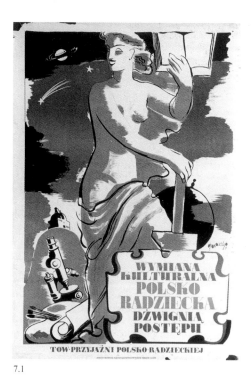

7.1

7.2

7.4

7.3

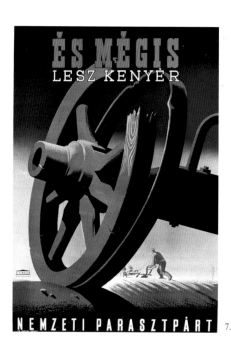

7.5

7.6

7.7

7.8

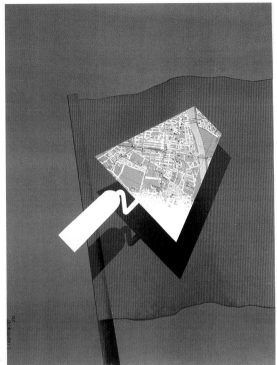

7.9

7.10

7.1
Tadeusz Gronowski, *The cultural exchange between Poland and the Soviet Union is the mainspring of progress*, 1947, Poland, Poster Museum, Wilanow.

7.2
Tibor Gönczi (Gebhardt), *The end of summer in the beautiful chalets of Balaton*, 1952, Hungary, Hungarian Museum of Contemporary History, Budapest.

7.3
Anon., *KSČ. Work mobilization for all members, 1–2 September 1945*, 1945, Czechoslovakia, Moravian Museum, Brno.

7.4
ŠAFR, *Spirit and fist. Honour to work!*, c. 1948, Czechoslovakia, Museum of Decorative Arts, Prague.

7.5
György Konecsni, *And still we'll have bread,* National Peasant Party, 1945, Hungary, Hungarian National Gallery, Budapest.

7.6
Kurt Fiedler, *The year of the Grand Initiative*, 1946, GDR, Berlinische Gallery, Berlin.

7.7
Tibor Gönczi (Gebhardt), *Forward with the Three Year Plan!*, 1948, Hungary, Hungarian National Gallery, Budapest.

7.8
Anon., *Your proposal, a building in stone. Ready in November*, 1950, GDR, Thomas Hill.

7.9
Tadeusz Trepkowski, *We build socialist Warsaw!*, 1950, Poland, private collection.

7.10
Jindřich Marco, *Ruins of the Warsaw ghetto*, March 1947, the photographer.

7.11
László Káldor, *Building a country*, Social Democratic Party, 1945, Hungary, Hungarian National Museum, Budapest.

7.12
Filo (Ilona Fischer), *Every hand should take part in the rebuilding*, Hungarian Communist Party, 1946, Hungary, Hungarian National Gallery, Budapest.

7.13
P5P (Working Fifth Programme), *Thirty years of the republic. Victory of the people's democracy. Five Year Plan. Way to socialism*, 1948, Czechoslovakia, All Trade Union Archive, Prague.

7.14
Tadeusz Trepkowski, *Warsaw*, 1952, Poland, private collection.

7.11

7.12

7.13

7.14

7.15

7.16

7.17

7.18

7.15
Gitta Mallász, *Hungary*, 1949,
Hungary, Hungarian National
Gallery, Budapest.

7.16
Jindřich Marco, *Ruins of the
chain bridge and the castle*,
Budapest, June 1945, the
photographer.

7.17
Anon., *Build Berlin!*, 1951,
GDR, Berlinische Gallery,
Berlin.

7.18
Jan Brukner, *Citizens build
their town. You help too!*,
1950, Czechoslovakia,
Moravian Gallery, Brno.

7.19
R. Barnick, *More current for the construction of socialism. Save current, avoid power cuts*, 1952, GDR, Thomas Hill.

KOMUNIZM
– TO WŁADZA RADZIECKA PLUS ELEKTRYFIKACJA

7.20

7.20
Mieczysław Berman,
*Communism – it is the rule of
the soviets plus electrification*,
1955, Poland, Museum of
Independence, Warsaw.

7.21
Klaus Wittkugel, *For the
peace treaty, for the peace and
unity of the nation*, 1961,
GDR, Academy of Fine Art,
Berlin.

7.22
Tibor Bánhegyi, *Home
insurance for each flat!*, 1965,
Hungary, Hungarian National
Gallery, Budapest.

7.21

Mit dem Friedensvertrag
zu Frieden und Einheit der Nation!

Mit dem Sozialismus
zum Glück des Volkes!

Wählt die Kandidaten der Nationalen Front!

7.22

minden
lakáshoz...

HÁZTARTÁSI BIZTOSÍTÁS !

tightest Soviet control, the parties within the Soviet sphere of influence always had their own national agendas which found their aesthetic expression in the political posters produced on their behalf. Parties not yet emasculated by the communists, such as the Social Democrats in Hungary, avoided explicitly socialist iconography. Many designs featured the pick rather than the hammer, and there were other very common motifs such as the wheel, the plough and the hoe which were utilized as emblems of the restoration of agricultural productivity (7.5–7). Typically, collectivization propaganda was forthright and grandiose and relied for its effect on exaggerated perspectives and distortions of scale.

In Poland and Hungary the trowel and the brick carried the metonymic force of reconstruction, and lent themselves to interpretation within abstracted designs by radical poster designers such as Tadeusz Trepkowski (7.9), László Káldor (7.11), Filo (7.12) and the Czech design group P5P (7.13). The city of Warsaw had been completely demolished by the Nazis and in the official rhetoric its name was the emblem of reconstruction (7.10, 14).

In Germany the imagery of reconstruction tended to dwell on the Nazi legacy of suffering and the cost of the war. The dispossessed, the 'returnees',[5] widows and orphans, and the concentration camps were prominent as part of political re-education.[6] The emphasis was on guilt and retribution. For example, few posters commemorate the heroic efforts of the *Trummerfrauen*[7] in the rebuilding of the devastated cities. Efforts at heroicization were directed at youth. *Build Berlin!* (1951) (7.17) encapsulates the image of the new generation in dislocated perspectives and an expressively dynamic style. It makes an interesting comparison with Jan Brukner's *Citizens build their town. You help too!* (1950) (7.18), where the task of reconstruction is related unproblematically to working-class labour in a design which makes effective use of photo-montage as a demonstration of an unsullied socialist heritage.

The communists set out to modernize the economies of central and eastern Europe, at first to bolster the Soviets' own war-ravaged economy, and later to compete with advanced Western capitalism. Electrification was one of their objectives. The policy was revolutionary in origin. Lenin addressed the Eighth Party Congress in December 1920 and coined the slogan: 'Communism equals Soviet power plus the electrification of the entire country' (7.19, 20). Electricity was the revolutionary and emancipatory light of communism made real. It signified an end to the darkness of ignorance, superstition and illiteracy, and embodied the triumph of scientific rationalism over nature. Electrification was a material metaphor for the

industrialized, scientifically planned and universal utopia that communism represented, and it offered designers the possibility of developing novel solutions to promote political agendas.

The first Five Year Plans were symptomatic of the integration of reconstruction into what David Crowley has called the 'core of the command structure of the planned economy, and the core of the Party's programme'.[8] Bold monumentalized numbers of the Six, Five and Two Year Plans provided the armatures for novel, relatively individualistic designs and were variously forged, transported, constructed and gave shelter. They signalled the heroic effort demanded by the new economic, industrial and agricultural targets required to bring about communism in practice. As numbers they conform to the picture of a controlled, quantified and measured society. In Hungary the design partnership So-Ky integrated into its vocabulary an iconography based on technical and architectural drawing (7.25). The clean lines and carefully controlled colour planes gave expression to the modernistic vision of communism, not simply as industrial and economic regeneration subject to scientific laws, but as a grand vision hinged on the idea of the national economy as a single giant manufacturing plant. For Marxism-Leninism, the factory was the model for society as a whole, subject to both rational order and centralized organization: it was also the blueprint for repressive totalitarianism. Striking though these designs are, they are the embodiment of the social order and they express the ideological premises of Marxism-Leninism more effectively, accurately and revealingly than more orthodox illustrations of party policy.

When Nicolae Ceausescu came to power in Romania, effort was directed towards the development of heavy steel and petro-chemical industries and in political posters images of industrial plant, scaffolding and cooling towers form the decorative motifs. Colourful and emblematic, they have a quality at odds with the experience of life as it was lived in a country where 'Draconian economic laws milked the working class and the peasantry, allowing the general secretary to boost his credit rating abroad while many went hungry in a country that was once the breadbasket of Europe'.[9] The disregard of the people may be indicated by the total lack of human presence in posters from the late 1970s.

Construction was important in communist rhetoric, and it was applied as much to the built fabric of society as to its political structure and spiritual well-being. Contrary to the elegant blandishments offered by Klaus Wittkugel, housing was a major political issue in the region, particularly in the German Democratic Republic, where it was an urgent problem for the government. The photo-montage *For the peace treaty, for the peace and unity of the nation* (1969) offers a mirage of industrial and domestic plenitude (7.21). The position was similar in Hungary: visions of building supported a dream of domestic and material security as part of a process of embourgeoisement promoted by the party in place of real political and economic achievement (7.22, 23). A few years later, critical poster artists such as Joseph W. Huber and Manfred Butzmann were to put their own gloss on life as it was lived in the GDR in simple, self-effacing photo-montage designs which placed the slogans of the party in juxtaposition with photographic images of the 'reality' of life (7.27, 28). In the Soviet Union, Viktor Pishii ruminated on the consequences of the grandiose gestures of the motherland (7.29).

In the 1920s and early 1930s the machine had stood for harmony and progress. But under Stalin it had been more or less completely superseded by the image of the hero. Represented in epic struggles against impossible odds, the machine became the tool of the Soviet hero. But in the post-war period technology made a comeback. Trains had been a favourite Soviet motif in the late 1920s, but as the geographical spread of the party increased and the historical lineage of the iconography extended, so their symbolism was enriched. Since the nineteenth century, throughout Europe and America, railways had been a symbol of industrial progress, speed of communication and the control of new lands. They were a powerful emblem in the wake of the destruction of war. Jo Brager's *Forward with the Two Year Plan!* (1948) (7.30) illustrates a train accelerating towards the future with almost expressionist verve, pushing aside economic saboteurs, the black market, anti-Soviet

rabble rousers, reaction, corruption and warmongers. A Polish poster by A. Werka, *Going to the west (recovered territory)* (1945) (7.32), cloaks the transportation of Poles from the east of the country to the part that was formerly part of Germany in an image of progress. Soviet examples are less abstracted and tend to include a human agency of command (7.33). Paradoxically, the heroic iconography is not individualistic and speaks of increasing concern with centralized control continuing well into the 1970s (7.34). But as those who opposed the Soviets were quick to point out, the train was also possessed of a dark anti-humanitarian side as it sped its way east to the primitive and life-threatening conditions of the Gulag (7.35).

Katerina Clark has described Stalin's project of modernization as an attempt to bring the city to the country. In the 1930s the struggle with nature was the most important Stalinist image as the 'machine was brought out of the city and into the garden': 'The great hydroelectric stations, which were the pride of all, were built to tame the arbitrary and destructive powers of the rivers. Collectivized, modernized agriculture would not be slave to the whims of climate. Drought was to be combated with dams, shallow waterways with canals and so on. The machine would triumph over elemental forces.'[10] Stalin was identified with these gigantist projects, and in his absence the colossal figure of a construction worker embodied the triumphant will of the people in posters demonstrating Soviet dominance over nature and capitalist exploitation (7.36). This poster by Viktor Koretsky was published in Soviet and national language versions and was meant as an example to follow. The common slogan was 'What the Soviet Union is

7.23
István Czeglédi, *91,000 newly built flats in Budapest in the fourth Five Year Plan*, 1971, Hungary, Hungarian National Gallery, Budapest.

7.24
Pohrib, *Day of Liberation, 23 August*, 1970, Romania, private collection.

7.25
So-Ky (László Sós and Éva Kemény), *The Twelfth Congress of the Hungarian Socialist Worker's Party*, 1980, Hungary, Hungarian National Museum, Budapest.

7.23

7.24

7.25

7.26
Miron Lukianov and Leonid Nepomniaschy, *To quality Five Year Plan. Working guarantee!*, 1976, three sheets, Soviet Union, Mikhail Avvakumov, Moscow.

7.27
Manfred Butzmann, *A place for trees,* 1978, GDR, the artist.

7.28
Joseph W. Huber, *Government Street, c.* 1985, GDR, postcard, private collection.

7.29
Viktor Pishii, *My homeland is not a pompous place, c.* 1990, Soviet Ukraine, Andrei Budnik.

7.26

7.27

7.29

7.28

7.30

7.31

7.32

7.33

7.34

7.35

7.30
Jo Brager, *Forward with the Two Year Plan!*, 1948, GDR, Berlinische Gallery, Berlin.

7.31
Jenö Molnár, *Following the example of the Soviet railway workers, we are building the socialist railway*, 1950, Hungary, Museum of Contemporary History, Budapest.

7.32
A. Werka, *Going to the west (recovered territory)*, 1945, Poland, Poster Museum, Wilanow.

7.33
V. Berezhovsky, *Forward to the new, great development of socialist transport!*, 1951, Soviet Union, Academy of Fine Art, Berlin.

7.34
Juri Golubev, *For the transport of loads. Exact rhythm and speed*, 1976, Soviet Union, Andrei Budnik, Kiev.

7.35
Anon., *You want to go to Siberia too?*, 1944, Hungary, Hungarian Museum of Contemporary History, Budapest.

7.36
Viktor Koretsky, *Peace will win! Kubyshev's power station*, 1950, Soviet Union (Czech version), private collection.

7.37
J. Kaiser and J. Koukolský, *Let us learn Russian. Let us learn from the Soviet peoples. Work, think, live in a new way*, 1951, Czechoslovakia, All Trade Union Archive, Prague.

7.38
Wojciech Fangor, *The friendship, example and help of the Soviet Union guarantee fulfilment of the Six Year Plan*, 1950, Poland, Museum of Independence, Warsaw.

7.36

7.37

7.38

7.39

7.40

7.41

7.42

7.43

7.44

7.39
Anon., *BAM (Baikal–Amur Railway)*, 1970s, three sheets, Soviet Union, Andrei Budnik, Kiev.

7.40
Anon., *Day of Learning, 12 June 1952. We teach, we learn, we struggle for peace*, 1952, GDR, Thomas Hill.

7.41
Valdemārs Valdmanis, *Science and work – foundation of the great harvest!*, 1949, Soviet Latvia, National Library, Riga.

7.42
Valery Viter, *Repairs have to be done to be ready for the spring front*, 1970, Soviet Ukraine, private collection.

7.43
Wolfgang A. Schlosser, *To help the country harvest. KSČ*, 1946, Czechoslovakia, Museum of the Working Class Movement, Prague.

7.44
Anon., Hungarian Communist Party, *More machines – more bread*, 1945, Hungary, Hungarian Museum of Contemporary History, Budapest.

7.45
Vadim Volikov, *Glory to the Soviet man. The first man in space, Vostock, 12 April 1961. Glory to Soviet science*, 1961, Czechoslovakia, Moravian Gallery, Brno.

7.46
Jochen Fiedler, *Juri Gagarin, 12 April 1961*, 1981, GDR, Thomas Hill.

7.47
Valentin Viktorov, *USSR, home of cosmonautism*, 1964, Soviet Union, Academy of Fine Art, Berlin.

7.48
Vladimir Potapov and V. Toders, *For country – the wish for security of energy!*, 1986, Soviet Union, Andrei Budnik.

7.45

7.46

7.47

7.48

7.49

7.50

7.51

7.52

7.53

7.54

7.49
Vladimir Chaika, *untitled* (devoted to the memory of the victims of Chernobyl), 1996, artist's edition, Moravian Gallery, Brno.

7.50
Juris Dimiters, *untitled*, 1988, Soviet Latvia, Moravian Gallery, Brno.

7.51
Jonas Gudmonas, *October. Progress of mankind!*, 1987, Soviet Lithuania, Moravian Gallery, Brno.

7.52
Jonas Gudmonas, *Love – protect!*, 1972, Soviet Lithuania, Moravian Gallery, Brno.

7.53
Juris Dimiters, *?*, 1981, Soviet Latvia, Phillip Granville, Lords Gallery, London.

7.54
Tadeusz Piechura, *Piece of earth, piece of sky, piece of bread … c'est la vie!*, 1985, Poland, Moravian Gallery, Brno.

7.55
Anon., *Stop Nagymaros,
Danube Dracula*, INCONNU
group, 1988, Hungary,
Hungarian Museum of
Contemporary History,
Budapest.

7.56
Joachim Thurn, *21 November
1989 on the second day of the
Wall. Action on the east side of
the Berlin Wall in Potsdamer
Platz.* (The photograph shows
Manfred Butzmann with the
poster *Citizens! Don't stop
long at the car feast!*), 1989,
GDR, Joachim Thurn.

today, we will become tomorrow!' Soviet supremacy was
asserted in every field of human endeavour as part of a
political, economic and polemical strategy designed to keep
the countries of the communist bloc in their place (7.37).
The friendship, example and help of the Soviet Union
guaranteed success, and in scale the figures embody the
epic and triumphant struggle between new socialist man,
geography and the elements (7.38). What none of these
posters can reveal is the human cost and the extent of the
work carried out under very difficult conditions not just by
'politicals' used as slave labour, but by an exploited and
downtrodden civilian work force.[11] The biggest civil
engineering project of the 1970s was the development of
the Baikal–Amur railway. The authorities encouraged a
revival of these iconographies and the whole project was
compared, metaphorically, with the achievements of Rus
bogatyri, or ancient knights who had unified the kingdom
under Ivan the Terrible, in a strategy devised to inspire the
younger generation, who, the authorities quite rightly felt,
were in danger of losing their communist faith (7.39). What
success it did have among the young was generated by the
high levels of pay, rather than by memories of national or
communist heroics.

Heroic struggle and the conquest of new frontiers was
not simply a battle of will against impossible odds.[12] The
command economy demanded careful planning, and in the
1960s, 1970s and 1980s the representation of the technical
and scientific intelligentsia competed with iconic images of
industrial and agricultural labour (7.40). The countryside,
for example, was increasingly collectivized with varying
degrees of success. Posters exalted the labours of the new

technocratic and scientific intelligentsia who brought
specialist knowledge and industrialized farming techniques
to promise ever more abundant harvests (7.41). Wolfgang
A. Schlosser's *To help the country harvest* (7.43) combines
photographic and schematic elements to illustrate the
relationship between the city and the country. In the
foreground, workers assemble outside their factory before
going out to help the collective farmers with the harvest.
The grain is taken to the rural village and the loaves of
bread roll back to the city in a projected cycle as ordered as
the universe itself. Despite the emphasis on mechanization,
Schlosser shows agricultural labour as a manual pursuit, in
contradiction to many posters relating to the rural economy,
where, if the posters were to be believed, fleets of tractors
waited on every collective farm (7.42, 44). According to
Edward Crankshaw, there were only 600,000 tractors in the
whole of the Soviet Union by 1950, and most of them were
unusable because of poor maintenance and the lack of spare
parts.[13] Even as late as the 1970s, Soviet and communist
leaders believed their own fraudulent statistics and thought
the excessive targets they had set themselves were possible
to attain. Such was the strength of that faith, that even
leaders in the West began to believe the communist
command economy capable of overhauling Western
capitalism.

Until the American moon landing in 1969, space
exploration was a key element in the propaganda of the
Cold War and a potent symbol of technological
achievement. The new frontier of space produced a
generation of Soviet heroes worthy of the aviators,
explorers and engineers of pre-war Stalinist popular culture.

7.55

7.56

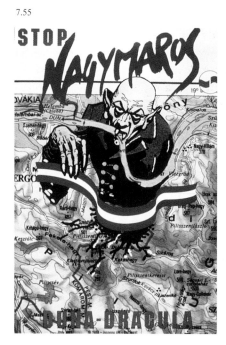

Many posters bore the likeness of Yuri Gagarin[14] (7.45, 46). Valentin Viktorov's *USSR, home of cosmonautism* (1964) (7.47) shows a fleet of rockets shooting out into space as notification of the scale of the assault on the new frontier. The poster takes as its inspiration the monument placed at the entrance of the Exhibition of the Achievement of the People's Economy in Moscow. At over 100 m in height, the titanium-coated monument to the conquest of space rises up to the sky in a giant streamlined sweep. But the propaganda effort was overblown and Muscovites quickly dubbed it the Impotent's Dream.[15] The space race and its ideology of scientific and technological progress were an illusion which obscured its value to the arms race and its cost to the people in depressed living standards.

The technological scientific dream finally came to an end with Chernobyl. The explosion at the nuclear plant in 1986 revealed the fragility of Soviet achievement and accelerated the process of *glasnost* and *perestroika*. Once the Gorbachev administration realized the extent of the disaster there could be no international, or even national, cover-up. A contemporary poster praised technological advance in bringing nuclear-generated electric power, and it was indisputably beneficial to the Soviet people (7.48). Even after the disaster it was necessary to keep the unaffected reactors working to provide essential power during the winter months. But five years later the benefits were far from clear, with poster makers tackling the impact on tourism and the long-term health of survivors (7.49). Computers were often used in posters to signal technological sophistication, but they were unloved by the *nomenklatura*, since the last thing they needed was accurate statistics or a class of computer experts who might undermine their control of figures in what was, by the 1970s and 1980s, a deeply corrupted command economy structured by the illusion of achievement (7.50, 51).

The illusion did not delude the people. Even the communist party was aware of the degree of cynicism abroad in the population and compounded it by allowing the production of posters which had their rhetorical origins in Western counter-cultural movements of the 1960s (7.52). Nuclear disaster is not the exclusive preserve of the communist bloc – any more than large-scale civil engineering projects – but the response of poster designers was a measure of increasing democratization. Ecological and green groups were increasingly tolerated in the 1980s and concern for the environment was indissolubly linked with issues of freedom of expression and movement. The emergence of these new modes of discourse combined with new stylistic strategies to challenge the limits of the officially defined (7.53). Poster design and its subjects became part of a wider reassessment of established conventions about the real and socialism, and the relationship between the two. Piechura's poster, for example, picks up on the iconography of the loaf of bread. No longer a sign of the abundant relationship between city and country, it signals man's relations with the environment as a whole (7.54).

Ecological issues were a focus of alternative politics in the 1970s in Europe across the divide. The widespread realization dawned, particularly among the young, that whole areas of Europe had become unhealthy, that many rivers and lakes had become barren of life and, most dramatically, that swathes of European forests had begun to die. Something of the very essence of what it means to be central European in folk myth and art was at risk. The promise of a golden future, of a technologically clean and utopian existence, could not be sustained in the face of statistics which showed air pollution to be four times worse in parts of Czechoslovakia and the GDR than in the West. Environmental awareness challenged the party's founding myths and was necessarily tied to political life. In the 1980s demonstrations against pollution in Poland were inextricably bound up with human rights agendas and the struggles of Solidarity. Similarly, in Czechoslovakia, Charter 77 made the ecological crisis part of its programme. Perhaps the greatest triumph in this direction was the achievement of the Danube Circle group in halting the Danube basin dam, a project supported by both the Hungarian and the Czechoslovak governments (7.55). Crucially, communist disregard for the environment bore a very real political price as poster designers and their public began to give expression to their disquiet (7.56).

The dominant rhetoric of progress and achievement was subjected to ironic and satirical treatment. From the mid-1980s poster makers were independently attacking the system which after so many years of broken promises and new Five Year Plans was still failing to deliver. Wolfgang Janisch's *Socialism: where the bright light is, is deep shadow* (*c.* 1985) (7.58), reduces the glow of socialism's dawn to a charcoal-black shadow where no light can penetrate. Januszewski's poster commemorating the twentieth anniversary of the Polish Workers' Party depicts a brick wall as the background to revolutionary graffiti (7.57) but later designs such as Joseph W. Huber's *Now – future* (*c.* 1985) (7.59) and Boris Mysliveček's *Go!* (1984) (7.60) make use of bricks to comment on the state of socialism as it really existed. The image of the wall was particularly significant in Germany, and it had become a physical expression of the division of Europe. Bricks, as we have seen, were an important part of the iconography of reconstruction, but here they have been fashioned into solid obstacles which impede progress and inhibit movement. It

7.57
Zenon Januszewski, *Twentieth anniversary of the Polish Workers' Party (PWP)*, 1962, Poland, private collection.

7.58
Wolfgang Janisch, *Socialism*, c. 1985, GDR, the artist.

7.59
Joseph W. Huber, *Now – future*, c. 1985, GDR, Moravian Gallery, Brno.

7.60
Boris Mysliveček, *Go!*, 1984, Czechoslovakia, Moravian Gallery, Brno.

7.61
Predrag Došen, *Stopped sands of time*, 1995, Croatia, Moravian Gallery, Brno.

7.57

7.58

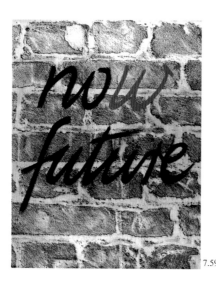

7.59

7.60

7.61

is worth remembering that the memorial to the dead of Stalingrad was also constructed of brick rather than the more usual monumental materials of bronze and stone. Similarly, Pedrag Došen's *Stopped sands of time* (1995) (7.61) mutates and continues the theme of the construction of the future with sandbags from the war in the former Yugoslavia.

NOTES

1   Quoted by Richard Stites, *Revolutionary Dreams. Utopian Vision and Experimental Life in the Russian Revolution* (Oxford, Oxford University Press), 1989.
2   The symbolism of the national anthem of the newly founded German Democratic Republic written by Johannes R. Becher and Hans Eisler in 1949 expressed the situation rather well. *Auferstanden aus Ruinen und der Zukunft zugewandt,* / 'Arisen from the ruins, turned towards the future, / let us serve you well, Germany, united fatherland. / We must conquer all need, and we'll conquer it together / And we'll yet succeed in making the sun shine as never before over Germany.'
3   David Crowley, 'People's Warsaw/Popular Warsaw', *Journal of Design History* special issue: *Design, Stalin and the Thaw* (1997) 203–24.
4   'A Kite in the Wind of History', unpublished ms, 1998.
5   Ethnic Germans expelled to the Soviet Zone in Germany by other national governments.
6   Images of the camps neglected to indicate their current use as places of internment for former Nazis and Wehrmacht troops.
7   *Trummerfrauen* was the word used to describe the women, literally 'rubble women', who helped clear the streets and rebuild the cities destroyed by Allied action.
8   Crowley, 'People's Warsaw/Popular Warsaw', 209.
9   Trond Gilberg, 'Romania in the Year 1990', in Joseph Held (ed.), *The Columbia History of Eastern Europe in the Twentieth Century* (New York, Columbia University Press), 1992, p. 290.
10   Katerina Clark, *The Soviet Novel. History as Ritual* (Chicago, University of Chicago Press), 1985, pp. 100–1.
11   See Stephen Kotkin, *Magnetic Mountain. Stalinism as a Civilization* (Berkeley CA, University of California Press), 1995.
12   The 3,500 km-long Baikal–Amur Magistral (BAM) cut through the eastern Siberian taiga. Three thousand bridges and 30 km of tunnels were built, and associated environmental and ecological damage went unheeded.
13   *Krushchev's Russia* (Harmondsworth, Penguin Books), 1962, p. 82. This figure should be seen in contrast to the 260,000 in Britain and the 2 million tractors in the United States.
14   As the first man in space he was granted the status of a hero of the Soviet Nation and his public return was marked by a symbolic welcome on Lenin's Mausoleum.
15   Jamey Gambrell, 'The Wonder of the Soviet World', *New York Review of Books*, 22 December (1994) 33. The Mechanization of Agriculture Pavilion was converted to the Space Pavilion in 1966 and the space outside which once sported a monument to Stalin now has a Vostock rocket. In 1993 the Space Pavilion became a salesroom for US cars.

Unsere Partei ist die Partei der Einheit

CHAPTER EIGHT

THE NEW SOCIALIST 'HAPPY' PEOPLE

Leonid Brezhnev stressed the continuity of the communist vision of socialist progress and
the new socialist people in 1977:

> The October Revolution and socialism have also enriched the history of mankind by bringing about the
> intellectual and cultural emancipation of the working people. … The working people began to take an active
> part in cultural life; they became the creators of cultural values. A new, socialist intelligentsia has emerged
> from the midst of the people, and has brought fame and glory to their country with outstanding achievements
> in science, technology, literature and art. A union which the best minds in history had dreamed of, the historic
> union of labour and culture, has taken place in the history of our country; in the history of world culture, this
> marks an event of tremendous significance.[1]

If the posters are anything to go by the population consisted of contented workers and voters, a proficient specialist technical and creative class, a vigilant military, enthusiastic youth and happy children. A typical poster shows a triumphant and youthful Red Army soldier holding aloft a red banner endowed with the portrait medallion of Stalin and Lenin (8.1). He is accompanied by a more mature skilled worker. His moustache attests to his experience. He wears overalls. He is usually a miner, steelworker or a building worker. A young woman wears a traditional headscarf and carries a sheaf of corn to denote the countryside. Her dress is decorated with a large floral pattern to indicate a domestic, comfortable and aspirational life.

The composition is hierarchical. Lenin and Stalin are at its pinnacle and provide spiritual inspiration and guidance; the soldier immediately below them is a sign of past victories and future security. Either side of him stand the young woman who is his physiognomic twin and the worker. Together they anchor the composition. The poster instantiates the relations of power between the people, the state and its forces of coercion. The urbane masculinity of industrial city life and the nurturing feminine of a productive countryside are overseen by the all-pervasive Soviet presence which is signified in the figure of the Red Army soldier and the banner. They are bathed in the light of success and health, and they look forward and outward into the future. Occasionally the triumvirate of types is supplemented by an educated man in a suit and tie. He usually wears a beard and holds the works of Marx and Lenin. He is representative of a new specialist class produced by the technological changes of the 1960s.

In the mid-1950s party polemicists promoted a vision of socialism as a complex weave of history and modernity. Rooted in specific traditions and directed towards the future, socialism was to transform agricultural peasant-based economies into industrial worker-based economies.[2] Under capitalism, cultural production and social leadership had been in the hands of a class-defined elite; under developed post-war communism the leading, organized sections of the working class were complemented by a stratum of experts drawn from its ranks.[3] This new specialist class was made up of the scientific and creative intelligentsia who were to play an important role in the race to surpass the West. Its presence is usually masculine, but, unlike traditional representations of the male, he is passive, rather than physically active. He does not struggle but thinks and he wears the clothes of a managerial class.

In one of the many paradoxes of communist rhetoric, there had been the need to create heroes since the time of Lenin. Originally the intention was to restrict them to the martyrs of the revolution, but the pantheon always included figures from world culture. In addition, by the end of World War II, scientists, artists and poets had attained official recognition in posters and public ceremonial. As role models they were part of the attempt to fashion a kind of Renaissance people schooled in the arts and sciences, dedicated to the party, politically class-conscious and antagonistic to Western culture. The anonymous Czechoslovak poster *Laureates of the International Peace Awards. Peace will always defeat war!* (1951) is a good illustration of the policy. The communist writer and hero Julius Fučik, who was executed by the Nazis in 1943, is awarded a laureate in deliberate emulation of the ancient Greeks and Romans. He is placed alongside a pantheon of heroes including Renato Guttuso, Paul Robeson, Pablo Neruda and Pablo Picasso.[4] Intellectual and cultural achievement was paralleled by physical prowess, and so sport was a significant subject for political poster artists, providing a model of male physique and an Olympian measure of individual and national achievement: 'sport for fighting readiness' was a much overused slogan (8.2, 3).[5]

(detail of 8.10)

8.1
Viktor Koretsky, *Our flag, victorious flag*, 1945, Soviet Union, Museum of the Working Class, Prague.

8.2
Čermáková, Čumpelík, Schoř, *State-wide Spartakiad*, 1955, Czechoslovakia, Moravian Museum, Brno.

8.3
Anon., *Members of a trade union exercise in Sokol. Through physical education to work and defend efficiency*, 1948, Czechoslovakia, All Trade Union Archive, Prague.

8.4
Jupp Alt, *Friendship for always. Month of German–Soviet friendship*, 1950, GDR, Berlinische Gallery, Berlin.

8.5
Karel Pekárek, *To the best ones in work. Vacation ROH (Revolutionary Trade Union)*, 1949, Czechoslovakia, All Trade Union Archive, Prague.

8.1

8.2

8.3

8.4

8.5

The Polish poster designer Maciej Urbaniec remarked, 'Sport and art are united by one of the most luminous humanistic ideas. Striving for perfection, attainment and the transcending of the limits of human powers lie at the core of that idea.'[6]

Posters were produced in direct response to official policy and provided an essential iconography of masculinity and femininity which remained in use in one form or another until the collapse of communism (8.1). Men were militarily efficient and vigilant, or were physically fit heavy engineers and construction workers (8.4, 5). Women, while appearing in these roles, did so much less frequently. Figures of both sexes are half- or full-length, frontal or three-quarter profile, and very happy (8.4). By the 1970s they are able, occasionally, to function under the emblems of their occupations and the state without the presence of the fathers of the revolution (8.6). People are pictured in shallow but anonymous exterior spaces, or they are contextualized against a montaged background of industrial plant or construction sites. Women are often pushed to the back of compositions, or are in a subsidiary relation to a dominant directing male. Often posters project a procession of ideal types, each representing republic or nation and occupying a valued place in the Soviet order as revolutionary, miner, soldier, shock worker, cosmonaut, tractor driver and athlete (8.11, 12).

Lukyanichin's *Tasks of the last Five Year Plan. Timely!* (1984) (8.6), as a late example of orthodox political poster making, presents a clear hierarchy of skills and trades. In the centre a man in early middle age instructs his colleagues; a woman of professional appearance reads over his shoulder; to his left and behind, a young man in a hard hat with an Asian appearance looks to him for guidance, as does the woman next to him. To the left of the woman, another young man in the casual dress of the professional specialist class offers advice. Another labourer, identified by his hard hat, gazes thoughtfully at the older man in the centre of the composition, whom we must take to be a manager. The gathering is relatively informal and lacks any of the decorative, if futuristic, stylizations of many posters from the 1970s. The figures are derived from photographs, and they stand against a panoramic view of the inside of a factory in a narrow stage-like space. They are on show. The composition presumes an audience and, despite the illusionistically rendered surfaces, the representation is not in any way naturalistic, unlike many high socialist-realist posters from the 1950s. Iconographically it is a presentation of good practice in an hierarchical composition which tells observers all they need to know about dress, deference and social position.

Posters depicting revolutionary collective action are relatively rare in communist-inspired political posters. One example is Edo Murtić's design produced in the aftermath of the Ustaše regime in Croatia for the Croatian Peasant Party (8.8) which illustrated a crowd in popular revolt: 'the peasant's connection with the land must not be severed, he must not be driven from the soil.'[7] Significantly, as a product of the anti-fascist movement in Croatia, it was not a communist poster. The communist agenda was one of domination and arbitrary power, exercised by *apparatchiks* and bureaucrats loyal to Moscow, and the last thing they desired was popular mass demonstrations. The preferred mode of mass assembly took the form of disciplined

8.6
Lukyanichin, *Tasks of the last Five Year Plan. Timely!*, 1984, three sheets, Soviet Union, Andrei Budnik, Kiev.

8.7
Vladimir Dobrovolsky, *The work of the party, the aim of our life, the welfare of the nation, the strength of our homeland. Union of Soviet Socialist Republics, Socialist Government of Workers and Farmers. Para. 1, Constitution of the USSR*, 1971, Soviet Union, Mikhail Avvakumov, Moscow.

8.6

8.7

8.8
Edo Murtić, *Steps of freedom*,
1945, Yugoslavia, Croatian
Historical Museum, Zagreb.

8.9
Andor Bánhidi, *All-Union
Sports Festival*, 1954,
Hungary, Hungarian National
Gallery, Budapest.

8.10
Murza and Panndorf, *Our
party is the party of unity.
Twenty-fifth anniversary of the
German Socialist Unity Party*,
1971, GDR, Academy of Fine
Art, Berlin.

8.8

8.9

8.10

8.11

8.12

8.11
E. Artsrunian, *USSR*, 1976,
two sheets, Soviet Union,
Mikhail Avvakumov.

8.12
D. Ikonnikov Cipulin, *Keep
the revolutionary step!*, 1987,
six sheets, Soviet Union,
Andrei Budnik.

8.13
Zdeněk Chotěnovský, *When
they proclaim 'Long live
progress!' always ask,
'Progress in what?'*, 1968,
Czechoslovakia, Moravian
Gallery, Brno.

8.14
Jan Sawka, *Patients. Teatr Stu*,
1976, Poland, the artist.

8.13

8.14

8.15
Péter Pócs, photo Péter Walter,
*Péter Pócs posters
1977–1987*, 1987, Moravian
Gallery, Brno.

8.17

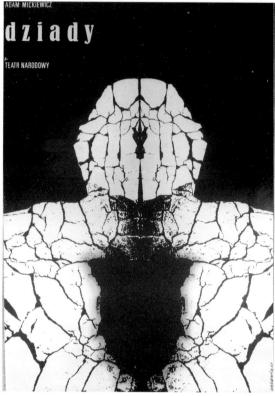

8.18

8.16

8.16
Jan Bokiewicz, *Bread, freedom, 1956, Poznań*, 1986, Poland, computer copy of underground poster, 1995, the artist.

8.17
Alexander Faldin, *Without words*, c. 1992, poster maquette, St Petersburg, Russia, the artist.

8.18
Roman Cieślewicz, *'The Forefathers' by Adam Mickiewicz. The National Theatre*, 1967, Poland, private collection.

8.19
Roman Cieślewicz, *Liberty = Freedom*, 1982, Poland, private collection.

8.19

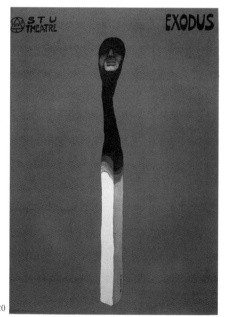

8.20

8.20
Jan Sawka, *Exodus. Theatre Stu*, 1976, Poland, the artist.

8.21

8.22

8.23

8.21
Jan Aleksiun, *Four at Wilanow*, 1976, Poland, private collection.

8.22
Marek Mosinski, *The Parliament and Council of the People rule through the will of the people*, 1969, Poland, Museum of Independence, Warsaw.

8.23
Jan Jaromir Aleksiun, *Tadeusz Rozewicz 'To the square'*, 1979, Poland, Moravian Gallery, Brno.

8.24
Karoly Schmal, *National Museum and Monument Month*, 1973, Hungary, Hungarian Museum of National History, Budapest.

8.24

8.25

8.26

8.27

spectacles dedicated to the service of the party and the state (8.9). More common still were posters showing the massed flag-waving participants in public ceremonials (8.10). Among others, the Plakát group in Czechoslovakia ably subverted these iconographies with posters such as Zdeněk Chotěnovský's *When they proclaim 'Long live progress!' aways ask, 'Progress in what?'* (1968) (8.13). The crowd as a metaphor for collective life was a powerful motif, and designers such as Jan Sawka in Poland and Péter Pócs in Hungary used it as the basis of critique and self-expression (8.14, 15). In 1982 the crowd formed the inspiration of the typographic design for Solidarity's emblem of popular resistance in a direct subversion of party claims to embody the will of the people. In 1986 Jan Bokiewicz, a Solidarity member, exploited the truly revolutionary potential of the crowd in an unofficial poster commemorating the thirtieth anniversary of the strikes and demonstrations which took place in Poznań in 1956. That event had led to some fifty people being killed by police and the poster uses a photograph of a crowd on the streets to draw an analogy between the present and the past (8.16). By the early 1990s with cynicism rife Alexander Faldin saw the crowd reduced to a queue of the self-serving (8.17).

Some of the more monstrous aspects of the ideology of the new socialist people had been broached in cultural posters which attracted political readings, simply because communism's ideals were so all-pervasive. The poster for Adam Mickiewicz's play *The Forefathers*, performed at the National Theatre in Warsaw in 1967, was designed by Roman Cieślewicz. It featured a giant figure to encapsulate what the designer saw as the volcanic will of the Polish people (8.18). Although Cieślewicz had left for Paris in 1963, his work continued to appear in Poland, and in 1982 the poster *Liberty = Freedom*, showing a grotesque distorted by the twists of fortune, received widespread circulation in the shadow of martial law (8.19). Jan Sawka's work for *Teatr Stu*, along with the other designers associated with New Culture, produced posters critically engaged with communist iconography (8.20). The poster for the exhibition *Four at Wilanow*, designed by Jan Aleksiun, illustrated in a dark monumental style a figure clutching a bare canvas leering out at the spectator (8.21). The poster was a variation of the metonymic but politically orthodox design by Marek Mosinski for *The Parliament and Council of the People rule through the will of the people* (1969) (8.22) in which the spectator is confronted with an expressionistic lithograph of a muscular worker's forearm clutching the 1952 constitution. In 1979 Aleksiun literally confronted the weight of socialist monumentalism in a design picturing a prostrate figure below a floating and crumbling block of masonry. The poster was widely regarded as a political statement (8.23). Karoly

156

8.28

8.29

8.30

8.31

8.32

8.33

8.25
Anatolii Volkov, *Let's go and thresh! My stomach hurts!*,1953, Soviet Union, Museum of the Working Class Movement, Prague.

8.26
Alexei Kokorekin, *Peace! Ties of friendship and solidarity with defenders of peace in all the world – unshakeable!*, 1953, Soviet Union, Museum of the Working Class Movement, Prague.

8.27
Viktor Koretsky, *Guarantee of five years of quality work!*, 1976, Soviet Union, Andrei Budnik, Kiev.

8.28
Anon., *To a large piece of bread!*, 1947, GDR, Berlinische Gallery, Berlin.

8.29
György Pál, *We ensure bread for the next year by produce delivery*, c. 1950, Hungary, Hungarian Museum of Contemporary History, Budapest.

8.30
Zdeněk Filip, *We fulfil commitments to the Czechoslovak Communist Party*, 1962, Czechoslovakia, Moravian Museum, Brno.

SEE PREVIOUS PAGE

8.31
Michał Bylina, *Bread for the homeland*, 1950, Poland, Museum of Independence, Warsaw.

8.32
B. Muchin and Boris Berezhovsky, *Produce high-yield cows!*, 1954, Soviet Union, Museum of the Working Class Movement, Prague.

8.33
Horst Naumann, *The year of the grand initiative to the people. More meat and fat*, 1954, GDR, Berlinische Gallery, Berlin.

8.34
P5P, *We work on our own, for ourselves. We vote communist*, 1946, Czechoslovakia, Museum of Decorative Arts, Prague.

8.35
Włodzimierz Zakrewski, *Forward! Let's fight for the Six Year Plan!*, 1949, Poland, Museum of Independence, Warsaw.

8.36
Gábor Papp and Károly Reich, *Exhibition of the Five Year Plan*, 1951, Hungary, Hungarian National Gallery, Budapest.

8.37
Klaus Schlicker-Weber, *Forward to new successes in our Five Year Plan*, 1951, GDR, Academy of Fine Art, Berlin.

8.34

8.35

8.36

8.37

Schmal's design for the National Museum and Monument Month in 1973 achieved much the same effect with a sculpturally rendered, boxed and divided head, the blank canvas of the Aleksiun forsaken for an interrogation of monumental propaganda and its impact on psychological well-being (8.24).

THE INDUSTRIAL AND AGRICULTURAL WORKER

In communist propaganda the workers and the peasants were to be as active in the struggle for social and economic transformation as the military. Labour was an ethical and moral category, capable of building the society of the future and forging new socialist man. Anyone who worked well was good, healthy and happy (8.29, 30); anyone whose work was poor was bad, afflicted and an enemy of the people (8.25). The productive union of the city and the country, of the party and the working class, was a staple iconographic motif (8.26, 27). From Hungary to the German Democratic Republic, and from Poland to Czechoslovakia, agricultural labour was represented as the force capable of liberating the people from hunger and producing wealth in alliance with industry (8.35). At first these designs were abstract or made use of photo-montage (7.44, 8.28). But by the 1950s socialist realism predominated. In Hungary, György Pál produced images of agricultural labour which combined all the conventional devices established in the Soviet Union in the 1930s, from gigantic figures to crushed and caricatured enemies. Occasionally the countryside was given an essentially bucolic character (8.31), without the rationalizing implications of mechanization, which in any case remained little more than a dream, giant cows and alert piglets aside (8.32, 33). Women were often identified with agricultural labour, but not nearly as often as in Soviet posters before World War II.[8]

Workers in the city were nearly always male, and in the immediate aftermath of war their occupations in posters were largely restricted to those of steelworker, miner, construction worker and, to a lesser extent, railway worker (8.34–42). A welder who has lost a hand in battle or in an industrial accident is not only pictured in employment but is placed against images of revolution and celebration. He appears to be almost hysterically cheerful (8.38). Happy in their work, these men look steely-eyed into the future and the certain dawn of a new age (8.39). Well muscled and always clothed, their skin glistens with the sweat of labour: the drill of the miner, the rod of the blastfurnaceman, the hammer of the construction worker are held like weapons to be used in the struggle for communism. But like their military equivalent, the gun, the tools carry an erotic and phallic charge similar to that described by Mikhail Heller when he quotes a passage from *Energy*, a part work published between 1932 and 1938 by the Soviet writer Fyodor Gladkov:

> The young worker Ivan grasped the drill. As soon as he felt the surface of metal he became excited and his whole body started trembling. The deafening roar of the drill hurled Sonya away from him. Then she placed her hand on his shoulder and tickled the hair behind his ear. … It was as though an electric discharge had pierced the two young people at the same moment. He gave a deep sigh and clutched the apparatus more firmly.[9]

8.38
Viktor Koretsky, *Welcome, work victories 1917–1953*, 1953, Soviet Union, Museum of the Working Class Movement, Prague.

8.39
Anon., *Through unified work to the blossoming of homeland, socialism, peace, 28 October* (Nationalization Day), 1950, Czechoslovakia, Moravian Museum, Brno.

8.38

8.39

8.40
Anon., *Fifteen years of
successful work*, 1964, GDR,
Thomas Hill.

8.41
Jan Marcin Szancer,
*Friendship and alliance with
the USSR assure the peace,
independence and prosperity
of our homeland*, 1953,
Poland, private collection.

8.42
Włodzimierz Zakrewski,
Party, 1955, Poland, Museum
of Independence, Warsaw.

8.43
Henning Wagenbreth, *PGH
Glühende Zukunft (Radiant
future), Head Office*, 1989,
poster maquette and postcard,
GDR, the artist.

8.44
Andrija Maurović, *Long live
elections!*, 1946, Yugoslavia,
Croatian Historical Museum,
Zagreb.

8.40

8.41

8.42

8.43

8.44

8.45

8.46

8.47

8.45
Zdeněk Filip, *Fiftieth anniversary of International Women's Day*, 1959, Czechoslovakia, Museum of Decorative Arts, Prague.

8.46
Juozas Galkus, *International Women's Day, 8 March*, 1968, Lithuania, Moravian Gallery, Brno.

8.47
Anatoly Grigorievich Rudkovich, *To the festival of 8 March*, 1973, Soviet Union, Mikhail Avvakumov, Moscow.

They are the shock workers[10] of communist construction and they are inspired by the leaders of the revolution and even the poets of the past (8.41). The communist male will vote and read a political tract or paper. He will be vigilant, but will only very rarely be seen at leisure, in simple enjoyment. There are some examples of posters from Hungary which are unusual because they promise not simply satisfaction at work through the pursuit of a greater cause but material benefit, the acquisition of material goods and a rich and fulfilled leisure life as a measure of successful economic development. Only in the final throes of communist domination did artists openly lampoon these iconographies (8.43).

WOMEN

Socialist posters have historically pictured women as allegorical figures, representing the abstract ideals of Liberty, Justice, Prudence, Industry, Fortitude, Temperance, Truth, Faith and Hope.[11] A Croatian poster from the immediate post-war period follows this tradition (8.44). Liberty towers above the people as she urges them to vote, but it was the exception to prove the rule. Occasionally, as in Zdeněk Filip's poster commemorating the fiftieth anniversary of International Women's Day published in 1959, a female figure is depicted in heroic mould (8.45). She sweeps across the composition wearing a sash and holding a red banner and flowers. In almost every respect she emulates the dynamic optimism of Delacroix's *Victory on the barricades* (1830), but unlike her French precedent she does not expose her breasts, nor does she wear a phrygian cap but instead sports a proletarian scarf. As a figure symbolic of the women of the world, her cause is a collective and revolutionary one based in Marxism-Leninism, divorced from either the allure of Liberty or the liberating nurture of nature. The figure of Liberty may have been associated with sexual freedom in early revolutionary iconography in western Europe, but in the communist poster she is fully clothed and is associated with proletarian liberation.

Before the war, communist parties largely abandoned the female iconography of revolution in favour of the male worker because the audience was supposed to be the male-dominated labour movement rather than the population at large. But in the 1940s and 1950s the figure of the woman as an embodiment of revolutionary beauty and zeal was rediscovered and posters dedicated to International Women's Day often featured elegant female profiles (8.46–48, 50). Revolutionary femininity was associated with motherhood and peace and was often accompanied by flowers and doves. In these posters it is blue, the colour of

peace, rather than red, the colour of revolution, which predominates. The posters are ideal pictures of socialism attained and bear no relationship to the actual lives of women under communism.

Women were habitually used as figures which symbolized the nation rather than revolutionary struggle. Dressed in traditional folk costume, women carry flowers and consort with Red Army soldiers (8.51, 52). By the end of the 1960s the female figure was so strongly equated with national identity that posters advertising the Lithuanina Folk Dance Ensemble, for example, featured an abstract design derived from a woman in national costume in the colours of the republic similar to Juozas Galkus's design for International Women's Day (8.46). Under Soviet rule, festivals of song and dance were the only occasions when people could gather together to show their national allegiance, albeit in veiled ways. As Anatol Lieven has pointed out, the connection between folklore and national identity stems from the intellectual history of the Baltic region and the work of the eighteenth-century philosopher, historian and critic Johann Gottfried Herder. For him, every nation had an essential spirit found in national folk art forms. It was an indigenous and romantic philosophy which stood against the Soviets' determined and coercive internationalism in favour of the assertion of national independence.[12] The Soviet pursuit of the popular in national folk forms carried with it the seeds of its own dissolution: in 1988 the national song festival, Baltika, saw the first open display of national flags, a phenomenon echoed in the subjects of the posters exhibited at the Poster Fest at Cesis near Riga.

The constitutions of the new communist states provided for equal rights and duties for all citizens. In Czechoslovakia the constitution stated: 'Men and women shall have equal status in the family at work and in public activity.'[13] Ideologically the communist parties were dedicated to female emancipation, to the improvement of the status of women, and to the state's responsibility in assisting with maternity and child care.[14] Posters from the late 1940s and early 1950s demonstrate commitment to this programme, exhorting women to vote and become part of the new communist order, even if elections were nothing more than a ritual of commitment rather than a meaningful democratic process (8.53, 54). The shortage of manpower created new avenues of work for women, and the emancipation of women was to be achieved by freeing them from housework and releasing them for productive labour outside the home (8.55–58). Added pressures to participate in political life and party organizations came from questionnaires directed at parents of schoolchildren and university candidates which asked about class origin

8.48

8.49

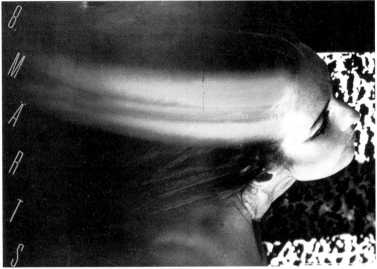

8.50

8.51

8.52

8.48
Nándor Szilvásy, *8 March.*
International Women's Day,
1975, Hungary, Hungarian
National Gallery, Budapest.

8.49
Lajos Görög, *8 March.*
International Women's Day,
1978, Hungary, Hungarian
National Gallery, Budapest.

8.50
Ruth Huimerind, *8 March*,
1988, Soviet Estonia,
Moravian Gallery, Brno.

8.51
Eduard Kalninš, *1 May*, 1946,
Soviet Latvia, National
Library, Riga.

8.52
Anon., *9 April. Day of peace*
and happiness. Union of
friends of the USSR, *c.* 1950,
Czechoslovakia, Moravian
Gallery, Brno.

8.53
Vasilii Tishchenko, *Everyone to the polls!*, 1951, Soviet Latvia, National Library, Riga.

8.54
Mikhailovich Soloviev, *'Such women could not be in old times.' J. V. Stalin*, 1951, Soviet Union, Academy of Fine Art, Berlin.

8.55
Wojciech Fangor, *8 March 1953. We greet women working for peace and the bloom of the homeland*, 1953, Poland, Museum of Independence, Warsaw.

8.53

8.54

8.55

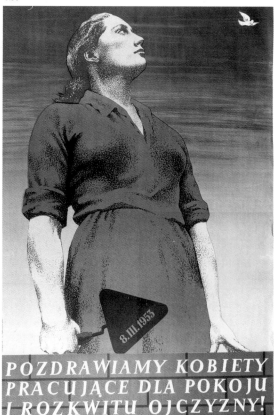

(working-class origin would accelerate advancement) and political activities.

The equation, however, had one serious flaw, since domestic work was not considered productive. When women are represented with small children it is in their function as politically active individuals, to which the child is but an adjunct (8.59, 60). The posters conceal the emotional deprivations and practical difficulties. Children are only supposed to be sweet, good and easy to care for. Inevitably, women were drawn into an existence where the tensions between wage work, domestic work and reproductive labour proved almost intolerable. At various times after 1948 the various governments of the communist bloc promoted higher birth rates or, alternatively, tried to keep women in the labour force and facilitated or prohibited divorce and abortion. But the necessary support structures were never fully put into place. Family incomes were assessed on the basis of both the father and the mother being in employment and maternity pay was calculated on that basis, so, no matter how generous the maternity leave or how long the period without fear of losing employment, poverty meant that most women had to return to work as soon as possible. Grandmothers functioned as unofficial childminders and home helps. The situation was worsened by the fact that even in societies not overburdened by archaic religious traditions rooted in patriarchal structures, such as Czechoslovakia and the German Democratic Republic, constraints on women's time and the fragmentation of their loyalties meant that their advancement in the workplace was difficult. The position of women was made all the more impossible by inadequate and cramped living conditions, the inadequacies of public transport, the lack of labour-saving devices in the home, and the sheer length of time needed to procure basic foodstuffs, particularly during times of shortage when queuing for long periods was commonplace. However, in non-political posters the state continued to promote women's roles in the context of domestic plenitude, rather than productive or political zeal in a manner directly comparable to Western representations of women in advertising and the press (8.61, 62). The posters position women in the market place and suggest that the state recognized their status as consumers in the economy.

These posters highlight the new-found status of women. But although they were active in the world of work, and despite ever higher levels of educational attainment, women were largely restricted to low-status jobs not only in construction and industry but also in areas of work traditionally associated with women such as catering, health, social services, education and research. The relatively high educational status of women is often referred to in the posters, almost by chance, as women are featured promoting the sale of books and championing a new socialist culture (8.64). One Polish poster shows a woman in national costume accompanied by a gesticulating worker. She carries in her hands volumes by Stalin, Bolesław Bierut, Właclysław Broniewski, Kollataj and Mieckiewicz, the romantic poet thought by many to be at the heart of Polish national identity (8.63).

By the 1980s it is possible to see how women are depicted as part of a new specialist and scientific elite with apparent independence (8.65). Such stereotypes, however, were hollow and easily subverted. Georgii Kamenskich and

8.56
Károly Sinkó, *Run to the help of your injured comrade. Attend the first-aid courses of the Hungarian Red Cross*, 1950, Hungary, Hungarian National Gallery, Budapest.

8.57
Gyözö Szilas, *Women and girls, come to work!*, 1950–52, Hungary, Hungarian National Gallery, Budapest.

8.56

8.57

8.58
D. Glinski, *Fifth Professional Competition for German Young Women and Men of the Metal Industry! For new working methods for the rapid fulfilment of the Five Year Plan!*, 1952, GDR, Thomas Hill.

8.59
György Pál, *Vote for the Popular Front. For peace and the future of our children!*, 1950–53, Hungary, Hungarian National Gallery, Budapest.

8.60
Anon., *Glory to women, fighters for peace and happiness on earth*, c. 1975, Soviet Union, Andrei Budnik, Kiev.

8.58

8.59

8.60

8.61
Pál Gábor, *It's not worth bottling. Buy tinned food!*, 1949, Hungary, Hungarian National Gallery, Budapest.

8.62
Anon., *Plan – save – buy*, 1966, GDR, Thomas Hill.

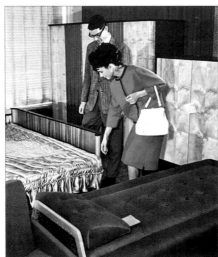

8.62

8.61

8.63

8.64

8.65

8.66

8.67

8.68

8.63
Witold Chmielewski, *We build the new culture for the prosperity of our homeland, to achieve world peace*, 1951, Poland, Museum of Independence, Warsaw.

8.64
Ilja Štikāns, *To each kolkhoz a bookshop*, 1951–53, Soviet Latvia, National Library, Riga.

8.65
Alexander Vaganov, *It's our and your earth, it's our biography!*, 1984, Soviet Union, Andrei Budnik, Kiev.

8.66
Georgii Kamenskich and Tatyana Nemkova, *Lift higher our heavy hammer*, 1989, poster maquette, Soviet Union, Alexander Lozenko.

8.67
Juris Dimiters, *untitled*, *c.* 1989, Soviet Latvia, Moravian Gallery, Brno.

8.68
Anke Feuchtenberger, *All women are brave! Strong! Beautiful!*, 1989, GDR, Moravian Gallery, Brno.

8.69
István Czeglédi, *Peace loan. Peace, Five Year Plan, flourishing country*, c. 1950, Hungary, Hungarian Museum of Contemporary History, Budapest.

8.70
Vladimir Sachkov, *Let the sun always shine!*, 1967, Soviet Union, Mikhail Avvakumov, Moscow.

8.69

8.71

8.72

8.70

8.73

8.71
Viktor Koretsky, *Talent's route under capitalism/Talent's route under socialism*, 1948, Soviet Union, Academy of Fine Art, Berlin.

8.72
Eva Hinze, *International Children's Day. In peace and democracy*, 1951, GDR, Academy of Fine Art, Berlin.

8.73
G. Shubina, *With a good nursery in the co-operative, Mother is content and the child is happy!*, 1949, Soviet Union, Academy of Fine Art, Berlin.

8.75

8.74

8.76

8.74
Anon., *National Party
Conference 13–14 October
1951*, 1951, Romania,
Academy of Fine Art, Berlin.

8.75
D. Sedláčková, *There stands a
man, and care of his welfare,
at the end of all our effort*,
1953, Czechoslovakia,
Moravian Museum, Brno.

8.76
Viktor Ivanov and O. Burova,
*With honour we meet the
festival!*, 1953, Czech
Republic, Soviet Museum of
the Working Class Movement,
Prague.

Tatyana Nemkova in *Lift higher, our heavy hammer* (8.66) combine the traditional iconography of the peasant female worker with the technologically progressive iconography of the monument situated at the entrance to the Exhibition of the Achievement of the People's Economy in Moscow. The poster places the true foundation of Soviet achievement not in a new liberated class of people but in the labour of exploited women. Juris Dimiters explored similar territory to different effect by visually aligning the physical work of women with prostitution, which was illegal but tolerated in the name of the pursuit of hard currency where legitimate labour had failed (8.67). Similarly, in the GDR, Anke Feuchtenberger mocked established stereotypes in a grotesquerie of overburdened women captioned *All women are brave! Strong! Beautiful!* (8.68).

YOUTH

Typically, the young are represented within frameworks defined by the party. Two very different posters from Czechoslovakia and Hungary demonstrate similar compositional and iconographical structures. A Young Pioneer stands in the foreground, the country and the city on either side. The male and female adults are not in the guise of mother and father but occupy the positions of role models in a microcosm of the ideal communist society. The child placed between the two adults provides the linchpin for the future productive unification of the urban and rural. The woman in the Czechoslovak poster is a symbol of the nurturing power of the party. Ears of corn identify her with the countryside and agriculture, but she also personifies 'Education': bearing the works of Lenin, she will inculcate the values of Marxism-Leninism into the younger generation. The woman is the symbolic source of the country's human, intellectual and material reproductive wealth. The Hungarian poster is almost exactly similar, though less epic: the worker gestures towards the building sites of the city, the woman to a blossoming suburbia (8.69).

The principal pedagogic device for the creation of the new socialist people was repetition and learned response established through communist ritual, ceremonies and festivals. Great emphasis was placed on the child's progress through early life to adolescence and adulthood, and it was plotted in official rites of passage from Young Pioneers through Union of Youth to full membership of the party and military service. Public ceremonial was but one aspect, and agitation and education played an equally significant role.[15] The emphasis on children and the attention paid to their education by the authorities helped to establish communist authority. Children were subjected to the will of the collective, individuality was derided and shamed,

discipline, obedience and compliance were rewarded (8.70). At school concepts of the enemy, paramilitary games and songs were introduced. The benefits of communism for young people were contrasted with the pitfalls and exploitative nature of capitalism. Viktor Koretsky produced a series of posters showing the fate of talent in the West (8.71). A young Western violinist is left to his own devices and busks alone for a living on the streets while his equivalent in the Soviet Union is provided for by the state and is supported within the collectivity of the orchestra. Other posters habitually follow a 'before and after' formula familiar from Western and pre-war advertising, and were especially prevalent in the GDR, where, as throughout the region, children and women are associated with peace. Eva Hinze's poster for International Children's Day (8.72), is a generalized anti-war statement which nevertheless makes it clear that the route to happiness is through youth and communism.

Children who could be encouraged to inform on their parents or relations performed an important function in undermining traditional society, which could then be replaced by party structures. Today, memories of the story of Pavlik Morozov, the communist hero and murdered patricide who informed on his parents, are likely to be met with derision or hilarity, but the purpose of the story was an important one: taught throughout the communist bloc, its moral supported the supreme authority of the party.

The poster *With a good nursery in the co-operative, Mother is content and the child is happy!* (1949) (8.73) pictures two oversize toddlers nurtured and educated outside the family, leaving the mother free to work. Similarly, a Romanian poster depicts children happily playing under the umbrella of various youth organizations, while in the background oil derricks and building sites rise out of virgin forest landscape (8.74). Iconographical schemes such as these had a long life throughout the region. The figure of the child embodies possibilities for the future, and is simultaneously the object of guidance and education by elders whose first allegiance is to the party (8.75–77). Furthermore, well-being was contingent not just on dedication to the party and the nation, but also on allegiance and friendship with the Soviet Union.

Children's lives are depicted as trouble-free and happy. Concessions were made to festivities such as Christmas which had always focused on children, but they are subtly modified to exclude the Christian message. A Czech poster by Dobroslav Foll has a Christmas table circumscribed by a giant and monumental figure 5: the abundance of the winter feast is seen to be entirely dependent on the production targets of the Five Year Plan, rather than on any thought of divine intervention (8.78). The domesticity of the scene is disrupted by the formal attire of the man and the working dress of the woman, who looks as though she has just stepped out of a canteen kitchen rather than a home. All reality is subject to the discourse of the party. The poster *We will win peace when we celebrate together* (1951) (8.79) depicts two children playing under a Christmas tree. The children are illuminated not by a heavenly source but by light emanating from the heroes of the revolution, whose portraits illustrate the book held by the little girl. Where there might have been cuddly toys in the foreground there are a tractor and a crane – symbols of the country and the city. Another Christmas poster produced in Hungary in 1956 follows much the same formula, but in the aftermath of the uprising the official policy was to mollify rather than repress the people at large (8.80). Parcels and a teddy bear await the family, and the caption urges, 'Merry Christmas, a peaceful, diligent new year'.

The first word a child was supposed to learn to read was 'Lenin', but repetition empties words of real meaning. The whole process gradually deteriorated into ritual incantation and mockery. Jokes about the 'father of the people' and 'Lenin's grandchildren' proliferated, and 'foreign' influences such as blue denim and youth culture began to take hold of the young (8.81–85). The process was accelerated by the introduction of compulsory military exercises for schoolchildren in 1973 in the Soviet Union and the GDR in 1978. The social analyst Viktor Zaslavsky ruminated on the parlous condition of Soviet youth:

> The liquidation of the consequences of the Stalinist cult and the desecration of state authority have given rise among the young to a negative attitude toward all authority, has produced false opinions with respect to discipline and democratic institutions and has sanctioned demagogery; in the last analysis, this could only translate into forms of indifference and nihilism toward the state, immorally dubious actions and in open violations of legality.[16]

Alexander Faldin, a poster designer from Leningrad, put it more succinctly when reminiscing on his youth: 'I paid no attention to school or education.'[17] Teachers were held in very low esteem because everyone knew that they knew they were not telling the truth. From Marx through Lunacharsky[18] to Pavlov,[19] communist ideologists believed man to be a machine, necessarily subject to rational control and manipulation. Young people, therefore, could be formed and moulded into perfect model citizens (8.82). The hope was that they would be resolutely patriotic in their love of the motherland, the Soviet people and Lenin, and respectful of the working classes of the world (8.83). The programme had changed little by 1980, when Bogdan Cywinski identifed four interrelated aims in the education of the young in Poland. The first and most important aim

was the inculcation of a Marxist view of the 'world, man, society, culture, economics and various contemporary and social problems'. The second was to establish an atheistic point of view. The third was to ensure an understanding of national interests, history and contemporary events in subordination to Soviet supremacy. The fourth was the socialist national state as the only one worthy of stirring up patriotic feeling.[20]

But in Hungary (and to a lesser extent Poland), where the process of westernization was interrupted by martial law, the authorities were aware that official attitudes would have to change if the old order were to survive. Wanda Szykszyan's *Revolutionary youth days* (1982) (8.86) made a gesture towards the fashion industry and Western youth culture of the previous decade. The order could not last unless the communists could take the young with them, and they turned in desperation to obsolete Western models to glamorize their agendas. But it was already too late. Youth organizations could not compete with a growing entrepreneurial culture based in popular culture. Designers in Hungary and Yugoslavia took established totalitarian iconographies and turned them to their own purposes. As the iconographies emptied themselves of meaning through endless repetition, so they became the object of play and the vehicles of apoliticized subversion in the display of affective and rebellious identity divorced from the worlds of work or party. The story was much the same in the GDR, where, despite a highly repressive state apparatus, the younger generation had developed a strong counter-culture. Even though it was heavily penetrated by the Stasi, the counter-culture formed an important focus for young people, and manifested itself in radicalized design groups such as PGH Glühende Zukunft (Shining Future). Henning Wagenbreth's poster *Cyclists, you have nothing to lose but your chains!* (1989) (8.87) mocks the communist *crie de coeur*, 'Workers of the world unite, you have nothing to lose but your chains.' It succeeds on both verbal and visual levels, depicting an unshaven and unheroic cyclist who champions not the cause of world revolution but cleaner air and a more humane way of life. Wagenbreth's poster owes nothing to a socialist heritage, but draws on Western popular graphic styles. More recently, however, styles simultaneously redolent of constructivism and early communist graphics have been appropriated by young Russian designers to advertise new businesses and to popularize political parties (8.88, 89).

Throughout the period, however, the posters betrayed a dark side to new socialist people, an obverse found in the propaganda against individuals who were insufficiently class-conscious. The depiction of those who were accused of black-marketeering, malingering, alcoholism or, more

8.77
Klaus Wittkugel, *Tenth
anniversary of the German
Democratic Republic*, 1959,
GDR, Academy of Fine Art,
Berlin.

8.78
Dobroslav Foll, *Happy
Christmas. Success of the first
Five Year Plan*, 1949,
Czechoslovakia, All Trade
Union Archive, Prague.

8.79
Hoerst Naumann Collective,
Dresden, *We will win peace
when we celebrate together*,
1951, GDR, Berlinische
Gallery, Berlin.

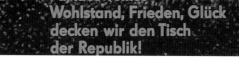

8.77

8.78

8.79

8.80

8.81

8.82

8.83

8.84

8.80
Anon., *Merry Christmas. A peaceful, diligent New Year*, 1956, Hungary, Hungarian Museum of Contemporary History, Budapest.

8.81
Rūdolfs Jansons, *We prepare for the first Republic Congress of Pioneers*, *c.* 1950, Soviet Latvia, National Library, Riga.

8.82
Klaudia Andrievna Kudryashova, *Young Pioneers*, 1976, three of five sheets, Soviet Union, Andrei Budnik, Kiev.

8.83
V. Konyuchov, *Be ready! Always ready! We fortunate children of the Soviet country will be a dignified rising generation for the homeland!*, 1988, three sheets, Soviet Union, private collection.

8.84
Horst Wendt, photo. Thomas Billhardt, *1818 Karl 1883 Marx 1983. Our ideas are reality. Vietnam – happy children in a socialist land*, 1983, GDR, Thomas Hill.

8.85
Vladimir Mikhailovich
Potapov, *Your name –
Komsomol*, 1982, Soviet
Ukraine, Andrei Budnik, Kiev.

8.86
Wanda Szykszyan,
Revolutionary youth days,
1982, Hungary, Hungarian
Museum of Contemporary
History, Budapest.

8.87
Henning Wagenbreth, *Cyclists,
you have nothing to lose but
your chains!*, 1989, GDR,
Moravian Gallery, Brno.

8.88
Elena Kitaeva, *IMMA Press.
Hope, support of top quality
typographic production*,
1992–93, Russia, Moravian
Gallery, Brno.

8.89
Igor Gurevich, *Your voice
[vote], your love, your power
to your future. Youth
movement Yabloko*, 1995,
election poster, three sheets,
Russia, the artist.

8.85

8.86

8.87

8.88

8.89

8.90
ŠAFR, *He who doesn't work doesn't eat*, 1945–46, Czechoslovakia, Museum of Decorative Arts, Prague.

8.91
Bronislaw Wojciech Linke, *Vodka contributes to poverty*, 1948, Poland, Poster Museum, Wilanow.

8.92
Isabelle Bindler, *Alcohol*, c. 1955, Soviet Lithuania, Juozas Galkus, Vilnius.

8.93
Anon., *Today he doesn't care! But what about tomorrow?*, 1955, Czechoslovakia, Museum of Decorative Arts, Prague.

8.94
S. Balčiunas, *Alcohol – poison*, 1986, Soviet Lithuania, Moravian Gallery, Brno.

8.95
Imārs Blumbergs, *Socialism.*
Is it our way of thinking?,
1986, Soviet Latvia, the artist.

8.96
Juris Dimiters, *Weathercock*,
1986, Soviet Latvia, poster
maquette, the artist.

8.97
Henning Wagenbreth, *PGH*
Glühende Zukunft. PGH
Blazing Future, *c.* 1990, GDR,
Moravian Gallery, Brno.

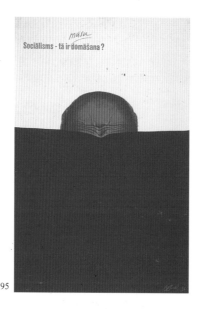

8.95

8.96

8.97

seriously, sabotage and spying reveals a dystopian underbelly to new socialist man. Optimism for the future characterized popular opinion in the 1960s but by the early 1970s, when stagnation began to set in, pessimism spawned cynicism and opportunism. Slowing growth rates created a sense of utopia postponed; shortages of most consumer goods and the long queues reduced material incentives. Simultaneously, political repression and the persecution of dissent were accompanied by the establishment of networks based on nepotism, favouritism and corruption. Under Brezhnev conditions were labelled the 'Little Deal'.[21] The worker was compensated for the lack of consumer goods through the possibility of working badly in a world of make-believe:

> The workers pretend that they are doing good work when they know their work is badly done but consider it their privilege to do bad work since they are paid very little and moreover can't buy anything with what they earn. ... The 'bosses' pretend because they are concerned only with the fulfilment of the plan, though they know the plan is a fiction. ... The country's leaders pretend because they are convinced that they ... can ensure the loyalty of the ... population by agreeing to let them do bad work.[22]

Unemployment was a matter of illegality, and a culture had developed of doing as little work as possible in defiance of official and exploitative work quotas. Under these conditions official representations condemning bad work effectively articulated passive and unconscious forms of resistance.[23] New socialist man was without blemish, yet his 'other' was all around him. The posters defined what he was supposed not to be but actually was in a society structured in corruption and mutual surveillance (8.90). Mikhail Heller quotes from an official document made public in 1983:

> the social type of 'worker' being formed 'at the present time in the USSR' does not correspond with 'either the strategic aims of an advanced socialist state or the technological demands of modern industry'. The document lists the qualities of 'Soviet workers' today: 'lack of labour and production discipline, attitude of indifference to the work being done, low quality of work, social inertia, a poor opinion of work as a means of self-realization, very marked interest in the acquisition of goods, a relatively low moral level. It is sufficient to recall the vast scale of the operation of the so-called *nesuny*, the prevalence of various "shady" deals at the expense of society, the growth of small manufacturing "on the left", dishonest accounting and the payment of wages irrespective of work done.'[24]

The first Soviet constitution written by Lenin had contained the line 'he who does not work shall not eat' and a Soviet joke quoted by Heller conjectures that if vodka interferes with your work then you should give up work. In fact the wages of transgression were exactly that: prohibition from society and the world of work. The shirker and the alcoholic are depicted in various states of domestic and social isolation. The dysfunctional family living in poverty-stricken conditions and the spiritual anguish and despair of individuals are depicted in rabid condemnation which implicitly recognizes the hopelessness of their condition (8.91–93). Paradoxically, these official posters provide a window on to aspects of life which were otherwise repressed and denied.

Alcoholism was a persistent theme in official posters, especially in the Soviet Union. It is interesting to note the large number of designers associated with the posters of *glasnost* and *perestroika* who took up this kind of commission.[25] Konstantin Geraimovich remarked in 1991:

> In those days, the party paid no small sum for posters, up to 500 roubles. They weren't stingy when it came to visual propaganda. … But the 500 roubles was a treat only for the chosen, and, to be among them, you had to be willing to draw the smiling faces of the toilers. I didn't feel like drawing workers' faces. So my posters were about the dangers of smoking and alcoholism, for which I was paid 120 roubles. But, as the soldiers say, 'clean shoulder straps – clean conscience'.[26]

The subversive iconographies of the poster of *glasnost* and *perestroika* found a home in the official representation of the problems of alcohol. A good example can be found in S. Baltiunas's *Alcohol – poison* (1986) (8.94), where a corkscrew doubles as a snake. The snake of temptation is the traditional emblem of the capitalist class in communist iconography, but the screw refers to Stalin's debased machine aesthetic. New socialist man has become less the screw in the machine than the screw in the bottle. As controls slowly relaxed in the Soviet Union under the pressures released by *glasnost* and *perestroika*, so designers turned their talents to the newly recognized enemies of inertia, the corruptions of the bureaucratic *nomenklatura*, political opportunism and the delusions of the past (8.95–97).

NOTES

1   Leonid Brezhnev, *The Great October Revolution and Mankind's Progress* (Moscow, Novosti Press Agency Publishing House), 1977, pp. 8–9, quoted in K. M. Dolgov, *Culture and Social Progress, Marxist-Leninist Aesthetics and the Arts* (Moscow, Progress Publishers), 1980, pp. 9–10.
2   Tadeusz Galinski, *Culture in People's Poland* (Warsaw), 1966, p. 32.
3   *Ibid.*, p. 69.
4   Others included were Václav Dobiáš, Nazim Hikmet, Candido Portinari, Wanda Jakubowska, Jean Richard Bloch and Mihail Sadoveanu.
5   The Czech national and Slavic organization Sokol (Falcon) was dissolved for the third time in 1948 by the communists; the first time was in 1914, the second was by the Nazis in 1938.
6   Maria Morawińska-Brzezicka, *Sport w szruce polskeiej 1945–1975* (Warsaw, Wydawnictwo Sport i Turystyka), 1975, p. 201.
7   Vladko Macek in Robert Bideleux and Ian Jeffries, *A History of Eastern Europe. Crisis and Change* (London and New York, Routledge), 1998, p. 456.
8   See Victoria E. Bonnell, *Iconography of Power. Soviet Political Posters under Lenin and Stalin* (Berkeley CA, University of California Press), 1997.
9   Mikhail Heller, *Cogs in the Soviet Wheel. The Formation of Soviet Man* (London, Collins Harvill), 1988, p. 213.
10   In Russian the word 'shock' applies to the firing mechanism of a gun, the hammer and the pin in the breech. The military comparison is etymologically present.
11   See Eric Hobsbawm, 'Man and Woman in Socialist Iconography', *History Workshop*, 6 (1978) 121–38; Tim Mason, 'The Domestication of Female Socialist Icons. A Note in Reply to Eric Hobsbawm', *History Workshop*, 7 (1979) 170–5; Maurice Agulhon, 'On Political Allegory. A Reply to Eric Hobsbawm', *History Workshop*, 8 (1979) 167–73; Sally Alexander, Anna Davin and Eve Hostettler, 'Labouring Women. A Reply to Eric Hobsbawm', *History Workshop*, 8 (1979) 174–82.
12   Anatol Lieven, *The Baltic Revolution. Estonia, Latvia, Lithuania and the Path to Independence* (New Haven CT and London, Yale University Press), 1993, pp. 115–16.
13   Sharon L. Wolchik, 'The Status of Women in a Socialist Order. Czechoslovakia 1948–1978', *Slavic Review*, 4 (1979) 583.
14   See Sharon L. Wolchik and Alfed J. Meyers (eds), *Women, State, and Party in Eastern Europe* (Durham NC, Duke University Press), 1985.
15   The number of people and institutions directly involved in political agitation should not be underestimated. Heller estimates that in 1975 there were 325 universities of Marxism-Leninism and about 3,000 town and district schools for party activists. *Cogs in the Soviet Wheel*, pp. 101–2.
16   Viktor Zaslavsky, 'The Rebirth of the Stalin Cult in the USSR', *Telos. A Journal of Radical Thought*, 40 (1979) 10.
17   Brno, 23–6 June 1998.
18   Anatoly Vasilyevich Lunacharsky (1873–1933), the Soviet Republic's First People's Commissar of Education and trusted friend of Lenin.
19   Ivan Petrovich Pavlov (1849–1936) is most important for his work on conditioned reflexes.
20   Heller, *Cogs in the Soviet Wheel*, p. 190.
21   See J. Millar, 'The Little Deal. Brezhnev's Contribution to Acquisitive Socialism', *Slavic Review*, 44:4 (1985) 694–706.
22   Heller, *Cogs in the Soviet Wheel*, p. 163.
23   See Miklós Haraszti, *A Worker in a Workers' State* (Harmondsworth, Pelican Books), 1977.
24   Heller, *Cogs in the Soviet Wheel*, pp. 175–6.
25   Gorbachev instituted a strict campaign against alcohol abuse in May 1985.
26   Unpublished ms, Moscow, April 1991.

CHAPTER NINE

INTERNAL AND EXTERNAL ENEMIES

Political posters played an important role in establishing the psychological barriers which reinforced the physical borders of the communist bloc. They were part of a state-sponsored propaganda programme aimed at those who tried to oppose the Soviet-defined just cause of socialism and were designed to strengthen resistance to external influence. The intention was to consolidate the body of the nation and the bloc into an ideological unity.

Accordingly, the visual satire and caricature used in the condemnation of internal and external enemies were vitriolic and full of hatred: the visual violence of the posters pictured a common enemy in justification of domestic coercion and the institutions of state security such as the people's army, the workers' militia, the secret police and the judiciary. As the party waged war against its own people the poster's task was to fortify the ideological fervour of the converted. The party's main weapons were its material powers of exclusion, its capacity to control employment and, if necessary, its power to physically eliminate, imprison or exile those who refused to conform.

(detail of 9.49)

In Czechoslovakia, as elsewhere, internal enemies were identified as those citizens who might be dangerous to the communist order.[1] Bourgeois or noble 'class origins' might betray a belief in the rights of private ownership in opposition to the Marxist-Leninist theory of the common ownership of property. The religious and representatives of the Church possessed a spiritual faith and institutional structure antipathetic to the communist atheist world view based on dialectical materialism. The legacy of World War II alliances with countries now considered enemies touched those who had participated in resistance groups associated with governments in exile and combatants from the western front. Like them, members of the former liberal and conservative political parties and so-called 'bourgeois' youth and sports organizations such as Skaut, Junák and Sokol (Falcon) were thought to offer an ideological threat. To be identified as a reform communist, or to be related to a political prisoner or emigrant, had serious implications for the individual and the prospects of their children. Similarly, the authorities curtailed the activities of the nonconformist artists, designers and art critics of the unofficial art scene. All these individuals were kept under surveillance by the secret police or suffered other kinds of harassment and persecution at their hands. In every workplace personnel cadres connected with the secret police compiled dossiers and recorded workers' class affiliation and political activities as 'positive', 'reactionary' or 'inimical', and on the basis of these classifications individuals were denounced to employers and the secret police.

In Czechoslovakia, during the 1940s and 1950s, many 'internal enemies' were executed, sentenced to long periods in prison or were used as slave labour in the uranium mines in northern Bohemia. The 1960s saw the release of the survivors, but they were not necessarily rehabilitated until after the collapse of communism, when they or their families could apply for moral and financial indemnity in law. The 1970s and 1980s were less draconian and 'politicals' such as Václav Havel and Lech Wałęsa in Poland received repeated short sentences. During this period the secret police still used torture, but the judiciary abandoned capital punishment and, instead, the state turned to political murder: the Polish priest Jerzy Popiełuszko was killed by the secret police in 1984 and the Czech prisoner of conscience, Pavel Wonka, was murdered in prison on 26 April 1988.

Stalin had demanded that the class struggle should continue after socialism had been achieved and the communist parties in the satellites took this as an opportunity to consolidate their power through the search for internal enemies. It became the subject of a major propaganda campaign. Everywhere in the communist bloc enemy agents and conspirators were said to have infiltrated the body politic and there was a frenetic hunt for conspirators within the communists' ranks in a mirror image of the communist witch hunts of the 1950s in the United States (9.1–4).

The campaign and the paranoia it displayed were partly stimulated by the threat that President Truman's Marshall Plan offered to Soviet hegemony, but even more significant was Tito's nationalist refusal to join the Cominform. The parties of the Soviet bloc slandered, provoked and pressured Yugoslavia. Branded agents of an English/American imperialist conspiracy, Tito and his followers were accused of treason and fascism. Tito's declaration of independence from Moscow gave Soviet-oriented communists the opportunity to attack national communists in the effort to bring the parties into line. Prominent party members whose credentials lay with anti-fascist resistance in World War II were criticized and accused of ideological deviation and political error. Rudolf Slánský, the General Secretary of the Central Committee of the Czechoslovak Communist Party, and ten of his colleagues were executed as agents of Western espionage after being

9.1
Alena Čermáková, *We build socialism, unmask evildoers and enemies of the republic, strengthen the peace front!*, 1950, Czechoslovakia, All Trade Union Archive, Prague.

9.2
Kra-Ma-Vot (Králík-Mařan-Votruba), *Do not talk about what you do, you do not know who listens to you*, 1952, Czechoslovakia, All Trade Union Archive, Prague.

falsely accused of high treason, sabotage and military treason in a high-profile show trial. Suspicion became a valuable attribute of class-consciousness and revolutionary vigilance (9.1). The trials served to promote the cult of Klement Gottwald in an atmosphere of bloodthirsty mass hysteria stimulated by the antisemitism inspired by the Treasonous Conspiracy Centre and the trial of the Jewish doctors in Moscow. Eleven of the fourteen defendants were Jewish. Czechoslovakia had been one of the foremost arms suppliers to Israel, but Moscow's policy of support had come to grief with the rise of a pro-American Zionist lobby. As a result, Soviet propagandists were presented with a ready-made and identifiable enemy linked with an international capitalist conspiracy, who in posters were often given stereotypically Jewish features in representations chillingly reminiscent of Nazi propaganda (9.41).

The crises of 1949 generated an atmosphere of fear and paranoia, and vigilance became part of official policy. Large numbers of posters promoted a permanent condition of watchfulness:

In the people's democratic countries state vigilance gains special significance – the vigilance of the proletarian dictatorship of the state. The principle of strengthening vigilance must be made through vigorous educational work. The office 'For permanent peace, for people's democracy!' in this respect summed up the tasks of communist and workers' parties in the paragraph 'To increase revolutionary vigilance!': 'Marxism-Leninism teaches that the party of the working class can successfully discover the enemy and strike him anywhere and at any time, let him conceal himself in whatever disguise, only so that it will systematically increase the political and ideological level of its cadres, to nurture in them a spirit of irreconcilability to all deviations from the path of Marxism-

Leninism; organizationally to strengthen its ranks, to suppress unmercifully all foreign elements in the party, in the course of time to reveal and defeat nationalist and revisionist deviations and to raise the level of class consciousness in the working class and the working people.

… In science, in literature, in painting, in music and also in film extreme vigilance is necessary, a standpoint which is irreconcilable with every tendency alien to the working class and opposed to the propaganda of cosmopolitanism!'[2]

Party members were screened to guard against infiltration and working-class credentials became more important than ever. But the real significance of communism's pursuit of its real or imagined enemies was that the hunt became a structural element in communist political psychology. The phenomenon was later reinforced by events in Germany in 1953, Poland and Hungary in 1956, Czechoslovakia in 1968 and Poland in 1981.

Václav Havel, as an influential member of Charter 77, was mocked for his bourgeois and elitist origins as part of a strategy designed to isolate him and his kind from the population at large. On 6 January 1977 Havel was detained by the StB and six days later an article by Jaroslav Kojzar, the principal strategist of the anti-Charter 77 campaign, appeared in *Rudé Pravó*:

In desperation the instinct of self-preservation drives the bourgeoisie to beat itself around the (non) head senseless(ly) [an untranslatable proverb with the double meaning of senseless violence and beating sense into], it makes anything possible and feels no strong dislike for anything which might stop the revolutionary process. International reaction will use any means. It corrupts no matter who, anyone is corruptible, it bribes, bulk buys and counts among its number apostates,

9.1

BUDUJME SOCIALISMUS
ODHALUJME ŠKŮDCE A NEPŘÁTELE
REPUBLIKY
POSILUJME FRONTU MÍRU!

9.2

NEMLUV O TOM, CO DĚLÁŠ

NEVÍŠ, KDO TĚ POSLOUCHÁ

ZACHOVÁNÍM STÁTNÍHO A VÝROBNÍHO TAJEMSTVÍ PŘISPĚJEŠ K BEZPEČNOSTI SVÉ VLASTI A UPEVNĚNÍ SVĚTOVÉHO MÍRU

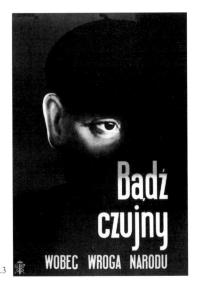

9.3

9.4

9.5

9.6

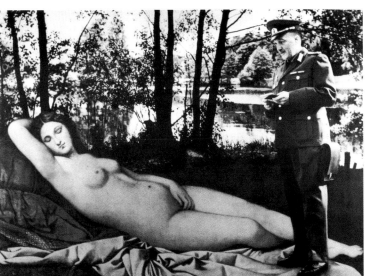

9.7

9.3
Tadeusz Trepkowski, *Be vigilant against the nation's enemy!*, 1953, Poland, Museum of Independence, Warsaw.

9.4
V. M. Lykov, *Always be vigilant everywhere*, 1960, Soviet Union, Historical Archive of the Czech Army, Prague.

9.5
Vytautas Kaušinis, *Eyes we have, but reality we do not see!*, 1963, Soviet Lithuania, Moravian Gallery, Brno.

9.6
Zdeněk Filip, *Charter 77*, 1977, Czechoslovakia, Historical Archive of the Czech Army, Prague.

9.7
Joseph W. Huber, *untitled*, c. 1985, GDR, Moravian Gallery, Brno.

deserters from the camp of the adversary. It recruits emigrants, and other wreckers living in the socialist countries, those who, whatever the purposes of their class, have reactionary interests, who, for the sake of vanity or the pursuit of fame, inconstancy and habitual spinelessness, consent to give their names even to the devil. In its inveterate fight against progress, international reaction tries to create the semblance of a broad anti-communist front. Belonging to this is the newest publication, the so-called Charter 77, a group of people not only from the failed Czechoslovak reactionary bourgeoisie, but also from the ranks of the failed organizers of the counter-revolution of 1968, made by order of the anti-communist and Zionist headquarters, controlled by certain Western agencies. It is treasonous, anti-socialist, anti-proletarian and demogogic slander, which rudely and mendaciously slanders the Czechoslovak Socialist Republic and the revolutionary achievements of its people. ... These authors despise the people, their interests and condemn the representative authorities elected to protect the people.[3]

A poster by Zdeněk Filip depicted Charter 77 as a band of luckless sailors adrift on a raft of anti-Sovietism about to be run down by the ship of peace – its toppled fountain pen mast revealing its insecure base in the dollar (9.6). Interestingly enough, the design apes Veniamin Markovich Briskin's anti-capitalist and anti-NATO poster from 1945 *Out of the way, instigators of war!* (9.41). Opponents were identified and mocked before being subjected to the forms of repression represented by the security forces and the judicial system (9.7). A plethora of laws against the gathering of information, subversive connections, treasonable disloyalty, sabotage, subversive organization of a group and agitation, resistance to government measures, unlawfully crossing borders, rowdiness, rioting, forming an organization with illegal goals, illegal contacts (talking to foreigners) and defamation of the state (including political jokes) were used very effectively against those who would not conform, particularly the young. The principle was one of divide and rule on both external international and internal national levels. The visual rhetoric, while passionate, was traditional and programmatic and would have been familiar to any nineteenth-century socialist, with its images of heroic revolutionaries, mythical monsters, snakes, fat capitalists and triumphant workers.

PEACE GUARDS

The communists called the Soviet bloc a 'Peace Camp' and the People's Army the 'Peace Army'. Etymologically *Mir*, the Russian word for 'peace', has a revolutionary resonance absent from its English equivalent, carrying the meanings 'community' in the rural sense (commune), 'world' and 'universe'. The word calls into play nostalgic longings for tradition, unity, stability and order – qualities which were,

of necessity, worthy of protection. 'Peace' was therefore a major cornerstone of communist rhetorical thinking with its reliance on structures of exclusion and inclusion. The mythicization of the peace guard was one of its products. Iconographically, the type owes its origins to revolutionary imagery and the single heroic figure of the anonymous insurgent. He stands alone, but armed, at the head of a crowd or astride the globe like some revolutionary colossus (9.9). Originally he epitomized the struggle of the Red Army against the White forces of reaction and in the post-war world he opposed those who would seek to undermine communist achievements from within and without (9.8). The figure often took the form of a militia man allied to contemporary and historical revolutionary traditions.[4] In Czechoslovakia the fight against the enemy within was visually aligned with the efforts of the Hussites in the fifteenth century (1.1). Similarly, in Poland the defeat of Nazism and the expansion of Polish territory westward under the Soviets were compared to the victory of a peasant army over the Teutonic knights at the battle of Grunwald in 1410 (9.10, 11). In Hungary the triumph of communism was historically paralleled with György Dózsa, the peasant leader executed in 1514 for his part in an uprising against the feudal lords. After the 1956 uprising, revisionist energies were condemned by István Prihoda's revolutionary poster of 21 March 1919, *You! Counter-revolutionary, hiding in the dark, spreading false rumours, tremble!* (1957). It was republished as a reminder of the founding energies of the short-lived Hungarian Soviet Republic prior to the country's partition in 1920. As a version of Alfred Leete's *Your country needs you* (1914), the poster called for Hungarians to root out counter-revolutionaries and played on patriotic memories of a greater and revolutionary Hungary. Communist man was armed, vigilant and dangerous.

After World War II borders and their guards had taken on a whole new set of meanings with the new geopolitical configuration and forced population displacements. Public knowledge of these shifts was suppressed, and while the peace guard protects against foreign incursion, he also confines, controls and watches the people he serves (9.12, 13). He – and the figure is always male – supplies the security necessary for well-being and happiness, and simultaneously reveals the repressions and delusions common to any patriarchy but strongly exaggerated in a dictatorship. He benignly dominates a worker or a peasant, and is himself subject to fatherly or brotherly Soviet guidance.

Assisted by the latest technology and weaponry, the military were cast in the image of protector and defender. Idealized assertive young men were presented with the

9.8

9.9

9.10

9.11

9.12

9.13

9.8
Viktor Koretsky, Viktor Ivanov, O. Savostyuk and Boris Uspensky, *Glory to the heroes of the Great October!*, 1954, Soviet Union, Andrei Budnik, Kiev.

9.9
Tibor Gönczi, *Long live Great October*, 1957, Hungary, Hungarian Museum of Contemporary History, Budapest.

9.10
Tadeusz Trepkowski, *Grunwald 1410 – Berlin 1945*, 1945, Poland, Poster Museum, Wilanow.

9.11
Włodzimierz Zakrewski, *Follow our ancestors*, 1945, Poland, Poster Museum, Wilanow.

9.12
Kra-Ma-Vot (Králík-Mařan-Votruba) *American agent cannot penetrate our village*, 1952, Czechoslovakia, All Trade Union Archive, Prague.

9.13
György Pál, *We will defend the peace!*, 1950, Hungary, Hungarian Museum of Contemporary History, Budapest.

9.14

9.15

9.16

9.14
Boris Reshetnikov, *Do not attack us – we will not attack you!*, 1954, Soviet Latvia, National Library, Riga.

9.15
Anon., *'The defence of the achievement of our republic is justice to the world.' Wilhelm Pieck*, 1954, GDR, Thomas Hill.

9.16
Hausler and Kleman, *Exhibition of the fortieth anniversary of the November Revolution*, 1958, GDR, Thomas Hill.

9.17
Anon., *Warm welcome*, c. 1965, GDR, Thomas Hill.

9.17

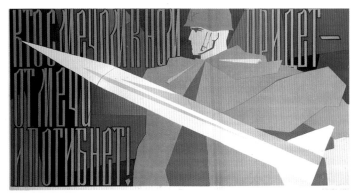

9.18

9.19

9.20

9.18
Alexander Mikhailovich Lemeshchenko, *Strengthen the protection of the homeland*, 1971, Soviet Union, Mikhail Avvakumov, Moscow.

9.19
Alexander Nikolaevich Dobrov, *Who comes to us with a sword dies by the sword!*, 1966, Soviet Union, Academy of Fine Art, Berlin.

9.20
Vladimir Sachov, *Learn to protect the homeland!*, 1987, Soviet Union, private collection.

9.21
Alexander Vasilovich Vorona, *I serve the Soviet Union!*, 1976, six sheets, Soviet Union, Andrei Budnik, Kiev.

9.21

9.22
John Heartfield, *Johannes R. Becher. Winter War*, 1954, GDR, Academy of Fine Art, Berlin.

9.23
Manfred Butzmann, *For example*, 1981, GDR, the artist.

9.24
Boris Bučan, *Voltaire, 'Candide'*, 1983, Yugoslavia, Moravian Gallery, Brno.

9.25
Andrei Sheliuto, Vladimir Cesler and Sergei Voychenko, *GZh-51560, Afghan* (unknown soldiers), 1989, Soviet Byelorussia, Moravian Gallery, Brno.

9.26
NSK, *United States of Europe. Laibach tour*, 1987, Yugoslavia, Moravian Gallery, Brno.

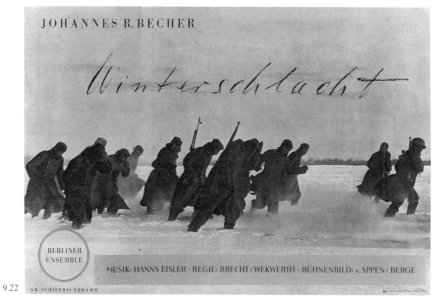

9.22

9.23

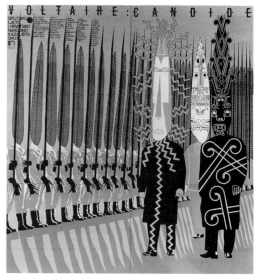

9.24

9.25

9.26

ZRÁDNÁ EMIGRACE VE SLUŽBÁCH ZÁPADNÍCH IMPERIALISTŮ

9.27

9.28

9.29

9.27
Anon., *Treacherous emigration serves Western imperialists!*, 1951, Czechoslovakia, private collection.

9.28
Anon., *Illegal border crossing from the republic*, c. 1955, GDR, Academy of Fine Art, Berlin.

9.29
Martin Hoffmann, *Concerning permanent emigrants*, c. 1985, GDR, Moravian Gallery, Brno.

9.30
D. Sedláčková, *Capitalism has one aim: to achieve the greatest profit through pauperization of the people and through war!*, 1954, Czechoslovakia, Moravian Museum, Brno.

9.30

9.31

9.31
Anon., *Through increase in market production – prosperity and security of peace*, 1960, GDR, Thomas Hill.

9.32
Anon., *Capitalism. Let's watch our factories carefully*, c. 1950, Czechoslovakia, Museum of Decorative Arts, Prague.

9.33
K. Pechánková, *For peace in Korea! Victory of the Korean people in their struggle for freedom*, 1952, Czechoslovakia, All Trade Union Archive, Prague.

9.32

9.33

9.34

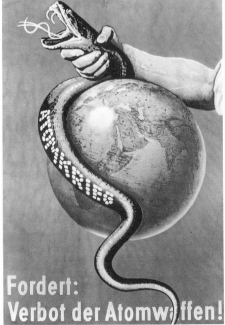

9.36

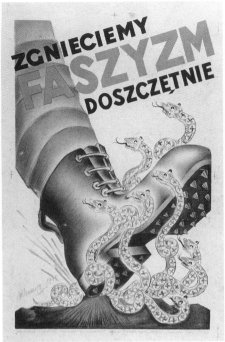
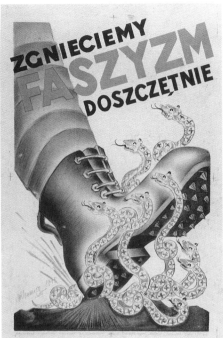

9.35

9.37

9.34
Filo (Ilona Fischer), *No!*,
1955, Hungary, Hungarian
National Gallery, Budapest.

9.35
Witold Chomicz, *We will
crush fascism completely!*,
1945, Poland, Poster Museum,
Wilanow.

9.36
John Heartfield, *Demand an
atomic weapons ban!*, 1955,
GDR, Academy of Fine Arts,
Berlin.

9.37
Viktor Koretsky, *We need
peace!*, 1950, Soviet Union,
Museum of the Working Class
Movement, Prague.

9.39

9.38

imagery of the military as an ideal to emulate. Military service, which was in any case compulsory, functioned as part of a rite of passage within various communist life stages from Pioneers to Socialist Youth Organizations in iconographies which continued with diminished authority until the collapse (9.14–21). This type of picture was challenged only rarely and never through the medium of the official political poster. Particularly telling is John Heartfield's 1954 design for the play *Winter War*, which was based on a photograph of Wehrmacht soldiers in the retreat from Moscow (9.22). Written by the Culture Minister, Johannes R. Becher, the play was performed at Brecht's Berliner Ensemble, the heart of the official German Democratic avant garde. The poster warned of the dangers of fascism and the price to be paid for aggression against the new masters in the Kremlin. The poster was all that, but it was more than that. Uniquely, it showed German youth as wretched and defeated, the dystopian character of the poster functioning as a critical statement, contrasting with representations of the armed forces as technologically advanced and cosmically ordained guardians of peace and security. Manfred Butzmann continued the tradition of critique, but his disarmanent poster fell foul of the authorities (9.23). Likewise, Boris Bučan used the medium of the cultural poster to draw attention to the primitive yet structural role of the military in contemporary Yugoslav society, risking a portrait of Tito as the 'big chief' (9.24).

The Red Army continued to trade on its defeat of fascism in World War II, but in the late 1980s posters about the war in Afghanistan began to undermine the unquestioned martial moral authority of the armed forces.

One poster drew attention to the scale of the casualties (9.25); another, published by Agitplakat in Moscow in 1988, and designed by J. Vertogradov, displayed the words 'Holding on in difficult times' and depicted a veteran amputee. A poster published by NSK advertising the *United States of Europe; Laibach tour* (1987) pictured an ambiguous, devilish figure with twin bayonets and a snake in the shape of a dollar sign (9.26). Simultaneously the poster aped the iconography of the peace guard and conformed to conventional anti-Americanism while participating in commercial popular culture. In Yugoslavia and in Hungary communist imagery carried with it a strong affective appeal for youth culture, where, in the wake of the virtual collapse of the Young Pioneers and Union of Youth as organs of party influence, the young were able to define themselves in terms of what they were not, as they openly mocked communist iconographies and emblems in posters promoting music and popular culture (5.31, 32).

ÉMIGRÉS AND ESCAPEES

Both before and after the construction of the Berlin Wall, 'the anti-fascist wall of protection', the authorities struggled with the desire of large sections of the population to leave for the West (9.27–29). Many were never to return. Some were shot by peace guards, others were arrested. In the German Democratic Republic propagandists played on the pathology and psychological burden of the border between the two Germanys, and exploited the fear and uncertainties of would-be *émigrés*.[5] After the 1975 Helsinki Accords, emigration was reluctantly permitted on humanitarian and

9.40

9.41

9.42

9.43

9.45

9.46

9.42
Sándor Ék (Alex Keil), *Nazi Germany will be destroyed soon!*, 1944, Hungary, Hungarian Museum of Contemporary History, Budapest.

9.43
Edo Murtiś, *Powerful allies pulling down Hitler's European fortress*, 1944, Yugoslavia, Croatian Historical Museum, Zagreb.

9.44
Anon., *We organize national resistance. Cast your vote on 15 October for peace, unity and a happy life*, 1950, GDR, Thomas Hill.

9.44

9.45
Wolfgang A. Schlosser, *The strong foundations of the Adenauer Company, formerly Adolf Hitler & Co.*, 1953, Czechoslovakia, private collection.

9.46
Wolfgang A. Schlosser, *Beware NATO. ... They shall not pass*, 1962, Czechoslovakia, Moravian Museum, Brno.

9.47
Anon., *May Day poster of Chiang-Kai Chek, 'Bearer of Culture', Wenceslas Square, Prague*, 1951, Museum of the Working Class Movement, Prague.

9.48
Wolfgang A. Schlosser, *To the fight against the American beetle. How we struggle against the American beetle*, 1951, Czechoslovakia, Museum of Decorative Arts, Prague.

9.49
After a caricature by the Kukriniksy group, Moscow, *Pest ridgeway in western Europe! Maximum vigilance and battle readiness protects our GDR*, 1952, GDR, Thomas Hill.

9.47

9.48

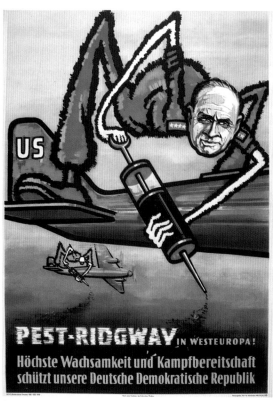
9.49

9.50
Alexander Vorona, *U2*, 1960,
Soviet Union, Academy of
Fine Art, Berlin.

9.51
Nikolai Petrovich Charukhin,
We will not permit!, 1969,
Soviet Union, Mikhail
Avvakumov, Moscow.

9.52
Boris Andreyevich
Reshetnikov, *We warn
revanchists!*, 1966, Soviet
Union, Mikhail Avvakumov,
Moscow.

9.53
Eryk Lipiński, *Down with
Truman's murders in Korea!*,
1951, Poland, Museum of
Independence, Warsaw.

9.54
Wolfgang A. Schlosser,
*Venceremos. Homeland or
death – we will win!*, 1962,
Czechoslovakia, All Trade
Union Archive, Prague.

9.55
Filo (Ilona Fischer), *Hands off!
Vietnam*, 1965, Hungary,
Hungarian National Gallery,
Budapest.

9.56
Sergei Raev, *Criminal –
responsibility*, 1970, Soviet
Union, Mikhail Avvakumov,
Moscow.

9.57
Jiří Figer, *No! No to American
aggression in Vietnam*, 1972,
Czechoslovakia, Historical
Archive of the Czech Army,
Prague.

9.58
Klaus Wittkugel, *In the name
of humanity*, 1970, GDR,
Historical Archive of the
Czech Army, Prague.

9.54

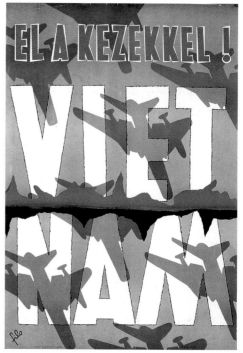

9.55

9.56

9.57

9.58

familial grounds; however, applicants were regarded as ungrateful enemies of the state. They were consigned to a kind of internal exile as they were forced to break off contact with relations and friends to protect them from harassment by the state. Posters warned of the fate awaiting them in the West: homelessness, despair and even death at the hands of criminals (there being no crime under communism). One poster published in Rostock in the mid-1960s, *Illegal border crossing*, plots the dramatic decline to certain death in the desert of capitalism (9.28). All that is left are the footprints in the sand. The physicality of the path from life to death is unmistakable, and the poster makes an interesting contribution to the nature of realism in communist political art. The question of absence and disappearance is evident in the work of unofficial designers such as Manfred Hoffmann, whose posters relating to emigration and human rights feature people as traces (9.29). It is as if the stress of living under close surveillance, and the strategies necessary for survival, made victims suffer guilt and reduced them to shades.

The official political poster pictured an unequivocal divide between a good and morally correct communist existence and a corrupt, decadent and essentially evil capitalist order in the West. One of the most effective means of accomplishing this strategy was graphic satire. Large numbers of posters relied in part on the techniques of the cartoonist. The language of the political cartoonist is a conservative one in any culture, rarely making use of anything other than a visual vernacular. Under communism graphic satire was radically conformist as it aped the policies of the state and its predetermined world view. The vocabulary is popular, easily understood and relies for its effect on the straightforward depiction of political slogans and a rhetoric dependent on figures of speech translated directly into visual form. As such it was amenable to the aesthetic tradition of socialist realism.

Drawing on the European tradition established in publications such as the German *Simplicissimus* (1896–1933), designers such as Aleksandr Apsit, Dmitrii Moor, Viktor Deni and later, under Stalin, the Kukryniksy group, Viktor Ivanov and Viktor Koretsky among others, elaborated the iconographies of the traditional *Lubok* and the revolutionary street celebrations of the Bolshevik years. They instituted pictorial formulas for the depiction of enemies, subjecting them to caricature and identifying them with a grotesque phantasmagoria of mythical beasts.[6] The technique was common throughout the region, where, as Mariusz Knorowski has pointed out, 'elements of barrack-room humour appeared beside the heroic, martyrological and humanitarian content. Caricatural overstatements, attempts at simple narration, made these types of

publications resemble the Soviet war propaganda known under the term "TASS windows".[7] The techniques of caricature and monstrous personification establish the capitalist enemy as a strange, alien, greedy aggressor (9.30, 31). Rapacious and violent, the enemy is reduced to a faceless 'other': a savage beast or a subhuman species without significance, certain to be defeated by the superior forces of communism (9.37–39).

The snake was particularly popular as a symbol of capitalism. Unpredictable, unseen and likely to strike at any time, the image of the snake fed the paranoia and fear generated by the perpetual search for enemies (9.32, 33, 35, 36). Often the fist and forearm put the monstrous reptilian foe to rout: nature is captured and controlled, subjected to the rational human will. The clenched fist salute was one of the most popular iconographic motifs of international socialism and communist-inspired national liberation movements. As a metonym of the power of the working class it embodied committed and rational control. We may see this idea represented in a poster by Viktor Koretsky *We need peace!* (1950) (9.37), which depicts the rather handsome figure of a worker towering over an international assembly of diminutive and grotesque Western leaders who smashes his fist down on to the conference table.

Ideological imperatives aside, this strain in communist propaganda offers direct parallels with political cartoons in the West. There is, however, one major difference: apart from the state-sponsored anti-alcohol and anti-shirking campaigns, where internal and external enemies were implicitly linked, poster makers in the communist bloc were unable to direct their skills at the domestic situation or the foreign political situation unless it was advantageous to the state. Criticism of the leadership, past or present, was not tolerated. Indeed, any such attack would undermine the essence of the totalitarian state, its claim to infallibility and its reliance on a mystificatory cult of the leadership. Overt criticism of the leader, and by implication the state, was not permitted even with *glasnost* and *perestroika*. Once allowed, it heralded the collapse of an entire system.

If the criticism of domestic leaders was prohibited, the skills of the graphic satirist were well employed in the demonization of Western leaders in a visual rhetoric defined by the titanic anti-fascist struggles of World War II (9.42–46). A Hungarian poster calling for an anti-war crimes tribunal depicts the three fists of Great Britain, the United States and the Soviet Union crushing the head of a hapless Hitler (9.42). But once former allies became rivals for world dominance in the Cold War, Western leaders were often directly identified with fascism and the figures of Adolf Hitler, Herman Goering and Josef Goebbels. An anonymous Czech poster directed against the Western

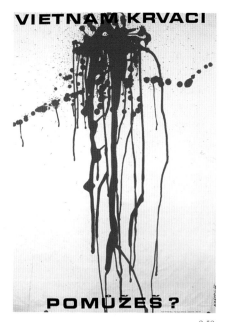

9.59

9.59
Jan Rajlich, *Vietnam*, 1966,
Czechoslovakia, Moravian
Gallery, Brno.

9.60
Alexander Zhitomirsky, *Out of
Vietnam*, 1971, Soviet Union,
Mikhail Avvakumov, Moscow.

9.61
Yevgeny Abramovich
Kazhdan, *Junta*, 1973, Soviet
Union, Poster Museum,
Wilanow.

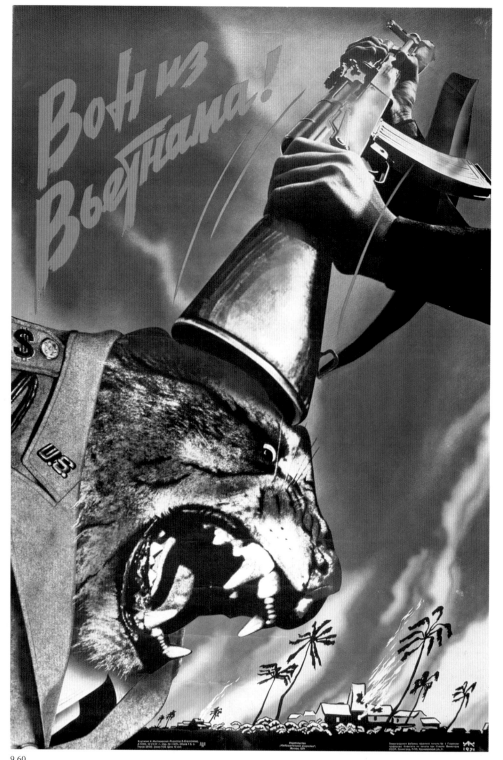

9.60

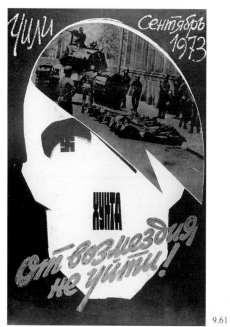

9.61

9.62

9.63

9.64

9.65

9.62
Juris Dimiters, *Welcome to Chile*, 1978, Soviet Latvia, Laimonis Senbergs.

9.63
Viktor Koretsky and Yuri Kershin, *Not just once defeated, they still scramble for a fight, but there is a collar for a wild dog! Warsaw Pact*, 1969, Soviet Union, Mikhail Avvakumov, Moscow.

9.64
V. Galba, *The inner nature of American freedom*, 1967, Soviet Union, Mikhail Avvakumov, Moscow.

9.65
Nikolai Petrovich Charukhin, *I am a man. Racism shame of America!*, 1969, Soviet Union, Mikhail Avvakumov, Moscow.

9.66
Tadeusz Trepkowski, *Fascism the American way*, 1952, Poland, Museum of Independence, Warsaw.

9.67
Zbigniew Lengren, *American shoe advertisement*, 1952, Poland, Museum of Independence, Warsaw.

9.68
Viktor Koretsky, *USA. American imperialism. It's war, slavery, racism*, 1968, Soviet Union, Mikhail Avvakumov, Moscow.

9.69
Witold Mysyrowicz, *Symbol and reality*, 1983, Poland, Museum of Independence, Warsaw.

9.66

9.67

9.68

9.69

9.70

9.71

9.72

GERMANIA 2000?

9.73

9.70
Jan Bohuszewicz, *From the
darkness of the Middle Ages.
Crusaders against Poland*,
1982, Poland, Museum of
Independence, Warsaw.

9.71
Vadim Volikov, *Racism terror.
We accuse!*, 1965, Soviet
Union, Mikhail Avvakumov,
Moscow.

9.72
Lex Drewinski, *Germania
2000. Against power and
xenophobia*, 1992,
Germany/Poland, Moravian
Gallery, Brno.

9.73
Manfred Butzmann, *Brother,
it's burning*, 1992, Germany,
the artist.

broadcasting stations such as the Voice of America, because they encouraged defectors, depicts the Western powers as a neo-fascist conspiracy, armed to the teeth and in cahoots with the former Nazi leadership and the Vatican (9.27). Similarly, Wolfgang A. Schlosser sees the Federal Republic of Germany and NATO as a house of cards supported not only by the United States and the forces of capital, but by the legacy of German militarism and the Third Reich (9.45).

As World War II became more distant, the United States became the subject of demonization. A photograph of a May Day parade from the early 1950s in Prague shows people carrying hand-made posters of the enemies of communism (9.47).[8] The largest of the posters shows a crazed, six-gun-toting Uncle Sam showering Korea with Colorado potato beetles in an act of biological warfare. In a campaign directed at the Americans, the Soviets accused them of spreading the pest along the Berlin corridor after a series of crop failures (9.48, 49). Uncle Sam provides the symbolic marker as a vehicle of condemnation. But, more often than not, the posters provided a guide for the identification of real-life enemies, just as Stalin had demanded, and promoted anti-American propaganda campaigns on the back of foreign policy blunders such as the international incident provoked by the shooting down of Gary Powers's U-2 spy plane over Soviet territory in 1962 (9.50).

Conventionally the monolithic power of American capital and imperialism was thwarted by the jovial strength of the armed forces and the solidarity of the working people (9.51). But as the Cold War developed, new patterns began to emerge which made greater use of photo-montage and exploited American domestic and foreign policy crises arising out of Korea, Cuba and the Bay of Pigs fiasco, the civil rights campaign, Vietnam, Chile and arms expenditure (9.53–71). Posters condemning American interference in the affairs of other nations represent the indigenous peoples as heroic and humane victims who suffer the anonymous and distanced onslaught of an inhuman enemy, reified in the caricatured body of its technological supremacy. A large proportion of these posters build on suppressed modernist techniques developed among others by John Heartfield, Gustav Klutsis, Alexander Zhitomirsky, Klaus Wittkugel, Wolfgang A. Schlosser and Viktor Koretsky. They never had wide exposure in the West but their language and technique are paralleled in the work of designers working from anarcho-liberal positions critical of American foreign policy and international capitalism, such as the poster artists of the anti-Vietnam War movement and individuals such as Klaus Staeck in the Federal Republic of Germany, Peter Kennard in the United Kingdom and John Yates in the United States. It was a two-way process. Ron Haeberle's photograph of the massacre carried out by American troops at My Lai in Vietnam which had provided the basis of the poster published by the Art Workers' Coalition in New York, *Q. And babies? A. And babies* (1969–70),[9] was also used in Czechoslovakia by Jiří Figer in 1972 (9.57) and in the German Democratic Republic by Jürgen Haufe in *Brother Eichmann* (1983), a poster commemorating both the Holocaust and the firestorm which had consumed Dresden in the last days of World War II.

The structures of exclusion and hatred have survived into the post-communist era, as has the commitment of

9.74
Anon., *Republicans against NATO!*, 1998, Czech Republic, private collection.

designers to social justice and political and economic reform. Lex Drewinski and Manfred Butzmann have directed their efforts against the rise of the extreme right in Germany, while in the Czech Republic the Republican Party has appropriated the stylistic vocabulary of the anti-nuclear movement of the 1980s to propagandize its nationalist and anti-NATO credentials (9.74).

NOTES

1   The following paragraphs on 'enemies' are based on information supplied by Marta Sylvestrová, January 1999.

2   G. Georgiu-Dej, 'The Jugoslav Communist Party in the Power of Murderers and Spies', Conference of the Information Bureau of the Communist Parties in Hungary, November 1949, translated by Marta Sylvestrová.

3   *Rudé Pravó*, 12 January 1977, translated by Marta Sylvestrová.

4   According to Nina Tumarkin the Soviets encouraged partisans to rise up against the enemy in the vanguard of their advance, but also ensured they had little support. Dead heroes were much more useful to Stalin than live ones, who might prove a threat to his designs on central Europe. See *The Living and the Dead. The Rise and Fall of the Cult of World War II in Russia* (New York, Basic Books), 1994.

5   See Hans-Joachim Maaz, *Behind the Wall. The Inner Life of Communist Germany*, translated by Margot Bettauer Dembo (New York, Norton), 1995.

6   See Vladimir Tolstoy, Irina Bibikova and Catherine Cooke (eds), *Street Art of the Revolution. Festivals and Celebrations in Russia 1918–1933* (London, Vendome Press, Thames & Hudson), 1990.

7   Mariusz Knorowski, *Forma i treść w plakacie polskim 1944–1955* (Warsaw, Muzeum Plakatu w Wilanowie), undated, unpag.

8   See Tolstoy *et al.*, *Street Art of the Revolution*.

9   See Francis Frascina in Paul Wood, Francis Frascina, Jonathan Harris and Charles Harrison, *Modernism in Dispute. Art since the Forties* (New Haven CT and London, Yale University Press), 1993, pp. 106–14; David Kunzle, 'Killingly Funny' in Jeffrey Walsh and James Aulich (eds), *Vietnam Images. War and Representation* (London, Macmillan), 1989, pp. 112–22; and Track 16 Gallery for the Study of Political Graphics, *Decade of Protest. Political Posters from the United States, Vietnam, Cuba 1965–1975* (Santa Monica, CA, Smart Art Press), 1996.

Even as products of a distasteful authoritarian political culture the sheer confidence of Stalinist posters and the later decorative achievements of Soviet designers have to be admitted. Furthermore, many of the most orthodox communist designers produced work which spoke for national agendas not wholly influenced by Moscow. The Polish poster school, for example, signified independent national accomplishment and served as a benchmark of autonomous achievement and quality throughout the period. National solutions emerged throughout the region. Some designers in Czechoslovakia adapted pre-war modernist strategies to new realist ends. In Hungary the fascist legacies of the 1930s were reinterpreted through the decorative qualities of *la moderne* to produce a poster art which was as confident as the impact of Russian occupation on indigenous culture was devastating. In the German Democratic Republic, for example, some designers drew on the vocabularies of the Weimar Republic while others such as Klaus Wittkugel developed the potential of photo-montage as a socialist-realist rather than critical medium.

Gradually the 'political' poster as a socially engaged medium separated itself from the official discourse and migrated to a site defined by independently produced art posters and spontaneous street graphics. Engendered by the transformation of the political, this shift saw a challenge to a monological dominant discourse. It was a change which can be usefully analysed by applying Jürgen Habermas's model of the liberal public sphere. For Habermas the public sphere is constituted by a free press defined by the point at which information as the circulation of a commodity is equivalent to an exchange of communications, where the primary purpose is neither propaganda nor profit but critique.[1]

But the reader should be warned that, as Zlavoj Žižek has observed, the imposition of the Habermasian model is in fact a measure of certain Western perspectives:

> Why is the West so fascinated by the recent events in Eastern Europe? The answer seems obvious: what fascinates the Western gaze is the *reinvention of democracy*. It is as if democracy, which in the West shows increasing signs of decay and crisis, lost in bureaucratic routine and publicity-style election campaigns, is being rediscovered in Eastern Europe in all its freshness and novelty. The function of this fascination is thus purely ideological: in Eastern Europe the West looks for its own lost origins, for the authentic experience of 'democratic invention'. In other words, Eastern Europe functions for the West as its Ego-Ideal: the point from which the West sees itself in a likeable, idealized form, as worthy of love. The real object of fascination for the West is thus the gaze, namely the supposedly naive *gaze* by which Eastern Europe stares back at the West, fascinated by its democracy.[2]

Habermas's model of the liberal public sphere presupposes the objective possibility of reducing structural conflicts of interest and bureaucratic decisions to a minimum. In practice these conditions never operated in communist states except at times of crisis and collapse and then only briefly and arguably. As we have seen, the

(detail of 9.64)

unofficial street graphics of the Hungarian uprising, the Prague Spring, the Polish August and the changes of 1989 provided the space for a critique of the rhetoric of domination. The corruptions of visual and verbal language found in the official political poster had a more constant corollary in the challenges to communist authority implicit in the counter-spheres of independent trade unions, dissident human rights campaigns, urban youth culture and the uncontrollable ramifications of *glasnost* and *perestroika*. The Solidarity logo was perhaps one of the most eloquent products of this engagement, as it simultaneously appropriated the colour red, the iconography of the crowd and the Polish flag in a manner which exactly mirrored the policies of Solidarity and its relations with the people, the communist party and the state.

Official political posters were the product of a large-scale industrial operation whose values were totally subjected to the power of the state. They do not partake of a public sphere because propaganda is contrary to public opinion. In contrast, art posters and street graphics are small-scale artisanal products of 'publicity' which, according to Habermas, once meant the subjection of political power to the public exercise of reason:

> Publicity was, according to its very idea, a principle of democracy not just because anyone could in principle announce, with equal opportunity, his personal inclinations, wishes and convictions – opinions; it would only be realised in the measure that these personal opinions could evolve through the rational-critical debate of a public opinion – *opinion publique*.[3]

Prototypically, the public sphere emerges during revolutionary crises as a guarantee of freedom. It can be produced by the formation of a consensus through the publication and public discussion of various viewpoints arrived at as the consequence of critical and rational reflection. In this liberal guise the public sphere serves as a corrective to the exercise of power and domination. Habermas argues that in Western democratic societies such perspectives result in personal financial risk. In communist societies financial risk is replaced by risk to personal liberty.

Official political posters are exhortations and intimidations, they are debased by subjection to police instructions and prohibitions. They are expressions of ideals coerced into existence through the mechanism of the communist state. Lenin had put in place a programme where the state control of language purified it of historical meaning. This was as true of the language of the 'nation' as it was of the language of 'revolution' and its antecedents in the Enlightenment and the French Revolution. 'Freedom', 'equality' and 'people' were words exposed as bourgeois corruptions of the class struggle, and as threats to the leadership of the party and the dictatorship of the proletariat. General statements were transformed into slogans and directives for action which provided the correct answer. A typical slogan might be taken from the constitution of the Soviet Union: 'The work of the party, the aim of our life, the welfare of the nation, the strength of our homeland' has no verb and is incontrovertible. Without a verb it has no meaning and its currency rests in its value as a slogan of the party. It is incantatory and ritualized. It has a magical quality, presenting what is desired as if it were real. There is no space for denial. To say it makes it true. Drawing on an Orwellian vocabulary, the first seminar of the Flying University in Warsaw noted:

> Besides trying to replace the classical language, [New Speak] also lays it to waste … preserving the appearances of classical meaning while in fact substituting a new one. … The degradations spread into specialised linguistic traditions such as the patriotic and the revolutionary. Everything is reduced to a formula or a platitude in which imposed value and ritualised incantation override meaning. New Speak destroys effective communication, particularly public communication, as it alters and neutralises formulations which stood for real meanings and real attitudes. New Speak disintegrates communication in an even deeper sense: it kills confidence in language in general.[4]

Alain Besançon suggests that Soviet words should be translated properly so that *kolkhoz*, for example, would no longer mean 'collective farm' but 'a serf plantation, run by an outside bureaucracy and under the surveillance of the apparatus of enforcement'. Or, when referring to democracy, elections and trade unions, it should be made clear that there are no such things in the Soviet Union in the Western sense.[5]

As part of the public face of coercive totalitarianism the slogans and the pictorial formulas are at once clichéed and threatening. The vocabulary is martial, laced with 'fronts', 'struggles' and the inevitable 'victories' in a Marxist-Leninist lexicon of dialectical materialism which dictates a condition of perpetual change in which opposites are identical. Quoting Engels, Lenin had written:

> The great basic thought, … that the world is not to be comprehended as a complex of ready-made things, but as a complex of processes, in which things apparently stable no less than their mind images in our heads, the concepts, go through an uninterrupted change of coming into being and passing away. … For dialectical philosophy nothing is final, absolute, sacred. It reveals the transitory character of everything and anything; nothing can endure before it except the uninterrupted process of becoming and of passing away, of endless ascendancy from the lower to the higher.[6]

Marxist-Leninist orthodoxies produced a rhetoric where dictatorship and democracy are one and the same and state power must be strengthened if it is to disappear. Society is classless but the class struggle must be intensified. Socialism is victorious and yet besieged by hostile states and an international capitalist conspiracy. Everything is fulfilled, targets are met and exceeded. The people are happy. But constant vigilance is a necessity, the enemy must be crushed and cut from the socialist body. The construction of socialism is complete and the building of communism must begin.

During periods of relative liberalism like that in Czechoslovakia in the 1960s or Poland during the 1970s, and throughout the region under *glasnost* and *perestroika* (with the possible exceptions, for different reasons, of Romania and the German Democratic Republic), many designers resorted to the grotesque and parody to engage in a visual critique of the spurious logic of dialectical materialism to create a kind of surreal rationality characterized by:

> Existential angst, urban man's romantic nostalgia for a bucolic soul, wryly realistic portrayals of everyday life, the individual's alienation from collective pressures, complex explorations of moral conflict, satires, comedies dealing with corruption and other symptoms of social malaise – all these themes found their way into the output of a vast cultural industry along with ones expressive of patriotism and socialist optimism.[7]

It cannot be argued that posters partake of rational discursive thought. But as street graphics and art posters they can help constitute the discourses of dissidence, opposition and critique as they take part in the struggle to re-establish a public sphere in communist societies. Wherever and whenever primitive markets and the developing discourse of civil and political society re-emerged, individual designers as both editors and publishers operated on a commercial basis without commercializing the product. The poster was not so much part of a commodity exchange for profit as part of an exchange of ideas in the pursuit of various individual, national and religious liberties. As individual expressions they were dialogical sites of ideological conflict and contestation. This was particularly true during periods of relative liberalization and during times of change and crisis: Czechoslovakia in the 1960s, Poland in the 1970s, the GDR, Yugoslavia, Hungary and the Baltic States in the early 1980s and in the Soviet Union at large after 1985. As the product of particular historical moments determined by wider historical conditions, these posters no longer function as mere vehicles of official approved information, but neither are they, in the words of Habermas, a 'medium for culture as an object of consumption'.

Destalinization had seen the rebirth of the intelligentsia as a public critical of the state. Identified by the kind of literature, plays and films they consumed, the intelligentsia were an educated, cultured and progressive group with a fluid relationship with the state as liberalizing trends were exchanged for more hard-line policies and back again. In the field of poster production, as in other fields, they made cultural products for the initiated rather than the politically defined 'people'. The Jazz Section, for example, produced a series of difficult to obtain but much thumbed books cataloguing officially prohibited jazz and rock music, theatre, literature, philosophy, film and nonconformist art. Such activities created space for parallel, unofficial, independent culture, connecting the semi-official with underground culture.[8] Motivated by the critical energies of the Prague Spring, poster artists such as Václav Ševčík in Czechoslovakia and, later, others such as Jan Sawka in Poland, became crucial figures in sustaining a more liberal and critical political poster practice coexistent with the orthodox. For as long as this section of the intelligentsia remained isolated and alienated from the general run of the population the authorities were prepared to contain their activities, but as soon as their public expanded to include larger sections of the community the intelligentsia regained the potential for meaningful intervention. A potential which did not go unnoticed by the party. On 11 March 1985 the State Security police entered Ševčík's private cultural evening of Prague intellectuals and took them away for interrogation, confiscating seventeen poster originals among other documentary material. Václav Havel was arrested for the last time in January 1988 for the symbolic act of putting flowers on the site of Jan Palach's self-immolation under St. Wenceslas monument during 'Palach Protest Week' when demonstrators were brutally suppressed by the state police. He was released only after considerable domestic and foreign pressure when Radio Free Europe listed the names of those who had signed the petition against his imprisonment.[9]

During the 1970s political and economic stagnation stifled political debate. Discontent found expression in the dissident movement which became a structural element in communist societies. Although attacked by the authorities for subversion and as a capitalist third column, the dissidents were rarely pro-capitalist. As they campaigned for more humane kinds of socialism they effectively became the authorities' repressed conscience. Opposition found much of its focus in networks of committees for civil rights and was Western-oriented only in so far as it advocated the indivisibility of intellectual freedoms, civil rights and economic progress. Official campaigns defined those critical of the regimes as class enemies, and their activities, which for most of the time lacked wide support among the population, often resulted in loss of status and access to privileged education, prosecution, imprisonment, exile, loss of citizenship, psychiatric treatment and a life of menial labour.

With the deployment of Soviet SS-20s and American cruise missiles rumblings of discontent were stimulated by the 'talk across the wall' in the German Democratic Republic. These events generated an explosion of anti-war and anti-NATO posters in a schematic style with a powerful European accent.[10] They suggest on visual levels ideological positions remote from both Moscow and Washington. Explicitly agitational in nature, posters in both East and West took part in a wider struggle against the prospect of a superpower struggle taking place on European, or more specifically German, soil. By the early 1980s a pattern had established itself throughout the region where the majority of public protests were organized by religious and ethnic groups supported by liberal human rights activists. The situation was aggravated by the effect of Western popular consumer culture on youth. Combined with its wider impact on the aspirational ambitions of young professionals, it brought about a state of affairs which outflanked the idealisms of the dissident intellectual community. In the end popular protest resulted in the uncritical appropriation of market values.

Political authority exercised by the state would wish to eliminate the development of a public sphere and to shape debate through the mechanisms of the mass media and the poster. Under these circumstances legitimation is acquired by the exercise of power rather than the common welfare the public sphere expresses. The messages that the official political poster carried were intended to inculcate ideas into the minds of the masses for the purposes of political education and indoctrination. Visual agitation gives no reasons, it simply states a politically defined condition with a view to stirring the people into action. Agitation relies on repetition and assertion rather than rational debate. As Lenin himself had written, 'It is not enough to explain to workers that they are politically oppressed ... agitation must be conducted with regard to every concrete example of this oppression.'[11] Official posters appeal to anxieties relating to health, prosperity and security, but they are ideological deceits. They are a cheat, a representation of a delusional reality at odds with existence. As Adam Michnik, the Polish dissident intellectual, observed: 'The communists who arrived at the end of the war succeeded in imposing false solutions because they succeeded in imposing their language ... .' Information is propaganda and propaganda is information. The state defines words and the contexts in which they appear to coin slogans which are vague in their meaning but are endowed with a single unambiguous party value.

In Poland the Social Self-defence Committee produced the document *Polish Censorship Exposed*. Focused on the *Book of Directives and Recommendations of the Central Office for Control of the Press, Publications and Performances*, it set out just what was and what was not allowed in official discourse. There could be no reference to the environmental and health threat posed by industry, the scale of alcoholism, shortages of nursery places or domestic failures of any kind. Mention of closer economic and industrial links with the West was forbidden and episcopal messages were tolerated only in so far as they were compatible with state policy. The adjective 'royal' was banned, for example. The media were forbidden to mention many events such as commemorations of the Warsaw uprising or the actions of the Polish Home Army in World War II. In 1975 reference to Katyń was allowed, provided that the date of death was placed before the Soviet occupation, so that the blame for the massacre of Polish officers rested with the Nazis. In March 1990 the Soviet Union finally admitted responsibility for the atrocity, forty-nine years after the event. Rational or critical debate did not exist, it had been legislated out of existence.

However, according to Habermas, once the framework of a legal bourgeois liberal state is established the need to take ideological positions lessens and polemic is abandoned for commercialism. Business efficiency takes priority over rational critical argument in ways remote from the strategies employed by the Plastic People of the Universe in Czechoslovakia, for whom Western popular culture had a symbolic significance far beyond the commercial,[12] or NSK in Slovenia, who embarked upon a critique of market-driven consumerism. In the liberal bourgeois state, 'Intelligent criticism of publicly discussed affairs gives way before a mood of conformity with publicly presented persons or personalities; consent coincides with good will evoked by publicity. Publicity once meant the exposure of political domination before the public use of reason; publicity now adds up to the reactions of an uncommitted friendly disposition.'[13] This process can be seen to take place with the poster of *perestroika* as it became increasingly popular in the West and designers produced work for a market besotted with Gorbachev. His reforms had generated a debate which found expression in posters critical of the state bureaucracy, the long-term implications of Stalinism and the legacies of Soviet versions of history. The posters of *perestroika* were exhibited in the liberal spaces of the art galleries, academies, theatre foyers and so on. As such they contributed to the debates which eventually led to the end of communist domination, but to produce them for a specific foreign market was a move at odds with the development of a public sphere. Following the revolutions of 1989 and the unforgettable spectacle of nations across central and eastern Europe taking back the symbolic spaces of their cities in the process of ousting the communists from power, it is premature to lament the passing of the tradition of political poster making as a mechanism of public debate and reflection. To this day designers continue to produce politically engaged posters in a part of Europe which still strives for an emancipatory modernity and which still takes culture seriously in the face of the new authoritarianisms of the market.

NOTES

1   For our purposes the definition will be widened to accommodate poster production as a branch of the media and publishing industry.

2   Slavoj Žižek, 'Eastern Europe's Republics of Gilead', in Chantal Mouffe (ed.), *Dimensions of Radical Democracy in Pluralism, Citizenship, Community* (London and New York, Verso), 1992, p. 193.

3   Jürgen Habermas, *The Structural Transformation of the Public Sphere. An Inquiry into a Category of Bourgeois Society* (Cambridge, Polity Press, [1962]), 1992, p. 219.

4   S. Amsterdamski, A. J. Jawlowska and T. Kowalik (eds), 'The Language of Propaganda', *Survey. A Journal of East and West Studies*, 24:4 (1979) 171.

5   Mikhail Heller, *Cogs in the Soviet Wheel. The Formation of Soviet Man* (London, Collins Harvill), 1988, p. 291.

6   V. I. Lenin, *Selected Works in Three Volumes I* (Moscow, Progress Publishers), 1970, p. 36.

7   Vladimir Anderle, *A Social History of Twentieth-century Russia* (London, Edward Arnold), 1994, p. 261.

8   The Jazz Section was founded by Karel Srp and Joska Skalnik in 1971. They were supported by membership subscription. Imprisoned in 1986, as the most important organization of nonconformist culture. Letter from Marta Sylvestrová, 19 February 1999.

9   Marta Sylvestrová, 19 February 1999.

10   The style is strongly reminiscent of 1930s design and the Swiss political poster designer, Theo Ballmer.

11   V. I. Lenin, 'What is to be Done?', in *Selected Works in Three Volumes I*, p. 164.

12   By the end of the 1960s the Plastic People of the Universe

were the best representatives of Czech psychedelic rock. In the 1970s they did not yield to normalization: they did not change their English name, cut their hair or alter their musical style as they were required. Instead their lyrics became political. As a result they lost their professional status and even private performances by them were severely restricted. They were imprisoned in 1976.

13 Habermas, *The Structural Transformation of the Public Sphere*, p. 193.

100+1 Years of Hungarian Poster Design 1885–1986 (Budapest, Müscarnok), 1986.

Ades, Dawn, *The Twentieth-century Poster. Design of the Avant Garde* (New York, Abbeville Press), 1984.

Agulhon, Maurice, 'On Political Allegory. A Reply to Eric Hobsbawm', *History Workshop*, 8 (1979) 167–73.

Albani, Maria Muscalu, *Romanian Contemporary Graphic Artists* (Bucharest, Fine Arts Union of the Socialist Republic of Romania), undated.

Alexander, Sally, Anna Davin and Eve Hostettler, 'Labouring Women. A Reply to Eric Hobsbawm', *History Workshop*, 8 (1979) 174–82.

Aradi, Nóra, *Politikai Plakát Kiallitas 1945–1965* (Budapest, Magyar Nemzeti Galeria), 1965.

Arvidsson, Claes, and Lars Erik Blomqvist (eds), *Symbols of Power. The Esthetics of Political Legitimation in the Soviet Union and Eastern Europe* (Stockholm, Almqvist & Wiskell International), 1987.

Aulich, James, and Tim Wilcox (eds), *Europe without Walls. Art, Posters and Revolution 1989–1993* (Manchester, Manchester City Art Galleries), 1993.

Avvakumov, Mikhail, *Is Stalin with Us?* (Moscow, Panorama), 1991.

Avvakumov, Mikhail, and E. Kazhdan, *Sovetskii Plakat 1970–1975* (Moscow, Sovetskii Khudozhnik), 1977.

Baburina, Nina I., *Twentieth-century Russia. History of the Country in Posters* (Moscow, Panorama), 1993.

Baburina, Nina I., *The Soviet Political Poster 1917–1980* (Harmondsworth, Penguin Books), 1985.

Baburina, Nina I., *The Soviet Political Poster* (Moscow, Sovetskii Khudozhnik), 1981.

Bakos, Katalin, 'Folyamatosság es Törés a Plakátmüvészetben', in Eva Standeisky, Gyula Kozák, Gábor Pataki and Rainer M. János (eds), *A fordulat évei. Politika. Képzömüvészet. Épitészét 1947–1949* (Budapest, 1956-OS Intézet), 1998.

Bakos, Katalin, *Musen und Kanonen. Ungarische Plakatkunst der Gegenwart* (Hamburg, Muzeum für Kunst und Gewerbe Hamburg), 1995.

Bakos, Katalin, *Plakát Parnasszus* (Budapest, Korona Galériában), 1995.

Bakos, Katalin, *The Signs of Change. Posters 1988–1990* (Budapest, Hungarian National Gallery), 1990.

Bakos, Katalin, *100+1 Jahre Ungarische Plakatkunst* (Dortmund, Cramers Kunstanstalt Verlag), 1987.

Baleka, Jan, *Angažovaný plakát. Druhá výstava tvůrčí skupiny Plakát* (Prague, Svaz čs. výtarných umělců nakladatelství Svoboda,Vystavní síň Čs. spisovatele), 1969.

Bartelt, Dana, *Contemporary Czech Posters* (Raleigh NC, City Gallery of Contemporary Art), 1990.

Bernik, Stane, *Poster and Sign. The Leading Themes of Modern Slovenian Visual Communications Design* (Ljubljana, Art Directors Club Ljubljana), 1988.

Boczar, Danuta A., 'The Polish Poster', *Art Journal*, spring (1984) 16–27.

Bogusz, Jerzy, 'Niektóre Problemy Polskiego Plakatu Politycznego' (Some Problems of the Polish Political Poster), *Przeglod Artystyceny* (*Arts Review*), 2 (1953) 24–40.

Bohrmann, Hans, *Politische Plakate mit Kommentaren von Margot Lindemann* (Dortmund, Harenberg Kommunikation), 1984.

Bojko, Syzmon, *The Polish Poster Today* (Warsaw, WAG), 1972.

Bonnell, Victoria F., *Iconography of Power. Soviet Political Posters under Lenin and Stalin* (Berkeley CA, University of California Press), 1998.

Borgs, Jānis, *Cartello della lettonia/Latvijas plakats/Affiche de la lettone* (Lugano, Forum Lugano), 1990.

Brodsky, Boris, 'uspesny debut sovetskeho vystavniho projektanta', *Tvar*, 12:10 (1961) 320.

Budnik, Andrei, *Youht [sic] Poster* (Kiev), 1988.

Causey, Sue (ed.), *Tradition and Revolution in Russian Art* (Manchester, Cornerhouse Publications), 1991.

Czestochowski, Joseph S., *Contemporary Polish Posters in Full Color* (New York, Dover Publications), 1979.

Demosfenova, G., A. Nurok and N. Shanyko, *Sovetskii Politicheskii Plakat* (Moscow, Izdatelstvo 'Iskusstvo'), 1962.

Dickerman, Leah (ed.), *Building the Collective. Soviet Graphic Design 1917–1937* (New York, Princeton Architectural Press), 1996.

Duis, Leonie ten, Annelies Haase and Jan Noordhoeck (eds), 'Graphic Design in Eastern Europe 1981–1991', *Zee Zucht*, 5:5/6 (1992).

Dydo, Krzysztof, *Masters of Polish Poster Art* (Bielsko-Biala, Buffi), 1995.

Dydo, Krzysztof (ed.), *Hundredth Anniversary of Polish Poster Art* (Krakow, Biuro Wystaw Artystycznych), 1993.

Efimov, Boris, *Asum-Plakat* (Moscow, Sovetskii Khudozhnik), 1986.

Erikson, John, 'Nazi Posters in Wartime Russia', *History Today*, 44:9 (1994) 18–19.

Fijalkowska, Janina, *Metamorfozy Plakatu Polskiego 1966–1972* (Warsaw, Agecja Wydawniczo-Reklamowa GRAFAG), 1991.

Fijalkowska, Janina, *Muzeum Plakatu ma 20 let 1968–1988* (Warsaw, Poster Museum Wilanow), 1988.

Fijalkowska, Janina, 'The Four from Wilanow', *Projekt*, 4 (1976) 113–17.

Fijalkowska, Janina, Stanislaw Tomaszewski-Mideza and Aleksander Gieysztor, *Warszawski Plakat Powstańczy/Warsaw Insurgent Posters/Affiches de l'insurrection de Varsovie* (Warsaw, Poster Museum at Wilanow), undated.

Finková, Dagmar, and Sylva Petrová, *The Militant Poster 1936–1985* (Prague, International Organization of Journalists), 1986.

Flügge, Matthias, 'Signs of the Times. Some Views on East German Art and the Artist Manfred Butzmann', in James Aulich and Tim Wilcox (eds), *Europe without Walls. Art, Posters and Revolution 1989–1993* (Manchester, Manchester City Art Galleries), 1993, pp. 73–86.

Forbes, Colin, in Jorge Frascara (ed.), *Graphic Design World Views. A Celebration of Icograda's Twenty-fifth Anniversary* (New York,

ICOGRADA Kodansha), 1990.

Fox, Frank, 'The Polish Paradox', *Affiche*, 11 (1994), 50–9.

Frach, Petra (ed.), *P40 Eine Austellung im 40. Jahr der DDR. Plakate von 1945 bis zur Gegenwart* (Berlin, Verband Bildender Kunstler der DDR), 1989.

Fraser, James, *Perestroika/Glasnost/Demokratika. A Catalog of an Exhibition of Printed Posters and Poster Maquettes from 1986 to 1989* (Rutherford NJ, Fairleigh Dickinson University), 1989.

Fraser, James, and Sandra Basens, 'Remarkable Posters from Latvia', *Print*, 39:2 (1985) 60–6.

Fraser, James, and Irene Dutton, *The Lithuanian Poster in the 1980s. A Catalog of an Exhibition* (Rutherford NJ, Fairleigh Dickinson University), 1990.

Gedminas, Antanas, and Juozas Galkus, *Lietuvos Plakatas* (Vilnius, Izdatelbstro 'Mintis'), 1971.

Ghozland, Freddy, and Beatrice Laurans, *Moscou s'affiche* (Toulouse, Ghozland), 1991.

Haiman, György, and Carol Stevens, 'Smiting the Eye', *Print*, 48:1 (1994) 12–14.

Hain, Juri, *Estonian Contemporary Posters* (Tallinn, Eesti Raamat), 1987.

Hellberg, Elena F., 'The Hero in Popular Pictures. Russian Lubok and Soviet Poster', in Rolf Wilhelm Brednich and Andreas Hartmann (eds), *Populäre Bildmedien. Vorträge des 2. Symposiums für ethnologische Bildforschung Rheinhausen bei Göttingen* (Göttingen), 1989.

Hellberg, Elena F., 'Folklore, Might and Glory. On the Symbolism of Power Legitimation', *Nordic Journal of Soviet and East European Studies*, 3:2 (1986) 9–20.

Heller, Steven, 'Glasnost Graphics', *ID International Design*, January/February (1991) 59–63.

Henrion, F. H. K., *AGI annals. Alliance Graphique Internationale 1952–1987* (Zurich, AGI), 1989.

Herzfelde, Wieland, *John Heartfield. Leben und Werk* (Leipzig, VEB Verlag der Kunst), 1961.

Hobsbawm, Eric, 'Man and Woman in Socialist Iconography', *History Workshop*, 6 (1978) 121–38.

Hornik, Susan, 'In Poland a Poster is a Fiery Art and a Way to Speak Out', *Smithsonian*, January (1993) 88–96.

Ihász, István, '… Toy of all Winds', *Poster and History 1944–1990* (Budapest, Hungarian Museum of Contemporary History), 1991.

International Exhibition of Graphic and Art Poster 'Fourth Block' (Kharkov, Culture Administration of Kharkov, Kharkov Union of Artists of the Ukraine, Kharkov 'Chernobyl' Society, Union Kharkov Art Museum), 1991.

International Poster Annual 1948–1949 (St Gall, Zollikofer), 1949.

János, Szintay, and János Fegyó, *Politikai Plakátok 1945–1948* (Budapest, Kossuth Könyvkiadó), 1970.

Karkanová, Hana (ed.), *Illustration, Typography and Type in Books, Magazines and Newspapers. International Symposium. Seventeenth Biennale of Graphic Design* (Brno, Moravian Gallery), 1996.

Knorowski, Mariusz, 'A Kite in the Wind of History', 1998, unpublished ms.

Knorowski, Mariusz, *Muzeum Ulicy Plakat Polski w kolekcji Muzeum Plakatu w Wilanowie* (Warsaw, Muzeum Plakatu w Wilanowie), 1996.

Knorowski, Mariusz, *Muzeum Ulicy Plakat Polski w kolekcji Muzeum Plakatu w Wilanowie* (Warsaw, Wydawnictwo Krupski i S-ka), 1996.

Knorowski, Mariusz, *100 Years of Polish Poster Art from the Collection of Posters Museum in Wilanow* (Warsaw, National Museum in Warsaw), 1993.

Knorowski, Mariusz, *Forma i treść w plakacie polskim 1944–1955* (Warsaw), undated.

Koščević, Želimir, 'War Posters from Croatia', *Affiche*, 5 (1993) 8–17.

Kraft, Perdita von, *Plakate aus Rüssland. Reihe: Plakate der Welt 6* (Cottbus, Brandenburgische Kunstsammlungen Cottbus), 1995.

Krichevski, Vladimir, 'Russian War Posters', *Affiche*, 11 (1994) 70–6.

Kroutvor, Josef, *Polselství ulice z dějin plakátu a promĕn doby* (Prague, Comet), 1991.

Kulinyi, István, *The Contemporary Hungarian Poster. A Selection of the best Posters of the last ten Years* (Budapest, Budapest Art Gallery, Muvelt Nep Book Distributors), 1986.

Kunzle, David, 'Killingly Funny. US Posters of the Vietnam Era', in Jeff Walsh and James Aulich (eds), *Vietnam Images. War and Representation* (London, Macmillan), 1989, pp. 112–22.

Landsberger, Stefan, *Chinese Propaganda Posters. From Revolution to Modernization* (Amsterdam and Singapore, Pepin Press), 1998.

Linsky, Robert H., 'Notes on "An Historic Event"', *Print*, 45:3 (1991) 17.

Litvinov, Viktor, *The Posters of Glasnost and Perestroika* (Harmondsworth, Penguin Books), 1989.

Lohr, Rolf-Peter, *Plakate gegen Gewalt und Fremdenhaas* (Berlin, Verband der Grafik-Designer eV), 1993.

Margadant, Bruno, *Hoffnung und Widerstand. Das 20. Jahrhundert im Plakat der internationalen Arbeiter- und Friedensbewegung* (Zurich, Lutz and Museum für Gestaltung Zurich), 1998.

Mason, Tim, 'The Domestication of Female Socialist Icons. A Note in Reply to Eric Hobsbawm', *History Workshop*, 7 (1979) 170–5.

Mauerkatalog. East Side Gallery (Berlin, Oberbaum), 1991.

McLean, Christine, *East Side Gallery. The largest Open-air Gallery in the World* (Berlin, WUVA), 1991.

McQuiston, Liz, *Graphic Agitation. Social and Political Graphics since the Sixties* (London, Phaidon Press), 1993.

M.L., 'politický plakát Bedřicha Votruby', *Tvar* 13:3 (1963) 85–93.

Morawinska-Brzezicka, Maria, *Sport w szruce polskiej 1945–1975* (Warsaw, Wydawnictwo Sport i Turystyka), 1975.

Moskovskie Plakatisty (Moscow, Moskva Sovetskii Khudozhnik), 1982.

Moskva Plakat 1945–1995 / adres: Moskva (Moscow), 1996.

Mroszczak, Józef, *Anti-fascist Posters* (Warsaw, WAG), 1977.

Mroszczak, Józef, 'O dalszy wzrost poziomu ideowo-artystycznego plakatu Polskiego' (For the Furtherance of the Level of the Ideo-artistic Polish Poster), *Przeglod Artysteny (Artistic Review)*, 3 (1953) 4–10.

Muratov, A., *Leningradskii Plakat* (Leningrad, Leningradskaia organizatsiia soiuza khudozhnikov RSfSR), 1990.

New Collectivism (ed.), *Neue Slovenische Kunst* (Los Angeles, Amok Books), 1991.

Nováková, Milada (ed.), *Orbis pictus. Picure World. International Symposium. Fifteenth Biennale of Graphic Design* (Brno, Moravian Gallery), 1992.

Paret, Peter, Beth Irwin Lewis and Paul Paret, *Persuasive Images. Posters of War and Revolution from the Hoover Institution Archives* (Princeton NJ, Princeton University Press), 1992.

Paskiewicz, Joanna, 'The ROSTA Windows. A Newspaper for Passers-by', *Affiche*, 12:3/4 (1992) 20–5.

Pavičić, Snježana, *Hrvatski Politički Plakat 1940–1950* (Zagreb, Hrvatski Pvojesni Muzej), 1991.

Perahim, Jules, Vasile Kazar, Mircea Popescu, Mircea Deac and Dan Baran (eds), *Militant Graphic Art in Rumania* (Bucharest, Meridiane Publishing House), 1963.

Peters, Robert L., 'Designing a New Russia', *Communication Arts*, March/April (1995) 82–93.

P.G.H Glühende Zukunft, *P.G.H Glühende Zukunft. Beck. Feuchtenberger. Fickelscherer. Wagenbreth* (Berlin, Galerie am Chamissoplatz), 1991.

Plakat Polski (Warsaw, WAG), 1956.

Plakats. VI, VII Baltijas Republiku Plakatu Triennales Laureatu Darbi. Retroplakati (Riga, Avots), 1989.

Poland is Not yet Lost, Forty-one reproductions of Polish posters (1980–81) and one poster by Klaus Staeck (Bonn, Edition Staeck), undated.

Politický Plakát 1945–1948 (Prague, Vydalo oddělení propagandy a agitace ÚV KSČ and Muzeum Klementa Gottwalda), undated.

Politický plakát proti fašismu a válce za mír a socialismus 1945–1985 (Prague, Vydalo Oddělení Propagandy, Agitace ÚV KSČ and Muzeum Klementa Gottwalda), 1985.

Politický plakát 1948–1960 (Prague, Vydalo Odděleni Propagandy a Agitacě ÚV KSČ and Muzeum Klementa Gottwalda), undated.

Politický plakát 1960–1970 (Prague, Vydalo Odděleni Propagandy a Agiticae ÚV KSČ and Muzeum Klementa Gottwalda), 1970.

Posters against Violence Worldwide (Edmonton, Alberta, Quon Editions), 1995.

Raban, Josef, 'Politická grafika W. A. Schlossera', *Tvar* 14:4 (1964) 51–7.

Rajlichová, Alena (ed.), *Social Responsibility of the Graphic Designer. International Symposium. Sixteenth Biennale of Graphic Design* (Brno, Moravian Gallery), 1994.

Risbeck, Phil, 'Contemporary Soviet Posters', *Graphis*, 46 (1990) 58–65.

Rothschild, Deborah, Ellen Lupton and Darra Goldstein, *Graphic Design in the Mechanical Age. Selections from the Merrill C. Berman Collection* (New Haven CT and London, Yale University Press), 1998.

Sahlstrom, Berit, *Political Posters in Ethiopia and Mozambique. Visual Imagery in a Revolutionary Context* (Stockholm, Almquvist & Wiskell International), 1990.

Schubert, Zdzsław, *Ogolnopolska Biennale Plakatu* (Katowice, ZPAP), 1965.

Schubert, Zdzsław, *The Polish Poster 1970–1978* (Warsaw, Kralowa Agencja Wydawnicza), 1979.

Seelig, Klaus, and Sabine Riedel, 'Student Culture Posters', *Novum Gebrauchsgraphik*, 9 (1987) 50–5.

Ševčíková, Zuzana, *Politicky plagát '87* (Bratislava, Slovak Union of Artists), 1987.

Skiba, E. A. (ed.), *Sovremennyi Plakat Latvii* (Moscow, Sovetskii Khudozhnik), 1989.

Sorvina, I. B. (ed.), *Zrelishchnyi Plakat 1986–1990. Bystavka Katalog* (Moscow, Soiuz Khudozhnikov SSSR), 1990.

Sovetskii Politicheskii Plakat (Moscow, Plakat), 1981.

Sovremennyi Plakat Latvii (Moscow, Sovetskii Khudozhik), 1989.

Staininger, Otto, *Die Geheimen Aufklarer* (Vienna), 1994.

Svirida, Inessa, *Panorama Izdatelstvo* (Moscow, Panorama), 1990.

Sylvestrová, Marta, *Český plakát 60.let* (*Czech Posters of the '60s*) (Brno, Department of Applied Arts of the Moravian Gallery), 1997.

Sylvestrová, Marta, 'Invisible Walls', in James Aulich and Tim Wilcox (eds), *Europe without Walls. Art, Posters and Revolution 1989–93* (Manchester, Manchester City Art Galleries), 1993, pp. 109–28.

Sylvestrová, Marta, *Sovětský plakát* (Brno, Moravian Gallery), 1988.

Sylvestrová, Marta, and Dana Bartelt, *Art as Activist. Revolutionary Posters from Central and Eastern Europe* (London, Thames & Hudson), 1992.

Szemberg, Henryk, *Plakat Polski* (Warsaw, Wydawnictwo Artystyczno-Graficzne RSW 'Prasa'), 1957.

The Polish Poster 1970–1977 (Warsaw, KAW), 1979.

The Poster in the Struggle for Peace, Security and Co-operation (Moscow, Plakat), 1985.

Timmers, Margaret (ed.), *The Power of the Poster* (London, V&A Publications), 1998.

Tippack-Schneider, Simone, 'Without a City Wall. Poster Art in the former GDR', *d'Affiche*, 3/4 (1992) 52–9.

Tolstoy, Vladimir, Irina Bibikova and Catherine Cooke (eds), *Street Art of the Revolution. Festivals and Celebrations in Russia 1918–1933* (London, Vendome Press, Thames & Hudson), 1990.

Track 16 Gallery for the Study of Political Graphics, *Decade of Protest. Political Posters from the United States, Vietnam, Cuba 1965–75* (Santa Monica CA, Smart Art Press), 1996.

Tupitsyn, Margarita, 'From the Politics of Montage to the Montage of Politics. Soviet Practice 1919 through 1937', in Matthew Teitelbaum (ed.), *Montage and Modern Life 1919–1942* (Cambridge MA and London, MIT Press), 1992.

Umblija, Ramona, *URNA Plakati* (Riga, Latvijas Kulturas Fonds), 1995.

Vladich, V., and I. M. Blyumina, *We Follow the Road shown by Great Lenin. Lenin in the Arts of Soviet Ukraine, Political Posters, Poetry* (Kiev, Goligrafkhiga), 1985.

Vlček, Tomáš, *Současný plakát* (Prague, Odeon), 1976.

Vo Imia Mira Na Zemle (Moscow, Plakat), 1986.

Vorsteher, Dieter, *Das Politische Plakat der DDR 1945–1970* (Munich, Sauer), 1995 (CD-Rom).

Waśniewski, Jerzy, *The Polish Poster* (Warsaw, WAG), 1972.

White, Stephen, 'Stalinism and the Graphic Arts', in John Shannon (ed.), *Politics, Society and Stalinism in the USSR* (London, School of Slavonic and East European Studies, University of London), 1998.

White, Stephen, 'Posters Mark a Soviet Turning Point', in Sue Causey (ed.), *Tradition and Revolution in Russian Art* (Manchester, Cornerhouse Publications), 1990.

White, Stephen, *The Bolshevik Poster* (New Haven CT and London, Yale University Press), 1988.

Wojciechowski, Aleksander, 'A Dyskusji nad i Ogólnopolską Wystawą Plakatu' (From the discussion at the First Polish Exhibition of Posters), *Przeglod Artystyceny* (*Arts Review*), 3 (1953) 11–18.

Yanker, Gary, *Prop Art* (New York, Darien House), 1972.

Za Mir i Sotsialhii Progress (Moscow, Plakat), 1989.

Zacharska, Anna, 'Religious Posters from Poland', *Novum Gebrauchsgraphik*, 10 (1984) 13–15.

Zaiiyeb, V., and A. Senkevych, *Plakat Naglyadnoy Agitatsii* (Moscow, Kamalog), 1979.

Zimmerman, Peter, *Die Stunde Null der 8 Mai 1945. Plakataustellung zur 50. Wiederkehr des Kriegsendes* (Berlin, Akademie der Kunste), 1995.

Zuffo, Dario, *CSSR-Plakate 1974–1985* (Zurich, Museum für Gestaltung), 1986.

Zuliani, Mariolina Doria de, *I manifesti della Perestrojka. Le mostra della Cassa di Risparmio 48* (Verona, Olograf Edizioni), 1990.

CULTURAL AND SOCIAL

Aczél, György, *Socialism and the Freedom of Culture* (Budapest, Corviana Kiadó), 1984.

Aczél, György, *Culture and Socialist Democracy* (Budapest, Corvina Press), 1975.

Ades, Dawn, Tim Benton, David Elliott and Iain Boyd Whyte, *Art and Power. Europe under the Dictators 1930–1945* (London, Hayward Gallery), 1996.

Adorno, Theodor, and Max Horkheimer, *Dialectic of Enlightenment* (London and New York, Verso, [1944]), 1979.

Aman, Anders, *Architecture and Ideology in Eastern Europe during the Stalin Era. An Aspect of Cold War History* (Cambridge MA and London, MIT Press), 1992.

Amsterdamski, S., A. J. Jawlowska and T. Kowalik (eds), 'The Language of Propaganda', *Survey. A Journal of East and West Studies*, 24:4 (1979) 166–79.

Anděl, Jaroslav, *The Art of the Avant Garde in Czechoslovakia 1918–1938* (Valencia, IVAM Centre Julio Gonzalez, Generalitat Valenciana Consellera de Cultura, Educacio i Ciencia), 1993.

Andrle, Vladimir, *A Social History of Twentieth-century Russia* (London, Edward Arnold), 1994.

Antonowa, Irina, and Jörn Merkert (eds), *Berlin Moskau 1900–1950. Bildende, Kunst, Photographie, Architektur* (Munich and New York, Prestel), 1995.

Aradi, Nóra, *A szocialialista képzömüvészet jelképei* (Budapest, Kossuth Konyvkiado/Corvina Kiadó), 1974.

Arendt, Hannah, *The Origins of Totalitarianism* (London, André Deutsch), 1986.

Balan, Ion Dodu, *Cultural Policy in Romania. Studies and Documents on Cultural Policies* (Paris, Unesco Press), 1972.

Banks, Miranda (ed.), *The Aesthetic Arsenal. Socialist Realism under Stalin* (New York, Institute for Contemporary Art, P.S. 1 Museum), 1993.

Bathrick, David, *The Powers of Speech. The Politics of Culture in the GDR* (Lincoln NE and London, University of Nebraska Press), 1995.

Berger, John, *Art and Revolution. Ernst Neizestny and the Role of the Artist in the USSR* (Harmondsworth, Penguin Books), 1969.

Bernhard, Michael, and Henryk Szlajfer (eds), *From the Polish Underground. Selections from Krytyka 1978–1993* (Philadelphia, Pennsylvania State University Press), 1995.

Binns, Christopher A. P., 'The Changing Face of Power: Revolution and Accommodation in the Development of the Soviet Ceremonial System' II, *Man. The Journal of the Royal Anthropological Society*, 15:1 (1980) 170–87.

Binns, Christopher A. P., 'The Changing Face of Power: Revolution and Accommodation in the Development of the Soviet Ceremonial' I, *Man. The Journal of the Royal Anthropological Institute*, 14:4 (1979) 585–606.

Bloch, Ernst, *The Utopian Function of Art and Literature. Selected Essays*, translated by Jack Zipes and Frank Mecklenberg (Cambridge MA and London, MIT Press), 1988.

Blomqvist, Lars Erik, 'Some Utopian Elements in Stalinist Art', *Russian History/Histoire Russe*, 2/3 (1984) 298–305.

Bourdieu, Pierre, *The Field of Cultural Production* (Cambridge, Polity Press), 1993.

Bourdieu, Pierre, and Alain Darbel, *The Love of Art. European Art Museums and their Public* (London, Polity Press), 1991.

Bown, Matthew Cullerne, *Socialist Realist Painting* (New Haven CT and London, Yale University Press), 1998.

Bown, Matthew Cullerne, *Art under Stalin* (Oxford, Phaidon Press), 1991.

Bown, Matthew Cullerne, and Brandon Taylor (eds), *Art of the Soviets. Painting, Sculpture and Architecture in a One-party State, 1917–1992* (Manchester, Manchester University Press), 1993.

Bown, Matthew Cullerne and David Elliott, *Soviet Socialist Realist Painting 1930s–1960s* (Oxford, Museum of Modern Art), 1992.

Brodsky, Joseph, *Less than One* (New York, Viking), 1982.

Brooks, Jeffrey, 'Socialist Realism in Pravda: Read All About It!', *Slavic Review*, 4 (1994) 973–91.

Brown, J. A. C., *Techniques of Persuasion. From Propaganda to Brainwashing* (Baltimore MD, Penguin Books), 1963.

Buck-Morss, Susan, *The Origin of Negative Dialectics. Theodor W. Adorno, Walter Benjamin, and the Frankfurt Institute* (Hassocks, Harvester Press), 1979.

Bushnell, John, *Moscow Graffiti. Language and Subculture* (Boston MA, Unwin Hyman), 1990.

Bushnell, John, 'The New Soviet Man turns Pessimist', *Survey. A Journal of East and West Studies*, 24:2 (1979) 1–18.

Calhoun, Craig (ed.), *Habermas and the Public Sphere* (Cambridge MA and London, MIT Press), 1992.

Carew Hunt, R. N., *A Guide to Communist Jargon* (London, Geoffrey Bles), 1957.

Caute, David, *Sixty-eight. The Year of the Barricades* (London, Hamish Hamilton), 1988.

Československo '89 (Prague, Panorama), 1990.

'Čeští fašisté útočí', *Týden*, 19 (1990).

Churchward, L. G., *The Soviet Intelligentsia. An Essay on the Social Structure and Roles of the Soviet Intellectuals during the 1960s* (London and Boston MA, Routledge), 1973.

Ciołek, Erazm, *Polska August 1980–August 1989* (Warsaw, Spotkania), 1990.

Ciołek, Erazm, *Stop Controla. Stocnia Gdanska Sierpien 1980* (Warsaw, Komiteta Wydawniczego NSZZ 'Solidarność' Region Mazowsze), 1981.

Clark, Katerina, *The Soviet Novel. History as Ritual* (Chicago, University of Chicago Press), 1985.

Clark, Toby, *Art and Propaganda. The Political Image in the Age of Mass Culture* (London, Weidenfeld & Nicolson), 1997.

Cohen, Abner, 'Political Symbolism', *Annual Review of Anthropology*, 8 (1979) 87–113.

Colton, Timothy J., *Moscow. Governing the Socialist Metropolis* (Cambridge MA and London, Belknap Press of Harvard University Press), 1995.

Condee, Nancy (ed.), *Soviet Hieroglyphics. Visual Culture in late Twentieth-century Russia* (Bloomington IN, University of Indiana Press), 1995.

Crowley, David, 'People's Warsaw/Popular Warsaw', *Journal of Design History*, 10:2 (1997) 203–24.

Crowley, David, 'Building the World Anew: Design in Stalinist and post-Stalinist Poland', *Journal of Design History*, 7:3 (1994) 187–201.

Cultural Policy in Hungary (Paris, Unesco Press), 1974.

Cygan, Piotr, and Rubem C. Fernandes, 'Secrets of Censorship in Poland', *Telos. A Journal of Radical Thought*, 38 (1978–79) 179–89.

Davies, R. W., *Soviet History in the Yeltsin Era* (London, Macmillan), 1997.

Davies, R. W., *Soviet History in the Gorbachev Revolution* (London, Macmillan), 1989.

Demontage … revolutionärer oder restaurativer Bildersturm? Texte und Bilder (Berlin, Kramer), 1992.

Dobrenko, Evgenii, 'The Disaster of Middlebrow Taste, or, Who "Invented" Socialist Realism?', *South Atlantic Quarterly*, 3 (1995) 773–806.

Dubuskas, Frank A., 'Leaders and Followers: Cultural Pattern and Political Symbolism in Yugoslavia', *Anthropological Quarterly*, 56:2 (1983) 95–9.

Dunham, Vera, *In Stalin's Time. Middle-class Values in Soviet Fiction* (Cambridge, Cambridge University Press), 1976.

Eagleton, Terry, *Walter Benjamin, or, Towards a Revolutionary Criticism* (London and New York, Verso), 1981.

Efimova, Alla, and Lev Manovich (eds), *Tekstura. Russian Essays on Visual Culture* (Chicago and London, University of Chicago Press), 1993.

Fehér, Ferenc, Agnes Heller and György Márkus, *Dictatorship over Needs. An Analysis of Soviet Studies* (Oxford and New York, Blackwell), 1983.

Feist, Gunter, *Kunstkombinat DDR. Daten und Zitate zur Kunst und Kunstpolitik der DDR 1945–1990* (Berlin, Nishen), 1990.

Fialkowska, Janina, *The Political Films of Andrzej Wajda. Dialogism in 'Man of Marble', 'Man of Iron' and 'Danton'* (Oxford, Berghahn Books), 1996.

Fitzpatrick, Sheila, *The Cultural Front. Power and Culture in Revolutionary Russia* (Ithaca NY and London, Cornell University Press), 1992.

Fitzpatrick, Sheila, 'Stalin and the Making of a New Elite 1928–1939', *Slavic Review*, 3 (1979) 377–402.

Flacke, Monika (ed.), *Auftrags Kunst der DDR 1949–1990* (Munich, Klinkhardt & Biermann), 1995.

Foucault, Michel, *Power/Knowledge. Selected Interviews and other Writings 1972–1977* (New York, Pantheon Books), 1980.

Freidin, Gregory, *Russian Culture in Transition. Selected Papers of the Working Group for the Study of Contemporary Russian Culture 1990–91*, Stanford Slavic Studies 7 (Stanford CA, Stanford University Press), 1993.

Fulbrook, Mary, *Anatomy of a Dictatorship. Inside the GDR 1949–1989* (Oxford, Oxford University Press), 1995.

Galinski, Tadeusz (ed.), *Culture in People's Poland* (Warsaw, Interpress), 1966.

Gambrell, Jamey, 'The Wonder of the Soviet World', *New York Review of Books*, 22 December 1994.

Gassner, Hubertus (ed.), *Agitation zum Gluck. Sowjetische Kunst der Stalinzeit* (Bremen, Temmen), 1994.

Geldern, James von, and Richard Stites, *Mass Culture in Soviet Russia. Tales, Poems, Songs, Movies, Plays and Folklore 1917–1953* (Bloomington and Indianapolis IN, Indiana University Press), 1995.

Gerner, Kristian, and Stefan Hedlund, *Ideology and Rationality in the Soviet Model. A Legacy for Gorbachev* (London and New York, Routledge), 1989.

Gleason, Abbott, *Totalitarianism. The Inner History of the Cold War* (Oxford and New York, Oxford University Press), 1995.

Golomstock, Igor, *Totalitarian Art in the Soviet Union, Fascist Italy and the People's Republic of China* (London, Collins Harvill), 1990.

Gomułka, Stanislaw, and Antony Polonsky (eds), *Polish Paradoxes* (London and New York, Routledge), 1990.

Gorky, Maxim, with Karl Radek, Nikolai Bukharin, Andrei Zhdanov *et al.*, *Soviet Writers' Congress 1934. The Debate on Socialist Realism and Modernism* (London, Lawrence & Wishart), 1977.

Great Soviet Encyclopaedia (Moscow, Progress Publishers), 1974.

Groys, Boris, 'On the Ethics of the Avant-garde', *Art in America*, May (1993) 111–13.

Groys, Boris, *The Total Art of Stalinism. Avant-garde, Aesthetic Dictatorship, and Beyond,* translated by Charles Rougle (Princeton NJ, Princeton University Press), 1992.

Gunther, Hans (ed.), *The Culture of the Stalin Period* (London, Macmillan), 1988.

Gunther, John, *Inside Russia Today* (London, Hamish Hamilton), 1958.

Habermas, Jürgen, *The Structural Transformation of the Public Sphere. An Inquiry into a Category of Bourgeois Society* (Cambridge, Polity Press), 1992.

Halász, Zoltán, *Cultural Life in Hungary,* Hungarian National Commission for Unesco (Budapest, Pannonia Press), 1966.

Haraszti, Miklós, *The Velvet Prison. Artists under State Socialism* (Harmondsworth, Penguin), 1989.

Haraszti, Miklós, *A Worker in a Workers' State* (Harmondsworth, Pelican Books), 1977.

Havel, Václav, *Living in Truth* (London, Faber), 1989.

Heibel, Yule F., *Reconstructing the Subject. Modernist Painting in Western Germany 1945–1950* (Princeton, NJ, Princeton University Press), 1995.

Heller, Mikhail, *Cogs in the Soviet Wheel. The Formation of Soviet Man* (London, Collins Harvill), 1988.

Hennig, Gerd, '"Mass Cultural" Activity in the GDR: On Cultural Politics in Bureaucratically Deformed Transitional Societies', *New German Critique*, 2 (1974) 38–57.

Herf, Jeffrey, *Divided Memory. The Nazi Past in the Two Germanys* (Cambridge MA and London, Harvard University Press), 1997.

Hermand, Jost, 'The "Good New" and the "Bad New": Metamorphoses of the Modernism Debate in the GDR since 1956', *New German Critique*, 1:3 (1974) 88.

Hoffmann-Curtius, Katherine, 'A Gendering of Germany. The Couple: Image-making for the National Unification 1989/90', *Oxford Art Journal*, 17:2 (1994) 78–90.

Howe, Irving (ed.), *1984 Revisited. Totalitarianism in our Century* (New York, Harper & Row), 1984.

Hutchings, Raymond, 'Soviet Design: The Neglected Partner of Soviet Science and Technology', *Slavic Review*, 37:4 (1978) 567–83.

Hutchings, Raymond, 'The Weakening of Ideological Influences upon Soviet Design', *Slavic Review*, 27:1 (1968) 71–84.

Institute of Art Criticism, Ethnography and Folklore of the Academy of Sciences of the Byelorussian SSR, *Cultural Policy in* the Byelorussian Soviet Socialist Republic. Studies and Documents on Cultural Policies, Paris, Unesco, 1979.

Jakubowicz, Karol, 'Musical Chairs? The Three Public Spheres of Poland', Media, Culture and Society, 12 (1990) 195–212.

James, C. Vaughan, Soviet Socialist Realism. Origins and Theory (London, Macmillan), 1973.

James, Harold, A German Identity. 1770 to the Present Day (London, Phoenix), 1994.

Johnson, Priscilla, Krushchev and the Arts. The Politics of Soviet Culture 1962–1964 (Cambridge MA, MIT Press), 1965.

Jowett, Garth S., and Victoria O'Donnell, Propaganda and Persuasion (Newbury Park CA, London and New Delhi, Sage), 1992.

Juhász, László, 'Rada pro průmyslové výtvarnictví v Mad'arsku' (Hungarian Board of Industrial Design), Tvar 12:2 (1961) 30.

Juvilier, Peter H., 'The Soviet Family in post-Stalin Perspective', in Stephen F. Cohen, Alexander Rabinowitch and Robert Sharlet (eds), Soviet Union since Stalin (London, Macmillan), 1980.

'K výstavě SSSR v Paříži' (Russian Exhibition in Paris), Tvar, 12:10 (1961) 316–20.

Kagan, Moisei, 'The Formation and Development of Socialist Art. The Logic of the Formation of Socialist Art in the Era of Capitalism', in Socialist Realism in Literature and Art. A Collection of Articles (Moscow, Progress Publishers), 1971.

Kagarlitsky, Boris, The Thinking Reed. Intellectuals and the Soviet State from 1917 to the Present (London and New York, Verso), 1989.

Kennedy, Michael D. (ed.), Envisioning Eastern Europe. Postcommunist Cultural Studies (Ann Arbor MI, University of Michigan Press), 1997.

Kideckel, David A., 'Introduction: Political Rituals and Symbolism in Socialist East Europe', Anthropological Quarterly, 56:2 (1983) 52–4.

King, David, The Commissar Vanishes. The Falsification of Photographs and Art in Stalin's Russia (Edinburgh, Canongate Books), 1997.

Klíma, Ivan, The Spirit of Prague and other Essays (Cambridge, Granta Books), 1994.

Koch, Hans, Cultural Policy in the German Democratic Republic (Paris, Unesco Press), 1975.

Komar, V., and A. Melamid, 'In Search of Religion', Artforum, May (1980) 36–46.

Korff, Gottfried, 'History of Symbols as Social History? Ten Preliminary Notes on the Image and Sign Systems of Social Movements in Germany', International Review of Social History, 38 (1993), supplement 105–25.

Koski, B., 'Documents from Eastern Europe. The Situation of Women in Poland', Critique, 8 (1977) 69–95.

Kostecki, Maria J., and Krzysztof Mreła, 'Workers and Intelligentsia in Poland during the Hot Days and in between', Media, Culture and Society, 4 (1982) 225–41.

Kotkin, Stephen, Magnetic Mountain. Stalinism as a Civilization (Berkeley and Los Angeles CA, University of California Press), 1995.

Kowalski, Tadeusz, 'Evolution after Revolution. The Polish Press System in Transition', Media, Culture and Society, 10 (1988) 183–96.

Kramer, Jane, The Politics of Memory. Looking for Germany in the New Germany (New York, Random House), 1996.

Kubik, Jan, The Power of Symbols against the Symbols of Power. The Rise of Solidarity and the Fall of State Socialism in Poland (Philadelphia, Pennsylvania State University Press), 1994.

Kuhirt, Ullrich, Kunst der DDR 1960–1980 (Leipzig, Seemann), 1983.

Ladd, Brian, The Ghosts of Berlin. Confronting German History in the Urban Landscape (Chicago and London, University of Chicago Press), 1997.

Lahusen, Thomas, and Gene Kuperman (eds), Late Soviet Culture. From Perestroika to Novostroika (Durham NC and London, Duke University Press), 1993.

Langer, Karel, 'Móda a socialistický životní sloh' (Fashion and Socialist Lifestyle), Tvar, 12:3 (1961), 65–6.

Lesnikowski, Wojciech, East European Modernism. Architecture in Czechoslovakia, Hungary and Poland between the Wars (London, Thames & Hudson), 1996.

Liehm, Antonin J., 'Franz Kafka in Eastern Europe', Telos. A Journal of Radical Thought, 23 (1975) 79–93.

Lifshitz, Mikhail, The Philosophy of Art of Karl Marx (London, Pluto Press), 1976.

Lindey, Christine, Art in the Cold War. From Vladivostock to Kalamazoo, 1945–1962 (London, Herbert Press), 1990.

Lunacharsky, Anatoly, On Literature and Art (Moscow, Progress Publishers), 1973.

Lunn, Eugene, Marxism and Modernism. An Historical Study of Lukacs, Brecht, Benjamin, and Adorno (London, Verso), 1985.

Maaz, Hans-Joachim, Behind the Wall. The Inner Life of Communist Germany, translated by Margot Bettauer Dembo (New York, Norton), 1995.

MacDonald, Dwight, Against the American Grain. Essays on the Effect of Mass Culture (New York, Vintage Books), 1962.

Majstorović, Stefan, Cultural Policy in Yugoslavia. Self-management and Culture (Paris, Unesco), 1980.

Marco, Jindřich, Soudruh Agresor (Comrade Aggressor) (Prague, Mladá Fronta), 1968.

Margolin, Victor, The Struggle for Utopia. Rodchenko, Lissitsky, Moholy-Nagy 1917–1946 (Chicago and London, University of Chicago Press), 1997.

Markham, James W., Voices of the Red Giants. Communications in Russia and China (Ames IA, Iowa State University Press), 1970.

Marxist-Leninist Aesthetics and the Arts (Moscow, Progress Publishers), 1980.

Mayer, Hans, 'An Aesthetic Debate of 1951. Comment on a Text by Hanna Eisler', New German Critique, 2 (1974) 58–71.

McLain, J., and J. Charles, 'From Ideology to Utopia. Ernst Fischer in Retrospect', Journal of Contemporary History, 17 (1977) 565–94.

McNair, Brian, 'Glasnost and Restructuring in the Soviet Media', Media, Culture and Society, 11 (1989), 327–49.

Mezhenkov, Vladimir, and Ewa Skelley, Perestroika in Action. A Collection of Press Articles and Interviews (London and Wellingborough, Collet), 1988.

Michaelis, Andreas, GDR Souvenirs (Cologne, Taschen), 1994.

Michnik, Adam, 'What we Want to Do and What we can Do', Telos. A Quarterly Journal of Radical Thought, 47 (1981) 66–77.

Millar, J., 'The Little Deal. Brezhnev's Contribution to Acquisitive Socialism', Slavic Review, 44:4 (1985) 694–706.

Miller, Frank J., Folklore for Stalin. Russian Folklore and Pseudofolklore of the Stalin Era (New York and London, Sharpe), 1990.

Miłosz, Czesław, The Captive Mind (Harmondsworth, Penguin), 1980.

Mitchell, W. J. T. (ed.), *Art and the Public Sphere* (Chicago and London, University of Chicago Press), 1992.

Modern Art in Hungary (Budapest, Corvina Press), 1969.

Morris, Pam, *The Bakhtin Reader. Selected Writings of Bakhtin, Medvedev, Voloshinov* (London and New York, Edward Arnold), 1994.

Muzeum dělnickeho revolučního hnutí Jižních Čech (Česke Budějovice), 1975.

Naimark, Norman M., *The Russians in Germany. A History of the Soviet Zone of Occupation 1945–1949* (Cambridge MA and London, Belknap Press of Harvard University Press), 1995.

Nehrlich, Ernst, 'odborná škola pro užité unměni v Berlině' (College of Applied Arts in Berlin), *Tvar* 12:3 (1962) 47–51.

Nove, Alec, *Glasnost in Action. Cultural Renaissance in Russia* (Boston MA, Unwin Hyman), 1989.

OKO (Pavel Meluš and Juraj Králik) *August '68 ... in Slovakia* (Bratislava, Editorial Series Slovakia in Photography I), 1990.

Pelczynski, Z. A., 'Solidarity and "the Rebirth of Civil Society" in Poland 1976–81', in John Keane (ed.), *Civil Society and the State. New European Perspectives* (London and New York, Verso), 1993, pp. 361–80.

Piccone, Paul, 'Czech Marxism. Karel Kosik', *Critique*, 8 (1977) 43–52.

Pike, David, 'Cultural Politics in Soviet-occupied Germany 1945–1946', *Journal of Contemporary History*, 24 (1989) 91–123.

Prokhorov, Gleb, *Art under Socialist Realism. Soviet Painting 1930–1950* (Roseville NSW, Craftsman House, G+B Arts International), 1995.

Raban, Josef, '40 let KSČ' (Fortieth Anniversary of the Czechoslovak Communist Party), *Tvar*, 12:7 (1961) 162–70.

Raban, Josef, 'Jubileum Vysoké školy uměleckoprůmyslové v Praze' (Jubilee of the Academy of Applied Arts in Prague), *Tvar*, 12:45 (1961) 99–158.

Rakovski, Marc, *Towards an East European Marxism* (London, Alison & Busby), 1969.

Ramet, Pedro, 'Disaffection and Dissent in East Germany', *World Politics*, 37 (1984/85) 85–111.

Reddaway, Peter, *Uncensored Russia. The Human Rights Movement in the Soviet Union. The Annotated Text of the Unofficial Moscow Journal, A Chronicle of Current Events* (Nos 1–11) (London, Jonathan Cape), 1972.

Reid, Susan E. (ed.), 'Design, Stalin and the Thaw', *Journal of Design History*, special issue, 10:2 (1997).

Remmer, Alexander, 'A Note on Post-publication Censorship in Poland 1980–1987', *Soviet Studies*, 41:3 (1989) 415–25.

Rogoff, Irit (ed.), *The Divided Heritage. Themes and Problems in German Modernism* (Cambridge, Cambridge University Press), 1991.

Rosen, Charles, 'The Ruins of Walter Benjamin', in Gary Smith (ed.), *On Walter Benjamin. Critical Essays and Recollections* (Cambridge MA, MIT Press), 1988.

Rosenfeld, Alla, and Norton T. Dodge (eds), *Nonconformist Art. The Soviet Experience 1956–1986* (London, Thames & Hudson), 1995.

Ross, David A., *Between Spring and Summer. Soviet Conceptual Art in the Era of late Communism* (Boston MA, MIT Press), 1990.

Rotenberg, Robert, 'May Day Parades in Prague and Vienna: A Comparison of Socialist Ritual', *Anthropological Quarterly*, 56:2 (1983) 62–8.

Rozwadowska-Janowska, Nina, and Piotr Nowicki, *No! – and the Conformists. Faces of Soviet Art of the 50s to 80s* (Warsaw, Fundacja Polskiej Sztuki Nowoczesnej Wydawnictwa Artystyczne i Filmowe Warszawa), 1994.

Saja, K., A. Rybelis, D. Mickevičius, A. Šimkúnas, Č. Ladukas and I. Zibucas, *Lithuania. Documents, Testimonies, Comments 1991.01.13* (Vilnius, State Publishing Centre), 1992.

Sayer, Derek, *The Coasts of Bohemia. A Czech History* (Princeton NJ, Princeton University Press), 1998.

Scriven, Michael, and Dennis Tate (eds), *European Socialist Realism* (Oxford, New York and Hamburg, Berg), 1988.

Sevchuk, G., *Cultural Policy in the Ukrainian Soviet Socialist Republic. Studies and Documents on Cultural Policies* (Paris, Unesco), 1982.

Shalin, Dimitri N. (ed.), *Russian Culture at the Crossroads. Paradoxes of Postcommunist Consciousness* (Las Vegas NV, University of Nevada and Westview Press), 1996.

Shlapentokh, Viktor, *Soviet Intellectuals and Political Power. The post-Stalin Era* (Princeton NJ, Princeton University Press), 1990.

Shlapentokh, Viktor, 'The Stakhanovite Movement. Changing Perceptions over Fifty Years', *Journal of Contemporary History*, 23 (1988) 259–76.

Siefert, Marsha (ed.), *Mass Culture and Perestroika in the Soviet Union* (New York and Oxford, Oxford University Press), 1991.

Šimek, Milan, and Jaroslav Dewetter, *Cultural Policy in Czechoslovakia* (Paris, Unesco), 1981.

Simmons, Sherwin, 'Grimaces on the Walls. Anti-Bolshevist Posters and the Debate about Kitsch', *Design Issues*, 14:2 (1998) 16–40.

Socialist Realism in Literature and Art. A Collection of Articles (Moscow, Progress Publishers), 1971.

Sopotsinsky, Oleg, *Art in the Soviet Union. Painting, Sculpture, Graphic Arts* (Leningrad, Aurora Art Publishers), 1978.

Staininger, Otto, *DAgegen Verbotne Ostkunst 1948–1989. Eine Ausstellung des Ostfonds des Bundesministeriums fur Unterricht und Kunst* (Vienna, Profildruck), 1991.

Standeisky, Éva, Gyula Kozák, Gábor Pataki and Rainer M. Janos (eds), *A fordulat evei. Politika. Képzömüvészet. Épitészet 1947–1949* (Budapest, 1956-OS Intézet), 1998.

Stanislawski, Ryszard, and Christoph Brockhaus (eds), *Europa, Europa. Das Jahrhundert der Avantgarde in Mittel- und Osteuropa I–IV* (Bonn, Kunst- und Austellungshalle der Bundesrepublik Deutschland), 1994.

Starr, S. Frederick, *Red & Hot. The Fate of Jazz in the Soviet Union 1917–1991* (New York, Limelight), 1994.

Starr, S. Frederick, 'Writings from the 1960s on the Modern Movement in Russia', *Journal of the Society of Architectural Historians*, 30:2 (1971) 170–7.

Stephan, Alexander, 'Johannes R. Becher and the Cultural Development of the GDR', *New German Critique* 1:2 (1974) 72–89.

Stites, Richard, *Russian Popular Culture. Entertainment and Society since 1900* (Cambridge, Cambridge University Press), 1992.

Stites, Richard, *Revolutionary Dreams. Utopian Vision and Experimental Life in the Russian Revolution* (Oxford, Oxford University Press), 1989.

Strigaliov, Anatoly, *Art and Revolution. Russian-Soviet Art 1910–1932* (Budapest, Palace of Exhibitions), 1988.

Sudau, Christel, 'Women in the GDR', *New German Critique*, 13 (1978) 69–82.

Sutyagin, A. (ed.), *The Bases of Marxist-Leninist Aesthetics* (Moscow, State Publishers of Political Literature, Institutes of Philosophy and History of Art of the Academy of Sciences of the USSR), 1960.

Szecsko, Tamas, 'Mass Communications and the Restructuring of the Public Sphere. Some Aspects of the Development of "Information Culture" in Hungary', *Media, Culture and Society*, 8 (1986) 199–210.

Szelenyi, Ivan, 'The Position of the Intelligentsia in the Class Structure of State Socialist Societies', *Critique*, 10–11 (1978–79) 51–76.

Tabor, Jan (ed.), *Kunst und Diktatur. Architektur, Bildhauerei und Malerei in Österreich, Deutschland, Italien under der Sowjetunion 1922–1956* I–II (Baden, Verlag Grasl), 1994.

Taylor, Brandon, 'Ways of seeing Socialist Realism', *Art Monthly*, 153 (1992) 9–12.

Thurston, Robert W., 'Social Dimensions of Stalinist Rule: Humor and Terror in the USSR 1939–1941', *Social Dimensions*, 24:3 (1990–91) 542–62.

Todorov, Vladislav, *Red Square. Black Square. Organon for Revolutionary Imagination* (Albany NY, State University of New York), 1995.

Tumarkin, Nina, *Lenin Lives. The Lenin Cult in Soviet Russia*, enlarged edition (Cambridge MA and London, Harvard University Press), 1997.

Tumarkin, Nina, *The Living and the Dead. The Rise and Fall of the Cult of World War II in Russia* (New York, Basic Books), 1994.

Tupitsyn, Margarita, *SOTS Art* (New York, New Museum of Contemporary Art), 1986.

Urban, Michael E., and John McLure, 'The Folklore of State Socialism. Semiotics and the Study of the Soviet State', *Soviet Studies*, 35:4 (1983) 471–86.

Volkov, Solomon, *St Petersburg. A Cultural History* (London, Sinclair-Stevenson), 1996.

Warneken, Bernd Jurgen, '"Forward, but Forgetting Nothing!" The Shift in Use and Meaning of Socialist Symbolism in East Germany since 1989', *International Review of Social History*, 39 (1994) 77–91.

White, Anne, *De-Stalinization and the House of Culture. Declining State Control over Leisure in the USSR, Poland and Hungary 1953–1989* (London, Routledge), 1990.

White, Stephen, 'The Effectiveness of Political Propaganda in the USSR', *Soviet Studies*, 32:3 (1980) 323–48.

Willett, John (ed.), *Brecht on Theatre. The Development of an Aesthetic* (New York, Hill & Wang), 1964.

Winzen, Matthias, 'The Need for Public Representation and the Burden of the German Past', *Art Journal*, winter (1989) 309–14.

Wnuk-Lipinski, 'Diomorphism of Values and Social Schizophrenia. A Tentative Description', *Sisyphus*, 3 (1982) 81–101.

Wolchik, Sharon L., 'The Status of Women in a Socialist Order. Czechoslovakia 1948–1978', *Slavic Review*, 4 (1979) 583–602.

Wolchik, Sharon L., and Alfed J. Meyers (eds), *Women, State, and Party in Eastern Europe* (Durham NC, Duke University Press), 1985.

Wood, Paul, 'Retreat from Moscow', *Artscribe*, 88 (1991) 48–53.

Wright, Patrick, 'Why a Pink Tank made Prague see Red', *Guardian Review*, 25 July 1991, 23–4.

Zaslavsky, Viktor, 'The Rebirth of the Stalin Cult in the USSR', *Telos. A Journal of Radical Thought*, 40 (1979) 5–18.

Zatenatskii, Ya P., D. G. Yanko and A. O. B'iunik, *Khudozhnik Ukrainii Narody 1917–1967* (Kiev, Vidaviitstvo 'Mistetstvo'), 1967.

Zhdanov, A. A., *On Literature, Music and Philosophy* (London, Lawrence & Wishart), 1950.

Žižek, Slavoj, 'A Leftist Plea for "Eurocentrism"', *Critical Inquiry*, summer (1998) 988–1009.

Žižek, Slavoj, 'Eastern Europe's Republics of Gilead', in Chantal Mouffe (ed.), *Dimensions of Radical Democracy in Pluralism, Citizenship, Community* (London and New York, Verso), 1992.

Žižek, Slavoj, *For they Know not What they Do. Enjoyment as a Political Factor* (London and New York, Verso), 1992.

Žižek, Slavoj, *The Sublime Object of Ideology* (London and New York, Verso), 1989.

Zvorykin, A. A., *Cultural Policy in the Union of Soviet Socialist Republics* (Paris, Unesco), 1970.

HISTORICAL

Ascherson, Neal, *The Polish August. The Self-limiting Revolution* (Harmondsworth, Penguin Books), 1981.

Ash, Timothy Garton, *In Europe's Name. Germany and the Divided Continent* (London, Jonathan Cape), 1993.

Ash, Timothy Garton, *We the People. The Revolution of '89 witnessed in Warsaw, Budapest, Berlin and Prague* (Cambridge, Granta Books), 1990.

Ash, Timothy Garton, *The Uses of Adversity. Essays on the Fate of Central Europe* (Cambridge, Granta Books), 1989.

Ash, Timothy Garton, *The Polish Revolution, Solidarity* (New York, Scribner), 1983.

Bahro, Rudolf, *The Alternative in Eastern Europe* (London and New York, Verso), 1981.

Bideleux, Robert, and Ian Jeffries, *A History of Eastern Europe. Crisis and Change* (London and New York, Routledge), 1998.

Childs, David, *The GDR. Moscow's German Ally* (London, Unwin Hyman), 1988.

Crampton, R. J., *Eastern Europe in the Twentieth Century* (London and New York, Routledge), 1994.

Davies, Norman, *Heart of Europe. A Short History of Poland* (Oxford and New York, Oxford University Press), 1986.

Djilas, Milovan, *Tito. The Story from Inside*, translated by Vasilije Kojic and Richard Hayes (London, Weidenfeld & Nicolson), 1981.

Djilas, Milovan, *The New Class. An Analysis of the Communist System* (London, Thames & Hudson), 1957.

East, Roger, *Revolutions in Eastern Europe* (London and New York, Pinter), 1992.

Fainsod, Merle, *How Russia is Ruled* (Cambridge MA, Harvard University Press), 1965.

Fejtö, Francois, *A History of the People's Democracies. Eastern Europe since Stalin* (Harmondsworth, Pelican Books), 1977.

Ference, Gregory C., *Chronology of Twentieth-century Eastern European History* (Detroit, Washington DC and London, Gale Research), 1994.

Gerber, Margy, and Roger Woods (eds), *Understanding the Past – Managing the Future. The Integration of the Five New Länder into the FRG. Selected Papers from the Eighteenth New Hampshire*

Symposia on the GDR, Studies in GDR Culture and Society 13 (Lanham MD, University Press of America), 1994.

Gross, Jan T., *Revolution from Abroad. The Soviet Conquest of Poland's Western Ukraine and Western Belorussia* (Princeton NJ, Princeton University Press), 1988.

Held, Joseph (ed.), *The Columbia History of Eastern Europe in the Twentieth Century* (New York, Columbia University Press), 1992.

Hupchick, Dennis P., *Culture and History in Eastern Europe* (New York, St Martin's Press), 1994.

James, Harold, and Marla Stone (eds), *When the Wall Came Down. Reactions to German Unification* (London, Routledge), 1992.

Kaplan, Karel, *Report on the Murder of the General Secretary*, translated by Karel Kovanda (London, Tauris), 1990.

Keep, John, *Last of the Empires. A History of the Soviet Union 1945–1991* (Oxford and New York, Oxford University Press), 1996.

Krushchev Remembers, translated by Strobe Talbot (London, Sphere Books), 1971.

Lieven, Anatol, *The Baltic Revolution. Estonia, Latvia, Lithuania and the Path to Independence* (New Haven CT and London, Yale University Press), 1993.

Litvan, György (ed.), *The Hungarian Revolution of 1956. Reform, Revolt and Repression 1953–1963* (London and New York, Longman), 1996.

Marcuse, Herbert, *Soviet Marxism. A Critical Analysis*, (Harmondsworth, Penguin Books), 1971.

Misiunas, Ronald, and Rein Taagepera, *The Baltic States. Years of Dependence 1940–1990* (London, Hurst), 1993.

Naimark, Norman, and Leonard Gibanski (eds), *The Establishment of Communist Regimes in Eastern Europe 1944–1949* (Oxford, Westview Press), 1997.

Neuberg, Paul, *The Hero's Children. The Postwar Generation in Eastern Europe* (London, Constable), 1972.

Nove, Alec, *Stalinism and After* (London, Allen & Unwin), 1975.

Pryce-Jones, David, *The War that Never Was. The Fall of the Soviet Empire 1985–1991* (London, Weidenfeld & Nicolson), 1995.

Remnick, David, *Lenin's Tomb. The Last Days of the Soviet Empire* (Harmondsworth, Penguin Books), 1994.

Róna-Tas, Ákos, *The Great Surprise of the Small Transformation. The Demise of Communism and the Rise of the Private Sector in Hungary* (Ann Arbor MI, University of Michigan Press), 1997.

Rupnik, Jacques, *The Other Europe* (London, Weidenfeld & Nicolson), 1989.

Rupnik, Jacques, Václav Havel, Petr Pithart, Jefim Fistejn and Dusan Neumann, '1968', *Týden*, 33 (1998).

Ryszka, Frantisek, 'Poland: Some Recent Revaluations', *Contemporary History*, 2:1 (1967) 107–23.

Schöpflin, George, *Politics in Eastern Europe 1945–1992* (Oxford and Cambridge MA, Blackwell), 1994.

Shipler, David K., *Russia. Broken Idols, Solemn Dreams* (Harmondsworth, Penguin Books), 1989.

Spekke, Arnolds, *History of Latvia. An Outline* (Stockholm, Goppers), 1951.

'Stát s odčiněním křivd nespěchá', *Týden*, 29 (1998) 3–15.

Stokes, G., *The Walls came Tumbling Down. The Collapse of Communism in Eastern Europe* (Oxford, Oxford University Press), 1993.

Sugar, Peter F., and Ivo John Lederer, *Nationalism in Eastern Europe* (Seattle WA and London, University of Washington Press [1969]), 1994.

Topolski, Jerzy, *An Outline History of Poland* (Warsaw, Interpress), 1986.

Ulc, Otto, 'The "Normalisation" of post-Invasion Czechoslovakia', *Survey. A Journal of East and West Studies*, 24:3 (1979) 201–13.

Vesilind, Pritt J., 'The Baltic Nations, Estonia, Latvia and Lithuania struggle toward Independence', *National Geographic*, November (1990) 24–49.

Volkogonov, Dmitri, *The Rise and Fall of the Soviet Empire. Political Leaders from Lenin to Gorbachev* (London, Harper Collins), 1998.

Voslensky, Michael, *Nomenklatura. Anatomy of the Soviet Ruling Class* (London, Bodley Head), 1984.

Walker, Martin, *The Waking Giant. The Soviet Union under Gorbachev* (London, Sphere Books), 1987.

Whipple, Tim D., *After the Velvet Revolution. Vaclav Havel and the new Leaders of Czechoslovakia Speak out* (New York, Freedom House), 1991.

White, Stephen, *Political Culture and Soviet Politics* (London, Macmillan), 1979.

CATALOGUES OF POSTER EXHIBITIONS

Brno Biennale, Czechoslovakia/Czech Republic.

Die 100 besten Plakate, Berlin, German Democratic Republic.

International Exhibition of Graphic Design and Communication, Zagreb, Croatia.

International Poster Biennale, Warsaw, Poland.

Moscow Triennale, Russia.

Poster Triennial Trnava, Slovak Republic.

Triennale Européenne de l'Affiche Politique, Mons, France.

JOURNALS

Affiche. The International Poster Magazine, Amsterdam.

Das Bildende Kunst, Berlin.

Interpressgrafik, Budapest.

Projekt, Warsaw.

Tvar, Prague.

Ukraine Journal, Kiev.

Note: page numbers given in *italic* refer to illustrations; 'n' after a page reference indicates a note on that page.